The Lima Inquisition

The Lima Inquisition

*The Plight of Crypto-Jews
in Seventeenth-Century Peru*

Ana E. Schaposchnik

The University of Wisconsin Press

Publication of this volume has been made possible, in part, through support from the Anonymous Fund of the College of Letters and Science at the University of Wisconsin–Madison.

The University of Wisconsin Press
1930 Monroe Street, 3rd Floor
Madison, Wisconsin 53711-2059
uwpress.wisc.edu

3 Henrietta Street, Covent Garden
London WC2E 8LU, United Kingdom
eurospanbookstore.com

Copyright © 2015
The Board of Regents of the University of Wisconsin System
All rights reserved. Except in the case of brief quotations embedded in critical articles and reviews, no part of this publication may be reproduced, stored in a retrieval system, transmitted in any format or by any means—digital, electronic, mechanical, photocopying, recording, or otherwise—or conveyed via the Internet or a website without written permission of the University of Wisconsin Press. Rights inquiries should be directed to rights@uwpress.wisc.edu.

Printed in the United States of America

This book may be available in a digital edition.

Library of Congress Cataloging-in-Publication Data

Schaposchnik, Ana E., author.
The Lima Inquisition: the plight of crypto-Jews in seventeenth-century Peru / Ana E. Schaposchnik.
    pages   cm
Includes bibliographical references and index.
ISBN 978-0-299-30610-6 (cloth: alk. paper)
1. Inquisition—Peru—Lima—History—17th century.
2. Crypto-Jews—Peru—History—17th century.
3. Peru—History—1548–1820.
4. Catholic Church—Peru—History—17th century.
    I. Title.
BX1740.P5S33   2015
272´.2098525—dc23
2015008394

ISBN 978-0-299-31344-9 (pbk.: alk. paper)

To

Raquel Cygiel

Contents

	Acknowledgments	ix
	Introduction	3
1	Heresy and Inquisition in the Iberian World	30
2	The Trial as a Setting for Confession and Repentance	53
3	A Cobbler and a Merchant	76
4	A Community under Trial in Colonial Peru	100
5	The Inner World of the Lima Prisons	131
6	The Plight of the Condemned	151
	Conclusion	181
	Notes	187
	Bibliography	257
	Index	281

Acknowledgments

This book would have not been possible without the assistance and support of educational institutions, professors, colleagues, editors, friends, and family. At the earliest stages of this project, I was fortunate to receive several awards that funded its preparation, research, and writing. At the University of Wisconsin–Madison I am thankful for the support of the Tinker-Nave Summer Research Grant from the Latin American, Caribbean, and Iberian Studies Program (LACIS); the History Department Foreign Travel Grant; the George L. Mosse Fellowship, the Robert and Beverly Natelson Award in Jewish Studies; the Vilas Travel Grant; and the George L. Mosse Advanced Dissertator Lectureship. I also received the Maurice Amado Research Grant from the University of California at Los Angeles. As an assistant professor of history at DePaul University, a teaching leave from the University Research Council, a summer research grant from the Office of the Dean, a Faculty Fellowship from the Center for Latino Research, and an award from the Vincentian Endowment Fund enabled me to conduct additional research in Lima and to complete the revisions to the manuscript. I am also thankful to the personnel at archives and national libraries in Madrid, Lisbon, and Lima, who kindly responded to my requests during several visits.

I am especially grateful for the guidance of my Latin American history professors at the University of Wisconsin–Madison. Steve Stern, Florencia Mallon, and Francisco Scarano generously shared with me their profound knowledge of Latin American history, theory, and methodology. In addition to their teachings, I want to thank Francisco for his warm sensitivity, Florencia for her constant encouragement, and Steve for challenging me intellectually, for offering professional guidance, and for his overall patience. From its inception they believed in the potential of my project, and they trusted I would finish it even when I doubted whether I would ever get to the end of the tunnel. Being their student has been a privilege I will never forget.

At the University of Wisconsin–Madison I also benefited from the knowledge, suggestions, and comments of Professors Susan Desan, Luis Madureira, Emiko Ohnuki-Tierney, Guido Podestá, Frank Salomon, and David Sorkin. In different settings, they all enriched my understanding, approach, and perspectives at several stages of this project. During my graduate education, I also profited from discussions with my peers in the Latin American History Program. Leo Garofalo, Solsiree del Moral, Ileana Rodriguez-Silva, Jaymie Heilman, Andrés Matías-Ortiz, Marc Hertzman, Ponciano del Pino, and Tamara Feinstein always helped me with affection and collegiality. Among them, I want to specially thank my dear friend and colleague Claudio Barrientos, who stood by me and encouraged me to pursue my intellectual growth and professional development even at the most difficult times.

After completing my doctorate, a position at DePaul University in Chicago brought new colleagues, friends, and additional support. In my new academic home, Félix and María Masud, Warren Schultz, Rajit Mazumder, Ogenga Otunnu, Scott Bucking, and Onie Green-Givens are colleagues and friends who created the supportive environment I needed to complete this project.

Throughout the development of this book I also had the support of friends and colleagues across countries and continents. At different stages, and in different locations, Ramiro Fernández Unsain, Inés Dussel, Bill Smith, Cynthia White, Gaby Castro, Elizabeth Miranda, Ted Sickley, Miguel Morales, Eileen Ewing, Naoki Kanaboshi, Sofia Erazo-Castrejón, Gregorio Kazaroff, Marina Paradela, Carlo D'Ursi, Adela Franze, Gabriel Sedler, Claudia Lederman, María Pita, Claudia Guebel, Alan Neumarkt, and Anthony Hollenback encouraged me to persevere in my endeavor.

Numerous colleagues in the field contributed in different ways. In addition to research seminars during my doctoral program, I presented papers at meetings of the Rocky Mountains Council of Latin American Studies and the Conference on Latin American History. At DePaul, the Faculty Symposium organized by the College of Liberal Arts and Social Sciences, the History Faculty Seminar, and the Center for Latino Research offered me opportunities to present my ideas and receive feedback. At different stages of my career and in either formal or informal settings I learned from suggestions and comments from many colleagues, such as Esperanza Alfonso, Martina Will de Chaparro, Miruna Achim, Pedro Guibovich Pérez, Fernando Ayllón Dulanto, Ana María Lorandi, Ana María Presta, Roxana Boixadós, the late Mónica Quijada, Miriam Bodian, Nathan Wachtel, Kris Lane, Robert Ferry, John Chuchiak, Rafaela Acevedo, Chris Stacey, and Lyman Johnson. Kimberly Lynn and Renzo Honores shared with me their unpublished work and their endless knowledge of archival materials. I am grateful to the anonymous readers who challenged me to rethink several aspects of this manuscript. Gwen Walker's expertise guided me in the process of preparation and revision, and Carol Roberts prepared the index. Jill Ginsburg provided fantastic copyediting services, which, as a nonnative speaker of English, helped me a lot.

Through long distance as well I received the loving support of many family members: my siblings, Ruthy and Alberto; my father, Saúl; my nephew, Martín; and my niece, Paula. From my extended family I want to especially thank my uncle Mario Cygiel and my cousin Ana Zigel.

Finally, this book is dedicated to the memory of Raquel Cygiel, my mother, who always celebrated the attainment of my dreams. Sadly, she could not see this particular one fulfilled.

The Lima Inquisition

Introduction

> Up to now I have been a Jew and from now on I am a Christian.
> **Rodrigo Váez Pereira**[1]

After a four-year trial, the Lima Tribunal of the Inquisition condemned Rodrigo Váez Pereira to death at the stake for the heresy of crypto-Judaism: practicing Judaism in secrecy while pretending to be a Christian. On the eve of his execution, he made one last effort to save himself. His trial had begun in 1635, and by the time it ended in 1639 he was about twenty-nine years old. Throughout the trial, Pereira's attitude changed frequently and in contradictory ways. He initially denied the accusation of heresy. However, when the tribunal threatened to send him to the torture chambers, he confessed that he had been practicing crypto-Judaism since his teens, when a relative convinced him to do so. Later, he revoked this confession, and the tribunal sent him to the torture chambers to establish if the truth was in the confession or in the revocation. In the chambers, Pereira gave a second confession that provided more details than the first one, but the next day he revoked the second confession, saying that he had lied in order to stop the torment. Unconvinced, the tribunal issued him a sentence of release to the secular authorities, usually referred to as the secular arm, a sentence that implied death at the stake. The night before his execution, Pereira voluntarily offered yet one more confession and begged for mercy so his life would be spared. But the Lima inquisitors, doubtful of the man's sincerity after so many changes in his story, left Pereira's death sentence as it had been issued.

Rodrigo Váez Pereira was one among eleven men who died on that same day in the Auto General de Fe performed in Lima in January 1639. Like many of the others, he belonged to a network of merchants of Portuguese origin who resided in colonial Peru, and also like the others, he bore marks of being a Portuguese New Christian. In the Iberian Peninsula and in the Spanish American colonies as well, a person designated as a New Christian (or a *converso*) was someone who had converted to Christianity, sometimes by his or her own decision or that of a close ancestor and sometimes by force, from either Judaism or from Islam. In a general sense, the religious sincerity of the New Christians was questioned, and they were suspected of a grave heresy: concealing their real religious identities and maintaining their previous beliefs, sometimes individually, sometimes in close secret groups.

The tribunal of the Holy Office of the Inquisition was first established in Spain in 1478 and, following the Council of Trent in the mid-sixteenth century, was expanded in 1570 to the Spanish colonies. The Holy Office was a royal tribunal that investigated and conducted trials, initially for the offense of heresy, and later also for issues of morality. According to Pedro Guibovich Pérez, the tribunal as it was established in Peru was intended not only to uncover and prosecute religious heterodoxy and provide moral control but also to strengthen the colonial state.[2] Situated in the viceroyalty's capital, the Lima tribunal initially had jurisdiction over the *audiencias* of Lima, Charcas, Chile, Quito, Panama, and Nueva Granada, a vast territory that corresponds to present-day Panama, Colombia, Venezuela, Ecuador, Peru, Bolivia, Chile, Argentina, Uruguay, and Paraguay.[3] This territory was reduced with the establishment of the tribunal of Cartagena in 1610, leaving only the audiencias of Lima, Charcas, Chile, and Quito under the jurisdiction of the Lima office.

Lima, called the City of Kings, was founded by Francisco Pizarro on the Pacific coast of the colony in 1535. By the late 1530s, the city boasted about 350 Spanish residents and already counted on the presence of some Catholic religious orders.[4] With about 25,000 inhabitants in 1614, the city grew into a diverse place with some 35,000 to 40,000 people by 1630, at the time Rodrigo Váez Pereira was under trial.[5] In theory, the various groups that made up the population were supposed to reside in separate areas, but instead, as Alejandra Osorio notes, "the city presented a mixed face and spatial arrangement with Indians, Africans, and *castas* living in close quarters with Spaniards and Creoles."[6]

With its close connection to the port of El Callao, and given the Spanish regulations for trade between the metropolis and the colonies, Lima also played a central role in international and interregional trade, as Margarita Suárez has demonstrated.[7] In this commerce, members of the Catholic orders took part, but the Church and its circles were by no means the only financial actors. Early in the seventeenth century *peruleros* (Peruvian merchants) founded financial institutions; Suárez notes that seven banks were established in Lima between 1608 and 1642. These banks received deposits, processed money transfers, and offered credit to individuals, to fellow merchants, and to the royal treasury. These operations gave merchants a visible presence in the city's social, cultural, and religious life and an indirect involvement in the conduct of local affairs. As Suárez and Osorio have pointed out, their combined possession of money, reputation, and connections, along with their participation in public events, allowed the merchants considerable social mobility and influence.[8]

During the first half of the seventeenth century, Peruvian merchants based in Lima participated in transoceanic, continental, and regional trade.[9] Once a year, the scheduled arrival of commercial fleets from both the Pacific and the Atlantic (via Panama and Portobelo) demanded exchanges of large sums, and merchants coordinated the circulation of silver and European commodities. This schedule set a rhythm for the commercial life of the city and lent economic strength to the entire viceroyalty. Within the colonial economy, silver extraction was central, but agricultural and textile production for local markets was important as well. In addition, slave ships docked in El Callao at various times of the year. The peruleros provided imported goods and also marketed and distributed local products. Because the return on an investment in the Atlantic trade could take five or six years, traders involved in such ventures diversified their activities and joined in business agreements with their fellows, not wanting to risk acting individually. The functioning of the important commercial consortiums over periods of years relied on the joint efforts of banks, merchants, transport companies, and producers, and on many others in the colonial economy, from wealthy traders who headed large consortiums in Lima to petty peddlers who distributed goods in the Peruvian highlands. Peruleros traded in slaves, pearls, pine pitch, tobacco, dyes, silk and other textiles, wine, cocoa, salted meat, wood, oil, and other commodities.

The merchants of colonial Peru were not all of Spanish origin. Among other foreigners, there were Portuguese merchants, like Rodrigo Váez Pereira. Generally speaking, they were called by the term used in Portuguese, *"homens da nação,"* literally, "men of the [Portuguese] nation." They belonged to a diasporic group that operated in maritime trade, in effect constituting "a nation without a state, a collectivity dispersed across the seas."[10] This collectivity was composed of about 20,000 people, scattered over many ports and cities across the Atlantic, according to Daviken Studnicki-Gizbert. The personal stories of those tradespeople who reached Peru, as recounted to Inquisition tribunals, were remarkable. In undertaking their financial endeavors they took advantage of shipping routes, employment assignments, and personal connections. Through these activities the merchants expanded their sphere of influence, so that by the seventeenth century cities such as Lima, Potosí, Mexico, Madrid, Seville, and others had Portuguese streets, quarters, or neighborhoods.

Religion and ethnicity were not discrete cultural categories in this historical past, although historians have attempted to define the distinctions by posing probing questions in their analyses of contemporaneous records.[11] The "men of the nation" were also noted for being New Christians—generally, descendants of Sephardic Jews who had converted to Christianity, by choice or by force, in either Spain or Portugal. Within the Lima viceroyalty, the conversos (either converts or the offspring of converts of Spanish or Portuguese origin) were suspected of practicing Judaism in secrecy. Regardless of whether allegations about their hidden religiosity were true, the suspects could be called before Inquisition tribunals, imprisoned, and subjected to trials of faith in which they were portrayed, accused, and punished as crypto-Jewish heretics. Clearly, their identity cannot be reduced to the definitions set down during the trials, but those definitions are but one part of the much broader records kept by the Inquisition. Considered together, the records give us material for a more extensive exploration of the topic.

In the Spanish American colonies, the presence of the "men of the nation"— potential crypto-Jewish heretics by definition—and the conduct and mandate of the Inquisition tribunals created a complex intersection between colonial Latin American and Jewish history, which I address in this book. I also recognize other focuses of the colonial Inquisition. Writing about viceregal power in colonial Lima, Alejandra Osorio states that "overall the numbers suggest that the focus of the Lima Inquisition in the seventeenth century was not heretics or witches but a poorly educated clergy and Old Christians."[12] Likewise, I recognize that the trial dossiers of crypto-Jews in Lima represent a minority of the trials conducted by the Lima tribunal during the seventeenth century. Despite this fact, I have placed this minority at the center of my research. While I do not question quantitative findings that demonstrate the tribunal's low volume of activity in cases of heresy, and the small number of heretics burned at the stake, I want to look at the cases we do have and suggest an alternative interpretation for those numbers.

In focusing on cases of crypto-Judaism, I present a tribunal that sought to discipline and shape culture not so much through frequency of trials or number of sentences as through the potency of individual examples. In examining trial regulations and institutional procedures, I seek to understand the experience and perspective of the prisoners in the Inquisition cells and in the torture chambers. In exploring the displacements of the Portuguese New Christians I analyze how their lives were shaped by the presence of Inquisition tribunals on both sides of the Atlantic. In addition to studying the prisoners' religiosity as portrayed in inquisitorial sources, I explore and evaluate their agency, limited though it might be, as illustrated by both individual behaviors and collective strategies. I explore how they used their knowledge of inquisitorial procedures in an effort to stall trials, confuse tribunal members, and mitigate the most extreme effects of the trial of faith. Finally, I analyze the 1639 Auto General de Fe in its own right. Looking beyond the ceremonial display of viceregal power as discussed by Osorio for several ceremonies, I see this Auto as a singular event—one in which we can trace the agendas of individual inquisitors and watch the drama of punishment and surveillance move from the dungeons into public spaces, where the plight of the condemned was exposed to the audience.

In developing this project I have relied on a vast body of scholarship, and for this reason the two sections that immediately follow discuss the historiography of the Inquisition and of the crypto-Jews.

Studies of the Holy Office of the Inquisition and the Lima Tribunal

Numerous scholars have scrutinized the Holy Office of the Inquisition in Spain and in the colonies. My goal in this section is not to address every work in that vast bibliography but to select and expand on what I believe to be the most relevant strands for understanding the tribunal. Here I will examine the theoretical and methodological aspects most closely related to my study of the Inquisition and explain how these works influenced my own.

The bibliography on the Lima tribunal is best understood in light of work that has been done on the Spanish institution, which operated between 1478 and 1834. A good starting point is the work of Juan Antonio Llorente, a man who worked for the Spanish tribunal toward the end of its existence. He became a supporter of its abolition and early in the nineteenth century wrote the four-volume *Historia crítica de la Inquisición en España*.[13] The historian Francisco Bethencourt argues that Llorente was the first to include in his study a broad approach to the institution that included a comprehensive description as well as quantitative analysis, the definition and articulation of religious and civil authorities, and the consideration of the Inquisition's impact on minority populations. Llorente's approach makes him a pioneer of Inquisition studies, whether or not his work reflects contemporary academic standards.[14] I have incorporated his description in the background information for my study but did not rely on his narrower areas of focus, such as his quantitative analysis. Henry Charles Lea's four-volume history of the Spanish Inquisition, first published in 1906, and his later history of the tribunal in the Spanish colonies were also key sources.[15] I believe Lea's work is still a valuable secondary source for understanding the Inquisition because of the depth and breadth the author brings to his extensive treatment of the structure, administration, bureaucracy, and practices of the metropolitan tribunal. As with Llorente, I used Lea's information to develop a context for my work.

Ricardo Palma and José Toribio Medina, two writers of the late nineteenth and early twentieth centuries with a focus on the Spanish American colonies, authored works that are now classics for the reader exploring the topic. Palma's *Anales de la Inquisición de Lima* was first published in 1863, and he later explained that he was thus able to consult documentation that was destroyed later, in 1881, when the Chilean Army occupied Lima.[16] Palma is concerned with the presence of the Inquisition in colonial Lima, without incorporating a broader continental view. As a writer, poet, and journalist, his priority was not the accurate reconstruction of the tribunal's history but the retrieval of verbal images from the period of its power. Thus, his text is highly engaging for any reader. Palma's prose is agile and spares unnecessary details; he explains inquisitorial activities in detail for the nonspecialized reader but at the same time criticizes the darkness of the institution and is outspoken in his anticlericalism. Modern scholars who have appraised Palma's work, such as Manuel Ballesteros Gaibrois and Teodoro Hampe Martínez, recognize that he was ahead of his time in seeing his source materials as a window into mentalities and social attitudes, an approach fully developed by historians only years later. Luis Millones also mentions that Palma's vivid writing is inseparable from his occasional humor and suggests these as key reasons that the *Anales* have retained their currency and relevance.[17]

The Chilean historian José Toribio Medina published several volumes on the Inquisition based on archival documents located in Spain. He covered all the colonial tribunals, organizing the volumes according to national boundaries.[18] His purpose, I believe, was to examine the Inquisition within each nation's narrative history. However, building as he does upon primary sources preserved in Spain, Medina does not provide clear archival citations. Paulino Castañeda Delgado and Pilar Hernández Aparicio find that the lack of precision in Medina's writing renders his work insufficiently rigorous in formal aspects.[19] However, I have used Medina's work because he provides a structural picture of the Inquisition in the colonies and addresses the sequence of events, but he also goes beyond these to describe the institution as it operated, the lives and careers of tribunal members, and conflicts between inquisitorial and other authorities (both secular and religious). He outlines the procedural aspects of trials and brings us to the site of Autos de Fe. Even though his work might today be perceived as overly reliant on empirical findings and correspondingly deficient in presenting a broad interpretative framework, José Toribio Medina is still essential reading for researchers interested in the topic. Scholars like Henry Charles Lea and Boleslao Lewin have used Medina as a core source in their works. Lewin in particular relied on Medina in presenting the extreme cruelty of the Inquisition and the terrible suffering of its victims and in demonstrating the extent and reach of inquisitorial power beyond the city of Lima over time, up to independence.[20]

Traditionally, scholarly studies on the Inquisition have emphasized the repression, violence, and terror exerted by this institution, creating the image of an irrational, unjust, extremely violent, and deeply illogical tribunal—the archetype of the Black Legend, and the deplorable outcome of Spain's unique cruelty and insatiable thirst for blood.[21] However, a large body of work produced during the twentieth and twenty-first centuries has questioned this depiction, because it is exaggerated and simplistic and also because it has led to the construction of stereotypes rather than to an accurate understanding of a highly complex institution. The Inquisition was active from 1478 until the 1830s in the Iberian Peninsula, and from 1570 to the 1820s in the Spanish American colonies. Clearly, its long existence demonstrates that it had a dynamic relationship with its own historical context and over the course of nearly three and a half centuries was "far less bloody than previously imagined."[22]

In *The Spanish Inquisition*, Henry Kamen maintains that the tribunal was a product of Spain, and not vice versa, insisting that both royal policies and local cooperation were the forces that put it in motion.[23] He argues that political controversies and conflicts led to the creation of the institution, and he explains the institution's longevity as a result of its adaptations to changing realities. A different perspective is that of Benzion Netanyahu, who explores the roots of the Inquisition, considering its religious, social, economic, and political aspects.[24] For Netanyahu, the underlying motivation of inquisitorial persecution was racial anti-Semitism, a notion that has recently been discussed by David Niremberg. However, Niremberg cautions us to be aware of "how different the uses, functions, and effects of these medieval ideologies were from modern ones."[25]

The theoretical and methodological shift in Inquisition studies has been accompanied by a grand quantity of academic production. Research now goes far beyond the discrete boundaries of the institution, and primary sources are no longer limited to documents produced by the tribunal. In addition to focusing on the description of the institution, its modus operandi, and the lives and religious experiences of its victims, scholars have asked broader questions and interrogated larger bodies of documents. They have formulated new questions in the effort to understand the role and effects of the Inquisition from a less judgmental point of view, to examine how the institution interacted with secular and religious authorities, and to consider what roles it played in the rural and urban worlds, how its victims conducted their personal and social lives while away from the eyes of the Inquisition, and how all of these changed over time. Some of these complex questions have been addressed by research teams who presented their results in collective publications. At the same time, foregoing the comprehensive approaches that researchers like Lea and Medina developed in their multivolume works, other scholars have turned their focus to specific areas of inquiry and deep analysis within those areas.

Studies now look not only at how the institution came to be but also at the logic and circumstances of its longevity. As expressed in the work of Ricardo García Cárcel and Doris Moreno: What did the institution do for nearly three centuries? Why did it last? Scholars have answered these questions by historicizing the institution and its victims, by addressing changes in inquisitorial practices and policies over space and time, by paying attention to tasks other than trials of faith that were conducted by the tribunal, and by connecting the institution with social, economic, and political realities. Some examples of these endeavors are studies by Antonio Domínguez Ortiz and Julio Caro Baroja on Jews, conversos, and the profile of the inquisitor and the works of Francisco Tomás y Valiente and Bartolomé Bennassar on the political-ecclesiastical duality of the Holy Office as an institution and the construction of inquisitorial power at the top and from there its reach throughout the system.[26]

According to Bartolomé Bennassar, the effectiveness of the Inquisition is rooted in the "pedagogy of fear"; he recognizes that through a combination of secrecy, infamy, misery, and powerful examples (the latter a key element, I think), the tribunal intended to deter specific practices.[27] Other scholars explain that the exercise of inquisitorial power was not limited to the top of any social or political ladder: the effort was accepted and locally sustained by lay personnel associated with the institution (*familiares*). In the case of Valencia, Spain, where the local elites did not support the tribunal's establishment, the familiares "provided a bridge between royal government and the popular masses" prior to the 1560s, according to Stephen Haliczer. This author also says that in later years it was petty nobility and distinguished citizens who predominantly occupied the post, which resonates with Jaime Contreras's discussion of the aristocratization of tribunal networks during the seventeenth century. Finally, Kamen observes that since the institution relied heavily on the cooperation of the local community, the familiares' role should not be overstated; although they sought out potential targets, they were not the only ones who provided denunciations.[28]

Adherents of these new viewpoints have examined, among other elements, the characteristics of the institution and its procedures, primary sources (the institution's own records), the demarcated stages of inquisitorial activities, the typology of its victims, the victims' practices, biographies of inquisitors, lists of prohibited books, and the concept of an inquisitorial mentality.[29] Some scholars have made in-depth studies of a single tribunal, either peninsular or colonial, in an attempt to set a base for comparative analysis.[30] On the global scale, the synthetic work of Francisco Bethencourt compares the Spanish, Portuguese, and Italian institutions using four analytical hubs: rites and etiquette, organizational forms, strategies of action, and systems of representation.[31]

The critique of primary sources deserves a separate mention. Inquisition trials were procedural and highly regulated, with each step recorded by notaries. As is common knowledge, the trials sometimes included the use of torture and threatened a potential outcome of death at the stake. Because of the emotional charge of that context, the structure and content of the primary sources that result from a trial present several challenges to any analyst. This is one of the reasons that scholars question the validity of the sources as a basis for research and have insisted on including sources external to the tribunal to obtain a different perspective. I will return to this topic in the following pages, but here I want to comment briefly that scholars have questioned the extent to which a particular practice or identity (like crypto-Judaism) can be reconstructed from confessions recorded during inquisition trials. An example of this line of research is Benzion Netanyahu's work, more precisely his assessment of the religiosity of the crypto-Jews based on documentation external to that produced by the Inquisition.[32]

The seminal work of Jean Pierre Dedieu, Gustav Henningsen, and Jaime Contreras remains a key reference for our current view of the Spanish Inquisition. These scholars applied statistical measures and tabulations to assess its impact and have provided a correction to previous errors in regard to the number of cases. Their work represents an especially important contribution in terms of both theoretical perspective and methodological approach. Most notably, their quantification of Inquisition cases has improved our estimates of how many people actually died as a result of a trial. In their pioneering work, Contreras and Henningsen establish that in trials held by the tribunal, whether on the Peninsula or in the colonies, the number of people who died was quite small. About 44,000 Inquisition trials were carried out between 1540 and 1700; for every 100 people put on trial, fewer than two (1.8) were burned at the stake in vivo (in cases of people absent during trials and Autos de Fe, there was the option of burning an effigy instead).[33] Inquisition documents are problematic in their erratic construction of numerical series, the evenness and completeness of the information, and the lack of homogeneity across records, all of which hamper synthesis considerably.[34] For this reason, all of these totals are estimates. Nevertheless, the proportional assessment of tribunal activities shows that across tribunals they were highly consistent, one might say uniform, with the tribunals of the Spanish American colonies offering no serious exception from the activities of their Spanish counterpart.[35] The work of Contreras and Henningsen allows us to focus even more closely. Initially the Spanish tribunal was organized in two *secretarías*, Castile and Aragon; the Lima tribunal belonged to the Secretaría de Aragón. For this secretaría, Contreras and Henningsen established that between 1540 and 1700 there were a total of 25,890 cases; of these, 942 (3.8 percent) were crypto-Jews. Of the crypto-Jews, 520 (2.0 percent overall) were burned at the stake.[36] For the 1,176 cases brought before the Lima tribunal between 1540 and 1700, 223 were crypto-Jews, and of these 30 were burned at the stake.[37]

In Peru, few people died as a result of Inquisition trials. Teodoro Hampe Martínez writes that during its two and a half centuries of activity (1570–1820), about 3,000 people endured trials conducted by the Lima tribunal, and about forty Autos de Fe (ceremonies of punishment, sometimes public) were performed. Of the estimated 3,000 people put under trial, 48 died at the stake.[38] Indeed, a vast amount of literature validates Hampe Martínez's estimates. René Millar Carvacho writes that between 1570 and 1820 the Lima tribunal issued sentences for 1,700 prisoners, of whom 50 were released to the secular arm. Of these, 30 were taken to the stakes in person (the rest were taken in effigy).[39] For a shorter period of time, between 1570 and 1600, 497 people were sentenced by the Lima tribunal; of these only 13 (2.61 percent) were burned.[40] These numbers do not make the Lima tribunal exceptional. With some minor variations in the totals, other scholars have validated these numbers, and analogous ones have been established for the Mexican office. Overall, it is clear that few people died as a result of an Inquisition trial in Lima, in the other colonial tribunals, or in Spain.

Quantitative analysis has opened doors for integrated studies. By correlating quantity, frequency, percentages, and proportionality, Bartolomé Escandell Bonet has been able to sustain that objective knowledge was possible and has offered guidelines for understanding collectivities as depicted in the sources of American tribunals. Pilar Pérez Cantó, for another example, has published tables illustrating the distribution of offenses, sentences, celebrations of Autos de Fe, and income and expenses for the Lima office.[41] The numerical analyses have also allowed scholars to assess how the institution changed over time, shifting from cruelty to accommodation, according to Dedieu. In the words of Contreras, it was "a very dynamic 'Inquisition,' that of Philip II, and a more calm [*reposada*] 'Inquisition,' this one of his successors."[42] On the basis of this approach and its results, scholars have portrayed a tribunal that after its early vigor became, for the most part, slow and bureaucratic, sometimes nearly dormant, and apparently not deeply concerned with the heresy of crypto-Judaism, with occasional exceptions. Such exceptions can be historically analyzed by considering several factors. Once social, political, and economic elements were incorporated into the logic and mission of the tribunal, religious orthodoxy remained a key element but not the exclusive one. Internal and external politics, as well as economic interests, had become driving factors.[43]

New research has also come from scholars who do not restrict themselves to statistical analysis of the Lima tribunal but instead build on it and from scholars who work on individual cases. In addition to the works of such historians as Marcel Bataillon, Álvaro Huerga, and Vidal Abril Castelló on the cases of Fray Francisco de la Cruz, María Pizarro, and the *alumbrados* (figuratively, "illuminated minds," those who questioned Christian dogma), new scholarship has come to focus on some lesser-known individuals.[44] Millar Carvacho, for example, establishes that between 1540 and 1700 Lima conducted 209 trials for sorcery. He also explains that the persecution had four distinct phases and that women were predominant among those brought to trial. Millar concludes that even though sorcerers were suspected of heresy, Lima did not consider sorcerers to be heretics and that they received lighter penances than did those accused of heresy.[45] Besides making creative uses of quantitative information, posing new questions to the primary sources, and expanding the scope of study to include "mentalities, ideas, attitudes, and behaviors," scholars have explored dimensions of life that are reflected in the documents of the Inquisition and can thus also inform us about the social and cultural experiences of those involved.[46] Gabriela Ramos used some of these approaches in a 1988 article in which she analyzed the *relaciones de causas* (case summaries) of the Lima tribunal for the years between 1605 and 1666, a total of 366 cases. Ramos considered the trials of Portuguese crypto-Jews—those involved in the so-called Great Complicity— of secondary relevance because of the exceptionality of those cases among the regular activities of the Inquisition. Indeed, Ramos's findings teach us that most of the cases brought under the Lima tribunal were for offenses related to superstition rather than heresy. Also, most of the victims were Old Christians rather than New Christians. Ramos concludes that, as a whole, the Lima tribunal devoted its energies to the moral education of the Old Christian Spanish population rather than to the harsh repression of heresies. In analyzing similar information, Millar Carvacho notes that the tribunal was initially concerned with heresy but later came to focus on the Old Christian population and explore the realm of catechesis.[47]

Scholars like Maurice Birckel, Alfonso Quiroz Norris, and Millar Carvacho have also studied the Lima tribunal's finances. The royal allowance, when present, was sometimes erratically dispensed, but a trial by the Holy Office could swell the coffers of the tribunal by sentencing the confiscation of an accused's property. These scholars have tried to understand the different sources of income available for the Lima office and the state of its finances in different moments. Research stemming from this effort focuses on profiles of individual figures, both tribunal members and prisoners, considering their financial profiles, their activities inside and outside the institution, and their cultural interests, sometimes even treating their appearances in trials of faith as secondary. These studies have contributed to our understanding of both accuser and accused and also of the participation of tribunal members in local politics and economic endeavors.[48]

Another scholarly innovation is the analysis of the relationship between the Inquisition and literature. Guibovich Pérez has studied library collections of the time and, more importantly, tribunal activities in the area of book censorship between 1570 and 1754. He finds that the Lima office followed instructions from Madrid in terms of both the rhythm and content of censorship and argues that Lima's exercise of book censorship was "intermittent and permeable," affected "production, circulation, and consumption of books," and had its peak activity in the first three quarters of the seventeenth century.[49] For the years between 1700 and 1820, however, Millar Carvacho maintains that the Lima office prohibited certain books at its own initiative, going beyond the instructions received from Madrid.[50]

With large sets of trials conceptualized as a unit of analysis, gender distribution and women's history have become additional avenues for exploring the records. In general, women are less present than men in the records of the Lima tribunal; this is also true for cases of crypto-Judaism. But women are not invisible. In their study of popular culture, the role of women in cultural resistance and syncretism, female piety, and the ways in which the tribunal exerted social control over young girls, Ana Sánchez and María Emma Mannarelli focus on information related to sorcerers, pious women, and orphans present in the records.[51]

In sum, the use of tabulations and numerical findings has opened the door to the historicization of the institution and invited scholars to pose questions related to elite and popular culture, women and gender studies, and the dynamics of inquisitorial power within colonial society, among other areas. Even though any effort to synthesize such a vast and sophisticated body of scholarship risks a certain degree of simplification, I think that recent scholarship in general agrees on depictions of a tribunal primarily concerned with moral control and preoccupied with book censorship, directed mainly at the Old Christian population, with dramatic but exceptional eruptions related to the persecution of religious heterodoxy (often with economic interest as a contributing factor). In these analyses, we see the tribunal's inefficiency and its drive to protect self-interest, including the economic interests of tribunal members, as the relevant forces behind tribunal activities rather than consistently applied zealotry. For example, Hampe Martínez recognizes this in a 1996 historiographical essay: "Among the most suggestive new outcomes is the image of the Lima tribunal as relatively inactive and inefficient, detached from vigilance in matters of faith and oriented instead toward promoting the commercial and financial interests of its own members."[52] In the same article, Hampe Martínez considers the relevance of the tribunal in broader social life and across the range of all inquisitorial functions. From this perspective, blasphemy, bigamy, gambling, and the like were at the core of the tribunal's preoccupations. To correct these misbehaviors and shape a colonial society inscribed within the lines of Roman Catholic moral patterns, the Lima tribunal exerted moral control over the population under its jurisdiction. It encouraged attendance at Mass, which meant a more systematic indoctrination, and it disseminated (or elaborated) lists of allowed books. In short, the tribunal was a disciplinary body devoted to social control and soft punishment within a relatively undisciplined society, and by exception concerned with heresy.

While these new perspectives have opened a broader understanding of the tribunal, they have also created, at the analytical level, a tension between quantity and quality—in other words, between relevance derived from quantitative summaries and an approach based on a close examination of sources in which quantity would have a much lesser weight. It is in this analytical tension that I situate my work. It is clear that the Inquisition evolved over time. Originally conceived as an agency of surveillance that looked after heretics, it lasted for centuries precisely because of its capacity to transition from dynamic to calm (*reposada*), as previously noted in Contreras's work. The historicization of the Inquisition has shown it to be a malleable institution, receptive to local and political realities. When new offenses emerged (such as those brought out in the trials of Protestants in Seville in the 1550s), the institution adjusted accordingly. As a moral guardian of the society in which it operated, it had to observe almost everybody and keep alert to a wide spectrum of activities. For that reason, it had to create and administer a broad system and a wide range of activity that would accommodate and tabulate both minor and major offenses, and a system of scaled punishments to correct all of them. Keeping this in mind, we can see that the Inquisition had to be able to cover both ends of the scale as well as hold the balance in the middle: a slap on the wrist for minor offenses, reconciliation for serious ones, and release to the secular arm (meaning death at the stake) for an abominable heresy. If heinous offenses and death at the stake did not characterize the bulk of the tribunals' activities, this is only to be expected.

On the other hand, as Bethencourt notes, executions affected minority groups in disproportionate numbers, meaning that the number of deaths takes on a different relevance if that number is considered within the demographics of a specific minority rather than against the full set of trials. Furthermore, our analysis of the impact of the institution should also consider sentences that did not include execution but imposed exile, property confiscation, and social stigmatization that affected several generations. It is this kind of information that is more difficult to quantify.[53]

Recent books that focus on the Lima Inquisition not only place the institution within a broader context but also delve into microhistory. In *Inquisición y sociedad en el virreinato peruano*, Millar Carvacho demonstrates that the modernity of the institution can be seen in several salient aspects: the tribunals' dispersion in the Peninsula and in the colonies, the centralization of its apparatus, the concentration of power at the top of the structure, and sometimes its financial autonomy. In *La Inquisición de Lima: Signos de su decadencia, 1726–1750*, the same author studies the last case in Lima in which the tribunal meted out a death sentence.[54] Irene Silverblatt, a scholar who has worked with inquisitorial sources in studies of gender relationships during the precolonial and colonial periods, has more recently focused on the Inquisition as an institution and on its role in broad historical change. In *Modern Inquisitions*, Silverblatt argues that through its combination of organized bureaucracy and racial thinking, the Lima Inquisition has had a particular place in the origins of the modern world: with the exception of Indians, it looked after all society members, projecting the notion of itself as "the empire's fairest court."[55] Silverblatt's argument invites further comparative study on a large scale. We might want to address, for example, the ways in which the Peruvian tribunal was different from that in Cartagena or Mexico, or both. This is not the area of my study, but in this book I do reach beyond the Lima office, posing questions in an effort to understand the connections between tribunals.

In this line of thought, François Soyer has noted in an article on the collaboration between the Spanish and Portuguese Inquisitions that the scholarship on both these Inquisitions is vast but that little work has been done regarding "the level of interaction and active cooperation" between them.[56] In this book I examine exchanges of information between Spanish, Spanish colonial, and Portuguese tribunals and consider how such exchanges affected individual trials. At the end of *Modern Inquisitions*, Silverblatt considers what might have been the overall force of the tribunal and how to gauge it, questions I have also pursued.[57] In trying to "gauge" the force of the tribunal (borrowing Silverblatt's expression), I have largely set aside the relevance of numbers so as to consider in combination the characteristics of tribunals and trials, the coordination among different tribunals, the experiences of individual prisoners, the presence of individual strategies and collective agency among groups of prisoners, and the overall impact of rituals of public punishment.

It is in the analysis of such rituals that my work both intersects and differs from that of Alejandra Osorio. In *Inventing Lima*, Osorio does not focus exclusively on the Inquisition but studies a variety of ceremonies performed in the City of Kings and the Autos de Fe celebrated throughout the tribunal's existence. She examines the Auto "not as a bloody act of punishment and paranoid repression but instead as a 'baroque machinery' [*maquinaria barroca*] or theater intended to heal the Christian body politic from its impurities."[58] In my work, I also contextualize celebratory aspects like ornaments, processions, staging, restoration of the honor of those wrongfully accused, and the overall unity of the Christian community, but my scale and focus of analysis are different. Instead of combining information from several ceremonies, I focus on one Auto General de Fe, performed in 1639, as a phenomenon in its own right, to examine the exemplary punishments and the irreversible penalties applied to alleged crypto-Jews (the "impurities," to borrow Osorio's expression). I analyze the primary sources, focusing on the impact of punishment and surveillance and the terror this ceremony generated, placing at the center the plight of the condemned.

Finally, a development contiguous to Inquisition studies, but one that falls outside the goals of this book, is the analysis of how indigenous religiosity was constructed and expressed in the colonial period. Campaigns called Extirpations of Idolatries targeted indigenous societies, using procedures modeled on trials of faith, although with different approaches to punishment. Did extirpation campaigns succeed? Authors like Pierre Duviols, Iris Gareis, Nicholas Griffiths, and Kenneth Mills have explored to what extent the activities of the Inquisition and the Extirpation of Idolatries were similar or different in structure and in outcomes and have debated whether indigenous reaction should be analyzed as the preservation of clandestine practices and resistance or understood as a process of selective assimilation of Christian elements and adjustment of their own religious conceptions. Here also, scholars have moved toward nuanced perspectives, understanding that there were never two clearly defined camps. For example, local populations acted as informants, but people who received punishments for idolatry were not made social outcasts (as happened with trials of faith). Also, regional and gender variations alert us to the problem presented by any broad generalization, as Iris Gareis and Irene Silverblatt have shown.[59]

In summary, the small proportion of people who died at the stake in the cases treated under the Lima tribunal for the offense of heresy invites scholars to work on other offenses and other kinds of offenders and to assess the activities of the tribunal from a broader perspective. I base my work instead on a closer look at individual subjects. Although I question neither the quantitative findings introduced in the previous pages nor the relevance of studying the Inquisition in all its breadth and depth, I want to consider the tribunal not only in light of the number of prisoners it condemned to death at the stake or the theatrics of the ceremonies in which it meted out punishment but also in light of the kinds of trials prisoners experienced and how they responded to them. The tension between quantitative and qualitative approaches is always a challenge for historical analysis. In taking up this challenge, I inverted my lens and looked not for numbers but for what I believe has singular relevance in terms of cultural and historical significance—that is, the few cases of crypto-Jews who underwent trials of faith in Lima.

Thus, I use in this book the small numbers and the analytical tension between quantity and quality to explore the impact of the activities of the tribunal. I have learned through extensive reading in the primary and secondary sources that the Lima Inquisition operated within the logic and rationale of the broader institution that spawned it—an institution developed on precedent, intent on its purpose, and huge in its presence over centuries. Following that logic and rationale, the tribunal looked after a vast array of offenses, classified and ranked problematic behaviors, conducted trials when deemed necessary, and punished according to the seriousness of the infraction. For lesser offenses and offenders, it was a merciful tribunal that assigned mild penalties and offered second opportunities, as vast scholarship has demonstrated. However, for cases of religious heresy, the most heinous offense by inquisitorial standards, the point was not the number of trials or their frequency but the long, secret buildup to them, with its regulated application of physical torment and its grim outcome in the Auto General de Fe as a principal form of the ritualized and awe-inducing theater of exemplary punishment identified by Osorio as central to the regime's power.

Seen as an element in the big picture of colonial expansion, the Lima Inquisition acted as a disciplinary body that watched over the population of European and African origins. For the broader colonial society, although the Inquisition reinforced the presence of the colonial state and brought moral control and cultural regulations, it probably had a very small direct impact in most peoples' lives. In the small (in numbers) picture, however, the Inquisition tribunal acted as a powerful body that persecuted, prosecuted, and punished religious minorities. Among New Christians, whether or not they had been singled out as crypto-Jews, the Inquisition instilled fear, fostered the birth of new identities, acted as a deterrent, and shaped human fates through secret trials that could lead to confiscation of properties and colossal public displays of exemplary punishment. The longevity of the tribunals, the sprawl of their operations in the Peninsula and the colonies, and the participation of secular and religious authorities at all levels in inquisitorial activities are key factors in assessing the impact of the institution. For example, there were university professors and members of the clergy who collaborated in the assessment of suspicious propositions, officers of civil courts who acted as defense advocates or participated in meetings to decide sentences, and viceroys who presided in person over ceremonies in which punishment was applied.

Through a combination of secrecy, infamy, misery, and power of example, the "pedagogy of fear" became the Inquisition's main enforcement tool, as Bennassar wrote (1984).[60] Among these four elements, the exemplary punishment applied at the public Auto de Fe was the most important one during the seventeenth century, because it revealed and brought home the outcome of the trials to the entire community. As such, examination of the plight of the condemned during the ceremony provides a unique and telling perspective to the study of such events. Evidence reporting leaks of information demonstrates that trials were not always conducted in absolute secrecy and that not all such trials ended in infamy and misery, although many did. In other words, even if secrecy was not completely preserved, and if infamy and misery were not the outcome of all cases, the tribunal could still showcase the result of its efforts in a major ceremony. Without the public Auto General, sporadically celebrated as it was, there would have been no spectacular ceremony to provide a religious and judicial climax to the trials—secrecy, infamy, and misery would have been experienced by individuals but would not have exposed the activity or the victim before the broader community. For this reason, I agree with Consuelo Maqueda Abreu when she writes that the Auto General de Fe clearly expressed the uniqueness of the Inquisition: the celebration was "profoundly alive, dramatic, overwhelming" and illustrates that quantity was not the Holy Office's primary concern.[61] Even though the executions did not occur during the Auto General but only after prisoners were released to the secular authorities, and the burnings happened at a different locale and not on the Auto's own central stage, it is clear that the ritual, punishment, and executions were integral to the Autos themselves.

Religiosity:
Crypto-Jews and Marranos

As they studied the institution, scholars have also focused on those persons brought before the tribunals, some of them prisoners, including the crypto-Jews. Here again, I do not attempt to cite every published work in the vast literature but rather to introduce the most relevant and influential strands for the analysis of the religiosity of people accused of the heresy of crypto-Judaism.

From a contemporary viewpoint it is not clear from the records if the prisoners were Jews, Christians, or somewhere in between. The location and nature of the division is blurred in other respects as well, because it entails a combination of lineage, religious beliefs, ethnic identity, dietary restrictions, funerary customs, and many other deeply entrenched aspects of social and personal life. New Christians' religiosity was obviously at the core of inquisitorial preoccupations, and as a research subject it has caught many scholars' attention. Several approaches have been proposed, developed, criticized, and reformulated. Taking a wide view, these approaches can be classified as supportive of one of two main contentions. On one side, there is acceptance of a hidden identity—either extant or potential, among those called crypto-Jews—preserved and reformulated while living under the eyes of the Inquisition in different countries and continents and across frontiers, oceans, and generations.[62] This contention accepts Inquisition records as a useful primary source for studying crypto-Jewish identities and practices. On the other side, there is the contention that the tribunal of the Holy Office of the Inquisition, by publishing edicts of faith that were read periodically during Mass, by using standardized questionnaires in trials, and by forcing confessions in the torture chambers, paradoxically cooperated in the definition, propagation, and corroboration of the heresy it aimed to eradicate.[63] A secondary product of these institutional practices is the way in which heresy and heretics are portrayed in Inquisition records. From that perspective, records generated by the Inquisition are not reliable sources for understanding the religiosity of its prisoners because of the context of their production. That context renders most available primary sources useless, or of very limited value.

In an attempt to avoid simplistic categorizations, scholars like Yirmiahu Yovel have recently moved toward more nuanced, flexible approaches that avoid trying to define an essential identity.[64] "The *conversos* were, like most groups of human beings, both diverse and inconsistent," wrote David Gitlitz in a book that synthesizes a vast array of sources related to this topic.[65] As Gitlitz looked into ways in which New Christians might have understood and defined their religious beliefs, he found evidence to suggest four basic types. First, there were the Christians, those who had sincerely converted. Second were the Jews, those who intentionally rejected the new religion and deliberately preserved the old one, some as defiant martyrs.[66] Third were those who oscillated between the ancestral faith and the new one, possibly seeking truth and comfort, but without a clear sense of direction. The fourth group consists of people who along the way withdrew from religion, those Gitlitz calls the "skeptical dropouts." Although Gitlitz also describes subgroups, I believe that the usefulness of his typology rests on his insights into the range of possibilities rather than on the allocation of individuals to one type or the other. In my analysis, I have tried not to label individuals as conforming to any single type, but I did consider that the individuals interrogated by the Lima tribunal could have been at different points along a broad religious spectrum but still identified as crypto-Jews by the tribunal.

Gitlitz clarifies the fact that crypto-Jewish religiosity included several elements that reflect a distinct religious experience, along with fragmentary articulations of both Catholicism and Judaism.[67] I found this study useful in identifying certain principles. First is the belief in a single God and the rejection of the Trinity. Second is the expectation that the Messiah had yet to come, which implies the rejection of Christ as a Messiah. Third is the hope that salvation could be achieved by believing in the Law of Moses, which carries elements of both religions through the incorporation of that law into the Christian framework of salvation.[68] Fourth is the relationship between Jews' behavior and their misfortune (or fortune)—meaning that collective suffering under the surveillance of the Inquisition was a consequence of their assimilation to the new faith, or that somebody's individual fortune was the result of a hidden adherence to Jewish beliefs, in spite of the possibility of painful (and perhaps irreversible) consequences. Fifth is the presence of Jewish saints as intermediaries between mankind and divinity and as miracle makers (again showing elements of both religions). Sixth is the unique location of the crypto-Jews between Christianity and Judaism and their comparative views of both religions.

Yovel and Gitlitz are not the only scholars using multilayered perspectives. Miriam Bodian, a scholar who has worked extensively on this topic, reflected in a recent article that "at the same time that crypto-Jews clung to biblical stories and the radical monotheism associated with them, their Judaism became even more imbued with a Catholic religious *sensibility*," whereas David Graizbord, Gretchen Starr-Lebeau, and Ignacio Pulido Serrano delve further into the multiplicity and flexibility suggested by such identities.[69]

Considering the characteristics of the documents and the complexity of the personal histories and religious identities, another challenge is how to approach fragments, or fragmentary information. The study of fragments is problematic, and not only because of the inherent intricacy of Inquisition records and the context in which they were produced. As with any historical subject, New Christians experienced change, within themselves individually and collectively over time. As Jonathan Schorsch wrote, they "do not necessarily maintain an identity over time and space."[70] The goal of the bureaucrats of the Inquisition was to conduct standardized procedures by asking uniform questions; answers were carefully recorded, but inquisitors did not seek to accumulate descriptive information along the way. In the words of Starr-Lebeau, "The power of the Inquisition came from its ability to construct difference out of ambiguity."[71] They would not, for example, have taken into account the differences between the religiosity of a Jew who opted for exile from Spain in 1492 and was forcibly converted in Portugal after 1497 and that of his or her offspring, quite possibly a New Christian of Jewish descent who was born after the establishment of the Inquisition in Spanish or Portuguese lands and had never experienced life in an open Jewish community, let alone in the colonies.

Yet, in spite of the restricted information in those trial records, many scholars have obtained important insights by considering the crypto-Jews through materials from the Lima tribunal. Francisco Maldonado de Silva, a New Christian of Portuguese descent who lived in Concepción, Chile, was imprisoned in 1625 and taken to Lima, and punished with death at the stake in 1639. The case has received the attention of several scholars (Boleslao Lewin, Günter Böhm, Nathan Wachtel, and Miriam Bodian).[72] Lucía García de Proodian took a different approach, using Inquisition documents to focus on the economic activities of the prisoners.[73]

Between 1635 and 1639 the Lima tribunal conducted a set of trials that their records call La Complicidad Grande (The Great Complicity). These were approximately one hundred trials of faith for the heresy of crypto-Judaism. According to the *Diccionario de Autoridades*, the word *complicidad* means company in the offense, in this case, heresy.[74] In general, the Inquisition used the term *complicidad* when referring to a group of people related by blood, friendship, hidden religiosity, and economic interest—whether or not the tribunal could demonstrate any relation to a particular plot or conspiracy (in our contemporary sense of the term). In using the term "Complicidad Grande" for the Lima trials of the 1630s, the tribunal meant to point to the great extent of both the New Christians' activities and their trading networks, and indeed the tribunal was preoccupied with the magnitude of the complicity.[75] The study of the Great Complicity has interested several scholars. Seymour B. Liebman surveyed secondary literature, summarized the main events, and considered whether there was sufficient evidence to posit a conspiracy among the Portuguese New Christians. Paulino Castañeda Delgado and Pilar Hernández Aparicio also look at the trials of faith in their comprehensive study of the Lima tribunal, and Silverblatt has discussed the fears attendant on these intense trials. When Castañeda Delgado and Hernández Aparicio center on the religiosity of these prisoners, they comment on the poverty of their practices given the absence of a proper Jewish instruction.[76] Harry Cross, Alfonso Quiroz Norris, and René Millar Carvacho contribute research on the financial impact of detentions. Although their book does not focus specifically on the Complicity, Linda Newson and Susie Minchin analyze some of the same historical characters, delving into the slave trips conducted by Manuel Bautista Pérez. Studnicki-Gizbert provides us with a portrayal of the Portuguese diaspora across the ocean, informing us of the broad commercial activities prisoners had conducted up to the time of their detentions.[77]

In my discussion of the topic, I have looked beyond the materials from the 1635–1639 trials and included source documents from prior trials. Although the imprisonments that began in 1635 were to my understanding the result of a discrete set of trials associated with specific tribunal decisions, I do not connect them to a discrete strand of crypto-Jewish practices among the Portuguese New Christians in Lima.

In *The Faith of Remembrance* Nathan Wachtel moves beyond materials from any single tribunal and takes a continental perspective, studying individuals from Peru, Mexico, and Brazil and bringing together a lively gallery of portraits, itineraries, social connections, and economic networks. He uses inquisitorial sources from the late sixteenth to the mid-eighteenth centuries as well as materials from interviews he conducted in the northeast of Brazil during the years 2000 and 2001. Conceptually, Wachtel builds on the notion of a potential toward a hidden identity present among New Christians (introduced earlier by Yosef Hayim Yerushalmi) and explores such potential in the religious experiences of crypto-Jews in the Spanish and Portuguese colonies through the concept of Marranism.[78] Wachtel mentions the consensus in the use of this term despite its pejorative meaning in Spanish (*puerco*, or swine), maintaining that the essence of Marranism was indeed in its tension between Jewish and Christian elements, beginning with the fact that people were initially Christians and at some point in their lives incorporated elements of a hidden, non-Christian, religiosity. Wachtel says that Marranism was a faith based on memories, "an objective reality, that of a particular 'religiosity,' . . . a set of concerns, practices, and beliefs, in a configuration made up of changing or even contradictory elements."[79] In this book, I employ the term *crypto-Jew* because I want to avoid the pejorative connotations of *marrano*.

The sources I have used in my own study of crypto-Judaism are a combination of transcriptions of trials of faith and summaries of such trials. In addition to the settings of confession and torture that limit the reliability of records in trials of faith, the trial summaries present another constraint. In such summaries prisoners' declarations are abridged, because these materials were produced primarily to report tribunal activities to other arms of the institution and, therefore, taken out of the trial's context. In seeking the best path for understanding the information available to me, I found Gitlitz's remarks highly appropriate, because they allowed me to discover in the sources important elements of crypto-Judaism—even where such elements appear disconnected and isolated from a broader religious framework—rather than a complete belief system. I also agree with David Graizbord when he writes that "the *basic credibility* of a given testimony is distinct from the *plausibility* of its literal content," and I have questioned the plausibility of testimonies when doing so seemed relevant.[80] To clarify, I do not argue that the specific complex of beliefs that Wachtel has defined and analyzed for individual cases did not exist among some New Christians in colonial Peru. Rather, I want to convey that I did not find information that was sufficiently detailed to support such an analysis, beyond one or two individual examples. For that reason, I have used an approach that provided me with more flexibility and allowed me to combine fragmented information pertaining to several individuals, drawn from a broad range of source materials.

Sources and Archives

To focus my study on the trials of alleged crypto-Jews in seventeenth-century Lima, with an emphasis on the Complicity and on the 1639 Auto General de Fe at which most of those accused received sentences, I conducted research in several locations. In Madrid, I found essential material in the Archivo Histórico Nacional (AHN) and the Biblioteca Nacional (BN); in Lisbon, it was the Arquivo Nacional da Torre do Tombo (ANTT); and in Lima it was both the Archivo General de la Nación (AGN) and the Biblioteca Nacional de Perú (BNP). I consulted published documents as well. Regarding the primary sources available for the scholarly study of the Lima Inquisition, it should be noted that the materials preserved are not complete sets; and I think it is for this reason that Lima has garnered less attention among historians than have other colonial regions where tribunals were active, like Mexico. In following regulatory procedures, however, the Lima tribunal commonly sent both summaries and complete transcriptions of selected trials to the Supreme Council of the Inquisition in Madrid. Although not even these materials provide a full record of the activities of the Lima tribunal, they are well preserved in the AHN and are accessible to scholars. In combining primary source evidence from a variety of archives and collections, I have included trials of faith, trial summaries, criminal trials carried out by the Inquisition, procedural guidelines issued to the tribunal, correspondence between tribunals, and chronicles of inquisitorial ceremonies.

I have also consulted published materials that were not generated by the tribunal, such as the diaries of colonial Lima written by Juan Antonio Suardo and Josephe Mugaburu and the descriptive writing of Pedro León de Portocarrero. These provided me with perspectives on the City of Kings and references to the Lima Inquisition as seen by contemporaries outside it. However, some writers, like Buenaventura de Salinas y Córdova, were indeed associated with or close to the tribunal.[81] Among the primary sources external to the tribunal, I should make special mention of the *Artes de la Santa Inquisición Española*, written by Reinaldo González Montes and published in Heidelberg in 1567. González Montes was an assumed name, and the author's real name is a matter of discussion among specialists. This writer clearly expresses his opposition to the tribunal and its practices, and for that reason I found it relevant to contrast his words with those of tribunal functionaries. Scholars have assessed González Montes's writings with comments that range from "a very shrewd analysis of inquisitorial procedure in all its aspects" (Bethencourt) to "morbidly pathologic" (García Cárcel).[82] Montes's voice is clearly different from any source internal to the tribunal, but it nonetheless refers to what are clearly the same institution and institutional practices. I do not think that Montes's opposition to the tribunal renders his text useless. His portrayal of tribunal practices and facilities resonates with internal documentation from the institution itself while reflecting another point of view.

To retrieve the story of the crypto-Jews who underwent trial in Lima, I also take a page from Michel Foucault to conceptualize the tribunal of the Inquisition as an "immaterial" panoptic.[83] That there were few heretics to validate the presence of the tribunal, few eyes watching over potential heretics, and few Autos Generales de Fe (great staged ceremonies for multiple trials, as opposed to smaller ceremonies for single trials, sometimes performed indoors) suffice to make an unequivocal point. The point of the Inquisition in the Spanish American world was not to have tribunals everywhere, but rather to locate the tribunals strategically in areas where potential offenders were likely to reside, mainly in capitals or port cities. Clearly, the point of the Lima Inquisition was not to launch frequent and exhaustive campaigns against heresy, as the work of Castañeda Delgado, Hernández Aparicio, and Millar Carvacho in its comprehensive consideration of all aspects of the tribunal from 1570 to 1820 illustrates.[84] The point was to punish selectively and eloquently.

Methodologically, a central question concerns how we read data and archival sources, and also how we focus and fine-tune adjust the lens of analysis. The internal and external ambiguities of all parties involved, the procedural secrecy, the articulation of secular and religious power, the hidden religious practices and suspicions surrounding them, legal and illegal trade, and many other factors contributed intentionally to a blurred context. Thus, to clear some blurring and present my study of the Lima Inquisition and the crypto-Jews, I place characters and events in a broader context and also change lenses and adjust focus throughout the text. My goal is not to re-create the Black Legend but to retrieve the human (or inhuman) experiences of these exceptional trials and their significance in our comprehension of the colonial history of Latin America.

Like Carlo Ginzburg in his study of materials from the Inquisition in Friuli, Italy, I have found that the historical characters I have come to know are to some extent "like us" and at the same time "very different from us."[85] I believe that the topic of this book, like that of the Spanish invasion and its impact, will continue to invite scholarly debate and the presentation of issues that perhaps cannot be resolved—this is a condition we all have to embrace.[86] It is important to acknowledge, as I have briefly done, that the nature and authorship of the information recorded by the tribunals, in trials of faith or descriptions of the Autos Generales de Fe, generate a permanent tension that must of necessity permeate the scholarly analysis, causing conflicts between principles of method, objectivity, and ethics, as Nathan Wachtel noted when reflecting on the difficulty of examining records from the torture chambers.[87] Given the exceptionality of these materials, I have made an effort to strike a balance between the standardized practices of the institution and the individual and highly unusual experiences of the prisoners, posing questions about how to integrate these elements in a way that captures the large picture and at the same time adds nuance to the understanding of the topic. Like Kenneth Mills in his study of idolatry in colonial Peru, I aim "to allow the richness of the source material to shine through the two main intervening filters, the inquisitorial genesis and formulaic recording of this evidence, and my own retelling and analysis."[88] As did Eric Van Young in his study of Mexican independence, I have recognized that "the idiosyncratic case and the individual experience are often just as important as the general statement."[89]

Although most of the primary sources are tribunal records, I have always considered in my research the perceptions and experiences of those undergoing trial and have tried to retrieve their perspective. Just one example: the procedural guidelines of the tribunal mandated a rapid process, yet Francisco Tomás y Valiente explains that tribunals held discretionary power regarding the speed—or prolongation—of individual trials.[90] At the same time, the records tell us that prisoners themselves were also ready to slow things down, bribing officials, finding loopholes to circumvent some stages of the trial, and altering the content of their confessions (although they thereby risked repetition of torture sessions), or even manipulating the actions of the tribunal at a key conjuncture. However, when misdeeds were noticed, the tribunal conducted additional criminal trials against those who were found to have violated its formal procedures.

As a historian, I could see in these records the ways in which the institution addressed its own corruption, but I also saw there the opportunity to explore how prisoners of a repressive body deployed their own limited levels of agency. I tried to understand prisoners' agency at both the individual and collective level. In analyzing the cases of the Lima tribunal, I repeatedly posed questions derived from several aspects of the trial of faith. Of course, I considered how each trial unfolded and, to the fullest extent possible, how each prisoner related to the inquisitors who conducted the trial, as should be expected from a study based on Inquisition sources. But I also placed under my scope the recesses of the world constructed inside the prisons of the Inquisition, which allowed me to pose three additional questions. The first: What happened inside the Lima prisons of the Inquisition during the duration of a trial? The second: How did prisoners relate to each other? And the third: How did prisoners relate to lower-ranking members of the tribunal who dealt with them every day and in basic human exchanges—the stewards, cooks, and janitors? These three questions allowed me to consider and observe interactions that did not occur in the official events of the trial of faith, or the hearings, or the torture chambers, and were not, therefore, recorded in the trials of faith. These interactions, recorded in internal documents such as correspondence and proceedings addressing institutional corruption also affected the development of the trials and the conduct of the Lima tribunal.

In its structure and narrative style, this book takes into consideration the reader who has little knowledge of the Inquisition, the specifics of inquisitorial procedures, the role of the institution in the colonial expansion, the presence of Portuguese New Christians in the colonies, the particularity of the Lima cases, and the 1639 Auto General de Fe. In the core chapters I articulate a logical progression from general to particular, focusing different lenses on each chapter.

Chapter 1 builds a context for the remaining chapters. Here, I discuss the process of creating the Spanish Inquisition in 1478 and its underlying rationale: it was to be a disciplinary body aimed at controlling heretical offenses against Christian dogma. I explore how the state and the Church acted together in the persecution and prosecution of heresy and how the tribunal created by the Spanish monarchy preserved essential characteristics of its medieval predecessor and also introduced some innovations: monarchical control and bureaucratic stability. This chapter also describes in detail the organization of the Tribunal of the Inquisition, addressing topics such as its bureaucratic structure, the specific tasks assigned to members, and its financial resources. The Lima tribunal was not an exact replica of the Spanish tribunals. Its geographic remoteness and scant corps of tribunal officers ensured it could not be, but it did follow Spanish guidelines whenever possible. Thus, this chapter places Lima within the Iberian world by presenting information on the tribunal in Spain as well as that of Lima. The Lima officers were integrated into the dominant colonial society and into the broader bureaucracy of the Inquisition, and on some occasions even climbed to the top of the inquisitorial bureaucracy.

In chapter 2, I inquire into the characteristics of the trial of faith and the phases by which it was mandated to unfold, with emphasis on the presumption of guilt, the regulations for the application of physical torment, and the overall importance of procedural secrecy. I juxtapose official regulations that emanated from Spain with materials from Lima trials of faith, with the aim of illustrating the tension between theory and practice within the institution. In the process I introduce the central figures to the reader.

Chapter 3 focuses on the local picture, using individual stories of Portuguese New Christians from Lima to anchor the narrative and to engage larger questions regarding the ways in which the Inquisition operated within the Spanish colonial expansion. Here I consider how the expansion affected New Christians: even though royal regulations prohibited their migration to the New World, they nonetheless moved to colonial locations and circulated across Spanish and Portuguese borders on both sides of the Atlantic. I consider agency at the individual level, as revealed in strategies articulated in prisoners' defenses, and I also explore how Spanish, Spanish colonial, and Portuguese Inquisition tribunals exchanged information in order to reconstruct the itineraries of Portuguese New Christians residing in Lima.

In chapter 4, I analyze the documents related to the Great Complicity. It is with this label that the Lima Tribunal of the Inquisition identified a set of almost a hundred trials brought against the Portuguese community of New Christian descent, most of whom resided in Lima itself in the 1600s. I present a social profile of the prisoners and connect them to the broader diaspora. Analyzing a variety of documents related to these trials—trials of faith, criminal trials, trial summaries, and correspondence between the Lima tribunal and the Supreme Council of the Inquisition located in Madrid, I show that although the Portuguese New Christians who lived in Lima evidenced many interconnections in their descent, their shared familial networks, and their transatlantic commercial activities, they were quite inconsistent and diverse among themselves in terms of religious beliefs.

In chapter 5, I introduce my lens into the inner world of the Lima prisons. I bring attention to the ways in which prisoners took advantage of the interstices left unguarded by organizational practices of the Lima tribunal itself and thereby deployed, at different levels, their own agency during the Inquisition trials. I widen my scope to compare information about the Lima tribunal with scholarship on Mexico, Spain, and Portugal, broadening my view to encompass similarities and differences in their collective and individual practices. Furthermore, I analyze how in this agency the imprisoned community of Portuguese New Christians relied on the familial and commercial ties they had developed prior to imprisonment. These ties also included bonds forged with the African population through the slave trade and the misconduct of tribunal officers themselves.

In chapter 6, I focus on the 1639 Auto General de Fe. Centering on the plight of the condemned, I look into how those condemned to death at the stake faced the end of their lives. In addition to the ceremonial aspects studied by Osorio, I emphasize and study in close detail how the trials of 1635–39 Complicity concluded, and the theater (encompassing staging, scenes of great drama and emotion, and multiple groups of actors) in which the sentencing and punishment of prisoners unfolded. Both the sentences meted out and the application of punishments support my argument about the primacy of these events, however numerically small, in the activities of the institution. In sum, I base this chapter on crucial aspects of inquisitorial activity that are not revealed in studies built on statistics and numbers. I suggest that the grandiose nature and awesome magnitude of the Auto General needs to be considered together with the most individual and singular dimension of the event: the end of selected human lives.

In the conclusion I return to the themes posed in these introductory pages and consider the implications of my work for Inquisition history, Jewish history, and colonial Latin American history. I seek moreover to build a continuing dialogue with scholars who work on issues of religion, colonial expansion, and historical change in Latin America.

1

Heresy and Inquisition in the Iberian World

Don Juan Antonio Suardo was a clergyman who from 1629 recorded in a diary the important events that occurred in the city of Lima. In an entry of May 1631, he wrote: "On the 12th, early in the morning in the streets of San Sebastián parish, there appeared some papers written by hand, full of thousands of heresies and blasphemies; these were later taken to the Holy Office. On the 13th, in the San Lázaro neighborhood, early in the morning, [it was found that] the crosses at the church cemetery and in other public locations had been removed, causing great turmoil. It is said that the *señores inquisidores* are conducting an inquiry into the case."[1]

Heresy was an offense to religious (Christian) law but affected the entire social body; according to Juan Antonio Llorente, this conception can be traced back to fourth-century Europe.[2] Since heresy was a matter that concerned religious and secular law, it fell under the judgment of both ecclesiastical and political authorities, and both participated in the repression. Inquisitors collected information, conducted trials, and applied the milder penalties; the more extreme punishments were applied after the judged were turned over to secular justice. During the early thirteenth century, the Church authorized inquisitorial campaigns in France (1209) and in Italy (1224). Those early tribunals did not sit on a regular basis but were established to cover a specific territory for a limited period of time; they collected information, evaluated evidence, carried out trials, sentenced the judged, and reported to the pope. Shortly thereafter, in 1227, the pope created a Tribunal of the Inquisition as a permanent body. By the fourteenth century the Church had a designated office (inquisitor) and a body of officers—inquisitors, set apart from bishops and their bishoprics—devoted to dealing with heresy and operating under the direct papal command.

Notwithstanding their provisional and itinerant aspects, the main features of inquisitorial activities were established during the times of the earlier tribunals.

During that period, the major characteristics and outcomes of the Inquisition trial (the trial of faith) were established: the requirement of an ecclesiastical sentence for punishing heresy, the involvement of the local population in the detection and persecution of heresy, the imposition of penitential garments (*sambenitos*) on offenders who were pardoned and reconciled, the confiscation of heretics' property, and the greatest punishment—burning at the stake—for the most serious offenders.[3]

Francisco Bethencourt notes that "the inquisitorial administrative culture was based on classification [of heresy] and identification [of heretics]."[4] The role of the Inquisition, he continues, "was to produce the means by which these heresies could be recognized, from the point of view not only of dogma but also of specific cultural practices."[5] Thus, inquisitors relied on regulated procedures to demonstrate the presence of heresy, following instruction manuals composed by and for them to guide them on how to fulfill their tasks. One of these was the *Manual de Inquisidores*, written by Nicolau Eimeric. This manual was not the first of its kind, and certainly not the last, but it was the first one to organize and systematize the task, providing for inquisitors a single set of guidelines so they would not have to consult a variety of decrees, laws, papal bulls, and other such documents.[6]

Nicolau Eimeric was born in Gerona (Aragon) in 1320 and entered the Dominican order at an early age. He held the office of general inquisitor of the Crown of Aragon from 1357. In the early 1370s Eimeric moved to Avignon, France, where the papal court was then located, and served as papal chaplain for Gregory XI and Clement VII. It was in Avignon in 1376 that he composed his most important work, the *Manual de Inquisidores* (Inquisitors' Manual).[7] First printed in 1503, the *Manual* had several editions, and in 1578 Francisco Peña, a Spanish specialist in canon law who lived in Rome, was put in charge of a new one, to which he added his own comments without altering the core.[8] According to the manual, the tribunal was to carry out a quick, straightforward procedure in cases of heresy, without paying attention to subtleties and solemnities.[9] In these trials, it was the type of behavior exhibited by the accused that constituted evidence of the severity of the offense. In his spectrum of offenses, Eimeric included blasphemy, sorcery, worshipping the devil, astrology, and alchemy. In addition, Eimeric stipulated that the Inquisition had to watch over other offenses that could not be exactly defined as heresies but still should fall under its jurisdiction.[10] It was generally considered that infidels to Christianity constituted a special category of their own; it included both Jews and Muslims as well as New Christians from both religions who had returned to their previous practices or persuaded erstwhile good Christians to do so. Eimeric also maintained that baptism conducted under a death threat or baptism as a minor child did not absolve an offender, although children were to be treated with less rigor.[11] The author of the *Manual* also placed under the tribunal's scope those who sheltered offenders in any possible way, including lenient officials and anyone who directly or indirectly obstructed inquisitorial activities.

In addition to defining categories of offenses and determining what fell into them, Eimeric outlined the guidelines of the Inquisition trial—the trial of faith—which will be discussed later in this book. He gave clear directions for conducting hearings, suggested different strategies for interrogating offenders and witnesses, warned inquisitors of attempts by the accused to deflect interrogations, and elaborated on the most commonly used defenses.[12] He summarized ways in which heretics attempted to equivocate when asked questions: adding clauses to slightly modify their answers, redirecting the question asked by the inquisitor, faking surprise or expressing indignation about the content of a question, diverting the direction of an interrogation, providing ambiguous answers, expressing lack of understanding, pleading physical weakness, simulating stupidity or dementia, or pretending to be a saint. These were all strategies to avoid answering the inquisitor's questions, Eimeric cautioned. An example from the *Manual*: "The second trick they use is the addition of an implicit condition, a restriction of the thought. When asked, 'Do you believe in the resurrection of the flesh?' they respond, 'Yes, if God so wants,' [as if] assuming that God would not want them to believe in this mystery."[13]

We see here how Eimeric alerted the inquisitors to the offenders' rhetorical tactics. According to these instructions, an inquisitor had to anticipate an intentional lack of precision and a proliferation of evasive answers. Such answers, in Eimeric's perspective, were the result of a strategy that aimed to detour the progression and outcome of the Inquisition trial. Eimeric also introduced the possible defenses heretics might offer, insanity for instance, and how to evaluate the truthfulness of such defenses. Peña, the canon law specialist, also gave careful consideration to the problem of pretended insanity.

The manual also treated the application of torture and laid out the steps by which it was to be applied and regulated within the trial of faith; these will be addressed later in this book. Eimeric carefully described the variety of penalties that could be meted out by the tribunal, such as the confiscation of property and the abjuration (a statement through which a prisoner would recognize mistakes and promise to stay away from such practices). In addition, Eimeric defined the appropriate punishment for different types of offenders including those who were to be released to the secular arm for burning at the stake.[14] The manual received approval from the pope and from all the tribunals of the

Inquisition, and it was accepted as the standard set of guidelines for inquisitors.[15] However, Inquisition theory and practice differed, and even when tribunals intended to follow standard guidelines, their actions sometimes drifted off in other directions. But in a general sense, we can state that the inquisitors of the Spanish institution (both peninsular and colonial) functioned with the guidance of a set of instructions.

During the years in which the Tribunal of the Holy Office of the Inquisition was developed, the Iberian Peninsula was going through changes that touched political, national, religious, and social spheres. In the year 711, let us remember, the Peninsula fell under Muslim domain, where it remained for centuries. In 1272 Portugal expelled the occupiers and started off on its own independent path. In what we now refer to as Spain (the term did not then represent a country, but merely a group of different kingdoms), a slow but steady process known as the Reconquista was taking place. Generally speaking, the Reconquista was the long process that led to the expulsion of the Moors from the Iberian Peninsula and opened the gate for the political and religious unification of Iberian kingdoms. The 1474 marriage of the Catholic monarchs Isabella of Castile and Ferdinand of Aragon was followed by the fall of Granada in 1492, marking the victory of the Reconquista and the end of Muslim Iberia. These events fostered many changes in a society that had been pluralistic, multicultural, and diverse for many centuries.[16]

The Sephardim were an integral part of these changes.[17] The Jewish population had lived in Spain for centuries; a Jewish presence in the Iberian Peninsula can be traced back to the Roman period. Jews suffered under the Visigoths but thrived under Muslim domain. In Al-Andalus, elite Jews participated in what Esther Benbassa and Aron Rodrigue have called a "Judeo-Arab symbiosis," leading them, among other scholars, to refer to the period as a "golden age" for Jews in the Iberian Peninsula. In Christian Spain, a strategy called by the same authors the "royal alliance" allows us to understand the Jewish presence in the Peninsula during and after the Reconquest.[18] Under the protection of a centralized power, Jews had special rights and could live in their own autonomous communities (*aljamas*). However, massive forced conversions carried out in 1391 had created a new cluster of people, known as conversos or New Christians.[19] The conversos, whether former Jews themselves or their offspring,[20] initially benefited from opportunities that had been closed to them as non-Christians. However, the adoption in the mid-fifteenth century of the statutes of blood purity (*estatutos de limpieza de sangre*) restricted the access of conversos and their descendants to government positions and limited their inclusion in the larger Spanish society. In short, there was a tension between change and assimilation. As Stuart Schwartz notes, "conversion was one thing, acceptance another."[21]

Questions of Blood Purity

According to the dictionary of Covarrubias, a man who is considered clean is an Old Christian who does not have Moorish or Jewish ancestry.[22] The blood purity statutes originated in Toledo during the mid-fifteenth century and continued in a process that was far from linear. However, the statutes were in place prior to the creation of the Spanish Inquisition, and the New Christian population on both sides of the Atlantic was affected by them in ways that I will show are interrelated.[23] Civil and religious institutions, nobles, commoners, and priests—all members of Ibero-American society contributed to shape these "genealogical fictions," requesting declarations attesting to purity from acquaintances and commissioning bureaucrats to collect and assess evidence. At the same time, those who did not have the pedigree that would have allowed them to blend in paid for tailored forgeries or bribed witnesses to sign or generate the required paperwork.[24]

Early in the seventeenth century in Madrid, a group of writers called *arbitristas*, who produced prescriptive social treatises and other types of essays, suggested a more lenient approach to the blood purity regulations. Their purpose was to gain New Christians' participation in what was then a problematic economy. A royal pronouncement issued in 1623 reflected their influence; it instructed officials and others to ignore rumors and verbal statements and instead to consider the issue resolved after three positive accreditations of blood purity conducted by reputable tribunals or other institutions, such as the Inquisition or the College of Salamanca.[25] Such ideas transferred to the New World as well, but not always in a linear way.

Even if just as a discursive formality, the relevance of pure blood in colonial Peru can be located in different sources, both internal and external to the Lima Inquisition. For example, the proper distinction between true and inauthentic Iberians received the attention of the Andean writer Guamán Poma de Ayala in the early seventeenth century.[26] Such a distinction is also expressed in the words of Fray Buenaventura de Salinas y Córdova. A Franciscan born into an aristocratic Lima family, he was sent by the order to Europe (Spain and Italy), and toward the end of his life came back to New Spain, dying in Cuernavaca. In 1630 the friar, who was a Holy Office *calificador* (assessor) as well, described the positive attributes of the faculty at the university in Lima, stating that in addition to being illustrious and celebrated, the professors were "*claros en sangre*" (of pure blood).[27] A third example of the attention paid to blood purity can be found in Lima later in the same century, when in 1673 the inquisitors requested the imprisonment of Sebastián de Aguilar because it was suspected he had provided false information for an appointment at the tribunal. He was released a month later.[28]

Once the Inquisition had become an established institution, no longer transient as in its early years, tribunals built facilities to store information pertaining to peoples' family trees. The relevance of this information for parties involved can be seen much later, when early in the nineteenth century the Lima *cabildo*, recognizing the impending abolishment of the Inquisition before the Spanish Cortes (parliament), requested that materials affecting the good fame and reputation of citizens persecuted by the tribunal be burned in public.[29]

Prior to the royal decree of expulsion in 1492, New Christians were not only subject to statutes that limited their social mobility and placed them under scrutiny but were also under direct suspicion of maintaining communication with Jews who had not converted and were still residing legally in Spain. It was alleged that social connections and communication between Jews and conversos, who might indeed have belonged to the same extended families, jeopardized the Christianization of the latter and by extension their full amalgamation into Spanish society.[30] The paradox was that the New Christians, suspect under the statutes of blood purity, could not fully merge into the broader society—whether they had such contacts or not. Indeed, *any* contact between conversos and unconverted Jews could raise speculation about the sincerity of their conversions and the likelihood of a religious turnaround. Once blood impurity was established on paper, then religious sincerity became a matter of investigation, not merely suspicion.

Many questions provided fodder for investigation. There were questions about the conversos' Christian sincerity, about whether they were using Christianity specifically to cover up their inner religious beliefs, and about whether the main aim of conversos living in Spanish lands was the opportunity to climb the social ladder. Were there any clues in the New Christians' behavior, any provable indications of heresy? These queries were not raised by regular bishops and other churchmen but by inquisitors, and they justified Isabella's and Ferdinand's request for papal authorization to establish a Tribunal of the Inquisition that would address questions raised about conversos on a case-by-case basis. In 1478 Pope Sixtus IV authorized a tribunal for the kingdom of Castile and in 1481 for that of Aragon. The papal authorization also granted to the monarchs the authority to appoint inquisitors, an essential feature of the peninsular tribunal that established royal command of the institution from its inception. In short order, the tribunal of Castile inaugurated its activities (1480), and the first Auto de Fe was performed in 1481 in Seville.

The Tribunal of the Inquisition:
A Body to Watch Offenders to the Faith

In the early 1480s, seven Dominican friars were designated as inquisitors. One of them was Tomás de Torquemada, born in 1420 in northern Spain, whose name is perpetually (and often fearsomely) associated with the Spanish tribunal.[31] He was appointed general inquisitor in 1483. Torquemada played a crucial role in the creation of tribunals, their bureaucratic configuration, and the delineation of the judicial procedures to be carried out by the Spanish Inquisition. From his initial appointment as general inquisitor to his death in 1498, Torquemada was the catalyst for the tribunals that proliferated in Castile and Aragon. During this period tribunals were itinerant, and their activity in these provinces followed the concentrations of conversos of Jewish descent, whose numbers increased after the 1492 edict of expulsion. Indeed, the only former Jews who remained in Spain were those who had chosen conversion to Christianity over exile. Thus, one of the major reasons for creating the Spanish Inquisition, the likelihood of a New Christian's reneging on his or her conversion under the influence of unconverted Jews, was resolved because, officially, there were no longer any unconverted Jews nearby—no such person was allowed to live in Spanish lands after 1492 according to the decree. However, the sincerity of the New Christians' conversions was still suspect, and that suspicion fueled inquisitorial activities. About 1493, the Inquisition tallied a total of twenty-three tribunals in Spain—the largest number in all its history.[32]

The establishment of an institution so peculiar and complex as the Inquisition was not a linear process, nor did it go uncontested. From the judicial point of view, the principles of the Inquisition conflicted with Aragon's laws and institutions. Although it is true that the papal Inquisition had been active in Aragon during medieval times, it was then itinerant and occasional, meeting only at specific junctures. At the end of the fifteenth century, however, Tomás de Torquemada was determined to establish permanent tribunals in this territory, and there he encountered opposition in Aragon, with two main objections against the establishment of the Inquisition. The first was technical: the methodology of Inquisition trials and the potential penalty of property confiscation contradicted the laws of the region. The second was political: the inquisitors were from Castile and therefore foreigners in Aragon, which also contradicted regional laws. In response to these objections, King Ferdinand pointed out that heresy could not be allowed to fall back on the protection of local institutions. He also remarked that the establishment of the Inquisition in Spain stemmed from a papal decision, one that the local courts of Aragon could not choose to defy and at the same time protect their region from heresy.[33] Llorente also mentions lack of support from the local population in Castile.[34] In spite of local objections and resistance, tribunals of the Inquisition were established and active in both Castile and Aragon at the end of the fifteenth and the beginning of the sixteenth century.[35]

After its first twenty years of activity, in the early 1500s, the Inquisition underwent some adjustment and reorganization. To achieve higher efficiency and lower costs, tribunals located in smaller cities and towns were closed, and tribunals located in the more important cities took charge of the entire jurisdiction. In consonance with the royal command of this institution, the geographic distribution of local tribunals followed Ferdinand's instructions, and inquisitorial districts were drawn with reference to secular borders (kingdoms and other political jurisdictions) rather than along diocesan or other ecclesiastical lines.[36]

The Tribunal of the Holy Office of the Inquisition operated in Spain for more than three centuries, from 1478 to 1834. Over this long period, the tribunal moved through different phases, cycles of activities, and targets.[37] Toward the end of the sixteenth century, it took on an important role in the Spanish Atlantic expansion. In the following pages, I present the tribunal's main features and the tasks of its members.

The Tribunal of the Holy Office of the Inquisition conducted investigations on matters of Christian faith. These investigations were called *inquisiciones* (inquiries), hence the tribunal's name. Technically, the Latin word *inquisitio* referred to a specialized type of procedure: "In the hands of a single public official lay the entire process, from investigation to accusation to conviction, and that official was guided by elaborate rules of procedure which could now be termed *inquisitorial* procedure."[38] The inquisitio bore parallels to the contemporary secular judicial procedure, in which "the judge is at the same time a police officer and an administrator of justice."[39] As already noted, the medieval Inquisition, transient in nature, was under papal command, but the Spanish Inquisition, under royal command, was an instrument of both religion and politics.[40] The institution created in 1478 inherited many characteristics of its medieval predecessor, but it also created new ones.

The main goal of the Holy Office was the prosecution of heresy, considered to be an error in the realm of Christian faith and defined as "both a sin and a crime."[41] This dual nature implies that heresy was subjected to both a forum of conscience and a forum of jurisprudence. Thus a person could be guilty in both realms. Following Henry Charles Lea, in the thirteenth century it had been decided that someone who received pardon of the sin in the forum of consciousness "would still remain to be punished in the judicial forum," like offenders to other human laws.[42] Someone who spontaneously confessed to heresy received pardon and absolution but was also persuaded to appear in front of the

Inquisition. There the person was expected to denounce him-or herself, and very possibly others, and endure proper punishment.

As a judicial forum that focused on religious matters, the Inquisition defined heresy as a complex crime with two basic subtypes: material and formal heresy. A person who committed an involuntary error on matters of doctrine was considered guilty of material heresy. Since the error was considered most likely to be the fruit of ignorance, material heresy was not subjected to inquisitorial punishment. Formal heresy was a very different matter.

From the tribunal's perspective, formal heresy was the effect of a voluntary and pernicious error that deliberately challenged Christian dogma and deserved punishment. Formal heresy was subdivided into internal (not manifested) and external (manifested) types, and there were further variations within the types. Formal external heresy was not always public as its name suggests: it could be occult (manifested in secret, to just one or two people) or public (manifested in any way to more than two people, or openly manifested to any larger number). Clearly, with its types and subtypes, heresy was for the Inquisition a label applicable to a wide range of practices and beliefs. The range stretched from the preservation of specific dietary habits that might reflect fragments of a hidden religious practice to the articulation of full-blown challenges to core Christian dogma. Heresy's boundaries were thus quite ambiguous; Lea calls the term "elastic" and suggests that it offered ample room for maneuvering; Eimeric says that on matters of faith, "heresy and error are perfectly synonyms."[43] Inquisitors themselves were often aware of the ambiguities. For example, Francisco Peña, a Spanish specialist in canon law, wrote a commentary on the issue of dietary habits and heresy, focusing on the consumption of pork. Someone who converted to Christianity as an adult might reasonably have difficulty in getting used to new foods and beverages, Peña stated, but this was not true of the offspring of a convert: such persons would have no reason to abstain from certain foods other than reverence for an old belief.[44] Given such fine points, how did the tribunal decide whether a person's actions qualified as material or formal heresy, internal or external, and so on? And who took the lead in making these appraisals?

At the most basic level, local tribunals were in charge of the appraisals. Tribunals had both paid and unpaid functionaries with clearly assigned responsibilities. As Tomás de Torquemada envisioned them, each tribunal was to have two inquisitors, a *fiscal* (prosecutor), a *calificador* (assessor), an *alguacil* (constable), *notarios* (notaries), and various other minor officials and professionals who carried out specific tasks. All these men were paid functionaries, whether they earned regular salaries or received one-time payments for performing specific tasks. To be appointed to any job by the Inquisition, every applicant had to demonstrate proof of his legitimate birth as well as his *limpieza de sangre*. This requirement applied as well to unpaid functionaries and to the wives and prospective brides of any man who worked for the tribunal.

In today's popular imagination, the *inquisidor* was a fundamentalist, a fanatic, always eager to preach to the mobs, a zealot ready to exterminate heretics en masse. This is an erroneous stereotype. In general, the inquisitor was a highly educated priest, expert in both theology and law, a member of the cultured elite.[45] In addition to writing instruction manuals, and to processing the internal paperwork and correspondence related to their specific tasks, some inquisitors also composed works for a broader audience. In these writings they discussed the origins of inquisitorial practices and argued in favor of the role of the Holy Office in assuring good governance and in protecting society from the dangers of heresy. According to Lea, it was not mandatory that an appointed inquisitor be an ecclesiastic. However, he also points out that those men who had attained the required qualifications for the office were most likely to belong to religious orders. Paulino Castañeda Delgado and Pilar Hernández Aparicio clarify that in Lima those who were not priests at the time of their appointment had to be ordained within six months.[46]

"In any given year in the later sixteenth or early seventeenth century, it can be estimated that from around forty to perhaps as many as seventy men were holding office as judges in the Spanish Inquisition's district tribunals and as councilors of the *Suprema*," says Kimberly Lynn.[47] According to the initial set of regulations, a man who aspired to be an inquisitor had to be at least forty years old, but this was later changed to thirty.[48] He must also have earned a university degree; a sample of eighteen inquisitors appointed in Lima between 1635 and 1696 illustrates the point: seventeen had degrees in law and one in canon law. A newly appointed inquisitor most likely started as a calificador, an unpaid position, evaluating the theological quality of beliefs and practices examined in a trial, or as a fiscal (prosecutor), compiling testimony and preparing accusations. Inquisitors were expected to gain experience in all tribunal procedures by learning from the body's senior members and to move from one location to another as they climbed higher in the ranks. From a post as inquisitor, an appointee could also move to a position outside the tribunal, as did Toribio de Mogrovejo, who became Lima's archbishop in 1579 after a time as inquisitor in Granada, Spain. It should be noted, however, that his previous connection to the Inquisition there did not exempt him from having confrontations with the Lima inquisitors.[49]

Inquisitors' salaries varied across tribunals and were higher in the colonies because of the higher cost of living. Of the New World tribunals, the Lima inquisitors were the best paid.[50] Writing in 1630, Fray Buenaventura de Salinas y Córdova, a Franciscan friar who was also a calificador, explained that from the foundation of the Lima tribunal the royal treasury had to pay its inquisitors a salary of 3,000 pesos per year. The same chronicler says that the bishoprics of Paraguay, Buenos Aires, and Santiago in Chile received, as ecclesiastic income, the same annual amount of 3,000 pesos.[51] The most successful inquisitors might rise to membership in the Supreme Council (Consejo Supremo) in Madrid or even become the general inquisitor of the kingdom, which during the seventeenth century frequently included serving also as a state advisor (*consejero de estado*). The various positions and progressions to advancement illustrate the fluidity between positions in the Inquisition and those in the royal administration.[52]

Obviously, any inquisitor would be well versed in theology; however, the post of inquisitor did not convey responsibility for assessing the theological quality of the beliefs and practices examined throughout a given trial. That task was assigned to a tribunal member of lesser rank, the calificador, whose task was to sort out what had or had not happened, what had or had not been said. As an example of the type of materials given to calificadores for appraisal, in 1619 in Lima, a Portuguese man named Manuel de Fonseca openly questioned Christianity's principles and asked, among other questions, how Christ could suffer if he was God, how Mary could be simultaneously a virgin and a married woman, and why the Church had rejected the practice of circumcision, considering that the Messiah himself had been circumcised. Such statements were not unique.[53] Stuart Schwartz retrieves the declaration of a Brazilian man who had lived in Angola, Jamaica, and Cartagena and toward the end of the seventeenth century told the Portuguese tribunal that "Christ had not been carried in Mary's womb for nine months, for he could not believe that in those 'nauseous entrails' [*bascosidades*] God would be incarnated. Mary had remained a virgin after the birth because God was all-powerful, and Christ had been conceived when Saint Gabriel had placed three drops of blood in the heart of the Virgin."[54]

The inquisitor himself operated as a man of law rather than of theology, because he was charged with making decisions on matters of evidence, testimony, innocence or guilt, repentance, sentencing, and punishment, rather than on whether or not someone's discourse contained heretical propositions.[55] Don Juan de Mañozca y Zamora, who worked for different tribunals in the Spanish colonies and acted as one of the leading inquisitors during the 1630s trials in Lima, is an interesting example.[56] Born in Spain in 1577, Mañozca belonged to a family that had had members in the Inquisition over different generations. He was a man of strong character, described as someone who did not avoid altercations, and crossed the Atlantic several times to take posts with the Holy Office and the royal bureaucracy. In 1596 Mañozca y Zamora earned a baccalaureate degree in Mexico City, where he lived with his maternal uncle Pedro Sáenz de Mañozca. At that time the Mexican tribunal, in which the uncle had a post as a staff member, was conducting the trials of faith of the Carvajal family for crypto-Judaism.[57] Lynn speculates about whether Mañozca y Zamora attended an Auto General de Fe conducted in 1596 in New Spain, and if so what impact this might have had in the development of his career. Early in the new century Mañozca was again in Spain. At the University of Salamanca, in 1600 and in 1608, he earned two more degrees: a baccalaureate in laws and a *licenciatura*, a higher degree, in canon law.[58] The year 1608 also saw the establishment of the colonial tribunal in Cartagena of the Indies (now Colombia); Philip III appointed Mañozca as inquisitor there in 1609. At the time he was thirty-two years old. It was the beginning of a prominent career.

Juan de Mañozca y Zamora's professional and family life were clearly connected to the activities of the colonial Inquisition. From Cartagena, he received a promotion to the Lima tribunal in 1624; this tribunal, seated as it was in the viceregal capital, was a more important one. Prior to taking over the post in Lima, Mañozca was also a royal *visitador* (inspector) in Quito. In this office, he conducted *visitas* (inspections) of tribunals and reported the wrongdoings of royal officers. He also alienated the local elites, who created a coalition to oppose the visitador. The Council of the Indies considered Mañozca's procedures imprudent and harsh and terminated his inspections in 1627; the council even considered revoking his appointment as inquisitor, according to John Leddy Phelan.[59] Referring to these events Juan Antonio Suardo recorded that the king designated another officer to complete the inspection in Quito.[60] But it was not the end of his career. Mañozca went on to occupy his post in Lima. By January 1639, when Lima celebrated an Auto General de Fe, he had advanced to become a member of the Supreme Council of the Holy Office. In his late years, Mañozca y Zamora held several top positions simultaneously: chief prelate of the viceroyalty, councilor of the Suprema, and archbishop of Mexico, where he died in 1650.

Mañozca y Zamora was not the only member of his family to figure prominently in an Inquisition tribunal. A younger cousin named Juan Sáenz de Mañozca y Murillo, the son of his maternal uncle, was an inquisitor of the Mexican tribunal during the trials of the Portuguese New Christians carried out there in the 1640s. This younger cousin had held an appointment at a lower rank in Lima in the 1630s and climbed up the institutional ladder, thereby reproducing the familial cycle. The chronicler Fernando de Montesinos, born in Seville but a resident of Peru from 1629, wrote that in the Auto General de Fe performed in Lima in 1639, yet another member of Mañozca's family, a lieutenant named Francisco Prieto, marched in the procession that accompanied the viceroy.[61] Another example of expanded opportunities, this time from the Lima tribunal, is the doctor don Juan Gutiérrez Flores, who arrived in the city in 1625 after having worked with the Holy Office in Mexico, Sicily, and Mallorca. Around 1629, Gutiérrez Flores had conflated the positions of inquisitor and royal visitador of the Lima audiencia and frequently accompanied the viceroy Conde de Chinchón at official functions.[62] However, the doctor died just five years after his arrival, in poverty.

The case of Juan de Mañozca y Zamora and his family is not unique. Also in seventeenth-century Peru, Juan Gutiérrez de Quintanilla was priest and comisario of the tribunal in Huamanga; he had relatives in the secular administration as well as in the tribunal. Nepotism at the top of tribunal ranks can also be appreciated in the case of Fray Antonio de Sotomayor, a Dominican born in 1557 who started his career as a calificador in Galicia, Spain, when he was thirty-four years old (in 1591). He became the confessor of Philip III's children in 1616 and state councilor in 1626. Sotomayor was Philip IV's confessor and general inquisitor between 1632 and 1643; at some time during that period one of his relatives was a member of the Supreme Council. In addition, the Galician tribunal had two inquisitors and a prosecutor who were related to the Sotomayor family.[63]

Transfers between posts and the conflation of high positions in the colonies were not exclusive to inquisitors. Indeed, their paths were similar to those of viceroys and bureaucrats at the top of the colonial administration, who arrived in Peru after appointments at other posts or left Peru for destinations at which they might advance.[64] Nevertheless, the examples of upward mobility mentioned here were not likely the general rule; certainly, not everybody reached the highest ranks of the bureaucracy, either royal or ecclesiastical. However, it is clear that during the seventeenth century many Lima inquisitors developed respected careers and sometimes used the post as a bridge to other positions in the royal administration.[65]

Although Torquemada had envisioned two inquisitors per tribunal, in the 1630s Lima had four. In order of the date on which they assumed their offices, they were Andrés Juan Gaitán, Mañozca y Zamora, Gutiérrez Flores, and Antonio de Castro y del Castillo.[66] Gaitán, born in Tordesillas, began his career in Spain as prosecutor for the tribunals of Cuenca and Seville. He later moved to Lima, where he remained for forty years, from 1611 to 1651; he left Lima in 1651 and died while traveling to Spain. Castro y del Castillo was born in Burgos and held university degrees from Salamanca and from San Marcos in Peru. After serving as a priest and a comisario of the Holy Office in Potosí for more than twenty years, Castro y del Castillo was appointed to the Lima tribunal in 1627, initially as a supernumerary, to work without compensation until such time as someone would leave and thereby create a vacancy. In September of 1647 he was named bishop of La Paz (now Bolivia). Both Gaitán and Castro y del Castillo had relatives in the tribunal as well.[67] It can be said that the Ibero-American world of the sixteenth and seventeenth centuries contained two parallel networks: kinship networks of Portuguese New Christians working in transatlantic trade, and networks of Spanish bureaucrats, some also linked by kin, working for Inquisition tribunals.

Interactions among inquisitors were sometimes contentious, due variously to disagreements on particular cases, rivalries and competitions related to their roles and careers within the institution, or simply to differences in personality. There might also be economic competition. Between 1587 and 1591 Don Juan Ruiz de Prado conducted an inspection of the Lima office that led to several confrontations with the inquisitor Antonio Gutiérrez de Ulloa, but during the same years the two men joined forces to confront the viceroy and declared his excommunication. Gabriela Ramos has found that, at the end of the sixteenth century, members of the Lima tribunal wrote to the Supreme Council accusing the inquisitor Pedro Ordóñez Florez of using tribunal funds for his own commercial endeavors. In the following century, the inquisitor Andres Juan Gaitán was Mañozca's senior; however, the latter was a senior at the post owing to his prior appointment in Cartagena, and, in practice, Mañozca had a more prominent role in Lima. By the same token, the articulation between the Holy Office and the civil authorities was far from seamless and harmonious. Issues of competence and arguments regarding immunity exposed the frictions between civil and religious members of government and were the cause of disputes between the tribunal and the viceroy. Issues of ecclesiastical jurisdiction and privilege created friction between tribunal members and the archbishop and bishop. At the end of the sixteenth century, as just mentioned, Lima tribunal members attempted to excommunicate the viceroy of Peru; in 1637, there were conflicts of jurisdiction between the Lima Inquisition and the Tribunal Mayor de Cuentas.[68] Furthermore, conflicts between the tribunal and the secular authorities were not exclusive of the Lima office. In his discussion of the conflicts between the Mexican tribunal and the officers of the royal authority, the historian Alejandro Cañeque concludes that "the inquisitors, rather than being a tool utilized by the monarchs to impose their authority, turned out to be trying and irritating rivals of that same royal authority."[69]

The position below inquisitor was the *promotor fiscal*, the prosecuting officer. This post was introduced by the Spanish Inquisition—it did not exist in the medieval institution. In theory, a prosecutor presented evidence in a trial, and the inquisitors listened and then judged, but in practice the prosecutor followed direct instructions from the inquisitor. During the seventeenth century in Lima, new prosecutors attained the post of inquisitors within an average of four years.[70]

Inquisitor networks also relied on the assistance of lower-rank bureaucrats and other officials who were not members of the Church but were most likely linked to inquisitors through family relationships. Other officials might have responsibility for overseeing or administering some aspect of tribunal finance: royal allowances, salary payments, or tribunal properties and investments. Also, every Inquisition procedure was carefully recorded, with names and genealogies, witnesses' accounts, trial records, meeting minutes, and accounts of confiscated property—everything had to be counted and itemized before being sold. These tasks were given to *secretarios* (secretaries), *notarios* (notaries), and *receptores* (receivers). The alguacil (constable) executed orders such as imprisonments and confiscations, with a salary of 1,000 pesos derived from confiscated properties according to Salinas y Córdova.[71] There were other lower-rank officials, such as the *contador* (accountant), the *alcaide de las cárceles secretas* (the steward of the secret prisons, who was in charge of the maintenance and security of prisons and prisoners), the *nuncio* (messenger), and the *portero* (janitor). Positions were not always so carefully defined: Bartolomé de Pradeda, the Lima alcaide in the 1630s, complained that at the time he had been appointed to his position (1615) he also performed functions of messenger and janitor because of the lack of other personnel.[72]

Other professionals who participated in a trial of faith were retained and paid for their services as such services were needed. These included attorneys-at-law employed as defense advocates (four are recorded for the Lima tribunal in the eighteenth century),[73] *verdugos* (public executioners) who administered torture, and health practitioners who examined the prisoners before and afterward and could be called on in case of an emergency. In 1638, after Antonio Morón fainted in the Lima tribunal's torture chambers, the session was interrupted and he was taken to his cell. A doctor and a surgeon were called by a tribunal officer to check on Morón's health. They concluded he had apoplexy and tried several remedies, such as bleeding the prisoner's foot, wet cuppings, and placing a mix of vinegar and pepper under his nose, until Morón came back to his senses. However, he died soon after.[74] Physicians' services were also required for specific assessments of prisoners' circumstances. When Manuel de Fonseca said under torture, in 1618, that he was a legitimate circumcised Jew (*judío legítimo circuncidado*), the statement had to be corroborated. A physician's counsel was also required in cases of prisoners who claimed mental illness before the tribunal to avoid liability; they might be called on to determine whether an insanity plea was justified, as in the cases of Lima detainees Enrique Jorge Tavares and Manuel Henríquez.[75]

The tribunal also made use of officials and associates who did not receive payment of any kind but probably benefited from the social recognition that stemmed from being connected to the institution; such connection carried prestige of course, but it also served to silence any challenges to their own blood purity and legitimacy. Among these officials were the *consultores*, the calificadores, and the familiares. According to 1630 sources, the Lima tribunal selected members of the royal court (Real Audiencia) to be consultores. The deliberations in which sentences were decided were called *consultas de Fe*, hence the term consultores.[76] Because they participated in the secret deliberations of Inquisition tribunals, secular judges had knowledge of the development of trials of faith and of upcoming sentences. Furthermore, in the viceroyalty it was the secular authorities who granted licenses for publishing, including the publishing of materials related to the activities of the Holy Office. In February 1639 the viceroy of Peru and members of the royal court and of the Lima tribunal approved the publication of the chronicle of the Auto General de Fe celebrated on January 23 of that year. There were three print shops in Lima in 1630, but the work was published in Madrid after being approved by the general inquisitor.[77]

The post of calificador was created in the mid-sixteenth century; his role was to provide assessments only, and he did not participate in the trial decisions. The calificadores were clerics who evaluated what qualified as heresy and what did not, controlled lists of censored books, and were expected to achieve the sincere conversion of imprisoned heretics during a trial by imparting catechism, discussing doubts, debating doctrinal points, and so forth. Between 1570 and 1600 nine calificadores were registered in Lima, although just two usually worked with the tribunal at any given time (the same number is recorded for 1621). The Lima calificadores could be members of the religious orders or the secular clergy. They might also be university professors (perhaps theologians), prominent intellectuals, writers, and owners of large private library collections. Even though some inquisitors had begun their professional careers in this post, other calificadores held the appointment for its honorific credit only.[78]

In cities outside its immediate area but still under its jurisdiction, a tribunal had designated priests who acted as *comisarios* (commissioners) and had executive functions only. According to instructions issued in 1569 for the Lima office, each head of the bishopric and each maritime port was to have a comisario, and inquisitors were supposed to make district inspections and oversee the comisarios's performance. In Peru, comisarios had more authority than they did in Spain because the mandated inspections by inquisitors did not turn into reality.[79]

Regarding the larger organization, each tribunal responded to the Consejo Supremo (the Suprema, or Supreme Council), which was based in Madrid and met five times a week. Initially, the Suprema had a role secondary to the general inquisitor, but over time it took on many of his responsibilities and others and came to hold almost absolute power over the tribunals. Local tribunals submitted monthly reports to the Suprema, informing the body about finances and cases, and the Suprema composed and revised instructions and advised on sentences, problematic prisoners, and on any other issue it considered of concern. Members of the Suprema could also be members of other royal councils, which again illustrates the peculiarity of that tribunal and the intersection of political and ecclesiastical functions in the activities of its members.[80]

In medieval times, armed guards protected the inquisitor and carried out his orders. According to Lea, these guards were close to the inquisitor and enjoyed recognition as members of his "family," thus the name familiares (familiars)—even though they were not relatives of the inquisitor.[81] The Spanish Inquisition kept the position's name, but the duties of the familiar evolved into something different, not attached exclusively to the inquisitor. In the Spanish institution, the familiares served the whole tribunal and performed whatever tasks were needed: for example, familiares acted as tribunal notaries in seventeenth-century Lima. In case of local opposition to the presence of the tribunal, the Crown used the network of familiares to develop a bond with local communities. Like the calificadores, the familiares did not earn a salary but enjoyed benefits such as immunity from secular justice and the social reputation usually associated with members of the tribunal. They had licenses to bear arms, could spy on suspected heretics and arrest them, and assisted in the persecution of fugitives.[82] In addition to the familiares, other people had authorization to carry weapons: Juan Antonio Suardo recorded that in 1630 in Lima, the viceroy ordered that only black *lacayos* (footmen) assigned to judges, court stewards, accountants and other royal bureaucrats, high officers of the army, inquisitors, and the tribunal prosecutor could carry swords; the highest-level representatives of the merchants' guild enjoyed similar privilege.[83] Instructions for the Lima tribunal established that the city would have twelve familiares (for comparison, there were fifty familiares in the city of Seville). Sometimes a tribunal member petitioned that a *familiatura* be granted to his sons as an initial step in a career in the institution. During the seventeenth century, the selection of familiares also took into account their economic position, which explains why some Lima merchants became familiares of the tribunal and why historian Jaime Contreras finds the peninsular institution increasingly aristocratic throughout the century.[84]

Financing the Guardians of the Faith

Nicolau Eimeric and his commentator Francisco Peña differ in their accounts of the payment of salaries to Holy Office members and the financing for maintaining the tribunals, and it is clear from reading their views that there was widespread variance of opinion on those subjects. One option put forth was that secular authorities should support the tribunal because the entire society would benefit from the eradication of heresy; another was that bishops would take care of inquisitors' financial needs as suggested by the pope. Other strategies called for allocations of various kinds of funds to be administered by each tribunal.[85] Indeed, each of these options was implemented by the Lima tribunal during the course of its existence. Financially, the Lima tribunal had had difficulties from its establishment in 1570—that is, until the confiscations related to trials for crypto-Jewish heresy toward the middle of the seventeenth century began to provide some income. Salaries were calculated annually and usually paid in installments during the months of January, May, and September. A subvention from the royal treasury covered the salaries of two inquisitors, a prosecutor, and a secretary, but for other salaries and for regular expenses such as the maintenance of poor prisoners, rental and upkeep of facilities, furniture, paper, ink, and any other necessary supplies, the office had to rely on other sources of income. Among these were fines and property confiscations imposed in sentences (civil court officers' salaries were also supplemented by fines and confiscations from civil trials). Even the royal subvention to the Holy Office was not issued automatically, however, and the funds obtained through confiscations were as variable as the trials of faith. One step in receiving the subvention required the tribunal to inform the viceroy of its finances, although inquisitors would have probably preferred to receive the royal subvention without further intervention.

The Lima office had additional sources of income from investments, monetary penalties imposed in some trials, and occasional donations. Even though in their letters to the king inquisitors insisted that they lacked funds to cover the everyday operations of the office, I agree with Maurice Birckel, Paulino Castañeda Delgado, Pilar Hernández Aparicio, and René Millar Carvacho in considering it plausible that they may have been exaggerating and that, as Birckel suspects, their complaints were probably sometimes formulaic. Nonetheless, these authors also demonstrate that since the flow of funds was unsteady, the tribunal clearly had challenges in organizing a budget. It must have restricted disbursements to the basics, and most of its members probably lived modestly, although some did not, according to reports written after inspections.[86] I will illustrate with a few examples, organized chronologically.

Following the 1573 celebration of an Auto General de Fe, a Lima tribunal member mentioned that income from earlier confiscations had been used to pay for the ceremony's main platform and for payments to the notary and other lower-rank tribunal members. In contrast, the Quito bishop in the following decade gave the tribunal 20,000 pesos for the construction of a chapel (1583).

After conducting an inspection of the Lima facilities between 1587 and 1591, Don Juan Ruiz de Prado suggested an annual allocation of 5,000 pesos to cover salaries, meals for poor prisoners, and general expenses, so that the office would not have to depend on confiscations. Ruiz de Prado also suggested the investment of confiscated funds.[87] In a 1594 letter to the king, the inquisitor Ordóñez y Flórez commented that buildings damaged by an earthquake needed repairs and that officers were serving without a salary. He proposed the tribunal receive an allocation of 100 indigenous workers to labor in the mines of Potosí so that the proceeds would come directly to the tribunal (the tribunal already held mining concessions there, but the concessions had been rented out to others). The inquisitor also proposed that the tribunal receive land concessions (*mercedes de tierras*) and other forms of assistance to generate income. By the end of the century, the royal subvention provided half of the tribunal's income; the other half came from various other sources. Records of investments made by the tribunal at the beginning of the seventeenth century suggest income from property confiscations, but a general pardon for heretics issued in 1605 instructed that confiscated goods be returned. The Lima tribunal initially complied with the instruction, but the inquisitors soon began to ask again for royal support. They reported to the king that the 1608 Auto de Fe had been celebrated at the cathedral cemetery because of lack of funds for building the stage.[88]

But during the 1610s, the viceroy received instructions to reduce the royal contribution to the Holy Office. In 1621, the king sent a letter saying that the tribunal would have to demonstrate that income from confiscations was insufficient to pay salaries before any royal subvention would be delivered. As a result, Lima received no royal funds from 1621 to 1625. The tribunal's numbers looked better around 1625 when they celebrated an impressive Auto and collected income from confiscations, and toward the end of that year, the tribunal did receive a royal contribution. However, there was a change of direction underlying these events: in a reversal of financial roles, the Supreme Council in 1628 requested a contribution from the Lima tribunal. In 1629 (Millar Carvacho situates the tribunal's prosperity in the years between 1629 and 1721), the Crown reiterated that the tribunal would have to demonstrate lack of other funds before it would be given any support; the Crown also criticized Lima inquisitors for their use of funds and excessive spending on the tribunal members' own residences. But even with these ups and downs, there was still sentiment for royal support. Shifts in the finances of the tribunal did not imply a total change in the financial dynamics and the payment of salaries. In January 1630, the issue of inquisitors' salaries came up in documentation external to the tribunal. According to Suardo, the Crown had instructed that inquisitors' salaries be paid by churches from within the viceroyalty instead of by the royal treasury.

In March 1631 the prior of the Dominican convent offered to cover the salaries, which had not been paid in the preceding two years. Heads of other religious orders (Jesuit, San Agustín, and La Merced) extended similar offers, and the inquisitors formally thanked each prelate.[89]

The income of the Lima office changed drastically as a result of confiscations following the trials of the Great Complicity (1635–1639) and the reconciliations of 1639–1641. Lea comments that "popular report estimated it as a million of pesos," a number close to what modern scholarship has established. According to Castañeda Delgado and Hernández Aparicio, the tribunal seized 1,204,174 pesos between 1634 and 1650. After deducting the cost of feeding inmates during their trials and fulfilling financial obligations contracted by prisoners before the incarcerations, the office was able to hold on to just over 30 percent of the initial amount. Reviewing tribunal records up to 1649, Millar Carvacho arrived at a very similar result: there was a total of 1,297,410 pesos at the time property confiscations were made (half of this sum was from the assets of Manuel Bautista Pérez, the wealthiest prisoner in the Great Complicity trials), and after deducting the cost of maintaining prisoners during the trials and liquidating pending debts and credits, the tribunal was left with just under 31 percent of the initial total. The main beneficiary of these accounts was the Lima office, which became financially independent after these confiscations and was able finally to send funds to the Suprema in Madrid.[90]

Life at Tribunal Facilities

"I was taken to a prison under the ground where no sky clarity could be seen but with lights night and day," wrote Manuel Henríquez, a man whose Lima trial started in 1635 and ended in 1664. He was not referring to the Lima facilities but to the jails of the Portuguese Inquisition in Coimbra, where he had had his first encounter with the institution prior to his migration to the New World.[91] The words of Manuel Henríquez echo those of Reinaldo González Montes, a man who lived in Seville in the 1550s and wrote a text opposing the tribunal. Montes says that offenders accused of heresy were assigned to small, narrow individual cells, and when imprisonments exceeded the tribunal capabilities, more than one person was placed in the cell.[92] In 1571 in Lima, a year after the establishment of the office, tribunal members reported to the Suprema that even though the cells were sound and had proper ventilation, prisoners fell sick with melancholy and were likely to die before the celebration of their public Auto General.[93]

Established in 1570, the Lima tribunal functioned in a provisional location until 1584, when it moved to its own facilities close to the University of San

Marcos; in this location the office operated until its abolition. The institution facilities required different types of cells (secret, perpetual, intermediate, and public) according to the type of accusation and the stages of each trial. For example, someone undergoing a trial of faith would be placed in a secret cell where communication with other people was restricted to a severe minimum. Someone who had been tried and received a sentence of perpetual imprisonment would be placed in a less restrictive cell, with less secrecy. In addition to cells, tribunal buildings had a kitchen and lodgings for the various officials who lived on-site: janitors, prison stewards, and at least one inquisitor. The complex where prisoners' cells were located also contained the hearing rooms, the torture chamber, and the storage area for records—this was the *cámara del secreto* (chamber of secrecy), a room locked with three keys, each in the hands of a different official.

Money to cover food and basic needs for prisoners, such as laundry, came from a combination of inmates' contributions and royal subsidies. These monies passed through a chain of minor officers and tribunal employees—*despensero*, *cocinero*, and *guarda* (dispensary clerk, cook, and guard)—before any part of them reached the prisoner.[94] As with secular jails, periodic inspections assessed the conditions inside the prisons, inquiring into their health and basic needs, such as food and clean clothes, the behavior of the guards, and the like. Peña recommended two monthly inspections at least, more if needed, and he also suggested giving permission for guests to visit a prisoner, assuming that would encourage a confession. González Montes, on the other hand, criticized the procedures of the Holy Office and questioned whether these periodic assessments brought any improvement to prisoners' circumstances or were mere bureaucratic formalities.[95]

As will be discussed in the following chapter, in theory, a trial of faith was to be short, fast, and straightforward. In practice, however, some trials dragged on for years and even decades, during which time prisoners lived—and sometimes died—inside the tribunal facilities. Inquisitors and prisoners met formally during a trial of faith, but lower-rank officials were in close, sometimes daily, contact with detainees. Such interactions generally did not enter into official records unless extraordinary situations arose, such as allegations of corruption, trial irregularities, or deaths in the secret cells. Even though secrecy and isolation were goals of the Inquisition as a disciplinary body, information did circulate among lower-rank officials, between these officials and prisoners, and also among prisoners. News also traveled outside of the prisons, to inmates' relatives and potential offenders. All of this verbal traffic probably influenced the development of a given trial. If notice of unauthorized interactions or the circulation of classified information reached the inquisitors, they could trigger a criminal trial of the perpetrators (also to be conducted by the Inquisition) and prosecute participants on the grounds of having helped the prisoners and thereby interfered with the tribunal's task.[96] In such trials, the interactions were often exposed in formal hearings, as in that of Manuel Bautista Pérez, who admitted to having paid a tribunal helper to take a message to another prisoner. The tribunal also pursued those involved in unusual events that happened in the cells. The same Pérez made cuts in his own groin with a knife and had to respond to an investigation of the incident afterward.[97] Taking advantage of the clandestine interactions among prisoners, the tribunal found ways to use them for its own benefit and sometimes positioned spies in cells to listen and report. The Lima tribunal, for example, placed a man inside Enrique Jorge Tavares's cell to assess if the prisoner was indeed insane or if he was pretending insanity to avoid harsh punishment.[98]

Neither the hunt for heretics nor the Tribunal of the Holy Office of the Inquisition, created in 1478 in Castile, was an invention of the fifteenth century. As a disciplinary body, the Spanish Inquisition was based on a considerable history of persecution and prosecution of religious heterodoxy in medieval Christian Europe. The Spanish tribunal introduced some modifications to the overall structure and procedures of the Inquisition but preserved the main characteristics of its medieval predecessor. No longer the medieval-era temporary tribunal that conducted exceptional inquiries, the Spanish Inquisition was a permanent disciplinary body directly under royal command and active for over three centuries in the Ibero-American world. Looking beyond the procedural details by which it conducted business, the central and remarkable innovation of the Spanish Inquisition was its stability, longevity, and the sprawl of tribunals on both sides of the Atlantic. With its specially trained personnel and its own facilities and finances (even though often strained), the Spanish Inquisition not only persecuted and prosecuted offenders but maintained an enduring presence in its host society's daily religious and legal life. For bureaucrats, it offered potentially grand careers—as well as the opportunity to gain from institutional corruption.

The Spanish tribunal was concerned with offenses to religious orthodoxy (Judaism, Islam, and Protestantism) and other offenses, and it was under royal rather than papal supervision. It also came to be an established institution, with its own facilities, bureaucracy, employees, merit system, and, certainly, corruption as well. In its regular operations, it demanded the same logistical support as any other legal authority and penal system. In practice, many of the tribunals carried out their functions in situations that were far from ideal, as Henry Kamen has pointed out.[99] As discussed in the previous pages, inquisitors found themselves addressing numerous complaints to the monarchy, demanding more money, better locations, and more personnel. Nevertheless, the very fact that Inquisition bureaucrats did attempt to bargain for better salaries and for assistance that would improve their operations does point to the tribunals' sense of their own importance and their integration into Spanish life, society, and politics.

In terms of specific tasks, the tribunals of the Inquisition were to lead the battle against heresy, blasphemy, witchcraft, and the like. To do so, the tribunal had to locate and imprison offenders and bring them to judgment with a trial of faith, a well-demarcated procedure that will be analyzed in the following chapter. Obstructing a trial or another activity of a tribunal was considered a serious offense. In case of people who did so, the tribunal carried out criminal trials, as happened in Lima in the mid-seventeenth century. Finally, the tribunal also exerted control over morality, listing, for example, bigamy as an offense, and over vehicles of potentially heretical ideas, such as books.[100]

2

The Trial as a Setting for Confession and Repentance

The trial was a carefully structured procedure that unfolded in a sequence of steps.[1] As described in Francisco Peña's 1578 revision and commentary on Nicolau Eimeric's 1376 *El manual de los inquisidores*, the trial of faith was strictly regulated by the Holy Office and proceeded in several defined stages.[2] The trial was called an inquisitio; it consisted of investigation, accusation, and conviction, all conducted by the same office, or even the same officer. Similar procedures were used in secular justice.[3] Events in a trial of faith took place inside the facilities of the Inquisition—only the ceremony of punishment, the Auto de Fe, was occasionally performed in public. The stages in a trial of faith followed a sequence: denunciation, deposition, imprisonment, hearings, accusation, torture, confession, defense, publication, sentence, and the Auto. A prisoner could confess at any time. Such a confession would alter the stages of his or her trial: a confession was of greater weight than witnesses' accounts.[4]

The tribunal communicated with the general population through the dissemination of *edictos* (edicts). In the case of itinerant tribunals, the publication of the edicto de Fe (edict of faith) preceded the inquisitors' arrival; for permanent tribunals, the edictos were read before the public at churches, cathedrals, monasteries, and convents during Lent. The reading of the edict of faith was itself a ceremony, announced prior to the event, and attendance at the reading was mandatory for anyone ten years of age or older.[5] As occurred at times during other kinds of ceremonies conducted by the tribunal, the reading of an edict could generate conflicts and heated disputes between tribunal members and officers of the civil authority, especially in regard to issues of protocol.[6] Edictos were also read as a formal part of the events surrounding a *visita* of inquisition officials to a tribunal district to exercise their oversight. However, the broader district covered by the Lima tribunal was not subject to the same kinds of visitas, so edicts for the Peruvian office and the Lima tribunal did not get as much visibility as for other tribunals, as Pedro Guibovich Pérez has argued. Furthermore, he notes that the reading of edicts, even in cities other than Lima, occurred with uneven frequency.[7]

Edictos were of two types: *generales* and *particulares*. Although the specific content of edictos generales varied over time and place, this edicto was most often employed by the Inquisition to alert members of the community to the spread of heresies or offenses that had taken place in their midst. The edicto might also offer a grace period (edict of grace) and varying degrees of benevolent treatment to those who had taken the initiative and confessed voluntarily before undergoing a trial of faith. The edictos also reminded local inhabitants that the tribunal expected the cooperation of the entire population and would administer penalties to those who obstructed its tasks. In addition to being read aloud, the edictos were posted on church doors, so as to inform all about improper or suspicious behaviors in their communities. The edictos particulares could address a specific offense or a specific book that was prohibited, and it required no special ceremony for its adoption.[8]

As I have noted elsewhere, heresy was considered an error in matters of faith. It was classified as material and formal, with types and subtypes defined by everything from the accused's behavioral traits and dietary habits to an articulated challenge to the core of Christian dogma. In practice, the boundaries of heresy were ambiguous, and for any accused person who stood in front of the tribunal, its members had certain room for individual interpretations.[9] However, in its written edicts (of grace and of faith) the Holy Office produced clear definitions of problematic behaviors. These varied over time, again demonstrating the historicity of heresy as a cultural construction. Initially, the Spanish tribunal addressed its edicts of grace to the presence of New Christians of Jewish descent; later, while the formulaic aspects remained similar, the major concern was the population of Muslim descent. In a similar progression, the edicts regarding rites, beliefs, and ceremonies were initially intended to target Judaism, then Islam, and later Protestantism, and even later to reflect the tribunal's concerns with issues such as moral offenses. In addition to scrutinizing dietary habits and the observance of the Saturday Sabbath, the edicts directed attention to private behaviors, such as the custom of shaving the beard or underarms of a dead person, burying the deceased in virgin soil, or eating on the floor during mourning as behaviors that indicated the heresy of crypto-Judaism. These and other practices are described by David Gitlitz in his survey of crypto-Jewish practices.[10]

In the edicts read in Lima over the sixty years between 1570 and 1630, the tribunal expanded the scope of these documents to include blasphemy and pacts with the devil among other moral offenses. An edict read in the City of Kings in 1629 centered on sorcery; an edict read in the city in March 1630 prohibited confessors from having improper conversations with women, and another in the same month exhorted residents of any quality and condition to take communion. In the same year, the tribunal also mentioned that people of Jewish or Muslim descent might have traveled to the colonies despite royal regulations against it.[11]

Moving Toward the Trial

Regarding the specifics of the trial of faith, the Spanish Inquisition followed the steps of its medieval predecessors but incorporated modifications, leaving its distinctive imprint on our historical perceptions of what the trial of faith and the Holy Office of the Inquisition actually were, as will be explained in following pages. When Tomás de Torquemada composed instructions for inquisitors between 1484 and 1498, he followed the general guidelines established by Eimeric, paying attention to the development of procedures and the broader institutional coordination; Torquemada also addressed matters of dispute or irregularity, such as the designation of advocates or the functions of ordinary inquisitors.[12] Other general inquisitors during the sixteenth century (Diego de Deza in 1500, Fernando de Valdés in 1561) also focused on the standardization of procedures: the roles of tribunal members, the conduct of proceedings regarding property confiscations, and establishing a steady income for tribunals. The underlying idea was that "the inquisitor would not be the interpreter of the Law, but only the agent who applies it."[13] In addition to the edictos, the inquisition issued guidelines and orders in the form of handwritten letters, called *cartas acordadas*, which were meant to be added as appendixes to the general operating instructions.[14] More remarkably, the Spanish tribunal took the Auto de Fe, the final stage of the Inquisition trial, to a new level, as I will discuss later in this book. For now, I will turn to the trial of faith to explore the procedures of the Spanish Inquisition in cases of heresy.

As Henry Charles Lea has made clear, "the procedure of the Inquisition was directed to procuring conviction rather than justice."[15] Heresy was considered a crime of *lesa majestad* (equivalent to treason) and as such could be punishable with the death penalty in a secular court once the offense was first dealt with under the jurisdiction of the Holy Office. The intent of a trial was to offer prisoners the opportunity to confess and express remorse, in which case the death penalty would be commuted to a lesser one, and the offender reconciled to the community. However, a prisoner who rejected the opportunity for confession before the tribunal would be transferred to the secular authorities for the application of punishment—in the jargon of the Inquisition, "release[d] to the secular arm."[16] Most often this meant the person would be burned at the stake. The person undergoing a trial of faith was by definition presumed guilty, an obvious sinner. Once it collected, reviewed, assembled, and weighed information that constituted evidence of heresy by inquisitorial standards, the tribunal would trigger a trial.

Given that the assessment of the evidence preceded the trial, the trial began with the prisoner's guilt already decided. From the perspective of the tribunal, the point of the trial was the prisoner's opportunity to confess, unburden his or her conscience, acknowledge mistakes, and accept the deserved punishment. Throughout the stages of the trial, the inquisition offered to prisoners the chance to admit their offenses against the Christian community and to make a humble request for forgiveness and reconciliation. In short, the trial of faith did not intend to uncover truth of any sort—its purpose was, rather, to confront the prisoner with the reality of heretical practices and beliefs and to decide on proper punishment.

The trial of faith had several stages.[17] It usually started with the *denuncia* (denunciation), which could be a self-denunciation, or a denunciation from someone else, whether the person was a tribunal member or not. In the words of Fernando de Montesinos, the Inquisition was the *Argos divino de la Fe* (the divine Argus of the Faith).[18] This metaphor alludes to Argus, the classical mythological character with a hundred eyes distributed all over its body.[19] Any member of the tribunal could collect information. Once the tribunal had heard the evidence and voted to pursue the case (*votos*), the content of the denunciation was recorded in a formal deposition, called a *testificación*. Always in front of a notary and another bureaucrat—either a commissioner or an inquisitor—the witness went over names, situations, conversations, locations, and every other possibly relevant detail about a suspect's heretical practices. The next step was imprisonment, and one or two weeks later began a set of hearings (audiencias). In cases of manifest heresy and other cases in which the tribunal had enough evidence for a conviction, the imprisonment also included seizure of properties.[20] Procedures for the conduct of the hearings were meticulously detailed. For example, writing in 1578 and commenting on Eimeric's *Manual*, Francisco Peña suggested that during the hearings the prisoner's seat had to be lower and simpler than the chair of the inquisitor and that the interrogation had to progress from general to particular.[21]

In the first hearing, the tribunal asked the prisoner about his or her name, age, occupation, ancestry, and lineage (Old or New Christian). There were also questions related to Christian indoctrination: if baptized, when, where, and by whom, and whether the prisoner regularly attended Mass, confessed, and could recite some prayers as a proof of Christian faith. In case of persons not born in Christian lands, the instructions were also specific: people who were not baptized and declared themselves as non-Christians could be assigned penalties but would not be treated as heretics, unless they had proselytized for another religion.[22] Following these were inquiries about whether someone else in the prisoner's family had undergone a trial of faith. A singular aspect is that all questions asked during a trial of faith of the Spanish Inquisition had to be so plain and intelligible as to be answered by a yes or no. In this way, the prisoner would not be confused or misled about the meaning of the questions. With its plain and intelligible questions, the tribunal captured clear information and used it to decide the path of the trial and, of course, the prisoner's fate. This precision is an innovation of the Spanish Inquisition, spelled out in instructions from the Suprema issued in 1518. In the less-regulated medieval tribunal sessions, deceit was considered a legitimate tool for obtaining confessions (in his commented version of Eimeric's *Manual*, Francisco Peña instructed inquisitors to avoid tricks and strategies based on deception).[23]

It was during the first hearing that the prisoner was asked to tell his or her personal story. In the *discurso de vida* (life speech or life story), the prisoner, guided by questions, recalled the main events of his or her life, including childhood, youth, marriage, migration, and other relevant milestones. Even though the context of the trial of faith itself mediated the content of the discurso—and its content was recorded by the notary, not the person relating it—the discursos are one of the few instances in which we have access to the prisoner's voice.[24] In assessing the validity of this material, I consider that at this initial stage any prisoner would likely omit information that might prejudice his or her case (for example, having New Christian lineage, or a prior incarceration), but I also consider the narrative trajectory of their lives and migratory paths, up to the initiation of the trial, to be nonetheless illustrative of who they were.

At the beginning of his Lima trial (1635), Manuel Henríquez was a thirty-four-year-old *mercachifle* (peddler). He said in his discurso that he was born in Lamego, Portugal, and that he had lived with his parents until the age of eighteen. From Lamego Henríquez moved to Castile to sell textiles, and starting about 1619 he traveled between Madrid, Valladolid, Murcia, and other towns, until in 1628 he married and settled in the Spanish capital. After several other moves within Spain, he boarded a ship to Cartagena of the Indies in 1633. In Cartagena Henríquez took a job with Antonio Gómez de Acosta, a Portuguese slave trader, and the work took him first to Paita in northwestern Peru and later to Lima. From this city, Henríquez traveled to Cusco and to Huancavelica selling clothes, until his imprisonment in December 1635.[25]

Antonio Morón was a merchant, aged forty-six or forty-eight, in 1635. His discurso reveals that he also was born in Portugal (in Fundão) and had lived with his parents until the age of seven, when they died. Together with his older brother Diego, he went to Lisbon, where the two embarked for Angola. About 1596 the siblings left Africa with a slave ship, this time headed for Bahia in Brazil. After selling the slaves and loading the ship with clothes and other local products, they sailed to Rio de Janeiro to complete the cargo and then returned to Angola, closing in this way the commercial cycle. They repeated this itinerary twice and afterward traveled to the Caribbean. Antonio Morón also recalled three trips to Spain, the last in 1613 when he decided to stay in Seville after his brother's death and his own marriage to a woman named Mayor de Luna. On subsequent commercial trips Morón went to Portobello (Panama) and to Lima, and in 1627 his wife Mayor and daughter Isabel Antonia came to the New World. The family settled in the Lima, where they had resided until the trials of faith.[26]

The first hearing typically concluded with an admonition. It was made clear to the prisoner that the Inquisition did not bring anyone to its dungeons without sufficient evidence. The criterion for this was based on a regulation that specified that two witnesses had to provide testimony before a trial could be initiated, as Francisco Peña's commentary on Eimeric's manual had confirmed in the 1570s.[27] In consonance with the presumption of guilt, the tribunal asked prisoners what knowledge they had regarding the reason that they had been brought in front of the tribunal, and if they had something to confess in order to unburden their consciences. At the end of the hearing, prisoners were summoned to return to their cells so they could reflect on their memories and thereby unearth the truth. The second hearing usually took place months after the first, and it included a repetition of the admonition regarding confession and repentance stated at the end of the latter. It was at the third hearing, again months later, when the fiscal introduced the accusation (*acusación*).

The accusation was built upon the information assembled during the testificaciones. It summarized all the charges and descriptions of all the offenses provided by witnesses, but it protected their identities, both those who had provided the initial accusations and those who had been asked or forced to provide further testimonies. The stories told in the depositions were presented as facts, and the prisoner was deprived of knowing the names of the witnesses. This is one reason that René Millar Carvacho concludes that despite its procedural similarities to secular trials, the trial of faith conceded fewer warranties to prisoners.[28] The accusations were framed in a fixed institutional discourse, but at the same time there was variation according to individual lives and contexts. Some accusations brought out unique details, as did that of Joan Vicente. His accusation by the Lima tribunal included the information that he had hung the sambenito (the penitential garment that was sometimes a component of inquisitorial punishment) he was given at a previous trial in Portugal from a tree and had stood throwing stones at the clothing.[29]

The accusation that Lima issued against the traveling merchant Francisco Vázquez on April 1637 had fifteen chapters. Charges included believing in the Law of Moses, following its rites and ceremonies, respecting the Saturday Sabbath, avoiding eating pork and fish without scales, holding conversations about these matters with other heretics in Lima, and concealing his accomplices' names. Charges also included being *mañoso* (cunning) and *astuto* (astute) in disguising his origin and faith, because "with the Castilians he becomes Castilian, with the Galicians, Galician, and with the Portuguese he is known as a New Christian."[30] When Christian devotional items were found in Vázquez's pockets, he was accused of using them to carry out the pretense of being a good Christian, and that charge too was cited in his accusation. According to a 1636 letter from the Lima inquisitors, carrying rosaries, relics, and Christian images was a common crypto-Jewish strategy, as was their ability to recite Christian prayers.[31] In the letter, the inquisitors also reported that the prisoners, after confessing their offenses and being interrogated about these objects and prayers, replied that they wanted to keep the objects close and wished to remember the prayers in case of need. From the perspective of the inquisitors writing the letter, this was evidence enough that the prisoners were hypocrites who aimed to pass as good Christians and mislead the tribunal. From my perspective, however, it also illustrates how fragments of both religions were articulated, as David Gitlitz has synthesized, and also how the tribunal's discourse constructed "difference out of ambiguity," as Starr-Lebeau has incisively mentioned.[32] Returning to the defendant, Vázquez was accused of bigamy and of hiding his true lineage as well as his real profession. He was a barber, but had declared in his initial hearing that he had earned his first moneys as a rural peon. Later in the trial he was also accused of planning to become a Holy Office familiar to prevent being apprehended.[33] The prosecutor demanded major penalties for Vázquez, but in the end he was reconciled (later in the proceedings, he contested the trial of faith, arguing that he was an Old Christian, which adds another layer of puzzlement to an already blurred context).

Manuel Bautista Pérez was the most prominent individual accused in the Complicidad Grande trials of the 1630s and was also close to the well-known Lima banker Juan de la Cueva. Pérez was the wealthiest merchant among the local Portuguese New Christians, the owner of a large library, and allegedly the leader of the Peruvian crypto-Jewish community. The Portuguese merchant and his wife Guiomar lived in an impressive residence and had hosted a weeklong celebration when Guiomar's sister Isabel Enríquez and her husband Sebastián Duarte arrived in Lima in April 1635. Duarte was also Pérez's business associate.[34] Just four months later, on August 11, Pérez was taken into custody by the Lima tribunal, and in February 1636, the tribunal issued the accusation against him, structured into thirty-four chapters. In addition to lighting candles on Friday evening and letting them burn until Saturday morning, and avoiding work and changing clothes and bed linens on Saturday, he was accused of preserving the faith of his ancestors by refraining from the consumption of pork and fish without scales, eating only the anterior part of an animal, and fasting on specific days as indicated in the Law of Moses. In addition, Pérez was described as a *fautor* (abettor), *encubridor* (concealer), *maestro* (teacher), *oráculo* (oracle), and *rabino* (rabbi) of heretics. At various points in the trial, he was also called the Great Captain, in allusion to his role as leader of the crypto-Jewish community. In Lima, a sign posted at the corner of the main plaza in 1627 indicated that whoever wanted to learn the Law of Moses had to locate Pérez. For the Inquisition this meant his activities were public knowledge and had been conducted publicly prior to his 1635 arrest. Above and beyond keeping religious books and observing dietary habits, Pérez was accused of failing to denounce to the Holy Office someone who had preserved funerary customs related to Judaism. He was also indicted for leading *juntas* (meetings) and *congregaciones* (congregations) related to the Law of Moses in his own home and was quoted as saying that salvation and prosperity were associated with this practice—in short, as proselytizing for heresy. Allegedly, either at these meetings or in other encounters with Portuguese New Christians and crypto-Jews, Pérez had retold and commented on Old Testament stories, underscoring the favors the God of Israel had done for his people. He was also accused of speaking in a different language in front of Old Christians so they could not understand the matter under discussion. Other charges included poking fun at the Catholic saints, at stories of miracles that had reportedly occurred in the Lima convent, and at Old Christians who regularly confessed their sins to the priest. It was also reported that Pérez had called Lisbon the best city in the world but then faulted it by pointing to the Portuguese Inquisition's rigor and cruelty; this comment was judged to have unveiled his hidden faith.[35] Finally, the accusation also stated that, just prior to his Lima imprisonment, Pérez had sent to Panama city, Portobello, Cartagena, and Spain amounts of gold, silver, and jewelry, hoping in this way to minimize the potential confiscation of his property. He had also concealed titles and legal paperwork. The prosecutor demanded Manuel Bautista Pérez's release to the secular arm and the confiscation of his properties. The prosecutor added that Pérez should be subjected to physical torment.[36]

The Uses of Physical Torment: Path to Reconciliation

After an accusation the prisoner was expected to respond to all charges in a hearing. If the prisoner confessed and provided information that satisfied the tribunal, the officials moved to mete out a sentence, which would be the end of the trial. However, if there was no confession, or if the confession did not satisfy tribunal members, the following steps would include torture, one or more publication of testimonies, and defenses. At any stage of a trial, the prisoner was permitted to request additional hearings for the purpose of confession, clarification, expansion, or retraction of anything previously said. As already stated, the purpose of the Inquisition trial was to offer prisoners the appropriate setting for a sincere confession and an admission of heretical practices and, therefore, to open the gate for reconciliation. It is important to understand that from the perspective of the Inquisition, torture served such a purpose. "The Inquisitor must not be in a hurry to apply torture," wrote Nicolau Eimeric.[37] The Inquisition did not apply torture for the sole intention of inflicting pain or as a punishment per se. Rather, for the Inquisition, torture was a method that enabled the prisoner to open up and release the truth. From this perspective, torture within the frame of the Inquisition is clearly different from the ordeal of punishment depicted by Michel Foucault in the opening pages of *Discipline and Punish*. In Foucault's scenario, physical torment *is* the punishment, because inflicting pain was the primary goal. The ordeal described by Foucault was the culmination of the judicial process and it was carried out in public, whereas the Inquisition applied torment in secret chambers during the judicial process.[38]

The Holy Office was not the only disciplinary body to use torture habitually: torture was a component of the procedure called inquisition (inquiry) used in civil trials as well as trials of faith.[39] However, Francisco Peña reasoned that if for other (civil) offenses people like doctors, soldiers, officers and their sons, children, and the elderly would not be tortured, there were no exceptions in cases of heresy, because the Holy Office looked after the entire population; at the same time Peña said that children up to fourteen years of age, old people, and pregnant women must not be tortured and further recommended that less rigor should be applied while torturing clerics and monks.[40] The use of torture during the trial of faith was thus controlled and regulated. Physical torment was applied during a special session that did not take place in the rooms where regular hearings were held but in the *cámara del tormento*, the torture chamber.[41] The verdugo (torturer) was usually the same person who applied torment in civil trials and was supervised by inquisitors (at least two had to be present, according to Torquemada's instructions). Notaries carefully recorded every step of the session. The sessions at the torture chamber also included the attendance of doctors who checked on the prisoner's physical conditions before and after. All these people surrounded and intimidated the prisoner.[42] However, the presence of a regulatory framework for the application of torture and the attendance of medical doctors should not undermine the fact that it was torture. Based on information from the sixteenth and eighteenth centuries, Millar

Carvacho explains that Lima applied torture only to prisoners who evidenced manifest heresy and that these were the minority of the cases he analyzed. Following Kamen, Irene Silverblatt says that "torture was applied selectively and fiercely: the bulk of its victims were Judaizers, Protestants, and *moriscos* (converted Muslims of Moorish ancestry)."[43] For the seventeenth century in Peru, Silverblatt writes that close to 75 percent of prisoners accused of crypto-Judaism were subjected to torture, a percentage similar to that tortured by the Spanish tribunal during the same century. Because of the prevalence of torture in trials of crypto-Jews, I want to analyze it at a deeper level, and examine its methods, reasons, and regulations.

Torture methods combined the use of ropes, wheels, pulleys, and water.[44] One of the torture techniques used in Lima was the *mancuerda*, in which ropes tied around the arms were connected to a wheel that controlled the tension. Other techniques were the *potro* (rack), the *tortura del agua* (water torture), and the *garrucha*. In the potro the prisoner's feet were inserted in the rack to secure the position, and then ropes were tied around the toes and also around the arms (again, ropes were adjusted during the session). In the tortura del agua, a restrained prisoner lay horizontally while water was poured into his or her mouth. When applying the garrucha, the prisoners' hands were tied behind the back (or above the head and neck according to some authors); then the prisoner was suspended in the air and let go abruptly, sometimes after a short period of time and sometimes after an hour, "the time being determined by the gravity of the crime," explains Karen Sullivan.[45] The fall was interrupted just before the prisoner's feet touched the ground.

The reasons alleged for the application of torture varied in consonance with the development of each case. In the absence of a confession during the course of the three stipulated hearings and the subsequent accusation, questions were asked in the torture chamber while the prisoner was being tormented. Initially, these addressed the heretical practices and beliefs of the prisoner. This was called torture *in capud proprium*.[46] If the prisoner had begun to confess his or her own heretical acts, but was reluctant to incriminate those with whom heretical practices had been shared, the application of torture continued, with those present asking questions about the practices and beliefs of others (relatives, acquaintances, business associates, etc.). This was called torture *in capud alienum*,[47] and it was directed to gather information that would thicken a current or potential case against a third person.

It is important to underscore that even though the application of torture took place in a secret setting (like most proceedings of the Inquisition trial), it was neither illegal nor clandestine. On the contrary, it was legal and a constitutive part of both trials of faith and civil trials. The application of torture was formally included in the trial of faith, and like every other step of the proceedings, it was regulated, controlled, and carefully recorded by notaries. Even though the entire trial was carried out in secrecy, the application of torment was executed in an atmosphere that took secrecy and isolation to a deeper level. Eimeric says that the executioners should undress the prisoner, all the while fostering uneasiness and anguish, pressuring to hurry the confession, trying to intimidate (him or her). Once naked, the Inquisitors were to take the prisoner to the side and request a confession offering leniency, if possible.[48] The uniformity among records from the torture chamber suggests the use of a "template," similar to what Martínez discusses in connection to the documentation related to blood purity.[49] Actually, documents from different times and places that address ways to apply torments and record sessions at the torture chamber confirm that this uniformity was intentional.

In the following pages, in addition to Nicolau Eimeric, I look at documents from different tribunals to describe and analyze such sessions, including a letter describing how torments are applied in Castile from 1662[50] and a document describing how a minister records sessions in the torture chambers from 1690.[51] Still another document, from the 1654 tribunal in Toledo, relates modifications on the application of torment.[52] If we read these documents and compare them with the records of the cámara del tormento from the Lima trials, we can see that the members of the tribunals carefully complied with formal instructions even in the secrecy of the torture chambers.

Instructions now preserved at the Archivo Nacional in Madrid show that the session in the cámara del tormento had to start in the morning. The following details had to be recorded as follows:

> This exercise of duty began at such-and-such an hour of the morning
>   Notice was given of the sentence of torment and [the prisoner] was told that if [he/she] appeals, the sentence will be executed nonetheless; then [the prisoner] was told to tell the Truth, for the love of God, as he would not want to see himself put through such a great burden.
>   *This was said.*
>   [Prisoner] was told to tell the truth or be commanded to go down to the torture chamber.
>   *This was said.*
>   And with that [the prisoner] was taken away to the torture chamber where the *Sres. Inquisidores* and the ordinary were, and once arrived there, the said [prisoner name] was [again] admonished, for the love of God to tell the truth and not put him/herself under such a great burden.
>   *This was said.*
>   [Prisoner] was told to tell the truth or have the Minister sent in.

> *This was said.*
> And then the Minister was called and came in
> *This was said* . . .
> [The prisoner] was told [again] to tell the truth, or he/she would be ordered to be undressed.
> *This was said.*
> [The prisoner] was ordered to undress, and [he/she] undressed and now naked, he/she was told to tell the truth and not put [him/herself] under such a great burden.[53]

In the previous fragment we see how admonitions to tell the truth preceded every step. The reading of these instructions preceded the prisoner's entrance into the torture chamber; the members of the tribunal would not yet have arrived, and the prisoner would not yet have been placed on the rack. The prisoner then received an admonition to reveal the truth or would otherwise be undressed. Once undressed, the prisoner received another admonition to reveal the truth; otherwise, he or she was warned, would be tied to the rack.[54] Once on the rack, the prisoner was again admonished to reveal the truth and warned that, in the absence of confession, the first round of the rope would be placed. Immediately after the first rope was placed, the prisoner was again admonished to reveal the truth; otherwise, a second rope would be placed. It was the same for each of the following ropes. In sum, each small step was preceded by an admonition offering the prisoner an opportunity to confess, and these admonitions continued throughout the entire session in the torture chamber. Owing to the presence of notaries, the whole dialogue of admonitions and responses was recorded in precise detail, including what prisoners said regarding the pain they experienced.

As we can imagine, this dialogue implied an extremely slow pace for the application of torment.[55] Furthermore, we can state that the procedure in the torture chambers unfolded almost as a script, with established steps that were systematically repeated in different places and times. In this script, two actions were always present at each step: one physical (the infliction of pain) and the other verbal (the interrogation).[56] On this matter, Nicolau Eimeric also suggested a progression for the questions: "The interrogation shall proceed beginning with the less grave points of which [the prisoner] is accused, because they confess more quickly to lesser offenses than to the more serious ones."[57]

In the scenarios that I discovered through the documents on applying torture, three main actors alternated in the physical and verbal actions: the inquisitor, the prisoner, and the torturer. At each step, the inquisitor asked a question and warned about the imminent pain if the prisoner did not confess, and the torturer inflicted the pain without asking any questions. Was the inquisitor, or the torturer, aware of how much the prisoner suffered? In the trial of faith of Antonio Morón, it is recorded that Morón spoke to a slave who was also present in the session, complaining about the pain. The notary who recorded the torture of Francisco Vázquez stated that he did not complain at the beginning but did complain about the pain as the session moved forward. The instructions and guidelines for the torture chamber covered more than the technicalities of how to use the torture instruments and the wording of the script. The inquisitor had to understand the goal behind the application of torment, and the guidelines prescribed the best way to achieve the goal: the prisoner's confession. The best way to obtain it was through the careful calibration of the pain that could be inflicted—not too little, but not too much.[58]

As we can infer from the guidelines, the anticipation of physical torment was also to be deployed in a convincing and gradually accelerating manner. In this way, the expectation of pain in itself would affect the prisoner's state of mind and thereby trigger the confession the tribunal sought. It is interesting to note that, officially, the Inquisition was not allowed to shed blood, and that a prisoner had to be in a generally good physical condition before the application of torture, usually verified by a physician.[59] However, it was advised that a prisoner who was judged not to be in sufficiently good condition still be taken to the session in the torture chamber and actually undergo the beginning of such a session as a strategy to provoke fear and elicit a confession.[60] Inquisitors and torturers knew it was the combination of psychological and physical torment that would overwhelm the prisoner's will and anticipated a variety of options for women or weaker prisoners.[61] If the prisoner did not confess, Eimeric suggested showing other pain-inflicting instruments to imply that all could potentially be used.[62] In any case, the tribunal issued different statements according to individual cases. In some, it stated that the accused had overcome the torment (*venció al tormento*). This expression indicated that the tribunal accepted that there was nothing to confess and that the prisoner had not spoken any lies to avoid or diminish physical pain. This was perceived simultaneously as a proof of both innocence and strength. In consequence, the offender was freed and the case suspended. But some prisoners who did not confess were still considered guilty, as the following example will demonstrate.

Manuel Bautista Pérez's session in the torture chamber began close to 9:30 one morning. According to the record, he was given six turns on the mancuerda, each preceded by the mandatory admonition to tell the truth. Throughout the session Pérez addressed inquisitor Mañozca, complained profusely about the pain, said he was dying, and repeated that he did not know anything and that the testimonies collected against him were untrue and his suffering unfair. Pérez continuously recited Christian prayers, said he was *Catholico Xpiano*

(Catholic Christian), and invoked the protection of Jesus, the Virgin Mary, and the saints. He also asked for water. After six turns and in absence of a confession, he was moved to the potro, with similar results. The session ended at 11:00 a.m. without a confession.[63] In this case the tribunal did not conclude that Pérez had overcome the torment; instead, it presumed that he had remained attached to heresy and persisted in lying, thereby refusing the opportunity afforded him by the inquisitors. Pérez was labeled as *negativo* (negative), which meant that further applications of torment could follow, or possibly a sentence of release to the secular arm and death at the stake. Also, in the case of prisoners who were inconsistent or contradictory in their confessions, the tribunal could repeat the torment sessions *para que se asiente en la verdad* (to get the prisoner to settle on the truth), as the documents said.

Paradoxically, the Inquisition did not accept a confession obtained under torture as irrevocable or even necessarily true, because its members were aware that pain, and the fear of pain, sometimes distorted rather than enabled the truth. Confessions obtained in the face of the *threat* of torture, or by showing torture instruments, were considered of absolute value because torment had not been actually applied. However, a confession obtained *during* the application of torment needed to be confirmed. For this reason, within twenty-four hours after the session at the torture chamber, the prisoner had to ratify the confession and validate its contents. Indeed, people could actually revoke what had been said under torture, state to inquisitors that pain and fear had misguided the confession and obstructed the truth, and change the contents of the confession. In such a case, tribunal members were required to hold a meeting to decide on the best course of action, which sometimes meant sending the prisoner to the torture chamber for a second time. If after a second session the prisoner revoked the confession again, there would probably be a third session. Regulations contemplated different scenarios, and tried to prevent a circular development *ad infinitum*. Eimeric mentioned that those who had been subjected to torment on repeated occasions resisted it better because their limbs became used to it, and also that some people would use sorceries to become insensitive to the inflicted pain.[64] Peña took this last consideration seriously, adding that sortileges included hiding pieces of vellum with fragments of the Scriptures written on them in the clothes, and for that reason complete nakedness was important in the torture chamber.[65] Peña insisted on avoiding cruelty and stated that a prisoner had been "sufficiently tortured" when the experts considered that he or she had endured torment equivalent in gravity to that of the evidence against him or her, even in the absence of a confession.[66]

To this point, I have considered the application of torture in the trial of faith from the perspective of the torturer (either the person or the institution).

Now, I want to consider the perspective of the prisoner. What did a prisoner know about torture in the dungeons of the Inquisition? Had prisoners seen the torture instruments before? While waiting in their secret cells, could they hear what was going on at the torture chambers? Would they have been able to talk to someone who had already been there? What did a prisoner "hear" when attending a session at the torture chambers? What did they understand as the admonitions and questions were delivered?

Some useful evidence comes from the trial of Bartolomé de Pradeda in Lima. Pradeda was the steward (alcaide) of the secret prisons of the Lima tribunal during the years of the Great Complicity (1630s). Also during these years the Inquisition opened a criminal trial against Pradeda himself, accusing the steward of repeated misconduct. In records of the trial triggered against Pradeda, we read that María de la Cruz "said that after a few days this witness [María] knew that torment had been applied to Antonio de Acuña because that's what the steward had told [her] in the kitchen, saying Jesus, what great pain that they had given him and that they had him for three hours and his arms are in pieces, and he said his name was Antonio de Acuña."[67]

As noted earlier, the same facilities housed Inquisition personnel and detainees (and trial records), providing a proximity that allowed interactions that may not have been recorded by notaries. However, these interactions likely had an impact on the development of a trial. As we can appreciate in the witness's account above, the consequences of the application of torture to a Lima prisoner could be a matter of comment between minor officials and other prisoners. It is hard to imagine that evidence of a fellow prisoner's torture and the recounting of the details after a torture session would not have affected the responses of other prisoners in their sessions.

Records of torture sessions, detailed as they were with adherence to instructions and prisoner responses, were systematically kept and incorporated into the trial. Notaries also recorded the sayings of a prisoner under torture, including their reactions to physical pain as well as any confessions. According to Elaine Scarry, writing on politically motivated torture in general, "The very question that, within the political pretense, matters so much to the torturer that it occasions his grotesque brutality will matter so little to the prisoner experiencing the brutality that he will give the answer."[68] Scarry's words do not refer to the Inquisition but seem pertinent to the following example. While undergoing torture in Lima, a prisoner could be completely disregardful of what he or she was saying or whether it was an answer to the question asked: "Asked if her mother and sister are Jews, replied that whatever they wanted to write there to do so, and said 'Jesus, I am dying, look I am bleeding a lot.'"[69] Mencía de Luna, a woman born in Seville who had a trial of faith before the Lima

Inquisition in the 1630s, not only complained about her suffering and bleeding but also told the notaries of the tribunal to write whatever they wanted in her declaration, so that her suffering would come to an end.[70] Even with the supervision of medical professionals, some prisoners did not survive the torture chambers, like Mencía de Luna, and Antonio Morón, who fainted under torture and died soon after.

In the trials conducted under the Great Complicity between 1635 and 1639, about a hundred prisoners passed through the dungeons of the Lima Inquisition. The duration of their trials of faith varied from months to years, or even decades. By the time a person had had three hearings, even before being sent to the torture chamber, we can infer that he or she had had enough time to learn what was happening in other trials and in the torture chambers to which many of them led. Beyond individual responses in the torture chamber, did prisoners of the Inquisition develop any sort of collective response to overcome the effects of torture? According to some references, prisoners sent one another help before a visit to the torture chambers. In the evidence collected against the steward Bartolomé de Pradeda, we read references to his providing such help. In the opening pages of his trial, a woman revealed the circulation of some pellets between the prisoners on the eve of their sessions at the torture chamber. In her declaration she described the pellets as *bolitas verdes* (little green pellets) and mentioned a note that accompanied them. According to the reading of a friar, the note included written instructions about taking one pellet the night before the session at the torture chamber. From these instructions, I infer that the pellets had some analgesic property, which made torture more bearable for the prisoners. According to the declaration of the same woman, a slave took the bolitas verdes, wrapped in a piece of paper (presumably the note with the instructions) and then wrapped again in cloth, from one prisoner to the cell of a person who was to be tortured on the following day.[71]

In sum, although the Inquisition regulated the application of torture, limited its duration, and mandated the presence of professionals to assess the health of the prisoners, there is no denying the fact that torture was the infliction of physical and psychological pain with the specific goal of obtaining a confession. At first glance, the guidelines for torturers suggest a picture in which torture was controlled and measured. If we consider the slow pace, the numerous admonitions and warnings, the precautions taken to oversee the condition of the prisoner, and concessions made to female prisoners, we might overlook the actual nature of the torture sessions and conclude it was a logical step, or a relatively minor detail, for someone undergoing a trial of faith. But it was not, because it marked a turning point in the effort to destroy the prisoner's integrity, and that was clear to both torturers and tortured.

Prisoner Defense

Throughout the trial, the tribunal offered various forms of support to the prisoner, mostly legal and spiritual counseling. This support was an innovation of the Spanish tribunal inspired by the presence of defense attorneys in secular courts.[72] The first support offered was the service of a defense advocate, an option that was not usually available in the medieval Inquisition. Francisco Peña commented that even in cases of grave suspicion—even that sufficient for issuing a sentence—the services of a defense advocate would be offered.[73] However, the defense advocate was first and foremost an official of the tribunal, and his main role was not to refute the accusations but to urge the prisoner to confess the truth. Ironically, the Lima inquisitors in 1570 expressed concern about the blood purity of the lawyers who lived in the city, and thereby questioned their eligibility for the task of defending Inquisition prisoners.[74] Nevertheless, attorneys offering assistance to detainees are clearly present in records of the Lima trials. Prisoners and defense advocates were not allowed to hold a private conversation; neither were they allowed to interrogate witnesses who had testified and incriminated the prisoner. In other words, the advocate's role was to serve the purposes of the trial of faith rather than those of the prisoner.

A prisoner who insisted on denying charges could undertake two different defense strategies: *abonos* or *tachas*. These strategies targeted issues of the honor of the prisoner and the witnesses. The concept of honor was extremely important in Spanish society and by extension in colonial Spanish America as well. It had two basic meanings. The first meaning, honor as status, was a combination of inherited traits (family name, nobility, legitimacy, and blood purity). The second meaning, honor as a virtue, implied the consistent adherence to certain behavioral patterns (honesty, courage, chastity) in both public and private life. The balance between inherited traits and behavioral patterns varied according to race, gender, and social rank. Indeed, in colonial Spanish America, a person's honor was not a rigidly fixed attribute; it could vary over time.[75] Within the context of an Inquisition trial, the honor of any person mattered because any hint of dishonor could taint the reliability of that person's testimony. Furthermore, being brought to the trial of faith had in itself a crucial effect on a person's honor; it called into question his or her blood purity and Christian virtue. This is why when a trial ended with a sentence of *"reconciliado con palmas,"* there was also an honor restoration, meaning not only that the accusation of heresy was mistaken but also that the suspicion of New Christian lineage and the assumed absence of blood purity had also been proven wrong.

Three years into his trial of faith, Manuel Bautista Pérez provided a list of people to answer nine questions about his Christian devotion, his generosity, and the debtors or rivals whose public ill will toward the wealthy merchant had led them to testify against him. The tribunal, however, incorporated the declarations of only thirteen of those presented, rejecting another twelve because they were either Pérez's relatives or individuals who themselves faced an impending trial of faith. Pérez was exercising a defense strategy called *abonos*, which was built upon the assertion of the prisoner's honor. A person of honor and good name, a good Christian, was by all means incapable of committing the alleged heresy. This defense required the introduction of reliable witnesses who would testify about the prisoner's reputation. The witnesses had to declare for how long they had known the prisoner and his or her family and what kind of relationship they sustained as well as contribute information to establish the detainee's honor and credibility.

The other defense strategy, called *tachas*,[76] questioned the standing and ulterior motives of those who had provided the testificaciones that formed the core of the accusation. With this strategy, the defense attempted to discredit and question the reputation of the prosecution witnesses and, by extension, to disqualify the veracity of the testimonies contained in the accusation. Eimeric wrote that during the trial of faith for heresy the prisoner could attempt to recuse the testimony of a mortal enemy, clarifying that "mortal enemy" was someone who had *already* made an attempt against the prisoner's life.[77] The accusation did not contain the names of those who had testified, but if a prisoner successfully guessed the name behind a specific testimony, then he or she could argue that this particular witness was a personal enemy, interested in providing false testimony for ulterior motives. Mencía de Luna asserted that her husband wanted to get rid of her so he could be with his mistress. She was imprisoned in Lima in November of 1635. (Enrique Núñez de Espinosa, Mencía's husband, had himself been in the Lima prisons since August of the same year, undergoing his second trial of faith under this tribunal.) A prisoner who had recently quarreled with someone who might have given testimony could bring that person's name to the trial, explain the motives behind the quarrel, and thereby disqualify the testimony. The defense of tachas was indeed a very difficult test but it still offered some possibility, and a number of Lima prisoners took the chance. In addition to Mencía de Luna, Manuel Henríquez, Antonio Morón, Francisco Vázquez, and Manuel Bautista Pérez all used this strategy, bringing up personal and business conflicts that involved Lima residents, other members of the Portuguese New Christian community, and also officers of the tribunal.[78]

Two additional forms of support were available to some prisoners. Prisoners under twenty-five years of age, and those considered incapable, received the service of a *curador*, a guardian who had to advise, protect, and steer the minor or incapable person throughout the trial, as happened in the case of Tavares.

This regulation, like many others, opened a window for prisoner manipulation, as in the case of Joan Vicente, a shoemaker who argued in front of the Lima tribunal that a previous trial of faith conducted in Portugal was not valid because he was a minor at the time and the Évora office had not provided the required assistance.[79] Irregularities, such as the absence of legal assistance or the application of torment without informing the bishop, are mentioned by Eimeric and Peña as grounds to recuse the inquisitor and perhaps appeal to the pope. However, both authors also clarified that this possibility should not be used as a protection for prisoners; and furthermore, Peña explained that a dossier with an appeal would be sent first to the general inquisitor instead of traveling directly to Rome.[80] A third form of support was related to the Christian indoctrination of the prisoner. After confession, a person who expressed doubts on matters of doctrine received the assistance of theologians (*patrones teólogos*). These theologians had to answer the offender's questions about the truths of Christianity and guide him or her in the process of reconciliation to Christianity.

Through certain pleas, a prisoner could limit the range of the Inquisition's actions, or at least improve his or her situation at the time of final sentences. One of them was proof of never having had a baptism; this meant that the prisoner was not a Christian, and thus did not fall under the eyes of the Inquisition.[81] For example, a Jew born outside of Spanish lands and never baptized could opt for this strategy. Another plea that could have a softening influence on the final sentence was insanity, which had to be verified by doctors. If declared insane, the person could not be released to the secular arm (for burning at the stake) because insane prisoners were not considered responsible for their acts. The sentence had to be postponed until the issue was resolved, as occurred in the cases of Enrique Jorge Tavares and Manuel Henríquez, albeit with different outcomes. Tavares was sent to the San Andrés hospital in Lima. Henríquez died at the stake.[82]

Once the defense had finished the exposition of its arguments, the names of the witnesses were unveiled (*publicación de testigos*) and the case moved toward closure (*causa conclusa*). However, if new evidence appeared, the prosecution could reopen it and submit the new evidence for consideration. Otherwise, it was time for the elaboration of the *sentencia* (sentence), which was pronounced after a meeting called *consulta de fe* (consultation of faith). To prevent arbitrary decisions, the consulta involved members of the tribunal and other officials.[83] Obviously, the inquisitors were there, but also the bishop from the diocese where the prisoner had lived, selected consultores who were specialists in law and theology, and members of the royal audiencia. During the consulta the participants heard the entire trial or at least a summary. In consonance with the character of the trial of faith, the consulta de fe was held in secrecy, and the resulting sentences were not published until later. But despite all the secret protocols of the Inquisition, sometimes the information slipped out and circulated, at least within the Inquisition facilities.[84]

Considering all the stages of the trial of faith together, we can see how the Inquisition deployed three tools throughout its trials to achieve a confession. The first tool was institutional alienation. In theory, and to a considerable extent in practice, a thick wall separated a person who entered the jails of the Inquisition from what had been his or her previous life. The second tool was deployed once the prisoner was inside the world of the Inquisition, and it was individual isolation. During the days and months between hearings, prisoners were confined to individual cells in an atmosphere that was supposed to enable silent introspection and profound self-scrutiny. They were expected to sort through their memories and examine their consciences, until they were ready to confess and ask for leniency from a benevolent tribunal. The third tool was bureaucratic secrecy, a key component in all the proceedings and a trademark of the Tribunal of the Inquisition. The French scholar Bartolomé Bennassar argues that the tribunal used a "pedagogy of fear" that combined secrecy, infamy, and misery and powerful examples.[85] From start to finish, the bureaucracy of the Inquisition hid from the prisoner information that would affect his or her trial, either positively or negatively, and communicated the sentences just before the Auto de Fe. By keeping prisoners alienated from the outside world, confined in individual cells, and ignorant about their own trials, the Inquisition aimed to build an arena of fear and confession that would bring the prisoner to open the door to repentance and punishment. In practical terms, this means that crucial parts of the trials did not occur at the hearings in front of inquisitors but in the cells where prisoners were confined. If we remember that trials of the Inquisition sometimes lasted for years and decades, we will recognize that the world created inside the facilities of the Inquisition can also be a subject for historical study. I will return to the world inside the facilities of the tribunal later in this book. For now, let me finish the discussion of the trial of faith with the description of the sentences.

Fitting Sentences to Offenses

According to the magnitude of the offense and the attitude of the prisoner during the trial, the tribunal issued sentences ranging from acquittal to death (expressed as a "release to the secular arm"). Acquittal was rare, because it implied that the Inquisition had made a mistake in targeting an accused person or that it had accepted inadequate evidence, but it was still a possibility. Rather than face an acquittal, the tribunal opted more frequently for the suspension of the trial (*causa suspensa*), which released the prisoner but in fact left the door open for a later development if additional evidence was made available. Among the other sentences and penalties, considered lighter, were a reprimand, imprisonment, reclusion, exile, and the mandatory use of the sambenito, a garment meant to shame the wearer. Sambenitos varied in color and patterns of decoration, indicating differences in the sentences. After the prisoner's death, the sambenito was hung in the local church (compliance with this regulation is reported by Lima bureaucrats at various times)[86] as a reminder of the offender's shame and the dishonor that would be cast on coming generations of his or her family. Regarding exile and the possibility of returns, a decree issued by the Catholic monarchs in Zaragoza in 1498 and reproduced in 1648 for the Toledo Inquisition states that those who returned to Spanish lands after a Holy Office sentence could be subject to execution and confiscation of properties, which would then be distributed in three equal parts: one part for the accuser, one for the justice, and one for the monarchy.[87]

The toughest sentences started with the abjuration. In cases where heresy was borne out in the trial, the abjuration was always present as a first step toward reconciliation. The prisoner had to read aloud a formal statement, in which he or she recognized guilt and expressed remorse, embraced the Catholic faith and rejected any challenge to Christian dogma, committed him-or herself to participate in the struggle against heresy, and acknowledged that, in case of a repeated offense, punishment would be harsher.[88] In cases of softer offenses, there was an "*Abjuración de Levi*," and in cases of serious offenses, there was the "*Abjuración de Vehementi*"; in case of a relapse and second trial, those formerly charged to perform the latter could receive a death sentence.[89] The abjuration opened the door for spiritual reconciliation, and it was combined with other penalties: galleys, exile, whipping, fines, and confiscation of properties. Confiscations were justified by the idea that heretics and idolaters were not allowed material possessions, and they were not exclusive to trials of faith—monetary penalties were also imposed in secular trials.[90] Technically, the confiscation was retroactive, effective from the day the prisoner had turned to heresy according to the evidence of the trial.[91] Confiscated items included personal belongings (furniture, clothes, linens, books, cookware, jewelry, and so on), merchandise, and commercial papers. Debts and credit were reassigned to the tribunal as representative of the king. Notaries carefully listed inventories, anticipating the revenue from the sale of objects in public auction and the future collection of debt.[92] Another penalty was excommunication and included prohibitions against obtaining a public post thenceforward, practicing medicine or law (with the prohibition extended to sons and grandsons in the paternal line), bearing arms, wearing jewelry or expensive clothing, and riding horses.[93] As noted earlier, heresy was a crime of lesa majestad and therefore deserved a death penalty as the most extreme punishment.

The trial of faith was conceptualized as an opportunity to confess, ask for forgiveness, and be reconciled to the broader community. For those who had not taken advantage of the gate opened by the trial, as well as people who had been reconciled in a prior trial but had returned to heresy (usually called *relapsos*, backsliders), the penalty was release to the secular arm for burning at the stake, which also included property confiscation. Today in Lima, there is a house named "La Casa de Pilatos," where Manuel Bautista Pérez and his family lived. However, regarding residences where heretics had held secret meetings, Peña instructed the tribunal to order the demolishing of the building, cover the plot with salt, and signal the event for posterity with an inscription.[94]

For offenders who fled before imprisonment and trial, the tribunal had the option of conducting a trial in absentia and applying the punishment to an effigy that represented the offender's body. Instructions also regulated how to carry on if someone died during the trial of faith. The Holy Office also conducted trials against the reputation and memory of a deceased person, as did secular tribunals in case of treason, and the sentences included exhumations, subsequent application of penalties at an Auto de Fe, and the confiscation of properties held by the deceased's offspring. Peña explained that the tribunal had the possibility of confiscating properties for at least five years after an accused's death; applying a sentence to the bones or to the effigy that represented the deceased person was without a time limit.[95] If the prisoner had expressed remorse before dying during the trial of faith, the effigy was reconciled. But if the prisoner had died without expressing remorse, one more accusation was added: dying as impenitent—without communion and confession—as happened to Mencía de Luna, who died in the Lima torture chambers.[96] If a prisoner committed suicide in prison, the suicide "was held to be confession of guilt and pertinacity," as happened in Lima with Garci Méndez de Dueñas.[97] Prisoners accepted for reconciliation learned about their sentences at the time of the Auto de Fe. Those who were going to be released to the secular arm learned about their sentences the night before the Auto, so they could prepare with the assistance of priests during the last night of their lives.

The decision about the sentence was not the end of the trial of faith. The trial of faith ended with a ceremony that sometimes was public: the Auto de Fe. An Auto General de Fe was a ceremony where the summaries of the cases and the sentences were read for the authorities (ecclesiastical and civil) and for the public. It was an impressive theatrical display that closed the trial of faith and reinforced the commitment of all members of the society to the struggle against heresy.

The trial of faith was a strictly regulated procedure that started after the tribunal had already collected evidence about the offense; given that fact, the procedure was necessarily built upon the presumption of guilt. Through several stages that combined long confinements, direct interrogations, veiled accusations, and torture, the Inquisition trial aimed to confirm the prisoner's guilt, facilitate his or her confession and reconciliation, and select the appropriate punishment. By implementing three tools (institutional alienation, individual isolation, and bureaucratic secrecy), the Inquisition aimed to instill fear and to inspire repentance. These tools, combined with the long duration of actual trials, also enabled the creation of an inner world, a world inside the prisons of the Inquisition. That inner world will be the subject of historical inquiry in another chapter of this book. In contrast with the secrecy that characterized the stages of the trial of faith, the Auto General de Fe that marked the culmination of the Inquisition trial and reinforced the commitment of the Church, the state, and the entire community in the struggle against heresy was a quintessentially public event. Finally, even though their distance from the Suprema meant that colonial tribunals were granted some extended discretionary power, it was necessary to consult on certain issues with the Suprema.[98] The information that survived from these exchanges is fragmentary; there are no complete sets of trials from the Lima tribunal available for scholarly inquiry. However, by comparing information from these exchanges, the written regulations and procedures, the information we do have from the trials of faith, the summaries of trials conducted in Lima in the 1600s, and some additional preserved materials, we can see that the tribunal, in general, complied with procedural guidelines while conducting trials of faith and respected the overall regulations governing the treatment of offenders. A different matter is the construction of inquisitorial jurisdictions in the New World, in terms of both geographical boundaries and the nature and history of the peoples under its surveillance. This difference will be addressed in following chapters.

3

A Cobbler and a Merchant

> All those Portuguese around the world who make so much noise. If they are not farmers or sailors, they are Jews.
>
> Álvaro Cardoso de Silba[1]

Up to 1570, all inhabitants of the Spanish American colonies were officially under the eyes of bishop-inquisitors. A royal decree issued in 1569 removed inquisitorial jurisdiction from the bishops' hands and regulated the creation of separate tribunals in the colonies.[2] In accordance with the earlier (1568) Junta Magna, which issued recommendations related to political, religious, economic, and organizational matters in the colonies, Philip II established tribunals of the Holy Office in Lima and in Mexico in 1570.[3] An important source for those early days is the Dominican friar Reginaldo de Lizárraga, born in Spain, who arrived in Peru at the age of fifteen (around 1560) and died in Paraguay in 1615. Lizárraga reported that two inquisitors were appointed for the creation of the Lima tribunal, the *licenciados* Serván de Cerezuela and Andrés de Bustamante, who traveled to Lima with the fleet of Viceroy Francisco de Toledo to proceed with the office's creation. Bustamante died in Panama in 1569, and Antonio Gutiérrez de Ulloa replaced him.[4]

Let us remember that the Spanish colonies were under the Royal Patronage, under which the Crown appointed ecclesiastical officers, as John Schwaller writes. This author further clarifies that it is because of the Patronage that "the Church in the Americas would be highly reflective of the secular state that supervised its activities."[5] The territorial jurisdiction of the Lima and Mexico tribunals followed the monarchy's administrative boundaries, in this case the viceroyalties of New Spain and Peru. It was the tribunals' job to identify and bring to justice the perpetrators of offenses such as solicitation, blasphemy, sorcery, and the practice of Protestantism, Islam, and Judaism. Cerezuela and Bustamante arrived in the colonies with instructions to watch over newcomers (from both Europe and Africa) but not Native Americans. In practical terms, restricting the tribunals' efforts to immigrants allowed the monarchy to concentrate its efforts. Even though colonial tribunals were nominally assigned vast territories, the exclusion of native persons allowed Inquisition officials to focus on the entry points where immigrants—and among them potential offenders—might arrive and the places where they were most likely to reside. Colonial tribunals were also among the bodies charged with certifying blood purity. This, again, made the location of tribunals in colonial capitals a reasonable policy.[6]

With regard to the indigenous population, the colonial administration tolerated the development over time of a syncretism, a certain fusion between Native American religions and Christianity. Members of religious orders were initially to introduce the native population to Christianity gradually, but at some critical moments, and in the face of the persistence of indigenous religions, those in charge of Christian instruction switched gears and turned to interrogation, repression, and punishment. In such cases, after 1570, a different sort of tribunal, dedicated to the "Extirpation of Idolatries," was created to place indigenous societies on trial. Modern scholars explain that these tribunals were similar to those of the Inquisition in terms of their composition and general procedures but stress that the two disciplinary bodies were not otherwise alike. The Extirpation, unlike the Inquisition, never turned into a permanent tribunal. Although both repressed religious offenders and deviations from Christian orthodoxy, gatherings for the Extirpation of Idolatries were exceptional rather than continuous and had a pastoral rather than a punitive purpose. Although extirpation campaigns did culminate in public ceremonies of punishment, people were not burned alive as the most extreme form of punishment. This established a crucial difference.[7]

Initially, the jurisdiction of the Lima tribunal was the entirety of the sprawling Peruvian viceroyalty, which included the audiencias of Lima, Charcas, Chile, Quito, Panama, and Nueva Granada (now Panama, Colombia, Venezuela, Ecuador, Peru, Bolivia, Chile, Argentina, Uruguay, and Paraguay). With the establishment of the Cartagena tribunal in 1610, the Lima office's jurisdiction was reduced to the audiencias of Lima, Charcas, Chile, and Quito only.[8] Lima was and remained the main port and a major trading center of South America, and it was here that foreigners (potential targets of the Inquisition) as well as books (vehicles of heretical ideas) arrived. But Lima was concerned not only with potential offenders who might enter Peru through the port of El Callao; the tribunal also had to monitor the unofficial migrations of Portuguese from Brazil to Peru and the activities of undocumented foreigners who landed at the Atlantic port of Buenos Aires and then circulated throughout the viceroyalty.

Royal instructions included that the Lima tribunal had to follow the peninsular model in inquisitorial procedures and also had to send twice-yearly *relaciones de causas* (trial summaries) to the Suprema (the Supreme Council of the Inquisition in Madrid). The tribunal was also required to consult with the Suprema in cases of split votes or releases to the secular arm. Upon settling in the City of Kings, tribunal members were also supposed to visit the lands under their surveillance or send delegates to fulfill the task; however, the visit of the territory under the jurisdiction of the Lima tribunal was not completed, as mentioned earlier.[9] Comisarios and familiares distributed throughout the main cities and towns of the viceroyalty were to support the tribunal's work. For example, twelve familiares were assigned to assist in the city of Lima.[10]

Viceroy Toledo assigned a fiscal property, at no cost to the Inquisition, to house the newly created office. Located near the church and convent of La Merced, it was remodeled to include hearing rooms, secret cells, torture chambers, storage space for records, and lodging for tribunal members and lower-level staff. However, the location and size of the property, even after these modifications, were not adequate to what the tribunal needed. The space was simply too small to configure for all these purposes. Only one of the two inquisitors could reside in the building, and the bedroom assigned to that inquisitor was divided to create the torture chamber. The room was selected for this purpose because it was the farthest removed from street noise and the possibility of casual intrusion. The prison cells were located off the main property, some in a rented house and some in a stable, according to Paulino Castañeda Delgado and Pilar Hernández Aparicio, who also noted that prisoners had to walk from their cells through a patio to get to the hearing room and thus could be seen from outside the compound, which created an inconvenience for procedures based on secrecy.[11]

Tribunal members wanted a placement suitable for their activities, removed from the city center and at a larger and more appropriate facility. Although the tribunal did collect revenue from property confiscations in the 1570s, it was of necessity applied to salary payment. During these early years of activity the Lima tribunal received an inheritance from Fray Pedro de la Peña, Quito's bishop. He donated money for the construction of a tribunal chapel, where he wanted to be buried. The tribunal used the money in the 1580s to move to new facilities somewhat removed from the urban colonial center and the Plaza Mayor but still in a well-located area. According to a 1630 chronicle, the University of San Marcos, to which Toledo had also assigned accommodations in the 1570s, functioned near the *plaçuela* (little plaza) of the Inquisition.[12]

The tribunal's earliest trials, with their findings of blasphemy, heresy, and pacts with the devil, justified its existence and clearly demonstrated that it had work to do. Among those trials were the cases of María Pizarro and Francisco de la Cruz. Autos de Fe had been celebrated in Lima prior to the 1570 creation of the tribunal: the first one in 1548 when a Flemish man named Juan Millar was released to the secular arm for being a Lutheran; the second and third ceremonies were celebrated in 1560 and 1565, after trials related to different offenses to Catholic orthodoxy that affected Spaniards, Indians, common people, and government authorities.[13] However, on November 15, 1573, the Lima tribunal celebrated its first Auto since being established in 1570. In this ceremony Mateo Salcedo was released to the secular arm and burned at the stake. Another Auto was celebrated in April 1578, and a third in October 1581; in the documentation for the latter, there are clear references to followers of the Law of Moses.[14]

Considering the territorial scope, from its inception it was clear that Lima would not be able to cover the great extension of territory and the varied settings, urban and rural, for which it had been made responsible in matters of religion. In 1577 Viceroy Toledo wrote to Philip II to inform him of the daunting tasks facing the tribunal. The viceroy pointed out that on occasions those who were denounced, as well as witnesses to their purported crimes, had to travel over long distances, which was expensive and difficult and sometimes left trials without a clear outcome. Also, the Lima tribunal had, comparatively, very few functionaries.[15] For example, familiares and comisarios usually resided in outlying locations and were relied on to communicate with the main office through periodic reports; the tribunal of Galicia alone had an administrative staff of 1,009 to field such reports, whereas the Lima office had just 250.[16]

When Toledo recommended the creation of more tribunals to distribute the workload, the monarchy considered the recommendations and off-loaded some of the Lima tribunal's tasks. In 1581, the Charcas audiencia (the jurisdiction to which Potosí belonged) was instructed to register the names, nations of origin, and occupations of foreigners and to inform of the presence of foreigners in Potosí without proper migration permits. The explanation for this action was that foreigners could lead the indigenous population into error.[17] Of the foreigners (that is, Europeans, excluding Spaniards) who arrived in the Spanish colonies in the early seventeenth century, the Portuguese were predominant.[18] Although the activities of the Lima office had been reviewed by the inspector Juan Ruiz de Prado in the years following Toledo's letter to the king (between 1587 and 1591), the viceroy's recommendation was not acted upon until the following century, when the Cartagena office was established in 1610.[19]

Furthermore, not all of Toledo's requests were addressed. In 1636, the Lima inquisitors were still trying to increase the tribunal staff, arguing that the number of familiares assigned to the city in 1571 (twelve) should be doubled to accommodate the increase in the urban population, probably as many as 35,000 to 40,000 people by the 1630s.[20] Yet, in spite of operating with insufficient staff and over a territory far beyond its capabilities, the Lima tribunal maintained its prominence and prestige. It was recognized among the most important bodies in the city and could count on the presence of the viceroy and his entourage at its public ceremonies. Also, members of the religious orders looked to the tribunal as a local authority. Fray Diego de Ocaña, who came to Lima in October 1599, noted that on his arrival he greeted first the viceroy, then the archbishop, and then the Lima inquisitors; and he includes the Holy Office among the prominent institutions of the city.[21]

In 1600 the inquisitor Pedro Ordóñez y Florez wrote a letter in which he echoed Toledo's concerns regarding the logistical problems of administering and regulating the huge territory under the Lima tribunal's surveillance. Ordóñez y Florez noted that the length of a trial commonly ran to two to three years, and even more. Once the information to prosecute was collected, he reported, it could—and did—happen that the potential prisoner had taken advantage of the delays to move somewhere else. If the offender was then found, there was a good chance that witnesses would have moved somewhere else too. During the long lapse of time, crucial witnesses might forget key points of their testimony. The Lima inquisitor also acknowledged that an efficient tribunal was more necessary than ever, pointing out that more and more people—especially non-Spanish, non-Catholic foreigners—were moving to the Castilian lands as the colonial project progressed. In this regard, he made special reference to Protestants and Portuguese, who according to Ordóñez were all Jews.[22]

Ordóñez's perception cannot be fully corroborated through independent sources. Even though the Portuguese presence in the Spanish colonies was documented in various censuses, the records are uneven and do not distinguish Old from New Christians.[23] Regardless, some sources seem to concur, like this reference from Gregorio Díaz Tavares, whose testimony was recorded by the Lima tribunal in the early seventeenth century: "Of one hundred Portuguese in Potosí, ninety-five of them are children of Jews."[24] A few decades later, in 1630, Fray Buenaventura de Salinas y Córdova, recounting the events of naval battles against the Dutch in El Callao, wrote that the main abuse to Spanish possessions was not on the maritime front but in the presence of foreign traders who lived among the local population in Lima, Huancavelica, and Potosí, profiting from commercial opportunities.[25]

Ordóñez insisted on the need for more tribunals and smaller territories for each of them. Lima alone, he reiterated, could not suffice for the surveillance of such a vast territory.[26] He proposed that a new office be established in La Plata

(Charcas, today Bolivia); in addition to its city of residence, it would cover Santa Cruz de la Sierra, Tucumán, and the Río de la Plata (these last two in Argentina). He proposed another tribunal to reside in Santa Fe de Bogotá (Colombia); it would cover that city, as well as Popayán, Cartagena, Santa Marta, and Venezuela, including the island of Margarita. If the new tribunals were established, Ordóñez argued, the Lima office would only hold jurisdiction over Lima, Cuzco, Quito, Panama, and Chile—a more manageable territory. To make their point, tribunal officials emphasized in their reports to the viceroyalty of Peru that it was not possible to deal with matters of faith in such a large territory, especially with an increasing (and increasingly suspect) population.

Ten years later, in 1610, modified versions of the various petitions for new tribunals were finally accepted and implemented, and a third tribunal was created in Cartagena de Indias, now Colombia. It was responsible for the provinces of New Granada, Tierra Firme, the Islas de Barlovento (the Leeward Islands), and Nicaragua. The activities of the tribunals of Mexico, Lima, and Cartagena would nonetheless be interconnected, as these bodies would need to work together to keep track of potential prisoners (for example, the Portuguese merchants) as they moved to and from the various trading posts and port cities. Also, tribunal officials themselves relocated between Mexico, Cartagena, and Lima as they performed their duties and also made progress in their individual careers.[27] Ordóñez proposed a fourth tribunal to cover Charcas, Tucumán, and the Río de la Plata; it was needed, he said, to prevent the entrance of undesirable immigrants through the port of Buenos Aires. Despite successive requests in 1619, 1620, and 1630, it was never established. Other cities were later suggested for a fourth tribunal: San Miguel del Tucumán in 1636 and Córdoba del Tucumán in 1640, 1662, and again during the eighteenth century.[28]

Colonial tribunals were responsible to the Suprema in Madrid and, in general, followed the procedural guidelines of peninsular offices.[29] However, there were important differences. Bartolomé Escandell Bonet finds that colonial tribunals shared five core characteristics that set them apart from their peninsular counterparts. First, colonial tribunals had more discretionary power, mainly for dealing with the logistical issues related to geographical distance. Second, these tribunals held no authority over indigenous societies, thereby leaving the majority of the American population outside of inquisitorial control. Third, the focus of the colonial tribunals was on the presence of foreigners in Spanish territories, primarily because of the interplay between the Counter-Reformation and the race for colonial possessions among European kingdoms. Fourth, tribunals were located in urban centers, mainly in viceregal capitals and port cities, with lower-level bureaucrats and inspectors deployed in seaports and also in towns of lesser importance. In Spain, on the other hand, tribunals were located in both urban and rural areas because they also looked after Spanish peasantry. Fifth, from their very inception, the New World inquisitorial districts overlapped with colonial civil and ecclesiastical divisions.[30]

Early Proceedings against Crypto-Jews: Joan Vicente

Information about early trials of crypto-Jews conducted by the Lima tribunal is scarce. We know through summaries sent to the Suprema of the 1581 reconciliation of Manuel López; the 1595 reconciliations of Duarte Méndez, Manuel Anríquez, Antonio Núñez, Joan López, and Francisco Váez Machado; and the trials of Duarte Núñez de Cea and Francisco Núñez de Olivera.[31] According to a trial summary sent to Madrid in 1596, Núñez de Cea was a Portuguese New Christian born near Lisbon, whose wife and in-laws lived in Venice openly as Jews; he confessed to crypto-Jewish practices but revoked his confession afterward. But for a few trials there are more detailed records, among them the proceedings against Joan Vicente, recently studied by Nathan Wachtel, and against Garci Méndez de Dueñas. Their cases give us some light by which to explore the workings of the tribunal in the early seventeenth century.[32]

Toward the end of 1601, Joan Vicente, a shoemaker born in Campo Mayor (Portugal), and his wife were taken to the Lima tribunal prisons. Vicente was a New Christian of Jewish descent on his maternal side and an Old Christian on the paternal one. Vicente's mother and sister had been burned at the stake after trials of faith under the Portuguese Inquisition, and other relatives had had trials with various outcomes. At the beginning of the Lima trial, the shoemaker declared that he was either forty-two or forty-three years of age and had been married since 1580 to Isabel Váez, a woman about ten years younger and from the same town, and also of mixed lineage. Similarly, several relatives of Isabel Váez's maternal line had undergone trials of faith, including her maternal grandmother who died in the prisons of the Portuguese Inquisition and was later burned in effigy. In 1601, at the time of the Lima imprisonment, Joan and Isabel had four children, two daughters born in Portugal (one already married) and two sons born in the New World. In the mid-1580s, both husband and wife had been reconciled after trials of faith in Évora, Portugal; thus their Lima imprisonment in 1601 meant that the couple would face a tribunal for the second time.

The Évora trials in 1582 and 1583 that affected the family unfolded after Joan Vicente approached the Holy Office of his own volition, he said, and had offered a confession. During several hearings held as part of his subsequent trial, he had provided evidence incriminating himself, his mother, siblings, wife, and other relatives and acquaintances. There is no record of physical torment having been applied to the shoemaker in Portugal. In Inquisition trials, a *curador* was typically assigned to prisoners under twenty-five years of age, like Vicente was at that time, so the prisoner would receive advice and protection during the trial of faith. With the assistance of his curador, Bento Cardoso, Vicente confessed to crypto-Jewish dietary practices, fasting, and prayers[33] in which he had participated in his hometown, together with family members and fellow crypto-Jews. He explained too that he was poor and could not avoid working on Saturdays. He spoke also of his in-laws' knowledge of Old Testament stories, such as Joseph's interpretation of Pharaoh's dream with its two sets of seven cows each and of his own rejection of Christian saints and images. As a result of his spontaneous confession, in 1584 Vicente was reconciled in Évora, abjured of his offenses, and told to wear a sambenito (the penitential garment that was sometimes part of the punishment applied in trials of faith) for some three years, until November 1587. His wife was also reconciled at that time and assigned to wear the degrading garment, although for a shorter period of time.

About four years after the reconciliation the family left Portugal behind, arriving in San Salvador da Bahia in the northeast of Brazil in June or July of 1588. They lived in that area for about three years. In the city Vicente first worked as a shoemaker, then moved to an outlying area where he was employed as the manager of a sugar mill, but he and his family later returned to Bahia. Working in his storefront shop, he met other Portuguese New Christians, among them some residents of the Gobernación del Tucumán, in what is today the Argentine Northwest. These men urged him to relocate to the Spanish colonies, pointing out that commercial opportunities were better in the viceroyalty of Peru, owing especially to the growing mining economy in the Peruvian hinterlands. Taking their advice, the Vicente family left Brazil in 1591 with their new acquaintances. After about two months in Buenos Aires, they moved on to Córdoba and Santiago del Estero (still then in Tucumán), making their way by selling clothes. The family then moved north, settling temporarily in Potosí and then circulating between Cuzco, Huaylas, Chincha, and Arica (Chile). Attracted by the fabled wealth of Potosí, the family moved once more.

Joan Vicente and his family lived in the Potosí area for about two years near the end of the sixteenth century. Writing some years later (1630) of the silver mountain of the highlands, now Bolivia, Salinas y Córdova declared that "Potosí gives bars to enrich Spain."[34] The Spanish settlement in Potosí had started in 1545 and had close to 14,000 people two years later. The population fluctuated with the level of mining activity: the villa likely had close to 160,000 inhabitants around 1610; ten years later, there were about 150,000, including miners, merchants, government officials, friars, Indians, and Africans.[35] Among them were also many foreigners, as is attested by local records.[36] The friar Reginaldo de Lizárraga gave his opinion about the presence of foreigners in Potosí: "From the foreign nations there are many men, and if there were not, nothing would the kingdom lose."[37] Yet, another writer, the Portuguese New Christian Pedro de León Portocarrero, marveled about 1620 at the display of wealth in Potosí and the profusion of merchants there who were associated with businesses in Lima, Mexico, and Seville and traded in commodities brought from Spain, Italy, Flanders, France, Mexico, and China.[38] As an economic magnet, Potosí was also linked to the Capitanía de Chile and the Gobernación del Tucumán, territories that sent cotton, candles, cattle, and slaves along the Lima-Potosí route and provided a market for imported commodities. This is also how the silver mountain and the Atlantic were connected, though illegally. The arrival of Portuguese merchants in the Peruvian highlands in the 1590s by way of Buenos Aires and Tucumán also meant that imported goods could reach Potosí from the Atlantic, bringing a growing importance to the roles of Tucumán and Chile in regional trade.[39]

Thus, Vicente's migratory path to Lima—Salvador da Bahia, Buenos Aires, and Tucumán, with a temporary stay in Potosí—seems chaotic, like Nathan Wachtel writes, but probably was not exceptional. It is noteworthy that at the time of his Lima trial it was hard to locate him to bring him to the tribunal. In July 1601 the Lima inquisitor Pedro Ordóñez y Florez sent an order to detain Vicente at Potosí, where it was thought the shoemaker was living. Unable to find him, the Potosí comisario replied to Lima that the accused might have moved to Trujillo, and in October of the same year Lima contacted the comisario of that region. Vicente had indeed rented a property in the Chicama valley close to Trujillo, and it was there that the Holy Office executed the arrests. For the second time, husband and wife were placed in secret prisons, this time in Lima in December 1601.

Isabel Váez died in a Lima prison in 1603, shortly after having confessed the couple's relapse into crypto-Judaism. Indeed, her death was similar in circumstance to that of her grandmother back in Portugal. Joan's trial, however, lasted for close to a decade. In 1603 the shoemaker asked the Lima tribunal for a hearing, knelt before the inquisitors Pedro Ordóñez y Florez and Francisco Verdugo, and confessed.[40] As in the Évora records, there is no information from Lima about physical torment being applied to Vicente. Following a subsequent conversation with his attorney, Vicente presented an argument in his own defense: the Évora trial had been a direct result of his spontaneous confession—not triggered by that tribunal. Thus, he could not be labeled as a relapsed heretic because this was not his second tribunal trial, but his first. Vicente and his lawyer repeated this argument in 1609, after the Lima tribunal had requested and received the Évora paperwork.⁴¹ In this second defense, Vicente also argued that Évora had not provided him with the curador, that is the legal assistance stipulated in inquisitorial procedures for detainees under twenty-five years of age. This type of defense was anticipated in inquisitorial regulations. In his 1376 manual of inquisitorial procedures, Nicolau Eimeric had specified that a prisoner could recuse an inquisitor if the latter had denied legal support. However, Eimeric also instructed that the inquisitor could take the trial a few steps back, correct the mistake by providing the required support, and in this way avoid the recusal.⁴²

In the materials attached to the archival folder of Vicente's trial, however, it says that Évora had indeed assigned him a curator, one Bento Cardoso, also mentioned as *portero* (janitor) of the Holy Office, and that the assignment had taken shortly after Vicente first approached the tribunal indicating his desire to confess in January 1582. Recorded also was the fact that Cardoso was present at the hearings, although there was no specific mention of his legal training.⁴³ It is unclear whether the questions raised in Lima about Vicente's legal support and Cardoso's training were ever resolved, but Joan Vicente was reconciled in Lima in 1612, with property confiscation. The ceremony was conducted at the tribunal's chapel owing to lack of funds for a public celebration, and here, for the second time in his life, he was ordered to wear a sambenito.⁴⁴ However, the reconciliation resolved Vicente's status only temporarily: he was to have one more encounter with the Holy Office. As Wachtel explains, the shoemaker underwent trial for a third time in Cartagena, where he was sentenced and burned at the stake in 1626. His sambenito remained on public display until 1658 at the office of the Cartagena tribunal.⁴⁵

Joan Vicente's trial in Lima allows us to explore the transatlantic dynamics of the colonial treatment of Portuguese New Christians and the Holy Office bureaucracy. What information was made available to the colonial tribunals, and how did it reach them? The colonial tribunal had testimonies related to Vicente as far back as 1595. As could be expected, witnesses declaring before the Lima tribunal informed inquisitors of Vicente's activities in territories in the Peruvian viceroyalty and outside — such as Córdoba del Tucumán, Potosí, and Brazil. As suggested above, the Lima inquisitors heard Vicente's claim that he had self-confessed and reconciled in Évora, then halted work on the case to gather more evidence. Beyond the records they received from Évora, witnesses had given testimonies recalling the rumor that in Portugal, after the reconciliation, the shoemaker had hanged his sambenito from a tree and thrown stones at the garment, as Wachtel analyzed in his portrait.

The Évora response to Lima, dated in 1609, arrived through Madrid and included transcriptions in Portuguese and translations to Spanish of Joan Vicente's confessions, sentence, and abjuration statement. The Évora tribunal even sent certification that it had no record of a permit Vicente would have needed to leave Portugal, given the fact that he had been reconciled by the tribunal. Vicente's transatlantic migration was thus an additional offense, and it was added to the infractions listed in his Lima accusation. In his *discurso de vida*, Vicente explained that four years after the Évora reconciliation he had been in Lisbon and planning a trip to Africa when he saw a poster stating that the king was offering free passage for families willing to travel to the New World. Vicente then changed plans and moved to Brazil with his wife and children. The shoemaker did not provide any details about what travel permits he might have carried, whether authentic or fake.

At different moments in his trial Joan Vicente described himself as a poor man. Although there is evidence of his inclusion and participation in Portuguese New Christian commercial networks in Brazil, Tucumán, and Peru, the records always describe him as a shoemaker, or as a minor tradesman, variously selling clothes or owning a *pulpería* (general store). In short, he appeared to be someone who switched directions according to the emergence of opportunities. Regardless of his economic position, tribunal officers in Évora, Madrid, Lima, and Cartagena paid considerable attention to Vicente and his family, verifying records and even translating the paperwork.

Even though not many records of the Lima trials of faith have survived, and those that have are sometimes fragmentary, we know this was not the only time that Lima had exchanged information with other offices. Lima bureaucrats had anticipated as early as 1569 that fugitives of Spanish tribunals were likely to be found in the New World.[46] By 1589 the tribunal had begun to record the genealogy of people reconciled and condemned, sending also to the Suprema denunciations affecting people who had left the colonies, because tribunals could still conduct trials against absentees and confiscate their properties if that was considered the proper sentence.[47] In 1597, Lima requested verification of an accused's *discurso de vida* from Mexico.[48] At the time of Vicente's trial, when Manuel de Fonseca declared in 1608 that he had not been baptized and therefore was not under inquisitorial jurisdiction, Lima requested information from both Lisbon and Mexico. Unable to verify Fonseca's claim, the tribunal found that their proceedings against him were legitimate and that he was indeed under its jurisdiction. It was also found that he was a relapse, based on a prior reconciliation he had made after being sentenced in Mexico in 1601.[49] Even in the 1630s, when the Lima tribunal was under pressure because of the volume of the Great Complicity trials (which will be discussed in following chapters), Inquisition officials there took the time to corroborate the facts related to the Portuguese peddler Manuel Henríquez and his prior trial in Coimbra.[50]

Proceedings against Garci Méndez de Dueñas

On January 12, 1624, at about 7:30 in the morning, the steward of the Lima prisons, Bartolomé de Pradeda, reported to the inquisitor Andrés Juan Gaitán that a detainee named Garci Méndez de Dueñas had been found dead, hanging in his secret cell with a cord around his neck and wounds on his face.[51] Pradeda recalled that the Portuguese merchant had been ailing and melancholic after his last hearing, speaking often about his numerous sins. The death was notarized and certified according to procedure, and the man was buried within the tribunal facilities, close to the steward's home.

Garci Méndez de Dueñas was born in the town of Olibença on the Spain-Portugal border. Imprisoned in 1623 in Lima, he had his first hearing shortly thereafter. He declared that he was fifty-eight years old, that his parents had lived and died in Olibença, and that those of his siblings who were still alive were in Portugal. He knew his father had Old Christian lineage but did not know his mother's background. Nor did he know of any family members who might have been punished by the Holy Office. Méndez de Dueñas also said he had been married to Leonor de Herrera, a woman born in Seville to Portuguese parents, for twenty-six or twenty-seven years. The couple's one daughter was probably twenty-five years old at the time of the hearing, but Méndez de Dueñas was estranged from them and assumed they still lived in Seville.

In his discurso, Méndez de Dueñas said that he was fifteen years old in 1580 when he moved from Olibença to Lisbon and from there to Guinea as a trader. His itinerary in the following years included several trips between Hispaniola, Cartagena, Spain, and Portugal. After a year in Seville, he married there and later went to France, Guinea, Cartagena, and Nicaragua, becoming a wealthy man. He declared he had lived in Lima for twenty years, since about 1603 approximately (meaning he arrived close to when Joan Vicente was confessing), residing in the city, with the exception of a year and a half spent in Acapulco, Mexico.

On the afternoon of November 27, 1623, Méndez de Dueñas had a hearing with inquisitor Gaitán, initiated at the prisoner's request. He knelt and confessed, as he would do in subsequent hearings. He argued there were false testimonies against him in connection to a shipment of pine pitch. The Portuguese merchant asked for mercy, explaining that his parents and siblings were devout Christians, but that his brother in-law had persuaded him to learn crypto-Jewish practices when they traveled together to Guinea in the 1580s. Since that time, he said, the heresy had been in his heart while he kept Christianity just to fulfill an obligation. He said he had never conducted or even attended many religious ceremonies, whether of the Law of Moses or the faith in Jesus. But he did reveal his lack of belief in a God-Father and a God-Son and stated that for protection he regularly prayed to the God of Abraham, Isaac, and Jacob.[52] He said his wife and her family felt the same way.

The accusation ran to twenty-seven chapters, and in addition to describing the crypto-Jewish practices common in such trials, it recounted events that had taken place in the accused's life in Europe, prior to his departure for the New World. To escape the Seville Inquisition, Méndez de Dueñas, together with his wife and in-laws, had crossed the Pyrenees into France, where they settled in the southern port city of Saint-Jean-de-Luz. Méndez de Dueñas had told the tribunal that he was estranged from his wife and daughter, but the prosecutor sustained that the statement was false on the basis of the testimonies that had been collected. The testimonies affirmed that it was public knowledge that both women lived in France and were known there as *"las sevillanas"* because they had come from Seville, that they received money from Méndez de Dueñas through his networks in Seville, and that he had arranged his daughter's marriage to another member of the crypto-Jewish network and provided a dowry. Further, he was accused of protecting heretics living in France by taking care of their businesses in Spanish lands. On a somewhat different matter, Méndez de Dueñas was also accused of offending Christian morality by living in Lima with a concubine while married.

Prior to his death, and in a series of confessions, Méndez de Dueñas recounted that he had first gone to Bordeaux to sell pearls, and then, finding that the cost of living was lower than in Spain, he had moved his family to Saint-Jean-de-Luz. He also admitted to having shared crypto-Jewish prayers in Bordeaux with other Portuguese merchants and to sending money to his family through Rui Fernández, a Portuguese trader from Seville. He talked about a shipment of pine pitch, which was used for lining wine barrels in Peru (pine pitch was one of the commodities that connected Central American and Peruvian economies during the seventeenth century).[53] This reference appears in several testimonies against the prisoner but he never admitted to concealing commercial transactions for other crypto-Jews.

Méndez de Dueñas confessed. Yet, since he killed himself before being reconciled, the tribunal declared him an impenitent and published an accusation that continued the trial, this time against his memory and reputation. The second accusation recapitulated events dating back to 1596, when Méndez de Dueñas and his family left Spain. At the time, the Seville tribunal was incarcerating many Portuguese. While he was in Saint-Jean-de-Luz, the accusation read, Méndez de Dueñas had read passages from the Scriptures in front of some two hundred followers of the Law of Moses, all Portuguese who had fled Spain. The prosecutor also characterized the merchant as diabolical and pertinacious in pursuing his errors to the point of killing himself and requested that his bones be exhumed, released to the secular arm, and burned. The tribunal voted to mete out the sentence as suggested and executed it in the public Auto de Fe of 1625.[54] At the ceremony, Bartolomé de Pradeda, the steward of the secret prisons who had found Garci Méndez de Dueñas dead in his cell, carried the silver coffer containing the sentences.

The trials of Joan Vicente and Garci Méndez de Dueñas have been discussed by other scholars, Vicente's quite recently by Nathan Wachtel in his gallery of individual portraits.[55] In addition to his detailed portrayal of the cobbler, Wachtel looks at Vicente's itinerary, at his relationship with other Portuguese New Christians (many wealthier than Vicente and his wife), and at the difficult fate this man suffered in trials under the Évora, Lima, and Cartagena tribunals. Wachtel introduces Vicente's displacements as almost chaotic.[56] In the following pages, we will look at both Vicente and Méndez de Dueñas to reveal what they can tell us regarding the larger picture.

The Wandering Merchants and New World Expansion

Beyond what they offer in terms of individual accounts and familial stories, religious practices, individual strategies of defense deployed during trials of faith, and the ways in which their lives ended, the travels of Joan Vicente and Garci Méndez de Dueñas invite us to pose questions about what the Holy Office encountered in the face of Atlantic expansion and how the institution accommodated and addressed its mobile targets. Portugal established its first three peninsular tribunals in 1536, at Lisbon, Évora, and Coimbra; a colonial tribunal in Goa, India, was created in the mid-sixteenth century. However, Portugal did not create tribunals in Brazil, although in 1622 the Portuguese general inquisitor discussed the need for one there. Periodically, inspectors crossed the Atlantic to collect information and, if necessary, detain offenders, who were then sent to Lisbon for a trial of faith.[57] Spain, on the other hand, created colonial tribunals in major cities between 1570 and 1610. These tribunals remained active until independence, although the intensity and scope of their activities were clearly uneven throughout the centuries. For the Inquisition in the colonies, the geography and the categories of colonial subjects were new. However, by the late sixteenth and early seventeenth centuries, tracking the activities of New Christians and alleged crypto-Jews of Portuguese descent was a well-established practice.

During the years 1580 to 1640, Portugal was aggregated to the Spanish Crown and, as Fernanda Olival, Joan-Lluís Palos, and Joana Fraga explain, governed under the alternating rule of viceroys and governors who resided in

Lisbon.[58] To solve its financial problems, the Spanish monarchy sought the support of Portuguese bankers, and the porosity of the border between the two kingdoms allowed for the arrival and circulation of Portuguese immigrants in both the Peninsula and the colonies. Even though royal decrees initially restricted passage to the Indies to Spanish Old Christians only, governing bodies issued authorizations to non-Spanish migrants, including some New Christians, well into the seventeenth century. Without it, however, Portuguese could legally travel to Africa and Brazil, like Joan Vicente and Garci Méndez de Dueñas did prior to their arrivals in Peru, but not to the Spanish colonies. Examples illustrating the circumvention of royal restrictions can be found in testimonies given in Lima. Manuel de Fonseca in 1618 and Álvaro Cardoso de Silba in 1623 (the latter as witness in the trial of Garci Méndez de Dueñas) admitted to having entered the Indies by assuming the names of persons for whom licenses had been issued.[59] Between 1500 and 1650, close to four hundred Portuguese obtained documentation as naturals (*cartas de naturaleza*). According to Jesús Aguado de los Reyes, to obtain this documentation a man had to demonstrate that he met certain requirements: he had lived for more than twenty years in Castile, he was married to a Castilian woman, he owned real estate investments above a certain value, and he had available to him significant moneys to invest. However, Tamar Herzog clarifies that in today's terms the outcome of this process, a royal decree of naturalization, resembles more closely a revocable residency permit than naturalization. The decree legalized domicile but did not imply the concession of rights equal to those of native members of the community.[60]

The history of the Portuguese New Christians was tied in many ways to Spanish history long before the Spanish annexation of Portugal. Jewish families that had opted for exile from Spain in 1492 to avoid conversion to Christianity and then moved to Portugal found themselves forcibly converted there in 1497. In 1506 these New Christians were targeted in a major massacre in Lisbon; after 1536 they were placed under the eyes of the Portuguese Inquisition.[61] Ironically, many of the offspring of those who had left Spain for Portugal following the 1492 royal decree found themselves living under the authority of Spanish monarchs in Portuguese lands. This meant that they were thus subject to the reach of the Inquisition not only along the Spanish-Portuguese border but on the other side of the Atlantic.

Regardless of which monarchy held power over Portugal, the leadership of the New Christian community frequently took initiatives and conveyed to the monarchs their concern about the distinctions between Old and New Christians and about the activities of the Holy Office. New Christian community leaders first tried to stop the creation of Inquisition tribunals in Portugal. Later on, they repeatedly tried to obtain a general amnesty from the Crown, or at least a certain degree of moderation in inquisitorial procedures and methods, like "the annulment of the policy of confiscating the property of people detained by the Inquisition," as Claude Stuczynski explains.[62] Among others, there were contacts and negotiations in the 1580s and 1590s, but it was in 1601 when a royal provision allowed the "men of the Portuguese nation" to sell their properties in Portugal and establish themselves in a place of their choice within the domains of the Spanish monarchy.[63] A general pardon issued in 1605 by Pope Clement VIII determined that prisoners of the Holy Office had to be freed unless sentences had been published within one year (in Europe) and within two years (anywhere else); further, if those time limits were not met, property confiscations would be reversed and the property returned to its original owner. In the hope of obtaining some modification of inquisitorial procedures, Portuguese New Christians had contributed 1,700,000 *cruzados* to pay for the negotiations that led to the pardon and to influence the Inquisition to modify some of its harsher procedures. The main donors were members of the New Christian oligopoly from Lisbon, close to forty families with strong participation in the Indian trading routes, but there were also contributions from New Christians living in Portugal, Spain, and the colonies. According to Stuczynski, detailed lists recorded the names of contributors; among them were representatives of close to six thousand New Christian families that had no record of an encounter with the Inquisition. Interestingly, this author also remarks that the lists of contributors were titled, in Portuguese, "*rol dos judeus*" (list of Jews). In any case, not only did the New Christians' hopes for modification of inquisitorial procedures go unmet, but in 1610 Philip III (Philip II in Portugal) annulled the concessions established under Clement's pardon just five years earlier.[64] In the meantime, the Lima tribunal had reluctantly accepted the instructions of Clement's 1605 pardon, and Joan Vicente was in their prisons during that time. However, Vicente could not benefit: pending the determination of whether he had had a prior trial in Portugal and was indeed a relapse, he was not eligible for pardon.[65]

Civil and ecclesiastical authorities knew that New Christians and crypto-Jews traveled between Spanish and Portuguese territories, crossed the Atlantic, and continued beyond Iberian domains. Among their efforts to manage these migrations was the 1581 instruction from the Crown to the audiencia of Charcas to collect the names, nations, and occupations of foreigners living in Potosí. Also, a royal decree sent to the Inquisition in 1619, now preserved in the National Library in Madrid, states that Portuguese were crossing to France with their families and properties to avoid inquisitorial punishment. The decree indicates that in the case of Portuguese travelers unable to present a proper permit at the Spanish-French border, they had to be detained with confiscation of their properties. The Spanish Inquisition had to promptly receive report of the detention and communicate it to the Portuguese tribunal, so the information about the travelers could be verified before letting them cross to France.[66] In the 1630s Philip IV sent an investigator from Spain to France to assess issues related to commercial and religious activities in these communities. It is important to note here that Jews had not been permitted to live in France since 1394. However, after 1550 the presence of Portuguese merchants in France was allowed or tolerated, thus opening a loophole. In France, the situation of these migrants was ambivalent: they observed Christianity externally and preserved Judaism within their community. This was a shaky proposition, as their status as baptized Christians would place them under the direct purview of the Inquisition if they were indicted in territories under the jurisdiction of a tribunal. Most often, they were not directly persecuted for this religious duplicity, but there were exceptions. In 1619, a sixty-year-old woman was burned in Saint-Jean-de-Luz. Circulation and migrations between France (mainly Bayonne, but also Bordeaux and Saint-Jean-de-Luz), Spain, and the Atlantic colonies have also been documented among crypto-Jews who eventually settled in New Spain. In addition, by the middle of the seventeenth century the peninsular exile communities in France had trading agreements with relatives in the Peninsula and in the Netherlands.[67]

The Portuguese aggregation did not convey the subordination of the Portuguese Inquisition to the Spanish tribunal; however, the tribunals did exchange information, including documentation on potential or confirmed heretics, across the border.[68] Cooperation among the Spanish, Spanish colonial, and Portuguese Inquisitions was not new in the seventeenth century: at least one extradition treaty between the Spanish and Portuguese tribunals was signed as early as 1544 and at least one other by 1570. Under the treaty of 1570, it is indicated that the Portuguese and Castilian tribunals could request from one another the imprisonment and submission to trial of offenders.[69] One exchange of information is recapitulated in a document now preserved in Lisbon in which the Portuguese Inquisition received excerpts from confessions presented before Spanish and Spanish colonial tribunals in Valladolid, Granada, Córdoba, Cuenca, Toledo, Seville, Cartagena, Murcia, Galicia, Navarre, and Mexico. In the excerpts, prisoners disclosed heresies that had been committed in Portugal. Although the document is undated and it is not clear just when it was sent, it is valuable for its references to confessions extracted in 1567 (Salamanca), 1589 (Mexico), and 1623–1624 (Córdoba and Ciudad Rodrigo). Even if the information was sent after the extraction of those confessions, the intent of the two tribunals to collect and share data is clear. Other documents now preserved at the National Library in Madrid illustrate a debate about whether the

Portuguese and Spanish tribunals exchanged not only information but prisoners held in their respective jurisdictions if it became necessary to return them to the place where the heresy had actually been committed. James Boyajian mentions information sent from Lisbon to Goa through Madrid in the 1630s and the impact this information had on the indictments made in Goa during the 1640s. Even if the implementation of treaties was not always smooth or consistent, the principle of cooperation was established.[70]

The conduct of the aforementioned trial of Joan Vicente and the testimony of Manuel de Fonseca in the proceedings against Garci Méndez de Dueñas provide additional evidence of cooperation. When Lima requested information from Mexico, from Évora for the trial of Vicente, and later from Mexico and Lisbon for the trial of Fonseca (himself a witness in the trial of Garci Méndez de Dueñas), the requests were not considered by Lima officials as exceptional but as part of the regular performance of their duties. In the trial of the peddler Manuel Henríquez in the 1630s, we can see that Lima's requests to Coimbra for information about an earlier reconciliation and the prisoner's allegations of misconduct in the procedures of the Portuguese tribunal are similar in kind to those made in the case of Vicente. Apparently, Lima did not base such requests on the social position of the accused or on its own economic interests: Vicente was a shoemaker and Henríquez a peddler, although both of them were connected to wealthier members of the Portuguese New Christian networks.[71]

It is a fact that these exchanges of information delayed the resolution of trials, contributing to its image as a slow-moving and often inefficient institution. Eimeric's manual for inquisitors urged that trials proceed in the most direct manner possible, but it would be hard to apply that ideal to many of the Lima tribunal's cases.[72] Nevertheless, the intention of the exchanges, however drawn out, was to verify the prisoner's story and to validate or invalidate his or her declarations. A request could result in evidence that would determine how a prisoner would be classified and dealt with (if there was a previous trial, if a previous encounter with the tribunal did or did not qualify as a trial, or if there had been irregularities in prior trials). At the same time, the exchanges gave some prisoners the time to seek loopholes to apply in their defense strategies. Nevertheless, the prisoner might still not succeed. When Joan Vicente argued for his spontaneous confession in Évora before the Lima inquisitors, the strategy gained reconciliation in Lima with a sambenito, but that resolution did not free the cobbler from the Inquisition's watch. He faced yet another trial, under another tribunal; his burning at the stake in Cartagena in 1626 came just two years after Méndez de Dueñas had committed suicide. In other words, colonial tribunals, despite the obstacles of a vast geography, limited staff, and inadequate financial support, were indeed able to fulfill many of their responsibilities.

The 1580 Spanish aggregation of the Portuguese Crown opened additional doors for many Portuguese New Christians, who probably took the opportunity to move away from the stigma of a past reconciliation into a new life. Like Joan Vicente, they relied on the support of a transatlantic network that helped them gain access to economic opportunities in the colonial economy. Or they found opportunities, as had Garci Méndez de Dueñas, to conduct trade in the colonies and keep up familial responsibilities from a distance, as Méndez de Dueñas did for his wife and daughter in France, through the services of the same network. Regardless of the migration route, and with or without required permission from the Inquisition to travel after their previous trials, Portuguese New Christians were likely to gravitate toward cities. Most often, they settled in or near entry ports and other commercial hubs such as Salvador da Bahia, Lima, Potosí, Córdoba del Tucumán, and Buenos Aires, as the lives of Joan Vicente and Garci Méndez de Dueñas illustrate. The conduct of proceedings before colonial tribunals was similar in many ways to that of the peninsular tribunals, and thus the travelers who came to their attention after experiences with Spanish or Portuguese proceedings might be aware of defense strategies and understand the conduct of the trials well enough to seek out procedural loopholes.

The Influence of Lima

Lima, where Garci Méndez de Dueñas lived for about twenty years, was often called "La Ciudad de los Reyes," the City of Kings, because the date of its foundation coincided with the Christian celebration of Epiphany. Located on the Pacific coast, Lima was the capital of the viceroyalty of Peru, which controlled the territories of Spanish colonial South America, from Argentina and Chile in the south to Ecuador and beyond in the north. As the head city of this colonial territory, Lima exerted political, administrative, judicial, and religious power over the inhabitants of the entire viceroyalty. As Alejandra Osorio writes, "the establishment of the viceregal court and archbishopric in Lima circa 1542, followed later by the Inquisition and the Extirpation of Idolatry, made Lima into the new baroque center of this civilizing and Christianizing mission."[73]

The city's architectural landscape speaks to its role in the Catholic hierarchy and its importance in Christianization within the viceroyalty. In the early seventeenth century, Lima hosted a splendid cathedral and more than forty churches and chapels, convents, and religious schools.[74] Among the most notable were a convent of the Dominican order (Méndez de Dueñas's home was next to it),[75] three Franciscan convents, and one convent each devoted to Nuestra Señora de Guadalupe, San Agustín, Nuestra Señora de la Merced, and Nuestra Señora de Belén. We can also mention schools and residences for Jesuit novices as well as six monasteries for secluded nuns. Public celebrations in Lima involved the participation of both civil and religious authorities and included celebrations of the Christian calendar, the entry of a viceroy, the funeral of a king, or the birth of a royal heir—and the public punishment of idolaters, heretics, and offenders of secular laws.[76]

Lima was at the heart of the viceroyalty's trading circuits. Dried fruit, milk, *chicha* (corn beer), almonds, and wine could be bought at the central plaza, and luxurious textiles and furniture were displayed in larger stores located on nearby streets. In addition to supplying its own population with such goods, the City of Kings also supplied the regional markets of Guatemala, Nicaragua, New Granada, Tucumán, and Chile.[77] Portuguese merchants were important in this commerce, but they were not the only group involved. "Everybody sells and is a merchant, even if through somebody else's hand and with dissimulation."[78] This comment about Lima comes from Portocarrero, who lived in the city for about fifteen years.[79] The city had close to 25,000 inhabitants in the 1610s, and as many as 60,000 in 1629.[80] Portocarrero noted that nearly every resident of Lima, including the viceroy and the archbishop, was directly or indirectly involved in trading activities, women as well as men. Black, mulatto, mestizo, and indigenous women traded in items for everyday consumption, and women's religious orders pursued financial endeavors. In her analysis of the colonial Peruvian economy, Margarita Suárez explains that the Church as an institution, as well as its members individually, participated in trading and financial activities.[81]

The diversification of civil and religious authorities into commerce was not an innovation of the early seventeenth century, nor was it exclusive to Lima. Grievances presented against the Lima inquisitor Gutiérrez de Ulloa in 1587 cited his commercial activities.[82] Carlos Sempat Assadourian found in his examination of such activities in Tucumán that governors, bishops, and members of the Holy Office participated in trade at different levels. This diversification made issues of trade regulation and administration an interest of both civil and religious authorities at the local level, not only the concern of a particular group or guild.[83]

In the seventeenth century, the Calle de los Mercaderes, where many Portuguese New Christians conducted their businesses, was considered the center of Lima's commercial life, as reported by writers of the period. The street housed at least twenty warehouses, forty stores carrying commodities from all over the world, and many smaller shops and stands. Merchants trading there had partners in Spain, Mexico, Africa, and China.[84] On a nearby block, Calle de las Mantas, a customer could find some thirty stores offering blankets and the less expensive textiles and flannels. The bank of Juan de la Cueva, one of the two most important financial houses in viceregal Peru during the first part of the seventeenth century, was located in the Calle de las Mantas; it was active there for twenty years. Méndez de Dueñas borrowed money from the bank in 1615, and in 1631 the Lima tribunal deposited money confiscated from him in the same institution. De la Cueva had properties in Lima, Callao, Huancavelica, Arica, Cajamarca, and Canta; his family and their eighteen slaves resided on an upper floor of the building in which the bank operated.[85]

The size and scope of the larger businesses conducted by Portuguese traders is indicated by the time it took the inquisitors to process the inventory of Garci Méndez de Dueñas's stores and the value they assigned to it as part of confiscation proceedings. It took twelve days to complete the inventory; the value recorded was 152,359 pesos. (For comparison, a chronicler writing in 1630 reported that the annual salary of an inquisitor in 1572 was 3,000 pesos.)[86] The final balance of the inventory was somewhat less after the liquidation of pending transactions, but the Lima tribunal collected enough revenue from the confiscation to expand its facilities and purchase houses for penitents. In fact, tribunal officials continued to work on Méndez de Dueñas's accounts until 1665—forty years after punishing his effigy in the 1625 Auto.[87]

According to Margarita Suárez, Juan de la Cueva had several paintings in his home, as would many prestigious men in Lima.[88] Lima's wealthy traders did not seclude themselves from the broader community: they were also patrons of the arts and urban cultural life. Furthermore, they contributed to the celebration of the 1625 Auto General de Fe—paradoxically, some of their own were among those receiving punishment. They also sponsored a lavish party at the end of 1630 to celebrate the new year. Given the street's vibrant buzz of commercial activity, merchants located in the Calle de los Mercaderes were often exposed to theft and other crimes, as Juan Antonio Suardo reported for August and September of 1629, September 1630, and March 1631.[89] Portocarrero described the great variety of local foods, underscoring the many kinds of fish (relevant for those who avoid pork) that made Lima attractive to newcomers.[90] He also noted that even Lima residents who were not wealthy always owned at least one silver piece and kept at least one slave for their service.

The Portuguese New Christians relied on transatlantic networks. The New World Inquisition tribunals also relied on an extended international network of administrators and other bureaucrats who kept track of potential offenders on both sides of the Spanish and Portuguese border and across the Atlantic. Although the inquisitors' procedure for requesting information from a Portuguese office through Madrid was probably just as slow and bureaucratic as an exchange of information with the metropolis conducted by the viceroyalty, the information in the end did cross borders and oceans. The setting was now transatlantic for all parties.

For the Spanish tribunal, exporting the Inquisition required drawing new jurisdictions. After the expulsion of the Jews and Muslims, it was widely assumed that everybody residing in the Peninsula was, or should be, a Christian, regardless of whether their baptisms had been by will or by force. In general, we can state that any lay adult (or minor with proper assistance) present in Spanish lands was under the surveillance of the Holy Office—even the king. Among members of the Church, secular clerics were accountable to the tribunal, but bishops remained untouchable. If a bishop were implicated in an act of heresy, the Inquisition was not to pursue the case but had to dispatch the evidence to the papacy. Members of religious orders were also under inquisitorial scrutiny, even though it was a matter of much disagreement and discussion.[91] In sum, with the exception of bishops, everyone was at least in theory subject to investigation by the Spanish Inquisition. Although the peninsular Inquisition had jurisdiction only over those who had been baptized—and theoretically everyone in Spain had been—its colonial counterparts conducted their work among large numbers of native people who were not under their jurisdiction. They also had to accommodate those native people as they were evangelized over time.

In political, social, and economic matters, Seville was the link between the Peninsula and the colonies, since it was from that port that the transatlantic exchange was articulated, starting in the early colonial days and continuing to the Bourbon reforms of the late eighteenth century. Garci Méndez de Dueñas and Juan de la Cueva were obviously not alone in having connections in Seville. In Seville resided the Consejo de Indias and the Casa de Contratación,[92] bodies that issued regulations concerning the Indies, controlled transatlantic trade, and also oversaw migration to the colonies. Prior to 1640, Portuguese immigrants probably constituted between 12 and 25 percent of Seville's urban population, but they were not the only immigrant community. To legally trade with the Indies, they could opt for a naturalization process. In addition, royal regulations prohibited the migration through Seville of New Christians—indeed, of anyone whose ancestors had been condemned in a trial of faith—but there were ways to bypass these regulations, as we have seen. Thus, there was a rationale for the establishment of Inquisition tribunals in the colonies.

On matters that pertained to the Inquisition, the nerve center of the Spanish presence on the American continent was not Seville but Madrid, where the Supreme Council of the Inquisition was located. The city was the connection point for tribunals of the Old World and the New, receiving reports of colonial tribunals' activities, dispatching requests from the colonies to Portugal, and so on. The Spanish Inquisition was a firmly established institution, and it had already had experience in transplanting tribunals to its colonial possessions in Sicily.[93] The Spanish Inquisition saw its challenge as how best to export and adapt to the New World an institution that was already present and functioning in Spain and its European colonies, not to create new bodies or change its longstanding organization. In this historical context, discussions about inquisitorial "jurisdiction" refer to both the territory to be covered by each tribunal and to the specific peoples to be targeted for inquisitorial procedures. The period during which the New World tribunals were established (1570 to 1608) coincides in general with the travels between Portugal, Spain, Africa, Brazil, and the Spanish colonies of Joan Vicente, who arrived in Brazil in 1588 and in the Peruvian viceroyalty in 1591, and of Garci Méndez de Dueñas, who left Portugal in 1580, traveled between Spain, Guinea, Portugal, the Caribbean, and the Peruvian viceroyalty several times, and arrived in Lima about 1603.

Overall, the pattern of establishing new tribunals and the nature of the exchanges of information among tribunals gives us the opportunity to track an expansion of the tribunals' capability and range of action. We can also see how expansion affected the tribunals separately and view in more detail the world in which they functioned. While any one tribunal might be understaffed, as many often claimed, the colonial Inquisition overall does not seem so. Each office dealt with only certain segments of the colonial population in fixed territories, and in cases of need it could contact officials of tribunals in other cities, as it did when it imprisoned Joan Vicente. Nor does it seem that individual tribunals were highly isolated, because tribunals were located where potential offenders were more likely to reside, and because individual tribunals could connect to others by way of the network articulated from Madrid.

The exact number of people who received extreme inquisitorial punishment is not part of this study's scope, but the fact is that the number was small—if we go only by records of the Autos. There is another way to consider these low reported numbers. Clearly, Lima could trace a person's activities on both sides of the ocean, and on both sides of the Spanish-Portuguese border. As a result, persons might meet the same fate as those killed at an Auto General without actually going through one. Someone like Joan Vicente or Garci Méndez de Dueñas could undergo a trial of faith, see his property confiscated, be sentenced with reconciliation and a derogatory garment, or commit suicide prior to the Auto General. Such a person would not be accounted for in the records of those receiving extreme punishment. In other words, quality and quantity—the numbers of those who died in Autos Generales and those who might have died as a result of other inquisitorial actions—are not directly correlated. In this chapter I used trials of faith to narrate individual stories but furthermore as a lens to analyze how the Inquisition approached the colonial expansion, and how tribunals articulated their networks across the Atlantic (like those merchants the Holy Office was trying to detect and imprison). In the following chapter I will use a different lens while analyzing trials from the Lima tribunal. Instead of focusing on individual trials, I will focus on a set of trials conducted in Lima during the 1630s, those labeled by the tribunal as "La Complicidad Grande" (The Great Complicity).

4

A Community under Trial in Colonial Peru

When the functionaries of the Lima tribunal talked about "The Great Complicity" (La Complicidad Grande), they were referring to the approximately one hundred arrests and trials that took place in that city between 1635 and 1639. Although complete records of only a few trials of the Great Complicity have been preserved, we do have trial summaries and other materials to draw upon. According to the records of the Lima tribunal, 90 people were initially imprisoned.[1] Mainly New Christians from Portugal or Spain, these men and women were accused of practicing the heresy of crypto-Judaism. Following their confessions, the tribunal imprisoned more suspects, bringing the total close to 110 people. The arrests began in April of 1635, and most of the prisoners received a sentence at an impressive Auto General de Fe celebrated at Lima's central square in January of 1639. Many were reconciled to the faith, accepting Christianity and convincing the inquisitors; they were punished with exile and confiscation of property. But eleven of the accused were burned at the stake. As a result of the Auto General de Fe, the community of Portuguese New Christians in Lima was decimated.

Lima tribunal records state that the evidence upon which its case for the Complicity prosecutions were built surfaced by chance, after a brief exchange between a store employee and customers shopping in the Calle de los Mercaderes in 1634. A few days after the exchange, one of those customers reported to the Inquisition a suspicious conversation that on its own soon triggered a number of imprisonments and trials. This unfortunate encounter occurred at a small store owned by Antonio de Acuña and Diego López de Fonseca and devoted to trade in imported textiles. It was at this store that Antonio Cordero worked as an employee. In the tribunal's narrative, a customer named Joan de Salazar Negrete walked into the store on a Saturday morning in 1634 and approached Cordero asking to buy some gauze.[2] To the customer's surprise, Cordero refused to perform the sale, giving the fact that it was Saturday as his reason. According to Salazar Negrete, when he returned to the store the following Friday early in the morning, he found Antonio Cordero having bread and fruit for breakfast. When Salazar Negrete asked Cordero why was he not having bacon instead, Cordero responded with a question: Since my father did not eat pork, why would I?[3]

In its historical context, and on the Calle de los Mercaderes, this last statement must have seemed unequivocally suspicious. The tribunal of the Inquisition had published in its Edicts of Faith a catalogue of the deeds that were considered crypto-Jewish markers. Avoiding commercial transactions on Saturdays and avoiding pork consumption were both on the list: together they sufficed to raise eyebrows, as probably happened with Salazar Negrete and those who accompanied him. Also, as previously discussed, the presence of Portuguese New Christians and alleged crypto-Jews was no secret. Indeed, it had been presented by the Lima tribunal as the rationale behind its creation in 1570, so a testimony of this sort would have raised suspicions, yes, but it would not have been unexpected in the 1630s. In his declaration, Salazar Negrete reported that he had consulted with a more knowledgeable man, who advised him to report the incident to the Inquisition, which Salazar Negrete did in August of 1634.[4] The denunciation was evaluated later, in a meeting of inquisitors that took place in March of 1635, and in April of that year Antonio Cordero was arrested. However, his properties were not confiscated. According to Fernando de Montesinos, the Lima tribunal held back from such action on purpose, guarding secrecy. Thus, for a while, nobody knew about Cordero's fate and could not be sure that he was in the tribunal's prisons. A known potential prisoner could have run away, disguised evidence, gotten rid of properties, or transferred ownership.[5]

Records of prior trials of faith demonstrate that the Lima Inquisition knew that crypto-Judaism had existed among the Portuguese merchants since the tribunal's creation, but much of what they knew likely came out of individual trials, not obviously connected in a way that would trigger a chain of imprisonments. In the 1620s a libel posted in the central plaza denounced Manuel Bautista Pérez as a crypto-Jew and announced with considerable sarcasm that those who wanted to learn and observe the Law of Moses had only to contact him and the others named. The Lima tribunal and the wealthy merchant had an initial encounter in 1624, with no drastic consequences. However, Pérez was incarcerated later, along with the other Portuguese New Christians who fell during the arrests of the Complicidad in 1635.[6] In a parallel example from Mexico, Solange Alberro mentions that in 1622 the Mexican tribunal received an anonymous denunciation about "the existence of a synagogue on Calle de Santo Domingo, just two doors down from the Inquisition's offices," but at that time the tribunal did not pursue such cases.[7] These two events seem to support scholarly depictions of a rather slow-moving Inquisition in the colonies, devoted in the long run to reprimanding minor offenses and to overseeing book censorship and focusing only exceptionally on crypto-Jewish heresy. These lesser pursuits were, as scholars like René Millar Carvacho, Gabriela Ramos, Teodoro Hampe Martínez, and Pedro Guibovich Pérez have written, the regular concerns of the Lima office.[8] On the other hand, historian Jaime Contreras, referring to the general structure of the Holy Office, explains that when evidence did result in a peak of activity in a particular tribunal, it would become clear that the Office had indeed been dedicated over time to the accumulation, organization, and presentation of such information, prior to the visible peak. For the Lima cases, this argument is supported in a 1636 letter from inquisitor Juan de Mañozca y Zamora to the Count of Castrillo, president of the Council of the Indies, explaining that in light of the number of Jews (in Mañozca's words) found to have immigrated to Lima from Portugal, the tribunal had secretly contacted comisarios in other parts of the district to calculate their overall numbers throughout the viceroyalty.[9]

In the 1630s the Lima tribunal did follow up on Salazar Negrete's lead. Antonio Cordero was placed under arrest, and tribunal officials devoted time and staff to investigate whether material heresy existed among Lima's Portuguese traders. In the letter mentioned above, Mañozca wrote that "from something that started out seemingly unimportant had been revealed the largest complicity ever seen."[10] We now see an awakened tribunal that for the following four years did not hesitate to devote itself to squashing the Complicidad Grande, putting almost one hundred people on trial. Salazar Negrete's denunciation clearly illustrates the workings of a specific mechanism set in motion by the tribunals of the Inquisition in the territories under their jurisdiction. It is that mechanism that leads me to contend that the Inquisition functioned as an immaterial panoptic.

Let us remember that in the Spanish American colonies, the tribunal held jurisdiction only over people of European and African origin, not over Indians. The patterns of European and African settlement meant that most of those the Inquisition could hold to account resided in urban areas. Thus, even though the territory of the Spanish American colonies was much greater than that of Spain, the Inquisition did not have to cover its full geographical extent, because not all its inhabitants were under inquisitorial jurisdiction. Thus, the colonial Inquisition did not need a huge number of tribunals and inquisitors but instead sufficed with tribunals settled where the populations under its direct purview resided—that is, in the port cities where merchants and slaves entered the colonies. Some additional staff, comisarios and familiares, were assigned to smaller cities and towns throughout the viceroyalty.

Also, the Inquisition had no reason to overflow suspicious communities with hidden informants or spies. Anyone who had undergone Christian indoctrination and regularly attended Mass could serve as the eyes of the Inquisition. Because of royal restrictions regarding who could migrate to the New World and who could not, all settlers of European origin who lived in the New World had to be Christians, Old or New, at least nominally, as permits were required for departure from their home countries. In other words, *anybody* could report suspicious talks or activities to the tribunal. Except for Indians, everybody was under the scrutiny of multiple inquisitorial eyes—those who reported as much as those reported on.

As part of its regular tasks, the Lima tribunal kept detailed notes in which the names and activities of potential offenders to Christianity were recorded, and the evidence against them compiled and assessed, before arrests were made. Strikingly, the web of Portuguese merchants of New Christian descent, as a discrete (and discreet) flock devoted to the hidden heresy of crypto-Judaism, does not appear in these notes as particularly suspicious. Even further, as the extent of the web was uncovered, it seems that the Lima tribunal was actually surprised by its magnitude and density. As successive denunciations bared a sizable crypto-Jewish network, the Lima tribunal had to apply itself diligently to clearing the prisons and making room for newcomers.[11] In addition, the Lima tribunal was instructed to proceed cautiously with the new arrests.[12] These facts suggest strongly that the tribunal did not know of the hidden network in advance, as its functionaries had received no call to clear space in the prisons in expectation of a string of arrests.

In the following pages, I will focus on a set of questions regarding the Great Complicity and attempt to uncover answers. First, who were these people? Second, in what were they complicit? Third, when the Lima tribunal accused them of crypto-Judaic heresy, what constituted evidence of their religious beliefs in the tribunal's own records? And to conclude, how do answers to these questions shape our understanding of the Lima Inquisition and the New Christians of Portuguese descent in Spanish America?

The Names and Faces of La Complicidad Grande

Of the approximately one hundred people imprisoned between 1635 and 1639, I was able to determine the birthplaces of only eighty (see table 4.1). Thus, any conclusions based on numbers will always be estimative. The majority (fifty-six) were born in Portugal, with a substantial minority (twenty-three) from Spain; only one was born in the New World, in Pernambuco (Brazil). Even though their numbers are slightly different, Paulino Castañeda Delgado and Pilar

Table 4.1. The Complicidad Grande: Birthplaces of Prisoners

Portugal

Birthplace	No.	Birthplace	No.
Alcains	1	Monte Mayor	1
Alpedrina (Castelo Novo, La Guarda)	1	Montemayor el Nuevo (Évora)	2
Ança (Coimbra)	1	Portalegre	1
Arronchas (Portalegre)	1	San Cobadan	1
Estremoz	2	Santa Marina (Coimbra)	1
Évora	1	Santarem	2
Feijo	1	Serpa	1
Fontecada (Lamego)	1	Suarzel (Évora)	1
Fundão (La Guarda)	1	Tomar	1
Guimaraes	1	Torre de Moncorvo	6
La Guarda	4	Vergança	2
Lamego	2	Villa de la Frontera	1
Lisbon	6	Villa Viciosa	1
Mirandela (Miranda)	1	Villaflor	2
Moncaraz	1	Villamean (Viseu, Coimbra)	1
Moncorvo (Braga)	2	Villamo	1
Mondi	1	Unspecified	2
Monsanto (La Guarda)	1	**Total**	**56**

Spain

Birthplace	No.	Birthplace	No.
Almagro	4	Pontevedra (Galicia)	1
Badajoz	2	Río Seco	1
Estela (Navarre)	1	Seville	9
Madrid	1	Villa Batua (Tordesillas)	1
Osuna (Andalusia)	2	Villarreal	1
		Total	**23**

Brazil

Birthplace	No.
Pernambuco	1
Total	**1**

Note: Of the approximately one hundred persons tried in the Complicidad Grande between 1635 and 1639, the birthplaces of almost eighty are listed. The table represents the individuals for whom information was available.

Source: Quaderno de la Complicidad del Judaísmo que se empeçó en esta Ynquisiçión De la ciudad de Los Reyes del rreyno del Pirú desde principio de Abril del año De 1635 (AHN–Inquisición, Libro 1030); *Auto que se celebro a los 23 de hen° de seys° y treinta y nueve y execucion de las sentencias* (AHN–Inquisición, Libro 1031).

Hernández Aparicio have found similar proportions, and write that about 70 percent of those who received sentences in 1639 in Lima were Portuguese.[13] This fact is related to the aggregation of Portugal by the Spanish monarchy between 1580 and 1640 and to the geographical circulation of the "men of the nation" discussed in the previous chapter. Of the eighty whose birthplaces we know, six were from Lisbon and the same number from Torre de Moncorvo, in the northeast of Portugal. The other Portuguese were from various other places, mainly in central and northern Portugal.

Of those born in Spain (23), more than a third (nine people) were from Seville, and many of them belonged to one of two extended families. One family consisted of the sisters Mencía and Mayor de Luna, their spouses Enrique Núñez de Espinosa and Antonio Morón, their offspring (Isabel Antonia, daughter of Mayor and Antonio), and their son-in-law (Rodrigo Váez Pereira, Isabel's husband). The other family was that of the Tavares siblings. Although in colonial Spanish America they were perceived as Portuguese, these people had in fact been born in Spain to Portuguese parents, or to their adult Spanish-born children. They lived as people of Portuguese descent, with Portuguese relatives, and very likely close links to people who lived in Portugal. An example is Enrique Jorge Tavares, a man born in Seville to Spanish parents. However, his paternal grandfather was from Castelo Branco and his paternal grandmother was from Fundão, both in Portugal.[14] The other prisoners were from scattered places in Spain, and all of the Spanish-born mentioned Portuguese parents or grandparents. In the tribunal's lists of prisoners, pairs or trios of siblings were also recorded, for example, Manuel, Jorge, and Antonio de Espinosa; Juan and Jorge de Silva; and Tomás and Luis de Lima, among others (the tribunal also took care to mention an additional partner, *su compañero*, who might have been associated with the siblings). In analyzing a larger sample of 358 individuals from Portugal who had trials under the three tribunals of the Spanish colonies, Studnicki-Gizbert found a similar lack of consistency in terms of the prisoners' places of origin.[15]

Two other facts known about the prisoners are their ages and marital status. The youngest was eighteen-year-old Enrique Jorge Tavares, and the oldest was sixty-year-old Luis de Valencia, whose son, born in Pernambuco, was also imprisoned. Of the seventy-five people who declared their age, most were male adults: twenty-five were between thirty and thirty-four years old, and sixteen were between twenty-five and twenty-nine. A third group, those aged forty to forty-four, consisted of nine people, and there were six between the ages of thirty-five and thirty-nine and another six between forty-five and forty-nine.[16] Castañeda Delgado and Hernández Aparicio sustain that even though the marital status of five of them was unknown, most of the men were single.[17]

They migrated alone if single, or if married either with their wives or alone. In many cases, the wives and children were left in the Iberian Peninsula, either with the intent that they would be brought to the New World once the migrant had settled, or in the expectation that the migrant would return to the Peninsula after attaining some economic advantage in the colonies. From these facts, we can infer that Portuguese New Christian women migrated to the New World with their parents or husbands, remained in the Peninsula with their parents, or waited for their husbands' call or return. The pattern for these women reflects that of the broader Spanish migration of women to the colonies.[18]

Gender deserves a separate treatment in considering the Complicidad. The only three women mentioned by name in the Complicidad cases are the sisters Mencía and Mayor de Luna and Isabel Antonia (Mayor de Luna's daughter). Their husbands, Enrique Núñez de Espinosa, Antonio Morón, and Rodrigo Váez Pereira, were also imprisoned. It has been argued that since public performances were forbidden, crypto-Judaic practice in the privacy of the home became more important than it had been prior to conversion, thus expanding the female role in crypto-Judaism from its place in traditional Jewish practices.[19] Based on the available information, the Lima cases involving women do not seem to fit this assumption. The number of women accused was very small. Two possible explanations, beyond the presence of single men among the Portuguese New Christians in the 1630s, are that the tribunal was unable to enter the private world of crypto-Jewish women in colonial Lima or that it considered the men more important for other reasons. In her study of the commercial activities of Jews in the colonies during the seventeenth century, Lucía García de Proodian found just seven cases involving trials of crypto-Jewish women: in addition to the three women mentioned above, there were Isabel Váez (introduced earlier with her husband Joan Vicente) and three others. In their analysis of the Lima tribunal inspections conducted by Juan Ruiz de Prado toward the end of the sixteenth century, Castañeda Delgado and Hernández Aparicio note that in twenty-six cases involving potential crypto-Jews brought to the tribunal's attention but not pursued, twenty-five of the accused were men plus a black woman from Panama.[20]

The paths of migration from Portugal to Spanish Peru reflect considerable variety. In some cases, the Portuguese New Christians migrated from Portugal to Spain, and later to the Spanish colonies of the American continent, as did Manuel Henríquez.[21] According to his statement before the tribunal, Henríquez was born in Lamego in northern Portugal to Portuguese parents and moved to Spain at the age of eighteen. He sold textiles in Madrid, Valladolid, and other small Castilian towns until he married and moved for three years to Villena.

Next, he returned to Madrid, and later moved to Seville, from where he took passage in 1633 on a slave cargo ship in the service of Antonio Gómez de Acosta. Henríquez arrived in Paita and later traveled to Lima.

Another migratory route began with a voyage by ship from Portugal to a Portuguese enclave in Africa, usually within the circuits of the Atlantic trade that linked Europe, Africa, and South America. Such was the case of Luis de Valencia. Before the tribunal, Valencia described his long itinerary, beginning in Lisbon and going on to Angola, Guinea, Cartagena, Pernambuco, Rome, Seville, Havana, Veracruz, and Caracas, among other locations.[22] Mencía de Luna, on the other hand, came directly from Seville to Peru to reunite with her husband in 1629, in the same fleet of warships that carried the viceroy, the Conde de Chinchón.[23]

Although the Portuguese were by no means the only foreign residents in Spanish lands, they are strongly represented in trials of faith. Historians have documented the presence of people from other European kingdoms (Italy, France, Germany, and England) in both peninsular and colonial Spanish territories. Bilateral agreements among kings regulated their presence and guaranteed a rather strictly limited acceptance that allowed non-Spanish men and women to live and work as foreigners.[24] However, among all the Europeans, the Portuguese were the closest to Spanish nationals. Their native tongue was closer to Spanish than any other Romance language, and many of them spoke Spanish fluently. In Lima, the similarity between Portuguese and Galician probably allowed someone from Portugal to pass as a Galician; this was noted by Juan de Acevedo and Bartolomé de León in their declarations in the trial of Francisco Vázquez in 1636. They described Vázquez as someone who could blend easily among Portuguese, Galician, and people from Extremadura as well.[25]

Whatever their home region in Portugal, many of the Portuguese merchants who lived in seventeenth-century Lima were part of broader transatlantic trading networks of the Sephardic diaspora. The networks included Jews who had left the Iberian world to avoid conversion to Christianity as well as those who had become New Christians and remained in Iberian territories. Among the latter were the crypto-Jews. The men of the nation were present in southern France, London, and the Netherlands and also in the Spanish and Portuguese colonies.[26] Living openly as Jews, as New Christians, or as clandestine crypto-Jews, they were found in both Catholic and Protestant lands. In Europe, monarchies developed different policies for keeping an eye on the religious practices of their subjects. In Spanish and Portuguese territories, New Christians accused of crypto-Judaism could be prosecuted. In the evidence compiled against Manuel

Bautista Pérez, it was brought out that he had called Lisbon the best city in the world but had added that he preferred not to reside there because of the rigor of the Portuguese Inquisition.[27]

Under British and Dutch domain, Jews had access to specific rights not available to them elsewhere at the time, and thus they were also found in Suriname. Although these rights did not make Jews equal to Christian subjects, Jews were allowed to practice their religion, to travel, and to trade. Members of the Sephardic diaspora circulated within Iberian lands and could also cross borders that divided Protestants and Catholics (and also those that divided Muslim and Christian lands). Even with its local and regional variations, this diaspora "constituted in both a metaphoric and an actual sense, a huge extended family."[28]

Scholars have explored both internal Inquisition records and official and personal correspondence to examine the Portuguese merchants' business and personal lives.[29] A merchant house, as an entity, was at the core of a network; it was a sort of cosmos unto itself, with specific internal dynamics. It usually contained about twenty or thirty members of an extended family, who were distributed among different residences. The four nuclear families that belonged to the house of Manuel Bautista Pérez constituted a cluster of approximately sixty people. In the Lima residence of Pérez, his wife Guiomar Enríquez, and their four children there also lived another nuclear family, this one composed of Guiomar's sister Isabel, her husband Sebastián Duarte, an apprentice, and about ten guests who stayed with the family for months or even years at a time. In his confession Luis de Valencia declared he had stayed as a guest at Pérez's house. Others connected to this extended family were Juan Rodríguez Duarte (Sebastián's nephew) and a sister of Pérez who was married to Luis de Vega, a silversmith from Lisbon who had also immigrated to Lima.[30]

As head of the household, a merchant was responsible to his family, his house, and the broader community. The physical space was a combination of residence—private rooms, family areas such as the kitchen and dining areas, a library of more than one hundred volumes, and an art collection of about the same number of paintings—and working areas, with studios and warehouses for family members, business associates and apprentices, slaves, and servants. Adding together the relatives, guests, employees, domestic servants, and slaves, Pérez's domicile probably accommodated around forty people and demonstrated to the community his wealth, generosity, and hospitality. Another example illustrates similar arrangements at a smaller scale: Gerónimo Hernández, who lived at a different residence, declared that he lived in a combined dwelling and working area with his nephew Antonio de Acuña, and that Diego López de

Fonseca, Bartolomé de León, Manuel de la Rosa, and Antonio Cordero lived in the same domicile.[31]

Merchants began their careers with an apprenticeship to an established trader, most likely a relative in some degree, learning the craft, building personal connections, and traveling with shipments when necessary.[32] With shared profits from a successful investment, or a loan from a trader at a higher rank, the apprentice could branch out by undertaking a trade activity of his own and then continue expanding his scope of work until he had established himself as a senior merchant. Born in Ança (northern Portugal), Manuel Bautista Pérez grew up with relatives in Lisbon and also had family in Seville and in Africa. On his first trip to Africa, in 1612, he was an agent for other investors and worked in partnership with an uncle. In December 1616 Pérez set out from Lisbon on a second journey that took him to Seville, Cacheu (in present-day Guinea-Bissau), Cartagena, Portobello, Panama, and Paita, and he docked in Lima in March 1619 with a cargo of 227 slaves. At some later point, his business reached a volume of 300 to 400 slaves per year. On this voyage, he represented the interests of investors who provided commodities to be taken to Africa, such as Indian textiles circulating via Lisbon.[33] As a result of multilateral connections among traders, associates, suppliers, and other correspondents, a merchant based in Lima, like Pérez, "traded directly with merchant houses situated in New Spain, Tierra Firme, Iberia, and West Africa."[34] Simón Váez Sevilla, based in Mexico City and among its wealthiest merchants during the same years, conducted business with traders located in Oaxaca and Guatemala and also in the Philippines. Merchants based in Lisbon and Seville linked the Iberian Peninsula with the Low Countries, France, the Mediterranean, and India through their trade activities.

In addition to the horizontal connections they made across two continents and across the Atlantic, the Portuguese merchant houses also achieved vertical integration as their activity ranged "from the highly localized and day-to-day business of street selling to the highest echelons of European finance and overseas trade."[35] In the urban environment, one found merchants, shopkeepers, and peddlers; each of these classifications was associated with typical tasks and held a mutually respective position within the network. On a larger scale, the verticality can be seen in the participation in the slave trade. Obtaining an *asiento* (a license for trade in African slaves) required the combined efforts of financial specialists and investors who stood behind the asiento holder. In addition to raising capital and obtaining licenses for the slave trade, the Portuguese networks controlled ships and points of sale, buying slaves from Portuguese traders who resided in Africa. Slave ships were exempt from regulations that set the annual schedule of colonial trade and could sail at will. They were not, however, exempt from official scrutiny. At different points along the trade circuit royal inspectors visited the ships, checking, for example, whether the number of slaves exceeded the number on the license the merchant had been issued (bribes were paid to cover discrepancies). Inquisition officials also visited the ships to check for unauthorized books and suspect passengers. Tribunal members charged four pesos for each visited ship.[36]

In spite of the limits and regulations that governed the Portuguese slave trade through Lima, traders had additional options: they could enter through other ports (after an asiento issued in 1595, these included Buenos Aires), or they could circumvent the regulations by trading illegally. In either case, the networks involved in the slave trade were complex.[37] On completion of a trading cycle, merchants could invest profits in tax farms or perhaps purchase monopoly rights for the distribution of a specific product (for example, tobacco), thereby extending and diversifying the Portuguese influence in the colonial economy. Harry Cross argues that the competition between Portuguese and Spanish trading networks was one of the reasons behind inquisitorial persecution in Lima. He bases his argument on the presence of members of the Merchants' Guild in the lists of Lima's familiares (tribunal members were recognized as people of pure blood). The tribunal had slots for twelve familiares; of those appointed between 1628 and 1637, fifteen were also active in the Merchant's Guild.[38] This correlation could have played a role in the collection of evidence. However, the familiares were unpaid members of the tribunal, and their specific duties varied as needed. Inquisitors, not familiares, made the decisions regarding imprisonments and trials.

The interactions between the men of the Portuguese nation and the royal court during the first half of the seventeenth century also deserve consideration.[39] During the 1620s and 1630s, Portuguese New Christians forged close relationships with the Count-Duke of Olivares, who occupied a powerful position close to Philip IV between 1621 and 1643. The Crown needed financial support, and the Portuguese wanted both investment opportunities and protection against potential trials of faith. This led to a period of negotiation and cooperation between the men of the nation, the ministers of government, and the Inquisition (mainly in Portugal) and even brought up the possibility of bringing the Portuguese New Christians who had moved to other kingdoms to avoid the Inquisition back to Portugal. There was also consideration of ways to better integrate them into the broader society. The Portuguese New Christians donated moneys to various branches of royal government in Madrid, received appointments to some key posts, obtained economic concessions, and were granted options for naturalization. Taking on an intellectual role, men of the Portuguese nation also wrote treatises proposing reforms in trade regulations, monetary policies, the composition of trading companies, and the role of merchants in the peninsular elite. The latter reform was associated with issues of blood purity and with restrictions applied to New Christians; these constituted a "legal inequality" that had been present in Iberian societies since the middle of the fifteenth century. Should such a reform have been achieved, it could well have meant that the Portuguese New Christians could attain the right of free relocation and the right to sell their real estate properties.[40]

In the early years of the reign of Philip IV (1621–1665) there was also the rumor that the Portuguese New Christians were soliciting another general pardon, similar to that granted in 1605 for those accused of heresy.[41] At the same time, they were formulating and presenting recommendations to Olivares for reforming the Inquisition. The recommendations included standardizing inquisitorial procedures between Spain and Portugal (this would have implied a certain restraint of the Portuguese office) and specific reforms regarding such issues as the penalties for false accusations, the possible absence of consequences in cases of self-denunciations, the need to improve the work of defense advocates, and the conduct of Autos de Fe annually to accelerate the resolution of Inquisition trials.

The discussions involved royal advisors and the general inquisitors from Spain and Portugal, and some modifications were introduced. Although Autos de Fe were suspended for a few months in 1621, a general pardon from Rome did not materialize. Instead, Philip IV passed an Edict of Grace in September 1627 and a concession of freedom of movement in 1629. Originally valid for three months, and then extended for another three, it allowed New Christians to leave Portugal but mandated a special permit for those going to the colonies.[42] The edict guaranteed that confessions made in front of inquisitors would not thenceforth result in confiscations, but it did not interrupt or change trials already initiated. Additionally, a set of questions would be attached to confessions made during the edict of grace; these related to accomplices and would permit the tribunal to conduct further prosecutions once the edict had expired. The edict also established that trials triggered after its expiration would carry a sentence of exile and a death sentence for one class of accused persons: these were the dogmatists, who proselytized or taught Judaism to their own children.

However, even the few protections set forth in the edict were not broadly supported. Arguments against the Portuguese New Christians dismissed their sincerity as Christians, "equating the New Christian, the Converso, and the Jew," emphasizing their "perversity" and depicting merchants who traded with foreign ports and houses, sometimes illegally, as persons who "deprived him [the king] of his rightful due" and might betray the kingdom at any moment.[43]

In contrast, the Count-Duke Olivares (with King Philip's apparent consent) was willing to allow New Christians of Portuguese descent to participate in the royal finances and to recognize their contribution despite issues of blood purity. Furthermore, Olivares was rumored to have had contacts with "real Jews" outside of Spain, and these facts have sometimes led to the depiction of Olivares as someone who favored Jews and Judaism.[44] Spanish historians now have a different perspective. Ignacio Pulido Serrano sustains that these elements are "too vague to endow him [Olivares] with the virtue of tolerance."[45] Bernardo López Belinchón concludes that both Olivares and the Portuguese New Christians behaved following their own dynamic interests and that their actions shifted accordingly.[46]

Once beyond the domain of the Crown, the migrations of these diasporic merchants were often related to the battles between European kingdoms for possession of colonial territories. As a minority, Jews found it efficacious to weave alliances with monarchs, who granted them residential and occupational permissions—a mixed blessing, since their relatively privileged status often earned them the animosity of the rest of the population.[47] On the other hand, Jewish and New Christian loyalty to royal houses was seldom taken for granted. Active as they were in a transatlantic commerce that crossed national boundaries, members of this diaspora were suspected of a two-tiered lack of loyalty: to the king of the country where they resided and to the Christian faith. For instance, Portuguese New Christians living in northern Brazil in the 1630s were presumed to be supporters of a Dutch invasion on the grounds that the Dutch might offer them religious freedom, even though the historical evidence is unclear on the matter.[48]

What was all this inquisitorial activity about? Why would a slow and semi-dormant body mainly concerned with book censorship and the control of public morality suddenly re-create itself in full force as a prosecutor of religious heterodoxy? Was the Lima tribunal responding to other interests, perhaps economic?[49] Given that the office had been collecting information since the 1620s, why did it not fully open its wings until 1635? There were many reasons for delays, some of them strategic. During the proceso of Bartolomé de Pradeda, a testimony stated that the Lima alcaide had commented that the tribunal's information against Manuel Bautista Pérez dated back some eight or nine years; however, the witness continued, "*Your Highness* [Mañozca] *did not want to catch him* [referring to Pérez] *so as to keep him for a better occasion.*"[50] But the reasons for the change remain less clear. The evidence does not lead us to the immediate motives that triggered the arrests, but the diligence of a tribunal in conducting the trials in "fast and fulminating mode" (paraphrasing Eimeric's instructions on how to conduct a trial of faith) can be appreciated. If we zoom our view to capture an area larger than the Lima tribunal's jurisdiction, and combine Lima, Cartagena, and Mexico, we can see peaks of activity in the Spanish colonies around the mid-seventeenth century: in Lima beginning in 1635, in Cartagena soon after, and in Mexico in the 1640s. In addition to the presence of merchants of Portuguese descent and suspect of heresy in these cities, and of the issues related to the Portuguese secession, the activities of the Peruvian and Mexican tribunals overlap with the professional career of Juan de Mañozca y Zamora and his posts as inquisitor in Lima, and later as archbishop in Mexico.[51]

As mentioned earlier in this book, for the Inquisition, the term *complicidad* conveyed the idea of a group of people related by blood, friendship, hidden religiosity, and economic interest rather than a specific plot or conspiracy. However, the geographic breadth of the New Christians' activity, spanning the Peninsula and crossing empires, gave rise to concerns about the size and scope that such a "great" complicity might have had in 1630 Lima, which Silverblatt notes.[52] In addition to practicing and quite possibly spreading heresy, Portuguese New Christians residing in Spanish lands could potentially ally themselves with the Portuguese nobility to plot a Portuguese restoration. Or they might secretly support French or Dutch invasions of Spanish possessions, hoping that a shift in the management of a colony would bring religious tolerance. As Studnicki-Gizbert points out, inquisitorial prosecutions of Portuguese merchants during the half century between 1610 and 1660 in Portugal, Brazil, Spain, and the Spanish colonies reflect this combination of national and religious concerns, which were indeed important to the colonial powers. However, while the combination of national and religious concerns in the entire kingdom explains the chronological frame of the trials, it does not fully explain the severity of the prosecutions undertaken by the Lima tribunal. When discussing persecutions in the 1630s, López Belinchón remarks that during that decade peninsular tribunals targeted Portuguese New Christian merchants but did not implement property confiscations. As a result, business operations of those indicted were not interrupted; family members or business associates remained in charge during the trials. Furthermore, with the exception of a man who was reconciled and dishonored in public, other sentences were less severe and some trials were suspended. The trials of the Complicidad Grande in Lima, on the other hand, clearly concluded with more severe outcomes. Paulino Castañeda Delgado and Pilar Hernández Aparicio suggest that the Lima tribunal acted independently from the Suprema, bearing in mind the probability of crypto-Jewish connections with the Portuguese or with the Dutch. René Millar Carvacho states that the exact motivations of the Lima tribunal in the 1630s are not indisputably clear; he considers that to the initial combination of national and religious concerns the tribunal probably added economic interest. Kimberly Lynn, who studied inquisitor Juan de Mañozca y Zamora as a protagonist of these events, writes that "the conspiracy was plausible in a number of ways" and mentions the unusual scale and drama of the application of punishments in 1639, while Alejandra Osorio analyzed the 1639 ceremony together with other Autos Generales de Fe from the angle of viceregal power.[53] Putting it all together, the monetary income derived from the confiscations combined with the harshest sentences administered to the Great Complicity prisoners resulted in an event that was a singular combination of scripted ritual and public spectacle, the Auto General de Fe. This event provided Lima inquisitors with a unique opportunity to shine, as will be discussed later in this book. For now I will turn to the discussion of how much danger these prisoners posed.

Most of the trials of faith associated with the Complicidad were finalized in January 1639. Portugal seceded from Spain in 1640. On the basis of the portrayal of the situation in official documents, it would have been plausible to think that Portuguese merchants were connected to a plot that would have led to a Portuguese secession. If this were true, the label "Complicidad Grande" would take on a different and broader meaning, as would the cases tried during its course. No longer directed solely toward preserving a hidden religiosity and familial and commercial ties, it might represent instead a broad-based political conspiracy in which the Portuguese merchants provided support to Portuguese secession from Spain (or a Dutch takeover of the colonies from Spanish hands). The information recorded in the trials of faith does not prove unambiguously that New Christians were involved in such plots, but a level of suspicion is clear.[54] On the other hand, a letter sent by the Lima inquisitors to the king early in the Complicidad trials (May 13, 1636) recommended that royal bodies in Madrid inform their Portuguese counterparts about the detentions and the gravity of the accused's offenses. This willingness to share information with the Portuguese tribunal suggests that at that point (1636) the Lima inquisitors did not suspect that the prisoners were party to a plot aimed at a Portuguese secession.[55]

Following Jonathan Israel, the connection between the Portuguese New Christians in the colonies and the Sephardim of Amsterdam preoccupied the Spanish authorities prior to the 1630 arrests, and I think that at the moment of the imprisonments the inquisitors were not anticipating a Portuguese secession. Rather, they were concerned with the possibility of a Dutch invasion. Furthermore, Israel also mentions that in November of 1639 Castilian and Portuguese forces combined their efforts against the Dutch in Brazil.[56] During the early seventeenth century there are references to the networks that connected the men of the nation, who resided in the Spanish colonies, with Amsterdam through Brazil and Portugal.[57] From tribunal correspondence and documentation from public sources, external to the tribunal, it is clear that the possibility of a Dutch invasion preoccupied both religious and secular authorities. Writing in 1630, Fray Buenaventura de Salinas y Córdova commended a priest who, in the middle of the 1615 battles against the Dutch (in El Callao), walked among soldiers carrying a crucifix, exhorting combatants to risk their lives defending the Christian faith. The priest himself died at the hands of the Dutch. In January 1630 Lima received notice of Spanish forces battling with the Dutch in the island of Saint Christopher (Saint Kitts in the Caribbean). Six months later, Buenos Aires alerted Lima to the presence of Dutch ships in the southern Atlantic, and at the end of July the Peruvian viceroy learned that the Dutch had seized Pernambuco in northern Brazil.[58]

The Holy Office was a tribunal under royal supervision, and because some inquisitors held positions in both the tribunal and the royal administration, they were especially aware of the potential Dutch threat. In November 1630, Quito informed the Lima inquisitor Juan de Mañozca y Zamora of battles involving seven ships from the Netherlands. Clandestine information also played a part: in a letter sent after the Complicidad trials, Antonio de Castro y del Castillo recounts that a spy placed in a cell with Isabel Antonia (one of the women accused in the Complicidad trials) recalled the prisoner talking about her relatives' communication with the Dutch, for whom they were waiting. In 1640, after the resolution of the Complicidad trials, the inquisitors from Lima and Cartagena reported to Madrid that they believed the crypto-Jews from the Spanish colonies to be in contact with the Jews of Amsterdam, which led to further investigations in the Peninsula, trying to find out if the Portuguese New Christians there also maintained such connections.[59]

Trials of La Complicidad Grande

When the Lima tribunal arrested him on April 1, 1635, Antonio Cordero was twenty-four years old. Because he was less than twenty-five he was considered a minor, and the tribunal assigned a curator to assist him throughout the trial. Fifteen days later, Cordero had his first hearing and was asked by the tribunal to present his life story, the discurso de vida. He said that he had been born in Arronchas, in the bishopric of Portalegre in Portugal, and that he had married a woman named Beatriz Brandon in Seville. As usual, the tribunal asked Cordero at the end of the hearing if he knew the reasons behind his imprisonment, or if his conscience prompted him to any confession. Antonio Cordero opened up at the end of that first hearing. He stated that he had learnt the practices of crypto-Judaism in Seville from another Portuguese, Antonio Suárez, who had come to Spain from Italy.

During April and May of 1635, in subsequent hearings and in the torture chambers (although no torture had yet been applied), Cordero expanded his confession. He revealed that his employers were also crypto-Jews and provided details about beliefs, prayers, and customs they shared.[60] He admitted to cooking meat with olive oil instead of butter, which indicated that he avoided the mix of dairy and animal products as stipulated in kosher law. When interrogated about how he addressed the God of Israel, he replied to the tribunal "that he did not know any prayer exactly, because he had no school, nor anyone who would teach them to him. The way he called on the God of Israel was to ask Him this: that as he had liberated Joseph from the prisons and the testimonies raised against him, and the people of Israel from captivity in Egypt and [the] power of the pharaoh, and those innocents from the oven in Babylon, and the people of Israel from the betrayal of a vassal of the King Ahasuerus, and the Ark of the Testament from the power of its enemies, that He in this same way liberate this prisoner from his burdens."[61]

In the end, the Lima tribunal sentenced Cordero with reconciliation, a relatively mild outcome. However, the effect of his trial went far beyond his sentencing: it moved the inquisitorial machine into high gear and set off the trials of the Complicidad Grande. Cordero's confession came on May 11, 1635; that same day the Lima tribunal incarcerated his employers, Antonio de Acuña and Diego López de Fonseca. According to the record kept by Juan Antonio Suardo, the tribunal arrested a merchant and several others on May 11 and seized considerable properties; on the 13th, tribunal functionaries imprisoned two or three more Portuguese traders.[62] In a letter a year later, the viceroy Conde de Chinchón described the decline of local commerce caused by these arrests. Another event, not directly related to tribunal activities, also affected the local economy. In May 1635, one of the most important banks in Lima failed. It was under the direction of Juan de la Cueva, who had close ties to Manuel Bautista Pérez. The inventory and property confiscation of de la Cueva's bank on Mantas Street was conducted on May 16, 1635, and the banker was held in a secular prison for the following ten years. This and other bankruptcies, combined with the imprisonments of the Portuguese merchants, had a strong impact on the local credit system.[63]

The documents related to the Complicidad tell us that Joan de Salazar Negrete, the disgruntled customer who denounced Antonio Cordero, presented his testimony at the end of August 1634, but the tribunal did not arrest Cordero until April 1635, seven months later. Therefore, the tribunal may not have shifted suddenly from dormant to aggressive following Cordero's arrest in spite of appearances to the contrary. There is good reason to believe that when the tribunal functionaries decided to arrest Antonio Cordero they were *already* planning to arrest Antonio de Acuña and Diego López de Fonseca. That would explain the fact that Cordero's confession and his employers' arrest happened on the same day. Even though Salazar Negrete's testimony clearly placed Cordero under suspicion but did not implicate the others so directly, the tribunal assumed that the store owners, also New Christians of Portuguese descent, were also involved.

Between the arrests of Acuña and Fonseca and the end of the following year (1636), the Lima tribunal arrested almost one hundred people. Together, they were labeled "La Complicidad Grande," and the prisoners were charged with the offense of crypto-Judaism. Initially, it may be difficult to believe that the tribunal was ready to arrest suspicious parties so quickly after they were mentioned in a random confession. Such a notion evokes a diligent and alert policing body, ready for a quick response, which hardly resonates with most of the literature about the Lima tribunal: it depicts a semidormant institution. However, we must consider this skepticism against what the protagonists of the story convey with their words.

In a letter written by the inquisitors Juan de Mañozca y Zamora, Andrés Juan Gaitán, and Antonio de Castro y del Castillo, they note that the accused are "sort of surprised and do not trust one another, because when they least expect they find themselves without partner or friend."[64] In a hearing conducted in 1637, a witness named Fernando de Espinosa remembered hearing the prisoner Francisco Vázquez say, "I swear to God that each day they apprehend more people—one by one they are going to take us all."[65] According to Espinosa, he had heard Vázquez say this after August 11, 1635, a day on which many of the Lima Portuguese were taken prisoner. Those who had not been indicted spoke to each other in tones of despair. Suardo's notes for the day show that at 1:00 p.m., the Lima inquisitors issued instructions to imprison and impound the properties of seventeen men. Because Suardo's record is external to the tribunal, it provides a way of corroborating Inquisition reports. He listed the names of the detained: Manuel Bautista Pérez, Sebastián Duarte (Pérez's brother-in-law), two siblings with the surname Tavares, Francisco Núñez Duarte, Roque Núñez, Rodrigo Váez Pereira, Rodrigo de Ávila (el mozo), Jorge de Silva, Antonio Gómez de Acosta, Manuel de Espinosa, Enrique Núñez, Antonio de Sosa, Jorge Rodríguez de Acosta, Duarte Núñez, Bartolomé de León, and Sebastián de Acuña. Suardo also noted a decree issued by the viceroy on August 14, 1635, to remain in effect for the balance of the year; the decree mandated that travel permits for those leaving the city by sea would require the approval of the Holy Office. On August 17, the tribunal celebrated an Auto at the Inquisition chapel; on the same day, another Portuguese man was imprisoned, and yet another on the day after.[66]

The imprisonments continued through 1635 and into the following year. Most of the arrests were made in Lima, but prisoners arrived from other parts of the viceroyalty as well. The tribunal's pace slowed a bit—nowhere else is there a record of seventeen detentions completed during a single afternoon—but at least twenty more people were detained and incarcerated before the end of the year. On November 21 alone, the tribunal imprisoned and confiscated the properties of seven people and moved a Portuguese priest named Coello, already being held in the city prison, to the cells of the Holy Office.[67] Four imprisonments are documented for December 4, six for December 10, and three more on December 19. During the same period, the Panama comisario sent some paperwork and some prisoners to Lima. If the public had not formerly been aware of the initial detentions (the tribunal tried not to publicize them in order to prevent escapes and transfer of property by the accused, although both did happen), they were now. People often waited in the plaza in front of the tribunal, or followed the inquisitors as they set out to execute the arrests.[68]

Suardo recorded details of more than thirty-five arrests during 1636, and in May of the same year a tribunal member affirmed in a letter that Lima's population was pleased with the indictments.[69] On January 10, 1636, Gaspar Fernández and Melchor de los Reyes, both Portuguese *mercaderes de cajón*, were imprisoned, followed by two others just a few days later. One of an additional three arrested in February was Francisco Vázquez (the man reported to have said that all the Portuguese would be taken). On February 22, the tribunal voted to imprison Vázquez, and just four days later he had his first hearing. During the course of 1636, eleven more people were imprisoned in March and April. In May four more men arrived in the tribunal prison: Mateo Henríquez, Mateo de la Cruz, Rodrigo Fernández, and Felipe Díaz, all of whom had been indicted in Huánuco, more than two hundred miles from Lima; an additional ten men were detained in the same month. Domingo Rodríguez and a son of Antonio Morón (the father was already in the tribunal cells) were imprisoned in June 1636; Manuel García was detained in July.

Kimberly Lynn reflects on how these events favored the career of Juan de Mañozca y Zamora, who was promoted to the Supreme Council of the Inquisition in 1637. The trials of the Complicidad unfolded between 1635 and 1639, even though in 1638 the Suprema had instructed the Lima inquisitors to avoid taking people to the secret jails.[70] Most of the prisoners were punished at the 1639 Auto General de Fe. Some were set free without punishment between 1637 and 1638, among them Alonso Sánchez Chaparro, Andrés Muñiz, Francisco Sotelo, and Antonio de los Santos. The local population applauded their release; their honor would be formally restored at the 1639 Auto General de Fe.[71]

Documentation of the Complicidad

In general, the trials of faith followed the standard procedures of the Inquisition and yielded a substantial body of written documents, as would be expected from such a bureaucratic institution. However, the complete set of trials is not available today. Many documents were sent to the Suprema in Madrid (Supreme Council of the Inquisition), sometimes as part of a regular report on the tribunal's activities, sometimes as part of an unusual case that required advice from the Suprema, and for other reasons as well. For that reason, the documentary collection most often cited in the study of the Lima Inquisition is in Madrid. These *procesos de fe* contain testimonies collected prior to the prisoners' arrests as well as those of the trials themselves. In the testimonies we can read declarations of Lima residents as witnesses and also those made by prisoners of the Complicidad. The latter made declarations throughout their trials (sometimes declaring against one another), and the tribunal continued to collect evidence as a trial progressed. The documentation preserved in Madrid includes trial summaries, records of property confiscations, and correspondence between Lima and the Suprema as well as correspondence between Lima and other tribunals, both colonial and peninsular. The records show that trials differed in duration (from several months to decades), length (from tens to hundreds of sheets), and the assignment of punishments. Because these documents constitute the empirical core of this chapter, it is important to consider some of their characteristics.

The documents associated with trials of faith, catalogued as procesos de fe, follow the order and structure of Inquisition trials previously discussed: denunciation and testimonies, imprisonment, hearings, sessions at the torture chambers, intervention of prosecutors and defense advocates, accusation, confessions, publication of testimonies, defense, consultation, voting, and sentencing. In this sense, the documents are uniform. On the other hand, the procesos do not provide direct access to the voices of the accused, because tribunal members and notaries mediated in the prisoners' statements and determined what would be recorded and what would not. Despite the intentional standardization that forced inquisitorial procedures and bureaucratic decisions into a codified format, we shall not forget that each trial represents the life and fate of a unique and singular individual.

We come closest to the prisoners' voices in their discursos de la vida, the summaries of their lives that the tribunal routinely demanded at the first hearing. The prisoner was asked to provide the circumstances of his or her birth, age and genealogical information, marital status, the names of close and extended family, occupation, and path of migration. This element of the Inquisition record can be considered to have two interwoven layers. The life story of the prisoner constitutes an inner layer, that of content. The format in which each life story is presented constitutes the outer layer, that of shape. As we can imagine, all the trials were similar in shape but different in content.[72] At some point during the trial a prisoner might receive a few sheets of paper to prepare a defense, using the strategies of *abonos* (asserting the prisoner's honor) and *tachas* (questioning a testimony based on the witness's motives). But only exceptionally, as in the cases of Antonio Morón and Manuel Henríquez, do we have access to pages that convey their voices.[73]

Through the correspondence preserved at Madrid, we get glimpses of other aspects of the tribunal's activities. For instance, it is clear that the bureaucratic machine that investigated and exposed the Great Complicity operated far beyond the territorial boundaries of the Lima tribunal as discussed previously in this book. As the tribunal functionaries executed imprisonments, hearings, and the extraction of confessions, they exposed a network of Portuguese migrants who had traveled across oceans and continents before settling in Lima. Sometimes evidence about earlier trials of faith, carried out by other tribunals, had to be retrieved and incorporated into the current trial. To unearth some of the personal and religious histories of its prisoners, the Lima tribunal relied on the cooperation of other tribunals and offices in both the Spanish American colonies (Cartagena) and the Iberian Peninsula (for example, Madrid and Coimbra). Paradoxically, as it collected this information, the bureaucracy of the Inquisition repeated the migratory path of those under its eyes, although in the opposite direction.

Crypto-Jews in Colonial Lima: Many Faces

Although the accusations against them were often quite specific, the religious identities of these prisoners were complex and dynamic, often changing during the course of their lives.[74] A general typology or classificatory approach is useful because it allows us to visualize the range of possibilities rather than fixate on singular unchanging identities. Taking the syntheses made by David Gitlitz as a point of departure, the spectrum of possibilities included Christians (sincere converts), Jews (who rejected conversions and were sometimes defiant martyrs), those who oscillated between religions, and those who turned to skepticism. The elements that allow us to understand crypto-Judaism as a distinctive religious experience include the rejection of the Trinity; the expectation that the Messiah will arrive and the denial of Christ as Messiah; adoption of a mix of both religions in the hope of achieving salvation (a Christian element) through belief in the Law of Moses; the connection of fortune, misfortune, and one's adherence or rejection of the new faith; the positing of Jewish saints and the unique perspective of crypto-Jews as they balanced themselves between two religious frameworks. People considered crypto-Jews by the tribunal could have been at different places within this spectrum and have lived very different religious experiences. These nuances are not discoverable from Inquisition documents. One reason is that the interrogations conducted at hearings followed a template, with questions that often directed the content of the answer or limited its scope. However, the records of the interrogations are valid for genealogical information, for sessions at the torture chambers, and for confessions issued with or without the application of torture, among other elements of the proceso. Furthermore, the information collected using templates generated documentation that strongly mediates the content of any particular confession. For these reasons, the allocation of individuals to one or another type of religious heresy is an elusive task, because religious identity is not static and essential. It changes and evolves throughout a person's life, with or without a repressive tribunal. However, I think the salient features of prisoners' identities, as summarized by Gitlitz and other scholars, are present in the records of the Lima trials. And even were the prisoners' voices to reach us directly, it is reasonable to think that they would have adjusted the content of their confessions to the circumstances.

The primary sources I used to approach more closely the crypto-Jews accused by the Lima tribunal and their religious lives have been studied by other scholars, and each has used them in different ways. Nathan Wachtel used them to construct individual portraits, for example, those of Francisco Maldonado de Silva and Manuel Bautista Pérez, whereas I examined information from different individuals and did not focus on one person exclusively.[75] Paulino Castañeda Delgado and Pilar Hernández Aparicio start from a different principle, organizing their analysis chronologically according to the cycles of tribunal activities; they discuss the materials related to the Great Complicity as a particular set.[76] I also used the trial records with the specific aim of understanding the perspective of the Lima tribunal, but in considering crypto-Jewish practices in Lima I expanded that framework to include materials prior to the Complicity trials so as to enrich the discussion. I think that even though the tribunal created a discrete group of people (those imprisoned in 1635), this does not necessarily mean that such inmates represented a particular strand of crypto-Judaism in Lima, separated from what prisoners could have declared before the same tribunal during the previous decade.

In its interrogations the tribunal aimed to establish just which practices and behaviors evidenced heresy, for example, Jewish prayers. They then used their list of practices and behaviors to determine whether or not an accused was guilty of heresy. There was not much room for doubt if a person was found to have performed such practices or evidenced such behaviors, and the effect was to reduce the prisoner's religiosity to the elements of the list. Manuel de Fonseca, punished in 1625 as a relapse (prior to the Complicidad trials), explained the organization of daily prayers using Hebrew terms such as *tefila*, *sama*, and *arbi*. Fonseca also referred to an encounter with another crypto-Jew in Huancavelica, in which they exchanged the Hebrew words of the quintessentially Jewish Shema prayer. As the Inquisition documents record his statement: "When the two men met in Huancavelica, he [Fonseca] asked Araujo if he knew some words in Hebrew, to which Araujo said yes. Araujo then asked him to say some words and he [Fonseca] said 'Shema, Yisrael.' Then Araujo said 'Adonai elohenu,' and he [Fonseca] said 'Adonai echad' and Araujo hugged him."[77]

But this kind of admission was not the general rule. Luis de Valencia initially denied any connection with crypto-Judaism and insisted that he had always been a Christian. Before breaking under torture he made one more denial: "Do you want me to be a Jew[?] I am not[!] I have always been Christian and will always be. . . . I cannot keep going. . . . What do you want me to be? I am Jewish, I am Jewish, I am Jewish, a thousand times, I am Jewish."[78] Immediately after his outcry, Valencia admitted that on a trip to Italy he had had a conversation with a man named Duarte de Acosta who insisted that the only true God was the God of Israel. Duarte de Acosta had also encouraged Luis de Valencia to fast in respect of the God of Israel.[79]

In the Complicidad trials, as in the trials of any Inquisition tribunal, after a confession, a section devoted to the actual heretical practices would follow. Questions posed at hearings and at sessions in the torture chambers examined practices and beliefs attributed to crypto-Jews, and the formal accusations in each case reflect the Inquisition's own idea of manifest evidence of crypto-Jewish heresy. What did the person do? Where, and with whom? At the bottom of his or her heart, did this person believe in the Law of Moses or in the Law of Jesus? Which attitudes and daily behaviors of the person reflected beliefs in one or the other? Was it diet? Was it the organization of the weekly calendar? Was it the ability to memorize and recite certain prayers? Or the frequency of one's attendance at Mass?

It is clear that the tribunal wanted principally to prove the presence of certain traits and habits that evidenced heretical practice. For the Inquisition, it was taken as fact that many New Christians followed the Law of Moses and held their communities together in the keeping of such law. Those who practiced crypto-Judaism regularly respected the Saturday Sabbath by avoiding work and commercial transactions and fasted on specific days.[80] Even if they could not avoid work on the Sabbath, the crypto-Jews wore clean clothes and also changed their bed linens and table covers.[81] On Friday evenings they lit candles, sometimes hidden, and celebrated with a special meal.

The Inquisition believed that crypto-Jews fasted on Tuesdays and Saturdays to honor their secret beliefs.[82] Over a given year, officials assumed that a fast would be held in February to honor Queen Esther and another in September to mark Yom Kippur, the Jewish Day of Atonement. The February festival, Purim, commemorates the biblical story of Queen Esther, who saved the Jews from slaughter in ancient Persia. Even though Queen Esther was a relatively minor heroine among a predominantly male list of biblical heroes, the crypto-Jews gave her a significant place in their representation of hidden Judaism, probably because the queen and her subjects' historical experiences of exile and captivity clearly resonated with their own.[83]

Another behavior that drew the tribunal's suspicion was peculiarities of food choice, to which they assigned significance in terms of religious identity. Among the suspect choices was the avoidance of pork and shrimp, as prescribed in Jewish dietary laws.[84] The varieties of fish and legumes available in Lima probably assisted those who wanted to follow dietary laws. "If we consider fish, there are few cities in Europe that enjoy during the whole year so much abundance as does this city of Kings," said Fray Buenaventura de Salinas y Córdova in his 1630 description of Lima.[85] For the inquisitors, these behaviors constituted manifest material heresy because they evidenced the preservation of belief in the God of Israel and respect for the Law of Moses.[86] In other words, such actions were viewed as intentional offenses to Christian law and doctrine, openly expressed in collective deeds and shared beliefs that challenged the dogma imparted by the Church.

Within their immediate families, the experiences of the Portuguese New Christians on matters of faith could be either heterogeneous or homogeneous. In some cases, several members of the same family were incarcerated in Lima, and delving into crypto-Jewish practices might also reveal familial connections. Such was the case with the sisters Mencía and Mayor de Luna, their respective husbands Enrique Núñez de Espinosa and Antonio Morón, and Mayor and Antonio's daughter Isabel Antonia and her husband Rodrigo Váez Pereira.[87] A different experience was that of Tomé Quaresma, a Portuguese surgeon whose wife had expressed to her confessor suspicions about the husband's crypto-Judaism. The priest's declaration was incorporated in Quaresma's trial as evidence, together with other testimonies. In the evidence against Quaresma, it is reported that he had conversations with other crypto-Jews, among them Manuel Bautista Pérez, but outside his own home.[88]

It was common that small children in crypto-Jewish families were not aware of the hidden religiosity of their elders, which was concealed from them, for obvious reasons, until they were judged old enough to know about it. In one example from Lima, a close relative disclosed the family's New Christian heritage when the child had reached thirteen or fourteen years of age and introduced crypto-Jewish practices as well. Such disclosures usually involved an invitation to join family members in some practice related to crypto-Judaism, such as a fast. After that initiating experience, the teenager gradually learned and incorporated more of the family's religious identity and practices.

I believe that this approach led the crypto-Jews of colonial Lima to assign a new layer of meaning to the Bar Mitzvah, the rite of passage of Jewish boys into adulthood. However, the disclosure of religiosity was not always conducted at the age of thirteen; it could have been at a different age.[89] In the context of crypto-Jewish life, adulthood implied not only taking on Jewish responsibilities but also assuming serious risks—it brought the young person into the purview of the Inquisition. Rodrigo Váez Pereira was a merchant from Monsanto in Portugal who conducted investments in the mines of Cailloma in southern Peru and, at the time of his imprisonment, had creditors in Cuzco, Lima, and Huancavelica.[90] In the following fragment, it is reported by tribunal scribes how an older family member told Váez Pereira of his family history: "When the prisoner was 13 or 14 years old, his cousin Duarte Rodríguez told him that he was a New Christian and asked if he dared to uphold the law of God in heaven by fasting for a whole day, and the prisoner said yes. Both fasted on that day until the night, when they dined on eggs, garbanzo beans, and the Friday meal."[91]

We will probably never know if a person like Váez Pereira would have suspected the religious identity of his family before he or she was told about it. Did young people who found themselves in this situation adhere to the hidden religious practice willingly and without question? As the result of the Christian indoctrination they would have received, would some of these children question the choices of their elders? For the same reason, might they reject their own family as heretics? The response of the children to a relative's disclosure of crypto-Judaism was not uniform, as might be expected. Francisco Maldonado de Silva did not belong to the cluster of Portuguese New Christians who resided in Lima but was incarcerated in the same prisons. His case illustrates my point. Earlier, Maldonado de Silva had revealed to his sister that he had followed their father into crypto-Judaism, and she had rejected the religious connection and her brother's heretical practices. She then revealed the secret to her own confessor, who for his part denounced Maldonado de Silva to the Lima Inquisition.[92]

In addition to the common familial connections, the communal networks of the Portuguese New Christians in Lima exerted direct and indirect pressure toward the preservation of crypto-Judaism as young people became adults. This seems to have been true for Manuel Henríquez. Born in Lamego (Portugal), he had business in Cailloma at the time of his imprisonment (as did Váez Pereira), buying wool and selling items from China.[93] Henríquez declared to the Lima tribunal that at an early age he had been reconciled in a trial of faith in Portugal. As described elsewhere in this book, the tribunal officials' verification of Henríquez's story through communication with the Coimbra tribunal proved to be a long process that delayed his trial for decades. Henríquez's trial began in 1635. He was sentenced in 1657 and died at the stake in 1664, nearly thirty years from the opening of the proceso. During its long course, he gave several confessions that were contradictory and therefore challenged the logic and modus operandi of the tribunal. It was even thought after a certain point that he might have gone insane, but this was never formally proven. At one moment in his trial, Henríquez insisted that his Coimbra reconciliation had come from sincere devotion and that he had not intended to return to the practice of crypto-Judaism in adulthood. In another, he stated that he had not been reconciled at all in Coimbra because his imprisonment there had occurred just a few days before an Auto de Fe—too late for him to be judged at the event. Then he claimed that he had undergone a trial of faith and that he had carried a candle during an Auto ceremony. Later, he claimed that the person reconciled in Coimbra was not him at all, but a cousin of identical name.[94]

Manuel Henríquez also recounted that he had found himself lonely and poor in Lima and had been told by other members of the Portuguese New Christian community that if he returned to the Law of Moses, the God of Israel would reward him. More specifically, he said that two men he identified as Simón Osorio and Pedro López Montesinos had told him they would help him if he returned to the practice of crypto-Judaism. Henríquez hesitated, he said, because he knew that someone who had been reconciled but later faced a second Inquisition trial would be considered a relapse and dealt with very harshly. A second trial of faith would almost surely lead to a death sentence, as it did for Henríquez himself when he was burned at the stake in 1664.[95] Henríquez said that when he found himself alone and in need, he had considered the advice and well-being of his wife and daughter, who had remained in Madrid and were awaiting his help.[96] In other words, his decision to return to crypto-Jewish practice was not solely a religious one; it was also driven by personal and social motivations, both complex and pragmatic. Following its mandate, the Lima tribunal paused the proceso to request from Coimbra the facts of Manuel Henríquez's trial before declaring him a relapse. Failing corroboration, Henríquez's claim was rejected, and the report from the Coimbra tribunal was added to the trial record.

It might appear that long-distance travel and frequent migration would present insurmountable obstacles for the preservation of a hidden religiosity, but this is not the case. While those circumstances may have made religious practice more difficult and driven it below ground, they did not destroy it. For the Portuguese New Christians imprisoned in Lima, the migrations and displacements across many countries did not preclude them from associating with crypto-Jews and performing crypto-Judaic practices. According to their declarations, they were able to locate people—in places as different as France, Italy, Angola, Mexico, and of course in Peru, both in Lima and in the countryside— with whom they could share some of their clandestine habits and beliefs.[97]

An unusual and perhaps unique example is that of Enrique Jorge Tavares. This man was imprisoned along with others during the Complicidad, but his trial did not end with theirs in 1639. It lasted until 1648, when he was declared insane and sent to a hospital. Throughout his trial, the tribunal had doubted Tavares's sanity, and to resolve the question sought the opinion of a doctor (Joan de Vega) in 1638. The opinion was inconclusive. In 1643 the tribunal tried a different strategy and placed another man in Tavares's cell for a month to observe him and later report to the tribunal on his sanity. Tavares admitted to the heresy of crypto-Judaism, but this was likely his strategy for concealing another offense prosecuted by the Inquisition: homosexuality.[98]

The physician of the Lima tribunal, assigned to examine Tavares to assess his mental health, interrogated the prisoner regarding some religious propositions that are at the core of Christianity. Did he, the doctor asked, know and understand the unity of God in the Trinity? He then wrote a report to the tribunal.[99] According to the doctor, Tavares had argued that God was one and not a trinity and had questioned the idea of God's seed participating in the conception of a human being.[100] These words sufficed for the doctor to establish Tavares's sanity, and the consistency of his heresies; however, he was ultimately declared not guilty. Another witness, in this case a Jesuit priest who was also a calificador of the tribunal, declared that Tavares had said that a person could be saved without baptism, just as the Native Americans had done prior to the arrival of the Spaniards.[101]

It has already been noted that the Portuguese New Christians who migrated to Lima did not come from the same region of their home country. This fact raises the question of how they might have met one another in various countries, established communal links, and disclosed among themselves their hidden religiosity. First and most evidently, many of them probably spoke with Portuguese accents that were immediately discernible in any conversation that might take place on board a ship or in a city square. Second, Portuguese origin itself was associated with a certain probability of being New Christians, and therefore crypto-Jewish, or at least of openness to persuasion to observe crypto-Jewish habits. In some confessions, the prisoners reported conversations among

Portuguese New Christians in which one side was trying to persuade the other of the importance of preserving crypto-Judaism.[102] A third and somewhat tentative answer is related to the very traits that the Inquisition and its collaborators elucidated in their denunciations; these may well have been used among fellow crypto-Jews to establish connections to each other. According to their confessions, the practices denounced could often be ephemeral and circumstantial, rather than definitive. One example might be sharing a fast for a special day. A fourth answer is that the Portuguese New Christians took advantage of their mobility to gather or work together in locations beyond the territorial jurisdiction of the Iberian Inquisition—that is, outside Spain, Spanish America, and Portugal—to learn and practice crypto-Judaism openly. Furthermore, they carried out crucial ceremonies or rites of passage in communities that offered a more developed and structured crypto-Jewish environment. In Manuel Henríquez's confession, it is stated (of another man) that he had been "in France and there they had taught him the Law of Moses, without saying in which place."[103]

More of the New Christians' transatlantic experiences can be found in the records of trials held before those of the Complicidad. Juan de Ortega, a man of Portuguese descent who was born in France and reconciled in 1625 in Lima, confessed that when he was eleven years old his parents had crossed the border with him into Italy and took him to Pisa, where he was circumcised.[104] Bernardo López Serrano, a man born in Portugal and also reconciled in Lima in 1625, brought into his confession a clear description of a two-stage wedding ceremony that took place in Bordeaux, France. A French cleric performed the first stage, according to Church rites. The second was performed later on the same day, indoors and in the company of family and friends. In the second ceremony, the groom put a gold ring on the bride's finger to indicate the union, and after the bride and groom had shared a celebratory cup of wine, the glass was shattered on the floor, "and that is how he got married according to the Law of Moses."[105]

In other cases, the Lima tribunal decided that the accumulated evidence revealed deeper religious conviction, as in the cases of Manuel Bautista Pérez and Tomé Quaresma. Both prisoners denied all accusations, even under torture, so we have no confession to associate with the tribunal's determinations. Nathan Wachtel, following a combination of information from the testimonies provided against Pérez and his own words, finds that the evidence suggests a duality of beliefs in Pérez's case.[106] Certainly, the Portuguese New Christians incarcerated during the trials of the Complicidad were not homogeneous in terms of religious identity. Nevertheless, we do find in these records clear suggestions of crypto-Jewish aspects in the lives of the accused, supported by evidence of social connections among them. Also strongly suggested is that many of those detained had an understanding of the inquisitional procedures under which they were being tried.

Life on a Pendulum

The cases of the Complicidad Grande share the principal features of many Inquisition trials: the format and content of the standard documents, the structure and development of the trials, the descriptions of the offenses, and the social profiles of the offenders. The Complicidad cases, and others as well, reflect the religiosity of the Portuguese merchants in Lima, in both qualitative and quantitative terms. Those imprisoned in the Complicidad were in the great majority adult Portuguese men who participated in both transatlantic commercial activities and kinship networks. When we consider the varied reasons and circumstances of their presence in the colonies, the diversity of their social status, and their degrees of alleged religious affiliation, we see that the Portuguese New Christians who lived in colonial Peru cannot be placed under a single label. On one level of the society in which they lived, they were members of an elite group of Iberian colonizers and active participants in the colonial project. I find it reasonable to think that in rural areas, or in places where indigenous communities were the majority of the population, the Portuguese New Christians were not perceived as radically different from the Spanish Old Christians. As members of the colonial elite, mainly merchants or professionals, they would have been identified as members of the middle and upper-middle classes, involved in transatlantic trade and participating in regional and local networks. In the Iberian cities where many Lima members of those classes were born, they and their families were likely perceived in terms of the nature and scale of their economic activities, and the New World was not so different in that regard. Some were people of substantial influence; others hung onto the lower rungs of respectability.

Impure blood was an ever-present concern in the lives of the New Christians and a constraint on their place in the community. Even though some belonged to the colonial white elite and controlled the higher levels of the slave trade, their descent marked them as different even as they interacted with Old Christians in business partnerships, political connections, social life, and the consideration of marital options. The paradox that results from this multifaceted and multiburdened social location leads us to describe Portuguese New Christians' life in the Spanish colonial world as a swinging pendulum. As the pendulum swung, one might live the life of a rich, well-connected merchant who owned a special license that allowed him to control the lives of others (slaves). He would also have had connections in colonial politics and enjoyed a high standard of living. But whether for this merchant, a less successful one, or a peddler traveling to remote towns, a swing of the pendulum in the other direction could bring stigma and even ruin. Even the most prominent among the New Christians could end up in the cells of the Inquisition—accused of heresy or under suspicion of betraying the monarchy by supporting foreign invasions. Their lives would now be in the hands of those who provided evidence against them and of Inquisition functionaries and judges.

This chapter has considered reasons for the imprisonments, the prisoners' social profiles, and the religiosity of the Portuguese New Christians who resided in colonial Peru. To argue that the crypto-Judaism of the prisoners was real or an artifact created by the Inquisition, and whether it represented a coherent Jewish practice or an incoherent array of fragments combined with Christian elements, leads to dead ends. The people accused of crypto-Judaism in colonial Lima were diverse and inconsistent among themselves. Some of them held a solid belief in the Law of Moses. However, others joined the network of Portuguese merchants either to gain wealth or to escape from necessity, and their participation in crypto-Jewish rituals was very likely due to peer pressure. The practice of their clandestine religion brought extreme risk, but they sought out opportunities to practice it in different places and continents. And some seem to have been confused, lost between the two religions—that, or they conveyed such a confusion by withholding from the tribunal (and from us, as contemporary readers of their words) a full description of their religious beliefs.

Although a description of the Lima tribunal as a slow institution mainly devoted to book censorship and moral control might have held true before 1635, the aggressive turn taken in the Complicidad trials that began in that year changed the picture. Between 1635 and 1639, we see a tribunal rapidly collecting and compiling evidence, incarcerating Portuguese New Christians in large numbers, subjecting people to long trials of faith for the heresy of crypto-Judaism. This picture does not reflect a semidormant tribunal. In spite of some corrupt officials and inadequate facilities, those in charge of the Lima tribunal between 1635 and 1639 actively persecuted and prosecuted religious heresy—they got their work done. And even though the volume and pace of the Complicidad trials marked an unusual peak of activity, those trials should not be set apart in the attempt at understanding the Inquisition—quite the opposite. The power of the Inquisition did not lie in the frequency of its accusations but in the terror it inspired. The analysis presented in this chapter, based on the trials of some one hundred people that lasted for four years, invites us to place the lens on the inner world of the Lima prisons during these trials, which is the topic of the next chapter.

5

The Inner World of the Lima Prisons

Upon its establishment in 1570 the Lima Tribunal of the Inquisition had a provisional location, but when the office received a donation from fray Pedro de la Peña, Quito's bishop, for the construction of a chapel, it purchased the facilities that hosted the institution from 1584 until its abolition in 1820. These were in a set of houses located three blocks east from the central plaza, close to the Universidad de San Marcos and the Hospital de la Caridad; thus the tribunal was not in a remote location. Because it consisted of a complex of three buildings, the small square on which the tribunal building sat was known as the plaza of the three cardinal virtues: faith, for the tribunal; hope, for the university, and charity, for the hospital. The tribunal buildings were remodeled to satisfy the institution's specific needs, and the construction continued for at least ten years after 1584; a document now preserved in Lima details all the payments made during 1584 and 1585 to the workers who participated in the project. Additional work was done after 1620 to improve the facilities and provide lodging for two inquisitors instead of one. Restorations were made after the earthquakes of 1609, 1655, and 1746 damaged parts of the buildings. After the abolition of the Inquisition, the cells served as a penitentiary, and the major houses were used by the Republican Congress. Since 1968, the facilities have housed the Museo del Congreso y de la Inquisición.[1]

Reinaldo González Montes, a writer from Spain who clearly opposed the Inquisition and its methods, commented in the 1560s about the darkness and harshness of the tribunal jails in the Peninsula, and on how much prisoners suffered during their detainments. The Augustinian historian Miguel de la Pinta Llorente describes the difficult conditions of the prisons but challenges González Montes, pointing to the periodic inspections of the facilities, the presence of physicians who assisted prisoners, and a general preoccupation with the well-being of the inmates on the part of the tribunal.[2] Current scholarship agrees on depicting the jails of the Holy Office as comparatively better than their civil counterparts, or at least no worse. In addition, there is evidence that some people tried to escape a civil sentence by speaking blasphemies so that they would be transferred from the civil to the Inquisition jails.[3] Therefore, it seems that the reputed harshness of the inner world of the tribunal prisons was related more to the unique characteristics of the trial of faith than to the material reality of the dungeons. Most likely, the same considerations apply to the use of torture, because torture was also part of civil trials. It is true that some features of the Inquisition's prisons had to satisfy specific regulations of the Holy Office; it is important to consider the character of one in light of the other.

In this chapter, I argue that because the Portuguese New Christians of colonial Lima belonged to a relatively cohesive community, they could devise and deploy collective strategies during the Inquisition trials. This is not to say that this community was a solid and perfectly functioning ensemble, and that all its members heroically helped one another, or that their combined actions held sway over the Lima tribunal. Frictions among the New Christians are reflected in the primary sources, for example, when Antonio Morón and Manuel Bautista Pérez in their respective trials questioned testimonies against them provided by other Portuguese New Christians. By doing so they exposed tensions related to commercial or personal issues with other members of the community.[4] However, the same allegiances that were present outside the dungeons of the Inquisition—mainly those of kinship and commercial networks, and probably of clandestine religious practices—enabled the Portuguese New Christians to develop a network of mutual support inside the world of the Inquisition, with the assistance of tribunal workers, servants, and slaves. They endured long and harsh trials, they deployed both individual and collective agency, and they stalled the progress and resolution of their trials. However, they could not in the end dictate the procedures of their judgment nor avoid the sentences issued by the tribunal.

Because the Lima Portuguese New Christians were already a discrete entity in the world outside the tribunal, they could deploy their networks inside it to take advantage of interstices and loopholes in the inquisitorial apparatus. The Portuguese merchants were a minority within the colonial elite because of two crucial markers: nationality (Portuguese among Spaniards) and the potential taint of impure blood (New Christians among Old). Under the eyes of the Inquisition, they were also a discrete entity viewed in a kind of opposition to Christian faithfulness (crypto-Jews among good Christians). Once the Lima tribunal incarcerated them, their social identity, theretofore somewhat invisible (at least in theory), was exposed, turning them into crypto-Jews among good Catholics, offenders among good Christians. Did the imprisonments destroy the previously established networks? If the accused knew each other, and sustained family, commercial, and religious networks, could they set those same networks in motion inside the prisons of the Inquisition? Clearly, they could: all they needed was to locate the appropriate venues and opportunities.

Records of the trials of the Great Complicity, as well as the correspondence between the members of the Lima tribunal and the Suprema in Madrid, bring to light many situations—some usual, some unusual—in which prisoners deflected or defied the main tools of the Inquisition trial. Prisoners, both individually and collectively, made the most of their circumstances for their own good. It is appropriate here to return briefly to the main characteristics of the Inquisition trial, those introduced in the second chapter of this book, and elaborate on the Inquisition's tools and how they could be applied—or circumvented.

The trial of faith was a carefully regulated procedure. As explained elsewhere, it was not a judiciary process in which discovery, proof, and truth were pursued as goals. Rather, it was a procedure that aimed for the full recognition of an already proven offense, with the expectation that the prisoner would request forgiveness and facilitate for the tribunal the calibration of the most appropriate punishment. In theory, three tools were introduced and applied, alone or in combination throughout the trial, each playing a crucial role in achieving the aims of the Inquisition trial.[5]

The first tool was institutional alienation. In lay terms, this was the notion of two strictly separate worlds: the outside (ordinary) world and the world inside the Inquisition. In theory, a near-impenetrable wall divided those worlds. Once a person arrived in the prisons, the Inquisition bureaucracy made sure that links between that person and the outside world were severed. The prisoner would be put out of sight and contact until the end of the trial. Relatives and friends of a prisoner would be given no information about what was happening inside the institution's confines. This tool was not exclusive to the Inquisition tribunal: other Catholic institutions, for example, convents, relied on a similar construction of institutional alienation in order to create an alternative world within their walls, although such walls were porous, as scholars have already explored.[6]

The second tool, also deployed inside the jails of the Inquisition, was individual isolation. Imprisonment was preemptive, the first step leading to a trial. Between hearings prisoners returned to the *cárceles secretas* (secret cells) that corresponded to the charges against them or to the status of their trials. Inmates in the secret cells were those undergoing trials of faith; inmates in public cells were undergoing trials for minor offenses, such as blasphemy. The *cárcel perpetua*, or *cárcel de la misericordia* (perpetual prison, or prison of mercy), also known as penitential prison (*cárcel de la penitencia*), had cells for those inmates who had already received sentence, and there they were probably allowed to interact with others. Finally, in the *cárceles medias* (intermediate cells) were tribunal members accused of transgressing regulations; they were also allowed to interact with others.[7] The secret cells were meant to create an atmosphere for silent introspection and profound self-scrutiny during the days and months between hearings. Prisoners were to remain isolated and reflect on their actions and beliefs. They were expected to sort through their memories and examine their consciences, until ready to confess and ask for leniency from a tribunal whose benevolent attention might result in life or death.

The third tool, bureaucratic secrecy, required the coordinated articulation of the whole inquisitorial machinery. Secrecy was a key component and a trademark of the tribunal of the Holy Office of the Inquisition. For example, when Lima inquisitor Antonio de Castro y del Castillo reported to Madrid about the tribunal's conduct of indictments in the 1630s, he mentioned that the secrecy of the first person to be imprisoned was so well preserved that the employers of the detainee contacted the local courts trying to find out if he was dead.[8] During the trial, charges were unveiled for the prisoner only after one, two, or even three hearings and probably a session in the torture chambers. In the actual accusation, the names of those who provided the testimonies were omitted (as were any specific chronological and locational markers) and unveiled only later on, at a stage called *publicaciones*. This omission had a specific rationale and opened the door for the tachas defense strategy: if the prisoner was able to guess and question the name of the person who had provided a given testimony, explaining a preexisting conflict, that testimony could be discarded. Finally, prisoners learned about their sentences only on the eve of the Auto de Fe. In short, the bureaucracy of the Inquisition withheld much of the relevant information that affected, positively or negatively, a prisoner's trial. By keeping prisoners alienated from the outside world, confined in their cells, and ignorant about their own trials, the Inquisition constructed for its operations an arena of fear and confession, guilt and betrayal, and punishment and repentance. Following Solange Alberro, the institution exerted psychological pressure through a combination of anxiety and boredom.[9]

But in reality, at least in the reality depicted in the documents yielded by the Great Complicity, secrecy was not constantly preserved, isolation was not strictly secured, and alienation was not completely guaranteed. On the contrary, it seems that a distinctive combination of circumstances and agency weakened these tools of the Inquisition trial. As we shall see, in spite of the tribunal's dedication to secrecy, those accused under the so-called Complicidad Grande— prisoners though they were—were fully aware of the special circumstances that surrounded their trials and maneuvered to affect these circumstances, when possible, for their own good.

Recent scholarship has demonstrated that the power of the Inquisition was built on the fact that not only was it a royal court but it was also constructed at the local level by the community. In addition to its own lay personnel (familiares), the Inquisition relied on denunciations from common people, which to some extent supported the viability of the institution. Scholars of the sixteenth-century peninsular Inquisition like William Monter on Aragon, Jaime Contreras on Murcia, and Gretchen Starr-Lebeau on Guadalupe explore how preexisting conflicts and family rivalries influenced the development of trials and trespassed into the prisons of the Inquisition. They also comment on how different networks and alliances used leverage to trigger or not trigger an Inquisition trial, bribe bureaucrats, or assist prisoners and how these efforts worked in the context of both large political rivalries and smaller-scale familial and personal conflicts.[10] If these contentions are applied to the Lima examples and to the larger political arena as well, it can be seen that the Inquisition was also a vehicle for the negotiation of local conflicts and rivalries. In the colonial context, historians who study indigenous resistance and accommodation to Spanish colonialism have presented parallel arguments with regard to the interactions between Indigenous communities and Spanish courts.[11] Civil and religious tribunals, even as they served the purposes for which they were created and modified, offered loopholes that could be manipulated by the local population, and sometimes by prisoners. Rivalries among merchants or merchants' families (as among indigenous groups for access to land or water) generated what was evidently manipulation of state institutions. However, the fact that any one person, family, or minority group manipulated royal tribunals, whether religious or civil, and thereby succeeded in stretching, delaying, or modifying trial outcomes does not render the tribunal a weak and ineffective institution. Rather, these facts broaden our understanding of the nuances and limitations of an institution's power and allow historians to place within their scope the dynamics of defiance, resistance, and agency.

There were many irregularities in Inquisition trials. One might consider corruption and wrongdoing in tribunal activities, prisoners' diversionary actions during the time of detainment, and their actions outside the formal hearings, sessions at the torture chambers, and meetings with defense advocates. One might also consider the prisoners' agency, limited though it was. Were the Inquisition's goals of institutional alienation, individual isolation, and bureaucratic secrecy indeed achieved? For an answer, I have questioned primary and secondary sources to assess their efforts against the overall development of the trials. My purpose here is not to focus on institutional corruption alone but to explore whether the Lima prisoners had knowledge of the procedures of the institution that was holding them, how much they had, how they might have acquired it, and how they used it to improve their difficult situations. What were they trying to achieve? I pose questions about the use of strategies, both individual and collective, by these prisoners. Finally, I ask whether the Lima prisoners were unique and whether similar wrongdoings by inquisitors and the use of similar strategies by prisoners have been documented for other tribunals of the Inquisition.

Inside the Lima Tribunal's Facilities

The Lima facilities were several interconnected buildings that operated as specialized units according to the various tribunal activities. There were locations designated for hearings and meetings, storage of documentation classified according to the stage of the trial—pending, suspended, sentenced, and information related to blood purity investigations—cells for prisoners, and the San Pedro Mártir chapel. The facilities also included lodging for at least one inquisitor, usually the most senior, and for employees in charge of maintenance. This layout was common to tribunals of the Holy Office and clearly related to the rationale of the trial of faith. When prisoners were led from the secret cells to the hearing rooms to meet inquisitors, there was no exposure to the public. The same lack of visibility extended to any request for consultation of secret records. Male prisoners were usually held in solitary cells, whereas females were more likely to be placed with other women. The formal instructions for incarceration indicated that accomplices and *negativos* (people who had not confessed) should not be placed in the same cell, so as to impede the circulation of details pertaining to ongoing trials. In the case of relocation to different cells, guards had to keep cellmates together.[12]

All penitentiary systems must arrange to feed their inmates and maintain their facilities. The person in charge of the Inquisition's prisons and prisoners was the *alcaide de las cárceles secretas* (steward of the secret prisons), and other staff assisted. The alcaide was not a member of the institution's bureaucracy but rather a lower-ranking official who usually lived close to the secret cells. His responsibilities included the preservation of the prisoner's safety and the maintenance of secrecy regarding procedures so that prisoners would explore their conscience without external influence during the development of their trials. Miguel de la Pinta Llorente transcribed instructions to alcaides dating from 1558, and Henry Charles Lea found instructions to alcaides dating from 1652: they were to visit the secret cells at the beginning and end of each day, verify the inmates' well-being, make sure the cells had no openings that would enable exchanges among prisoners, and check to see whether inmates had hidden anything. As guards completed their chores, they had to lock one cell before moving to another. If prisoners needed scissors or knives, these had to be used in front of a guard. Alcaides were not authorized to discuss the development of the trial with the prisoners, and since it was common that alcaides resided close to the secret prisons, the restrictions were also extended to their families.[13]

Prisoners contributed to their own sustenance. In addition, there was a royal allowance for assisting poor inmates. In case of confiscated properties, the tribunal also had to feed the family that was dismembered. If the prisoner died while under trial but the trial continued, the tribunal looked after the family for the duration of the trial.[14] Lea explains that there was no standardized ration. Upon arrival at the prisons, tribunal members assessed the financial situation of the newcomer and used it to estimate an allowance for meals. Sometimes food was delivered daily or every two days in pots, to avoid wrapping paper (so they could not write messages), and prisoners prepared their own meals. On other occasions assistants and cooks prepared meals that were delivered to the cells.

During the trial of faith, inmates and tribunal members, whether inquisitors or defense advocates, held meetings that were dedicated to a single purpose and formally scheduled. In preparation for their defense, prisoners could ask for paper and receive a certain number of sheets. On the other hand, inmates and personnel in charge of maintenance and their assistants, and also slaves, saw each other almost every day, and perhaps more than once a day. These encounters were much more frequent and probably more casual too. It is reasonable to think that the chores required for maintenance offered windows for interactions between inmates and those charged with guarding and maintaining them. And it is also reasonable to think that this interaction enabled a venue for favors and counterfavors, bribes, and corruption, with a variety of outcomes. The Inquisition was immune neither from such irregularities nor from breaches such as prisoners communicating through holes in the wall, as did Antonio Morón.[15] Nor was Lima an exception.

Following tribunal regulations, inquisitors had to inspect the prisons at least twice a month to review prisoners' needs and the overall conditions of their detainment. Periodical inspections were also conducted at secular prisons.[16] Notice of anomalies might surface in regular or occasional inspections (visitas), or in criminal trials that addressed a particular problem. In an article published in 1984, Castañeda Delgado and Hernández Aparicio analyzed the record of an inspection conducted in the Lima tribunal between 1587 and 1591 by don Juan Ruiz de Prado and his assistant, in which all kinds of irregularities were discovered.[17] Ruiz de Prado extended his stay in Lima until 1594, after completion of the inspection, and tried to remain permanently as the local inquisitor (he acted simultaneously as inspector and inquisitor during the assessment). This fact invites us to question whether the gravity and magnitude with which Ruiz de

Prado portrayed the irregularities of the Lima office were related to his own ambitions. However, in a general sense the reported misdeeds seem plausible and comparable to irregularities reported for other tribunals. For example, among the two hundred complaints against Lima inquisitor don Antonio Gutiérrez de Ulloa are the charges that he conducted commercial transactions for his own benefit and that he had had illicit relationships with women. Observations from the inspectors also discuss poor recordkeeping and faulty development of trials; the lack of required signatures and ratifications of witnesses; the granting of permission to defense advocates to see original materials instead of copies; allowing advocates to take these materials to their homes, or even worse, to the secret cells; and unfairness in sentencing, in both directions. There are also more complicated, and quite possibly more serious, criticisms of Gutiérrez de Ulloa, including nepotism and the trafficking of influence. Inspectors also found that prisoners in the secret cells had scissors, knives, money, and paper, and even access to properties that had been confiscated from them. Prisoners' servants circulated in and out of the prisons. These irregularities not only jeopardized the proper conduct of trials but also opened multiple venues for corruption. Grievances from some twenty prisoners exposed the poor quality of the attention they received and also complained about the inquisitor and the tribunal secretary. The inspection also provoked conflicts with higher officials: the discovery of irregularities extended to the standing inquisitor, the inspector-inquisitor, the viceroy, and other Lima residents. Later grumbling also uncovered irregularities committed by Ruiz de Prado himself.

Examples from other tribunals demonstrate that Lima was not an exception. Reinaldo González Montes, the early Spanish critic of the institution, described two men who held high positions in Seville's prisons at different times during the 1550s. One, moved by the presence of a mother and her two daughters in the dungeons, authorized the women to see each other for half an hour. Fearful later that the women would expose him in the torture chambers, he confessed his own transgression. The second character described by González Montes is a guard who profited from funds assigned to prisoners' food and laundry, subjected those who complained to additional ordeals, and omitted to transmit prisoners' requests for hearings to the inquisitors (prisoners awaiting trial could complain to tribunal members about unusually poor treatment). Montes tells us that both men received punishment.[18]

Lea mentions an alcaide in Barcelona who in 1544 accepted bribes, left the prisons unguarded at times and at others under somebody else's supervision, and committed other transgressions. Contreras reports that an alcaide of the Galician prisons frequently invited wealthy inmates to share a meal, where he informed them about the state of their trials; the wife and daughter of another alcaide were in touch with prisoners' relatives and would update inmates about family news. Alberro comments that alcaides of the Mexican tribunal received jewelry, clothing, and money from prisoners in exchange for certain indulgences.[19] In his discussion of the dossier of Lucrecia de León, whose five-year-long trial (1590–1595) was brought by the Toledo tribunal for her prophetic dreams, Richard Kagan found that de León's cellmate helped her to maintain communication with another prisoner. Kagan also mentions that inquisitors gave her special concessions, met with her outside of scheduled hearings, and that one of the inquisitors even expressed wonder at her arrest. Legal maneuvers related to the trial of de León and some of her associates included questioning whether the Holy Office was the appropriate court for a case that was clearly political as well as a subsequent appeal addressed to the papacy. These efforts had some temporary success in delaying the early stages of the trial. In fact, notices of its irregularities triggered an inspection of the Toledo tribunal itself, which upon confirmation of its transgressions redirected the trial and decided on the departure of the inquisitors and on the construction of another prison.[20]

Even though regulations emphasized that secrecy was crucial for the development of trials, and tribunals punished those who violated it, the tribunals themselves evidenced a certain ambivalence on this matter. Aware that prisoners exchanged messages, tribunals also placed spies to document what inmates told one another. This is how, during the trials that took place between 1635 and 1639, the Lima tribunal received information about a connection between the Portuguese New Christians and the Dutch, as reported by Isabel Antonia's cellmate, which provided for inquisitors the link between heresy and treason and justified the detentions as well as the seriousness of the procedures.[21] In Mexico during the 1640s, a spy named Gaspar de Alfar reported to the tribunal the conversations between two prisoners, with detailed information about their discussions on matters of religiosity. Considering this information in light of tribunal regulations, I agree with Solange Alberro who argues that placing spies in cells to record private dialogues was a more efficient method for collecting evidence than sessions at the torture chambers, which in addition to the obvious pain, generated content that could technically be revoked by a prisoner afterward.[22]

While conducting the Complicidad Grande trials, the Lima tribunal also carried out a criminal trial against the alcaide Bartolomé de Pradeda.[23] Paulino Castañeda Delgado, Pilar Hernández Aparicio, and Pilar Pérez Cantó have summarized this and other similar documents to be examples of the obstruction of normal tribunal tasks by members of its own ranks. Offenders included clerics who did not preserve the required secrecy; people who assisted prisoners, for example, in allowing conversations among prisoners or facilitating exchanges with the outside world; clerics who resisted cooperation with the tribunal; members of local cabildos or other holders of other public offices who spoke recklessly about the tribunal or its members; and people who intentionally ignored a clear instruction of the Holy Office, as well as those who provided false testimonies, forged documents, or posed falsely as authorized to speak in the tribunal's name.[24]

Bartolomé de Pradeda became the tribunal's alcaide in the cárceles secretas in 1615 and is thus closely connected to many of the cases discussed in this book. Pradeda's fate changed during the trials of the complicity because his own conduct was placed under investigation, and he was interrogated by the tribunal. Following procedural regulations as it generally did, the Inquisition also proceeded against those who obstructed the tribunal's tasks, no matter who they were. In this context, the trials held were criminal trials, rather than trials of faith, although it was before the Inquisition tribunal that the case was brought and not the civil court. At the time, the tribunal separated Pradeda from his functions as alcaide and designated a replacement; Pradeda's criminal trial then continued after the 1639 Auto.[25] The record of his criminal trial fills some 185 sheets, which are housed in the National Archive in Madrid. In general, the document depicts a trial whose procedures were similar to those of the trials of faith as carried out by the same tribunal. Only the offenses addressed in the trial were different: they concerned Pradeda's alleged misconduct in the fulfillment of his duties as the steward of the secret prisons, not a religious heresy.

Porosity, Corruption, and Agency in the Jails of the Inquisition

According to the trial record, Pradeda's performance as a prison steward was called into serious question because of his many transgressions. Grievances such as those against him affected the security measures of the Lima tribunal and serve to illustrate the tribunal's level of corruption. We can also consider how this corruption affected the development of the trials themselves.

As portrayed through the court testimony and the accusations against him, Bartolomé de Pradeda repeatedly contravened the security measures of the Inquisition, disregarding written instructions, overlooking his obligations, and breaking secrecy.[26] The enumeration of his transgressions is fairly long. The initial charges included leaving doors unlocked so prisoners could talk and share the developments of their trials[27] and allowing prisoners' servants to bring food and messages into the prisons. On receiving the food, clothes, wine, and other gifts brought to the prisoners by their families, he reportedly gave the inmates only a few of the items, presumably keeping the rest for his own family and friends. Other transgressions included discussing trials with prisoners and offering input on how to handle them, listening to inquisitors' consultations through a window, telling both guards and prisoners of upcoming developments, permitting some Lima residents who had expressed concern about specific imprisonments into the facilities to see the inmates, and revealing the names of those who had been imprisoned while secret trials were still under way.[28]

Another set of Pradeda's alleged wrongdoings relates to the honor and public reputation expected of those associated with the Holy Office. The testimony reports that he had intimate relationships with an underage girl and with female prisoners as well as women he had brought from the outside into the tribunal facilities. He was accused, too, of giving to these women items originally brought for prisoners as gifts. Finally, it was also noted that Pradeda carried out in his home, which was within tribunal facilities, other businesses incompatible with his function of alcaide of the cárceles secretas.[29] In the testimony presented at his criminal trial, sometimes including material pasted from individuals' trials of faith, members of the complicity admitted to sending and receiving messages through Pradeda, or one of his helpers, and to the payment of bribes for these services.[30] These charges illustrate how, even in cases brought under the complicity, the institutional alienation of prisoners was not completely guaranteed. It is true that this weak point was common to all tribunals, since prisoners always had to eat and Inquisition trials were often long. But in the Lima cases, these everyday needs opened a space to defy all three of the Inquisition's most repressive tools. So what of the second tool, the individual isolation?

Pradeda did not work alone at the chores related to the maintenance of prisons and prisoners. Inmates held for minor offenses, along with maids and African slaves, assisted the alcaide with these chores. As mentioned earlier, many of the prisoners of the complicidad had participated in the trade in African slaves. As Portuguese merchants, they represented a wide range, from the powerful merchants who held asiento licenses (for slave trade) to the lower-ranking employees of the transcontinental shipping companies that brought slaves from West Africa to colonial Lima. As the merchants explained to the Lima tribunal in their discursos de vida (when prisoners told their life stories in front of the tribunal), some of their patterns of migration followed their activities in the slave trade (from Portugal to West and West Central Africa and from there to the New World).

African slaves interacted with the Inquisition in different ways, as Paulino Castañeda Delgado, Pilar Hernández Aparicio, Ruth Magalí Rosas Navarro, Robert Perry, and Jonathan Schorsch have found.[31] Africans too could be put under trial for offenses to the faith. For example, in Lima between the late sixteenth and the early seventeenth centuries, slaves represented 26 percent of those condemned for blasphemous expression, most often committed in situations of physical abuse. Penalties ranged from a public lashing of a hundred to two hundred *azotes* to a simple reprimand following on a formal abjuration (in cases of *de levi*, suspicion of minor heresy), the latter seemingly more common as the seventeenth century progressed.[32]

However, the interactions between Africans and the tribunal were not limited to the role of offender and accuser. Slaves owned by members of the tribunal or its lower-ranking bureaucrats, such as town criers, cooks, cleaners, assistants, and construction workers, participated in tribunal activities. The list of expenses for the construction of tribunal facilities in Lima in 1584 mentions black slaves receiving compensation for tasks as sawyers and builders, among other trades.[33] In cases in which a prisoner's sentence included property confiscation and several years in jail, the prisoner's slaves could be transferred to the tribunal or sold under tribunal auspices.[34] Slaves outside the tribunal could provide denunciations and incriminating testimony against potential heretics, as in the Lima trial of Antonio Morón. In an interesting parallel, Ana Cannas da Cunha notes that in Portuguese Goa, the colonial tribunal relied on the cooperation of African slaves to denounce the New Christians, thereby making the New Christians wary of the domestic slaves in their own homes.[35] Similar situations are documented for Lima and for tribunals located in such diverse places as Lisbon, Mexico, and the Canary Islands. These situations raise questions about how open or secretive masters might be in front of their slaves and whether slaves' denunciations were connected to the context of their enslavement, or even entangled in conflicts among slave owners, as mentioned by Schorsch.

But slaves were not always ready to denounce their masters. Indeed, there is also evidence indicating something much different—slaves supporting their masters in activities concealed from the tribunal. The assistance of slaves in hidden activities probably did not occur first inside the cells of the Inquisition. Nathan Wachtel writes that in Mexico City a domestic slave from the house of Simón Váez Sevilla, the most prominent crypto-Jewish merchant in the local community, sometimes circulated through the city streets dressed in significant colors, announcing in this way an upcoming concealed ceremony.[36] However, it is inside the cells that the activities of slaves directly affected the development of the trials. As can be surmised, and as Inquisition officers found out, the proximity of Portuguese New Christians to African slaves exposed the former to the languages of the latter. In discussing the slave activities related to cases of the Mexican tribunal, Wachtel, Alberro, and Schorsch point to some female inmates of New Christian descent who probably had never been involved in the slave trade but had learned African languages in their childhood homes from domestic servants. Even if the New Christians' knowledge of African languages was fragmented and minimal, it was enough to build a somewhat discreet communication channel. Whereas this channel included Portuguese New Christians and African slaves, it excluded many others, both prisoners unconnected with the slave trade and tribunal members. Similarly, a spy placed in the cells of the Mexican tribunal reported that prisoners talked to one another in Nahuatl; the tribunal added a second spy who understood this language. From Lima, events like these are reported in the letter that Antonio de Castro y del Castillo sent to the Suprema in Madrid some years after the 1639 Auto General de Fe. According to the inquisitor, the African slaves who worked as servants inside the prisons during the trials of the Complicidad Grande also carried messages between prisoners, sometimes spoken messages, sometimes messages written on small pieces of paper printed with ink prepared with lemon juice or scribed in smoke from candles on torn pieces of fabric taken from shirts or sheets. For the prisons of peninsular tribunals, Richard Kagan and Lu Ann Homza have noted the use of burned paper and paper inscribed with invisible ink made from fruit juice for exchanges of messages. Furthermore, the trick was not exclusive to prisoners; Ignacio Pulido Serrano wrote that a man sent on a royal commission from Spain to France during the 1630s sent letters to the king in Madrid that looked like pieces of blank paper but when observed against the light of a candle revealed inscriptions written in lemon juice.[37]

In the list of accusations found in records of the trial against Bartolomé de Pradeda, we find a reference to domestic servants who carried messages into the prisons. In other sources, there are records of messages sent out from the prisons. With the assistance of lower-ranking prison officers, a prisoner named Jorge de Silva contacted his brother Juan Rodríguez de Silva, exhorting him to approach the tribunal with a spontaneous self-denunciation, which the latter did. In the end, however, Jorge was reconciled to the Christian community and Juan was released to the secular arm in 1639. These irregularities, or similar ones, were documented for Lima and for other tribunals as well. In Mexico during the same century, a woman who was worried about the imprisonment of her husband asked one of her female slaves to establish contact with a male slave from the Mexican tribunal to learn the husband's fate. The members of the Cartagena tribunal, after a torture session, allowed one of the slaves of the man who had been tortured to spend some time with the prisoner, although the Suprema subsequently questioned the decision and suggested the presence of someone without previous ties to the prisoner.[38] The historian Jonathan Schorsch collected examples of interactions between "jailed judaizers" and their African servants throughout the period of the colonial tribunals and discussed how their relationships changed according to the dynamics of the situation.[39] My interest regarding this information, however, is not to focus on the relationship between African slaves and crypto-Jews but to understand the strategies used by the latter while in the jails of the Lima Inquisition.

Another relief to the prisoner's confinement and isolation came from the avenues afforded by leniency, bribes, and corruption. Lower-ranking functionaries in most frequent contact with prisoners might leave cells closed but unlocked, thereby allowing prisoners to converse;[40] circulate information to prisoners related to the trials of others; and keep part of the food that was destined for prisoners. The assistance with prisoners' everyday needs, lenient or lax supervision by the prison's steward, and the special connection between the Portuguese New Christians and the African slaves were three factors that weakened the tools of the Inquisition trial in the cases of the Great Complicity. But these openings and unguarded spots were not the only ones that fostered some agency by prisoners. Another circumstance of the Complicity opened an even bigger breach. The issue was the prisoners' accommodations during their trials.

As already described, the Lima tribunal had from 1584 operated in a compound of three houses. In the middle house were the secret cells, the room used for hearings, the secret chamber used for records storage, and other rooms used to hold paperwork related to accounting and other administrative records.[41] The sixteen cells available to the Lima tribunal in the 1630s did not suffice for the people implicated in the Complicidad, and the Inquisition found it necessary to expand into additional facilities and neighboring houses. At a cost of 29,250 pesos, probably obtained from property confiscations, the tribunal commissioned alterations to create additional secret cells. After the resolution of most of the trials in the 1639 Auto General, they had to restore the original layouts and also acquire additional facilities for perpetual cells. The latter did not need to be close to tribunal members since people allocated to them were fulfilling sentences and did not need to be in the isolation required prior to a trial.[42] We can assume, however, that the de facto secret cells located in neighboring houses failed to provide the level of isolation required by those awaiting an Inquisition trial; we can also infer that the low level of isolation provided special opportunities to the prisoners already judged in the Complicity.

As mentioned in an earlier chapter, the inquisitor Antonio de Castro y del Castillo reported that the arrests increased at a pace that soon overwhelmed the existing accommodations of the Lima tribunal. It was not the first time: something similar had happened in 1581 when inquisitors had reported that because of lack of space they were postponing arrests and submitting the dossiers to Spain for consultation in the meantime.[43] Jaime Contreras has described a similar occurrence in Galicia between 1607 and 1609, when the tribunal conducting trials of Portuguese crypto-Jews decided to add nine cells, six close to the inquisitors' chambers and three close to the alcaide's, although the construction was stalled owing to internal conflicts.[44] In Lima during the 1630s, a first step to solving the space problem was to expedite the resolution of impending cases and thereby vacate cells for incoming prisoners. However, the tribunal did not issue a sentence for all inmates, and at least one trial for crypto-Judaism did not end at this point: Francisco Maldonado de Silva, a surgeon born in Tucumán in 1592 who had been in the Lima prisons since 1627, remained in the prisons while the trials of the Complicidad Grande unfolded. He also had the opportunity to interact with those prisoners.[45] In any case, it appears that the solution was more effective in theory than practice; between 1635 and 1636 the number of arriving prisoners was much higher than the development and resolution of the trials. The tribunal understood that the cases of the Complicity were interconnected; therefore, a fast resolution of any single case was not realistically possible. When the tribunal ran short of cells, something more was needed. We see again in Castro y del Castillo's letter what followed the resolution of such a large number of pending cases during the Complicity: "[This tribunal] found itself with such a number of prisoners, with sixteen cells where more than a hundred were needed, that neighboring homes and homes owned by the tribunal were taken, and their doors and lodgings carved out *not with the proper dividers, as was required, but with* [only] *the accommodation that time and urgency allowed.*"[46]

In a second step, the Lima tribunal extended its holding cells onto other properties it controlled as well as to neighboring houses. In a short period of time the Tribunal remodeled these houses to its own purposes, opening some spaces and closing others and adapting rooms in the houses to make Inquisition cells. The new prisons were ready by December 1636, as there is evidence indicating that the prisoner Enrique Jorge Tavares was moved into one of the cells.[47] Considering the architecture, the location of the doors, and the rapid makeover, we can assume that the infrastructure of these edifices made them less secure than a prison built specifically for that use. The walls of the neighboring houses would have been thinner than those earlier designed as Inquisition cells, and the new cells would de facto fail to offer the same degree of security. There was concern not only with the number of cells but how the construction of new cells might facilitate communication between prisoners. For this reason, Enrique Jorge Tavares was moved to another cell.

It is reasonable to think that the prisoners of the Complicity would seize the opportunities offered by their new sort of prisons and the somewhat improvised cells. In regard to communication among prisoners, Antonio de Castro del Castillo's letter offers the following: "On other [occasions, the prisoners] used stones to knock, signaling one for *a*, two for *b*, and so on for the other letters; and when they arrived at the letter they wanted to use for the communication they rang a bell, and he who was listening to the knocks wrote [the letter] on the floor or on the wall, and with all letters together they could put together the entire message."[48]

By this system of knocking stones and with the assistance of African slaves as messengers, the prisoners were able to transmit, albeit slowly and likely with unforeseen delays, messages to one another and thereby circumvent their individual isolation. References to this method of communication also appear in the 1647 accusation brought against Manuel Henríquez, wherein it is said that he had learned the knocking trick during his previous experience as a prisoner of the Coimbra tribunal and that it was he who had taught it to the Lima prisoners.[49] Communication between cells at inquisitorial prisons by tapping the alphabet has also been documented among prisoners of the Mexican tribunal in the 1640s and among inmates of the Portuguese Inquisition in the eighteenth century.[50] These experiences suggest that even though the tribunal emphasized secrecy, inquisitorial procedures over the long years of the institution's existence were not always a mystery to prisoners or potential prisoners.

When one considers together the corruption inherent in the system, the lack of sufficient cells and the inadequacy of the quickly remodeled ones, the assistance of the African slaves in passing messages, and the presence of a prisoners' communication code, we can see how the New Christian Portuguese merchants, as inmates of the Lima tribunal, were able to build alternative channels of communication and otherwise access information by their own agency. The information obtained through these channels allowed them to deploy collective strategies during their trials. It is well worth our time to explore the uses of these channels and the content of the messages. What were they telling one another? According to the letters exchanged between Lima and Madrid, the coded communication enabled prisoners to create and execute collective strategies, generally aimed at amending the paths of their own trials and obtaining a better outcome. For instance, the code could reveal if a prisoner had been broken at the torture chambers, or if a prisoner's confession had denounced others. In this way, the prisoners could make collective guesses at the names of incoming prisoners. The Lima–Madrid correspondence also suggests that some members of the complicity plotted to use this communication to denounce Old Christians so that they too would be brought to the dungeons. Enrique Jorge Tavares confirmed the existence of this plot in a hearing held at his request.[51]

More supporting information comes from records of the trial against Bartolomé de Pradeda. According to witnesses' declarations, the Portuguese New Christians took Bartolomé de Pradeda's leniency and the cooperation of their African slaves for granted. They were even able to combine those advantages to strengthen their cases or protect themselves from some extremes of torture. In both the testimonies and accusation against Pradeda, there are references to the circulation, inside the prisons, of *"pelotillas redondas mas gruesas algo que granos de maíz"* (small pellets a bit larger than a grain of corn). Such pelotillas presumably diminished the pain of torture. Let me translate here how this is described in the accusation against Pradeda: "And the blacks that served [Bartolomé de Pradeda] had so much freedom of movement that they entered the jails by themselves and communicated with the prisoners, and it happened that one black man dropped a knotted piece of cloth and someone picked it up to see if it contained a note sent from outside for one of the prisoners, and in it were four small balls of what looked like incense . . . the paper explained how the small pellets were to be used on the day on which one was to be tortured."[52]

The night before a prisoner's session at the torture chambers, the pellets were wrapped in paper and a slave took the paper to the prisoner's cell. Unfortunately, the documents do not provide more information on the name of the main agent in these pellets, or on how the pellets worked to reduce pain, if they did indeed do so. But nowhere in the record of Bartolomé de Pradeda's trial is there a challenge to the existence of the pellets or to the reality of such a chain of communication and support among the prisoners of the Complicidad Grande, or to specific strategies addressing the application of torture. Nicolau Eimeric, who authored a *Manual* for inquisitors in 1376, mentioned that prisoners who suffered torture several times used sorceries and sortileges in hopes of becoming insensitive to pain. Furthermore, in his 1578 comments to Eymeric's *Manual*, Francisco Peña (a Spanish specialist in Canonic Law) mentioned that for the same purpose, prisoners hid in their garments pieces of vellum containing fragments of the Scriptures.[53] Therefore, inquisitors probably expected that prisoners would deploy such strategies.

In one of his hearings, Manuel Bautista Pérez admitted he had corresponded with his fellow prisoner and brother-in-law Sebastián Duarte by writing notes on small pieces of paper (*papelicos*) carried by Pradeda's slaves from one prisoner to another. In this correspondence, Duarte told Pérez he was worried for himself because there was a long list of unnamed witnesses in his trial of faith. Pérez replied, encouraging Duarte not to confess to what he had not done, even under torment, and also suggesting that Duarte declare against those who had declared against them. The messages were written in a numerical code. The tribunal intercepted the messages, but inquisitors were unable to decipher its contents. When interrogated about the specifics of the numerical writing, Pérez explained he had received the code from the outside (also through slaves) and sent it to Duarte, so they could both understand the messages. Furthermore, he asked the tribunal to track down these exchanges by interrogating the slaves to find out if there were false testimonies provided intentionally.[54]

Another strategy of the Portuguese New Christians imprisoned during the trials of 1635–1639 involves the manipulation of the trial of faith itself. Starr-Lebeau in her study of the Inquisition trials in Guadalupe has discussed steps like the modification of confessions and supplications for mercy.[55] As already stated, during the trial of faith, the prisoner had twenty-four hours following a confession to ratify or revoke its contents. If the prisoner ratified, the tribunal considered the confession as established truth and moved forward. If the prisoner retracted the confession, the tribunal still had to establish the truth in future steps (a meeting among tribunal members had to decide about another hearing or another session in the torture chambers and order other steps to be repeated). The trial was not a single act, but a set of highly controlled procedures. Initial instructions dating back to 1376 recommended a fast trial, but tribunals held discretionary power regarding the length and speed of the process. If a prisoner changed the content of his or her confession, the trial stalled until truth was established. In Lima, Rodrigo Váez Pereira, the man mentioned in the introduction to this book, was imprisoned and had his first hearing in August 1635, received the accusation in November, confessed in April of the following year (after receiving the admonition or threat of torment but not torment itself), and ratified his confession. However, in January of 1637 Váez Pereira retracted most of his confession, mainly the sections that implicated others, saying that the fear of torment had guided his words. The tribunal then issued a second accusation, of which he denied everything, and the inquisitors responded by issuing a sentence of torment in August of 1637. This second time Váez Pereira was tortured and confessed, after which the tribunal decided to sentence him with an abjuration, a sambenito, property confiscation, perpetual prison, four hundred lashes, and ten years in the galleys. Váez Pereira changed his declarations again, and in January of 1639 the tribunal modified the sentence for a release to the secular arm and property confiscation; these punishments were applied in the 1639 Auto General de Fe.[56] Considering that the indictments of the complicity included some one hundred prisoners, and that many other trials evidence similar circumventions, the trials of the 1630s clearly challenged the Lima inquisitors.

In the official account of the sentences issued at the 1639 Auto General, Fernando de Montesinos (a priest born close to Seville who arrived in Peru in 1629 and settled in Lima in 1636) wrote that Enrique Núñez de Espinosa was an extremely pernicious prisoner because he had informed others of how the tribunal procedures worked.[57] In short, he gave them information that might suggest how to revoke a confession in an advantageous way. Actually, in the trials of 1635–1639, the revocations were fairly common. Why did so many people revoke? Did they know a revocation probably meant another session at the torture chambers? One explanation was the sense of impending doom: according to the inquisitors of the Lima tribunal, there was a day on which these prisoners heard construction noises and assumed that a stage for an Auto General de Fe was being built. From this, they inferred that their sentences were almost decided and that the trials were coming to an end. This inference— mistaken, because the construction noises were coming not from the mounting of a stage for an Auto General but from the replacement of a door in the tribunal's chapel—triggered another collective strategy. Many prisoners revoked their confessions and made multiple modifications to their declarations. This back-and-forth occurred at different steps of the procedure and stalled trials and delayed sentences. According to the inquisitors, delaying the sentences was indeed the prisoners' goal for this strategy: the Portuguese New Christians schemed to postpone the resolutions of their trials in the hope of a general (royal and papal) pardon, similar to the one issued in 1605.[58] The 1605 pardon specified that after one year in Europe and two outside of Europe, prisoners who had not yet received a published sentence had to be let go and their confiscated property returned. Indeed, the behavior of these Lima prisoners was not unique among prisoners in similar circumstances; rumors of a general pardon under Philip IV are discussed elsewhere in this book. Such rumors also circulated in Lisbon around 1620, when offenders from Brazil arrived at the Lisbon prisons of the tribunal after an inquisitorial inspection (there were no tribunals in Brazil, so offenders were sent to Lisbon).[59] In any case, the delays certainly affected the resolution of the sentences and the organization of the 1639 Auto General in Lima.

❧

Even though the Lima tribunal attempted to follow inquisitorial regulations regarding isolation, alienation, and secrecy in the secret cells, the Portuguese New Christians, as prisoners, took advantage of bureaucratic corruption, insufficiently secure cells, and potential helpers to exert a certain degree of individual and collective agency. This agency relied in part on the creativity and bravery of those detained but also on two other factors. One factor is how the fissures and glitches of the inquisitorial system offered spaces to the prisoners awaiting trial. The number of prisoners contributed to the irregularities; a large number was not anticipated when the prisons were built. When the resolution of impending cases failed to afford enough space for incoming inmates, the Great Complicity triggered the hurried construction of new (and inadequate) cells.

The other factor is that the Portuguese New Christians, before their imprisonments, already belonged to a discrete network. Even in recognizing their internal rivalries and tensions, they could count to a considerable extent on one another. They could also count on the cooperation of many Africans who worked as prison servants or alongside some lower-ranking personnel of the tribunal. When the Lima tribunal learned of the direct and indirect participation of these lower-ranking bureaucrats in such maneuvers, it initiated criminal trials for those found to be obstructing Inquisition tasks, separating the bureaucrats involved from their posts and replacing them. Lima was not the first or the last tribunal to experience corruption and wrongdoing. The prisoners of the complicity trials exploited these factors; defied the alienation, isolation, and secrecy of the Inquisition by devising their own strategies and communication codes; and successfully manipulated the duration—although not the outcome—of many trials.

6

The Plight of the Condemned

In the city of Lima, kingdom of Peru, on January 23, 1639, there was an Auto General de Fe with seventy-two prisoners.[1] Literally, auto de fe means "act of faith." In the Inquisition context, the phrase names the ceremony that marked the culmination of a trial or group of trials. As Juan Antonio Llorente observed, the Auto de Fe was the public and solemn reading of the summaries of the cases and the sentences by inquisitors, with the attendance of the penitents, the civil and religious authorities, and all other respectable groups of society.[2] The Auto General de Fe was a public event demonstrating the cooperation of the tribunal of the Holy Office and the civil authorities (the secular arm) in the struggle against heresy. During the ceremony, prisoners with sentences of death at the stake were formally handed over to the state (literally *relajado al brazo secular*, "released to the secular arm"), and the latter implemented the executions. The historian Alejandra Osorio has looked at the Autos performed over time by the Lima tribunal to consider how they were used as displays of viceregal power.[3] As she notes, the celebration had all the makings of a great public spectacle to celebrate the successful culmination of a battle.

As a ceremony, the Auto de Fe was not a creation of the Spanish Inquisition. A similar, although simpler, ceremony has been described for the medieval Inquisition that operated in thirteenth-century France. That ceremony was a solemn act called Sermo Publicus (Public Sermon) or Sermo Generalis de Fide (General Sermon of Faith) and consisted of a sermon, the reading of the sentences, and the meting out of punishments to penitents.[4] Francisco Bethencourt notes that the great difference between the medieval ceremonies and those organized by the Spanish and Portuguese Inquisitions was that the latter ceremonies were "regular and collective events."[5] Over time, the Spanish Inquisition embellished every detail of this ceremony with liturgical, dramatic, and ornamental elements. On this new and much grander scale, it sometimes delivered a public punishment to hundreds of people at one time.

In its specific implementations, the Auto de Fe varied in scale according to the number of people punished and the number and hierarchical status of the authorities who attended. It also varied in the location where the ceremony was performed. It might be an Autillo (one person, usually conducted at the hearing rooms of the tribunal), an Auto Singular de Fe (held at the church, or perhaps at the public square, depending on the nature of the sentences), an Auto Particular de Fe (various penitents and authorities; in Lima, these were usually performed at the Church of Santo Domingo), or an Auto General de Fe in which a large number of penitents would receive sentences according to their guilt. The last-named ceremony would be attended by the entire apparatus of religious and civil authorities as well as numerous local onlookers.

Both dimensions of the Inquisition, judicial and religious, were on display in the Auto de Fe.[6] Trials that had unfolded over years, through testimonies, hearings, accusations, torture, confession, and sentencing, were in this act concluded, and sentences were carried out. Those who were able to refute the tribunal's accusations and demonstrate their innocence were rehabilitated and their honor was restored. Those who either confessed and admitted to the charges or were unable to refute the accusations received the assigned punishment. According to the seriousness of the offenses, some had to abjure, some were reconciled to the Catholic faith, and some were released to the state to die at the stake.

A public Auto General de Fe could last for an entire day or even more. Its much-elaborated rituals demanded the attendance of the highest civil and religious authorities, the concurrence of religious orders, the participation of brotherhoods and guilds, and the public exhibition of all the penitents. In brief, the Auto General was a public ceremony that marked the final stage of a set of cases, a colossal display that made sure and visible the application of punishment.[7] Throughout the ceremony, there were processions of tribunal members, civic and religious authorities, and prisoners. There was a Mass and a sermon, followed by an open reading of the cases, and finally the public execution of the sentences. It was an Auto General de Fe that was celebrated in Lima in 1639, devoted mainly to the closure of the cases tried under the Complicidad Grande. Another Auto General had been celebrated in Lima in 1625, and during the intervening fourteen years Autos of lesser importance, held to end cases or to vacate the prisons, were performed in closed spaces away from the public eye.

According to Alejandra Osorio, the "larger, baroque purpose of the auto de fé was first to ritually restore the moral fabric and religious purity of the city and the polity." A second purpose was "to accentuate and disseminate the exalted status of Lima as Guardian of the Faith, to the Crown, and the Empire." Considering several ceremonies celebrated in Lima, she concludes that "the auto de fé celebrated the triumph of the Catholic faith but more importantly 'the preservation of peace.'"[8] In this chapter, I will diverge from Osorio's work to examine the 1639 celebration in its own right, and from a somewhat distinctive position. I focus here on the application of punishment to specific historical subjects during a single event rather than on the elements of viceregal power common across other ceremonies, Autos or not. Doing so allows me to anchor my analysis to the plight of the condemned and the terror the institution exerted as it attempted to restore the moral fabric of its society. In the following pages, I will examine the relationship of the 1639 Lima Auto General with the trials leading up to it (trials analyzed in previous chapters), and I will also consider its impact on the tribunal organization and finances, its ritual aspects, and the plight of the condemned—the terror the tribunal imposed over the persons it targeted and those who feared the same might happen to them.

Eye Witnesses to an Act of Faith

Diego de Ocaña was a Spanish friar who traveled in the colonies at the very end of the sixteenth century and at the beginning of the seventeenth. He arrived in Lima in October 1599 and set out to visit the rest of the viceroyalty. Upon his return to Lima he fell sick and prolonged his stay there. In combined visits, he spent about twenty-four months in the City of Kings. Ocaña commented that the city did not host enough secular festivities to entertain the local population but noted that the extensive celebrations conducted at churches, of which it is reported that there were forty by 1630, filled the void.[9]

Ocaña recorded the events of the Lima Auto General de Fe of 1605, in which twenty-three Portuguese crypto-Jews received sentences, three of them burned at the stake. Ocaña was impressed by the magnitude of the ceremony, which began at seven in the morning and ended at eight in the evening. Although the friar did not estimate the number of participants, he did observe that the central stage was large enough to accommodate the viceroy and his entourage, the judges of the high court, and members of the religious orders and the local universities, as Osorio has noted. Ocaña, himself a man from a small village in the Iberian Peninsula, compared the Autos he knew of in Spain to the 1605 event in Lima: in Spain, he said, if the king was not present, the Autos were not so noteworthy as the one that unfolded before him.[10]

Fray Buenaventura de Salinas y Córdova, a Franciscan born into the Peruvian aristocracy and a Holy Office calificador, recorded his observations of Autos Generales in a chronicle written in 1630. At the time of writing he had attended two but chose to focus on the later one. The Franciscan friar recaps the ceremony performed in Lima on Sunday, December 21, 1625, early in the Southern Hemisphere summer and seventeen years after the previous public Auto in the city (June 1608): "The majesty with which these grand Ministers celebrate the General Autos de Fe in this city has no comparison: and thus they have been much admired and supported by the viceroys in whose administration they took place."[11] Salinas y Córdova's description of the 1625 ceremony is concise, but he mentions that more than twelve thousand participants fit onto the central stage. The viceroy and his military companies, tribunal members, city residents, knights wearing their best clothes, officers of the city government—all participated in the ceremony and witnessed the sentencing and punishment of twenty-one penitents, including two persons and two effigies released to the secular arm.[12]

The ceremony was not only an occasion for punishing heretics. In its pomp and grandeur, it served to reinforce and validate the Holy Office of the Inquisition itself—its commitment to the struggle against the enemies of the faith and the active participation of the entire Christian community in such a struggle. In this historical context, heresy was constructed as the most extreme and heinous offense not only to the Divinity but also to the entire community. Therefore, the reparation and punishment, both enacted at the Auto de Fe, had to reach a level of intensity equivalent to that of the offense. The ceremony was a complex and elaborated ritual that combined pedagogy, drama, spectacle, and violence. It was a simultaneous display of rigor and mercy, severity and forgiveness, pain and remorse, deviation and defiance.

The Auto General de Fe was of necessity a theatrical performance. The main public plaza of a leading city—as was Lima—provided the perfect location to present and heighten the drama. It was a location that everybody knew, with plenty of entrances from different streets, usually surrounded by buildings with high balconies and front windows, almost a prebuilt amphitheater. The theatrical component was subsumed into the civil and religious nature of the ceremony: theater was the medium, not the goal. Nonetheless, the ceremony was a spectacle that provided entertainment for local crowds.[13]

Autos Generales were not the only events held at Lima's central plaza. On regular days, the plaza hosted a local market where indigenous, mestizo, black, and mulatto women sold fruits, bread, milk, cheese, prepared foods, and *chicha* (corn beer), among other items. Other vendors offered figs, raisins, almonds, fruit preserves, and wine.[14] At least twice before 1629, Lima's central square was the setting for bullfights, as reported by Antonio Suardo.[15] On special days, the plaza was the stage for ceremonies that highlighted the viceroy's role in the colonial mission of civilization and Christianization; similar displays of public performances have been documented for Mexico City, Potosí, Cuzco, and many other colonial cities.

In any calendar year, public festivals, both religious and secular, were frequent.[16] Some, like those honoring the Virgin Mary, could last for up to eight or nine days. In addition to religious services, the festivals offered popular entertainment with parades, dancers, street theater, and fireworks. The city plaza and its adjacent streets were cleaned up and adorned for such occasions, and those who attended wore their best garments. Religious images, portraits, and large figures representing historical and mythological characters were also decorated, and horses wore accessories as well. Around the plaza were hung leaves and flowers for their beauty and aroma. Mirrors and metallic objects hung from poles, and trees reflected the sun and added sparkle to the proceedings. Buildings were decorated with elegant textiles, as were the ornate balconies that offered viewers a preferential location for viewing the spectacle. The colorful and elaborated ornamentation could, for example, transform Potosí's arid landscape into a warmer environment, even if just for the duration of the fiesta. As Osorio and other scholars have discussed, religion was not the only reason for a public festival. Events in the royal family (births, marriages, coronations, and deaths), military victories, the arrival of viceroys, the appointment of higher authorities, the location of new sources of income (such as mines)—these were also events that triggered public celebrations, the adornment of urban streets for general entertainment, and the attendance of all social actors.

Civic festivals were elaborate and expensive. They also began with a Mass, but they included parades of dignitaries, games and competitions for the socially prominent and others, bullfights and cockfights, presentations of comedies and Greek tragedies and plays recalling the events of the conquest, musical and dance performances, and of course, general dances for all the public. Spectators wore costumes and masks, guilds contributed funds and organized games. Like the religious festivals, these civic celebrations could last for several days. In 1556, when Philip II's coronation was celebrated in Potosí, the festivities went on for twenty-four days. The planning and execution of the celebrations, whether religious or secular, was not exempt from quarrels among participating social groups, institutions, and governing bodies, but in the end the festivals entertained everybody, enforced the core structures of colonial society, highlighted economic status and social hierarchies, promoted local consumption, employed artisans and construction workers, and offered opportunities to artists of Spanish, Indian, and African descent to display their talents.[17]

Before the eighteenth century colonial cities did not have street lights. A chronicler setting down the story of a galley that caught fire during the battles against the Dutch in El Callao wrote that "it was such a huge fire and explosion that in this City of Kings a letter could be read after nightfall, which is when the fire started."[18] In such a place, the lights, candles, and fires that shown over the main plaza during festivals had a tremendous visual impact, and the entertainment that took place in the glow often continued well into the night. Celebratory explosions, bells, choirs, church music, and the noise of the crowd also contributed to the festive atmosphere.[19]

Church regulations mandated that a number of religious festivals were to be celebrated annually in colonial Peru. Of these, thirty-seven were mandatory for Spaniards and twelve for Indians. The festivals commemorated significant events in the Christian calendar or honored individual patrons and saints. Gifts to local *cofradías* (confraternities), guilds, and brotherhoods linked to a particular figure provided the opportunity to partake in a public celebration. The participation in cofradías was common to all members of colonial society. Indeed, these associations overshadowed the religious aspects of the devotion because they provided in addition a social forum and mutual assistance and fostered local sodalities.[20] Apart from the Church-mandated festivals were those organized locally for a specific purpose, such as the inauguration of a church or its reconstruction after an earthquake. Festivals were also held to celebrate beatifications and canonizations, like that of San Ignacio de Loyola, celebrated in 1624 in Potosí. Events such as the arrival of a relic sent by the pope as a gift to Lima's main church (as happened in 1649) were also occasions for mounting a festival.[21]

The Holy Office had its own saint in the figure of San Pedro Mártir de Verona, an Italian man born into a family of heretics who converted to Christianity and became general inquisitor in Milan in the 1230s. He was killed by two delinquents in 1252 and canonized in 1253.[22] In 1625, San Pedro Mártir's banner, made of fabric woven with golden threads, led the procession that inaugurated the Lima Auto General. Following the banner was a caravan of six hundred members of the religious orders, two choirs, and tribunal personnel. Just behind the main procession was the vicar of Santo Domingo, carrying the Green Cross.[23]

The annual fiesta of San Pedro de Verona was on April 29. Each year, the senior inquisitor received 1,000 pesos for the performance of the Mass at the church of San Pedro on that specific day. On April 29, 1636, while the tribunal was conducting the Complicidad Grande indictments (three arrests in March and eight in April), the celebration at the tribunal chapel was a solemn one.[24] The celebration held the following year was bigger and conducted with more ostentation. In 1639, on the day before the much-awaited Auto General, the procession departed from the San Pedro Mártir chapel, with a provincial from the Dominican order and the governor of Chile carrying the main emblems.[25]

Civil and religious bodies, local guilds, individual benefactors, and respected members of local society donated funds or lent their jewelry for the adornment of religious images, and they participated as well. Regulations mandated that work was forbidden to faithful Christians during the festivals so that they could attend and enjoy them. If they were absent, penalties were applied. In addition to their doctrinal functions, these festivals contributed to the reinforcement of religious and civil authority, to the preservation of unity within this Christian colonial society, to the immersion of Native Americans and Africans into the new religion, and to the ratification of social hierarchies. Of course, they also provided diversion and a space for sociability to all who attended.

The Auto General de Fe, as a celebration, shared elements with both religious and secular festivals but was clearly distinct from them. Although it was a religious celebration, it was not part of an annual cycle like many others, nor was it attached to the commemoration of a particular saint, even though it was sometimes celebrated in conjunction with a saint's day. For example, the 1639 and 1664 Autos Generales in Lima were both performed on January 23, the day of San Ildefonso. The Auto de Fe was not anchored to a particular person or family (as were those dedicated to events in the royal family or a saint's day), but the participation of royal authorities gave status and relevance to the ceremony as a public event. The celebration of Autos Generales de Fe, like the ceremonies related to extirpation of idolatries, was not a frequent occurrence. The Lima tribunal had been active since 1570, and there is record of celebration of an Auto prior to the tribunal's creation (1548). The announcement of an Auto General implied that the tribunal had at least one trial of faith with a sentence of death at the stake.[26]

A singular outcome of the celebration of the Autos Generales de Fe was the emergence of a literary genre: the *relación del auto de fe*, a narration or chronicle of the ceremony. In the early years of the tribunal, observers recorded events informally, addressing their notes to their relatives or acquaintances. Also, tribunal officers noted the observances and inserted them into reports to the peninsular authorities. The relación of the 1578 Auto in Lima consists of two folios (sheets of paper), written on both sides, and states that the ceremony began early in the day and ended at two in the morning on the next day. It also mentions that the *tablado* (staging area) accommodated the public of all social locations and that the event had the majesty and grandiosity one would more likely expect in an important location in Spain. Likewise, the document recapitulates the sequence of the celebration and summarizes the sentences of those punished.[27] In later years, official writers took charge of reporting what happened at each Auto de Fe. These longer accounts were dedicated to the authorities and published with formal licenses.

The historian Pedro Guibovich Pérez has classified printed materials produced in colonial Lima into four categories, with the largest (54 percent of all writings) being ecclesiastical works. Lima residents also read printed works that were not produced locally, such as novels of chivalry, prayer books, musical works, and art books imported from Spain. The genre "ecclesiastical writing" includes a variety of works: sermons, laws (bulls, edicts of faith), proceedings for beatifications and canonizations, and devotional literature such as hagiographies, treatises, instruction manuals, and dictionaries. Under this label are also found accounts of religious festivities and celebrations, such as a relación del auto de fe.[28]

Doubtless, the "official" account of an event conveys the message promoted by the hosting institution and its patrons, but as a primary source such an account can also be mined for less official information embedded in the event's description. For the Lima Auto General of 1639, we have a detailed text written by the Spanish priest Fernando de Montesinos. Born in Osuna, close to Seville, he was ordained before moving to Peru and traveled there in the same fleet as the Conde de Chinchón and his wife in 1629 (Mencía de Luna, one of the Lima tribunal detainees, was also on the ship). Montesinos was interested in mineralogy and wanted to learn the location of El Dorado. He lived, among other places, in Trujillo, Potosí, the Atacama Desert, Cusco, and probably Huancavelica before settling in Lima in 1636; there he became the administrator of a property of the Holy Office. After the 1639 Auto General, Montesinos left Lima and traveled through Andahuaylas and Cajamarca, briefly settling in Quito. He returned to Spain in 1643, where he died ten years later, after trying without success to return to the colonies.[29]

Although Montesinos wrote other works, he thought of his *Auto de la Fe Celebrado en Lima a 23 de enero de 1639*, published in 1640 in Madrid with the license of the General Inquisitor of the Supreme Council, as "one of the high points of his career."[30] The published document has twenty-eight folios containing the narration itself in addition to the opening sheets that reflect the necessary bureaucratic approvals. To analyze the 1639 Lima Auto General, I will use this primary source combined with other documents.

Far from the Public Eye

The everyday tasks of the Inquisition that occupied tribunal members on more typical days included the assessment of evidence, imprisonments, hearings, interrogations at the torture chambers, recordkeeping, meetings to discuss current and upcoming cases, and exchanges of correspondence with the Suprema in Madrid. All these tasks were kept in secrecy for procedural reasons, as has already been pointed out. Although Inquisition bureaucrats very likely participated in many public events in the colonial city, they thus had few opportunities to showcase their own activities and the results to the broader community or to the civil authorities that supported their mission. The same applies to the highest-level administrators sent to the colonies: the Autos Generales, even though they were rare events, offered them the opportunity to demonstrate their support for the tribunal in a public arena. For example, the viceroy Conde de Chinchón held office in Lima from January 1629 to December 1639: during his ten years as the highest royal delegate in Peru, he attended only one Auto General—no others were held. The ceremonies of 1631 and 1635 that occurred during Chinchón's tenure were minor ones, performed at the tribunal's chapel.[31] The Lima inquisitor Andrés Juan Gaitán saw only two Autos Generales (1625 and 1639) during his forty years of service.[32] Lower-ranked members of the tribunal had similar experiences. Bartolomé de Pradeda became the tribunal's alcaide in 1615. He participated in the 1625 Auto General, but prior to the 1639 ceremony he had been removed from his post because of allegations of corruption as discussed earlier. The inquisitor Juan de Mañozca y Zamora, one of a family of inquisitors, was an exception. He moved among cities and tribunals throughout his life and attended ceremonies in Cartagena, in Lima, and in the vast viceroyalty of New Spain.[33]

Procedural secrecy was mandatory for tribunal staff inside tribunal facilities. In case of violations, the tribunal could bring one of its own to a criminal trial for obstruction of the Inquisition's tasks. Inquisitors were highly educated men, with academic degrees from prestigious universities, and members of a royal tribunal. Bethencourt notes that "inquisitors ventured out increasingly rarely," and their public appearances were carefully regulated. However, tribunal members of all ranks, to some degree, participated in the activities of the larger society. In Lima, inquisitor Juan Gutiérrez Flores was also a visitador of the Lima audiencia, part of the entourage that accompanied the viceroy on his journey to Lima in 1629. Two years later, the inquisitor declared null the election of a professor of theology. The same year, Juan Gutiérrez Flores and two other Lima inquisitors, Andrés Juan Gaitán and Antonio de Castro y del Castillo, attended a debate put forth by an Augustinian friar, an event that was dedicated to the Holy Office functionaries. In October 1630 Mañozca and Castro y del Castillo traveled out of the city to receive the captain bringing the official announcement of the prince's birth. And on the day after Christmas of the same year, the inquisitors greeted the new viceroy and his wife, following in line after the audiencia members and the archbishop.[34]

Inquisitors and other tribunal members regularly attended Mass and probably enjoyed a privileged location or assigned seats at religious and civic ceremonies, the recognition of their status as members of a royal tribunal.[35] On September 6, 1634, the tribunal as a group visited the viceregal couple to extend condolences for a family loss.[36] They also participated as a discrete column in processions at important events. In a 1666 procession, during the ceremony associated with the funeral of Philip IV, tribunal bureaucrats—including familiares, consultores, calificadores, secretaries, and accountants—filed together in a group, followed by the constable carrying the banner with the Green Cross. Three inquisitors walked at the back of the group: they were don Cristóbal de Castilla, don Álvaro de Ibarra, and one señor Huerta; they wore very long cloaks of black Holland cloth, dragging the ground; and all the rest also wore their long cloaks of heavy flannel.[37]

In the intervals between Autos Generales, ceremonies of a lesser scale conducted at the chapel provided closure for cases that did not have a sentence of release to the secular arm. These were usually attended by religious and civil authorities, and perhaps the viceroy, but not the broader public. Reports state that the 1631 Auto, performed at the Inquisition chapel, took place in the presence of the viceroy, his wife, who was accompanied by the ladies of her entourage, and some special guests.[38] In short, Autos Generales, as large celebrations hosted by the tribunal of the Holy Office of the Inquisition, placed the institution, its bureaucrats and supporters, and prisoners in an unaccustomed limelight. It is this fact that lends distinction and importance to the Auto General.

In regard to the Auto General de Fe, the historian Consuelo Maqueda Abreu found that this ceremony was the essence of the unique nature of the tribunal of the Inquisition.[39] She noted that the tribunal and the Spanish civil courts of the same historical period shared important judicial features, like the presumption of guilt as a point of departure, procedural secrecy, and the use of torture.[40] But Maqueda Abreu also sees a crucial difference between the civil courts and the Inquisition that emerged once an Auto General de Fe was in the picture. In civil justice, an equivalent public ceremony was rare and exceptional, because punishment was usually administered in secret.[41] Sources that inform us of public punishments in colonial Lima, for reasons unrelated to the Inquisition, generally mention torture, galleys, scourging, the use of the garrote, and hanging (sometimes one after the other) as penalties for rebellion, theft, escape from prison, murder, homicide, and treason. Some sources have reported public attendance and displays of solidarity and empathy with the condemned.[42] Outside of the tribunal's Autos Generales, burning at the stake in the City of Kings is mentioned only twice in the seventeenth century: once for a mestizo and a mulato who had committed sodomy on a raft and were burned in 1629 in El Callao, and once for the 1674 execution of Gabriel del Palacio, who forged currency. These accounts do not describe any grand ceremony in the days building up to the executions, but they do report how people were killed and mention public attendance.[43] In contrast, while the tribunal did hold private ceremonies for smaller-scale offenders, it also celebrated a magnificent public

Auto General de Fe when the characteristics of the cases and the seriousness of the offenses justified it. A key element was the magnificent theatrical display, through which the Inquisition showed their world—the civil and religious authorities, nobles and common people, good Christians and potential heretics—what the power of the Inquisition had done, and could do. The point of a magnificent public ceremony was to turn inquisitorial punishment into exemplary punishment.[44]

It is interesting to note that the public nature of the Auto General clearly contravened the other dynamics that shaped the Inquisition as an institution. An essential characteristic of the Inquisition was the extreme secrecy and reserve it deployed through every stage of a trial. As the grand ceremonial stage for the procedures of the Inquisition, the Auto General de Fe clearly broke with the secrecy, the isolation, and the alienation of other inquisitorial activities. It was a ceremony performed in an open space, with the support and attendance of both religious and civil authorities as well as the public. It was widely publicized, prepared with anticipation, and performed as theater to highlight the results achieved by the Inquisition. In short, the Auto General constituted a social arena in which power, religion, and entertainment (tinged with certain morbidity) were simultaneously present. All these elements interacted with people's public and private lives, since the entire society participated in one way or another. This is why Maqueda Abreu correctly contends that the Auto General was the element that essentially defined the peculiarity of the Holy Office of the Inquisition and made it the unique institution it was. It was because the Auto General de Fe was so spectacular that it made an impact on the broader society.[45]

In the conduct of an Auto General, we can appreciate the hybrid nature of the tribunal of the Inquisition—a religious tribunal under the control of the Crown. It had its own prisons and a self-contained judicial bureaucracy in charge of a systematic procedure for persecuting and punishing religious and moral deviations, but it did not administer the full range of sentences itself. Since the Church was not allowed to kill, the Inquisition had to release its worst prisoners to the secular arm. And in the Auto General de Fe, all the forces that shaped the tribunal and its struggle to control religious belief and moral actions appeared in public to reinforce their commitment and support.

Fifty Days in Advance: Preparation

It has already been pointed out that prisoners, especially those tried under the Complicidad Grande, were able to deploy individual and collective strategies for delaying or confounding the progress of their trials while in the prisons of the Lima tribunal. They established communication channels, challenged the expected isolation of Inquisition trials, delayed the resolutions of their trials by revoking and altering the content of their confessions, and plotted and provided unreliable information to bring Old Christians to the cells. According to the tribunal's own documents, the prisoners' strategies also interfered with the preparations for an Auto General. For this reason, the Lima tribunal kept the decisions about the Complicidad Grande sentences and the organization of the ceremony under wraps.[46] It was not until December 1, 1638, that the tribunal issued the formal notice announcing the celebration of the 1639 Auto General.[47]

As we have established in earlier chapters, the Portuguese New Christians exerted some degree of agency during the Complicidad Grande trials. Their knowledge of African languages (owing to Portuguese participation in the slave trade) allowed the prisoners to elaborate a communication channel between themselves and the Afro-Peruvians that excluded others and to use the Afro-Peruvians as messengers between cells and also to communicate with people outside. The tribunal, aiming to prevent the use of strategies by the prisoners and to avoid delays and detours to the celebration its officials had planned, had to find a way to break off the communication between the prisoners and the Afro-Peruvians. Montesinos knew of this effort and reported on it as follows: "Before publishing the auto, all the blacks who served in the prisons were locked up, in a place where they could not hear, know, or find out about the publication, so they would not give the news to the prisoners, even though the Inquisition takes pride in its newly arrived black *bozales* . . . They were *ladinos* to the Portuguese, since they had brought them from Guinea they knew their languages and that helped them a lot."[48]

In other words, even though the Lima tribunal had newly imported African slaves who had not met the Portuguese New Christians prior to their trials of faith, officials still considered it necessary to confine the Africans in places where they could not learn of the plans for the upcoming Auto. Separating the slaves was intended to prevent the disclosure of confidential information by the Afro-Peruvians to the Portuguese New Christians. With this precaution in place, the preparation of the ceremony began on December 2, 1638.

The celebration required that cases be prepared and made ready for the assignment of sentences, that adequate funds be secured, and that a special area or tablado for the performance to come be constructed. It also required informing and gaining the support of the civil and religious authorities as well as the advance broadcasting of the event to a large audience. In the last quarter of the sixteenth century, the viceroy announced that the city was responsible for the expense and also that wood kept from a previous ceremony could be reutilized. For lack of money, previous ceremonies of the Lima tribunal had been performed at the cemetery or indoors. The cabildo and the city's merchants had contributed money to construct the tablado for the Auto of 1625.[49] It is also recorded in the Lima cabildo's proceedings that there must be steps taken to ensure that wives of its members had assigned seats to attend the ceremony, with enough room to include an additional woman (it could be the mother, daughter, or sister of the wife). The same held for members of the merchants' guild and their wives.[50]

In 1639 the situation was clearly different. The tribunal had funds obtained from the property confiscations connected to the Complicidad Grande trials and could host an impressive celebration. The historian René Millar Carvacho says that in 1639 the seizures totaled 1,297,410 pesos. However, he also explains that the tribunal had to comply with obligations previously contracted by the detainees and pay off pending charges, plus provide for the prisoners' care and food during the trials. In examining financial records up to 1649, Millar Carvacho concludes that only 31 percent of the value of confiscated assets entered the coffers of the Inquisition and gives the sum of 401,124 pesos and 6.5 reales for the closing balance of the Complicidad Grande confiscations. Millar Carvacho also clarifies that Philip IV, once he had been informed of the proceedings and the confiscations, requested from the Lima tribunal the restitution to the royal treasury of the monies that body had paid out in the past for tribunal salaries. While he has not found evidence of compliance with this royal instruction, the Lima tribunal did send 48,000 pesos to the Suprema in Madrid. The rest remained in the Lima office.[51]

The tribunal merged the proceeds from the confiscations with its other assets and invested them. During the second half of the seventeenth century, the investments generated an annual income of 40,000 pesos, making Lima one of the healthiest (financially speaking) tribunals of the Holy Office, fully independent from the royal treasury. As noted elsewhere, it had been stipulated since 1572 that the inquisitor's annual remuneration was 3,000 pesos, and between late 1630 and early 1631 the prior of the Dominicans (seconded by those of the Jesuits, San Agustín, and La Merced) offered to pay tribunal salaries because they had not been paid in the previous two years.[52] Thus, it is clear that the impact of the Great Complicity trials on the finances of the Lima tribunal was drastic. Although the trials of 1635–1639 were clearly exceptional in many ways, two facts deserve special attention: the small number of victims who received death sentences is not directly proportional to the historical relevance of the events, and the trials had such a sweeping economic effect that the financing of the Lima branch of the Holy Office subsequently became independent of the royal treasury.

In spite of Millar's finding that less than a third of the value of the confiscated assets remained in possession of the Lima tribunal, officials could still afford a large celebration in 1639. The expenses began with the construction of the tablado (the central stage), a common element in Autos Generales. The tablado was rectangular, of considerable height and variable dimensions, and sometimes exceeded one hundred by two hundred feet.[53] The tablado was built and mounted in the plaza and dismantled immediately after the ceremony. Francisco Bethencourt and other historians have studied carpenters' notes related to the construction of tablados. According to this historian, after examining materials preserved at the National Library in Lisbon "we learn that there were secret passages for the inquisitors, leading directly to their palace or to the church behind, so that they would not have to enter by the same route as the prisoners; there were also internal rooms where special guests and the members of the tribunal could wash and eat during the ceremony; and there were special exit passages that brought the condemned to the place of execution."[54] They must have anticipated a long ceremony. Unfortunately, I have not located equivalent information for the Lima tablado, but it is logical to suppose similar pragmatic aspects. Montesinos mentions a *passadiço* (passage) but does not describe it as a secret tunnel; from his description it evokes a covered hallway that facilitated circulation during the summer celebration. Medina mentions *pasadizos* in the stage of the 1625 Auto, but it seems a transitional area rather than a secret passage. Portocarrero, on the other hand, mentions a pasadizo in the viceregal palace, although Lohman Villena says that Portocarrero made a mistake in the palace location.[55]

In the months prior to the ceremony, some prisoners of the Complicidad Grande, overhearing some random construction noises, concluded that a tablado was being built and erroneously inferred that the celebration of an Auto General was imminent. Local workers joined in preparing for the ceremony, among them carpenters, tailors, and candle makers. The urban population awaited the celebration with great anticipation, most likely whetted by what they could see of the construction of the main stage.

Nonetheless, the tribunal attempted to keep the event, or at least its details, secret until the special day. Juan de Moncada was hired to prepare the badges, sambenitos (penitential garments), *corozas*, crosses, and effigies. In addition to swearing to secrecy, Moncada's assistants had to relocate to the house of the prison's steward within the tribunal facilities so that none of the public could see what they were crafting until the day of the ceremony.[56] Also, the tribunal relied on artisans with whom the institution had worked before, men who understood its regulations. Fray Buenaventura de Salinas y Córdova noted that the City of Kings had more than three hundred carpenters in 1630. From among them, the Lima tribunal chose Bartolomé Calderón to build the tablados for the Autos Generales of 1625 and 1639.[57] Eighteen workers, two of them construction masters and sixteen of them Afro-Peruvian workers, participated in the erection of the tablado for the 1639 Auto General, which measured about 36 feet by almost 130 feet.[58]

At the laterals of the tablado, two benches served to organize the ceremonial space. One was the bench of honor, where the authorities sat; the other was the bench of infamy, for the prisoners.[59] The bench of honor consisted of ascending steps, with elaborate decoration at each level, and an abundance of symbols that represented the Church, the Inquisition, and the monarchy. The bench of infamy was also a series of steps, these dreadfully decorated with images of horrendous demons.[60] In practical terms, this distribution of the ceremonial space facilitated the unfolding of the ceremony and the circulation of its participants. At the center of the stage, an altar formed a sacred transitional area between the two benches; here members of the secular clergy and functionaries spoke and prisoners abjured.

In addition to its practical functions, the distribution of the space on the tablado served as the symbolic theater of the Auto General. It presented for the viewer in the clearest terms an interaction between two opposing and irreconcilable forces, inquisitors and heretics, as Francisco Bethencourt has pointed out. The viewer saw "on one side justice, purity, and divine inspiration, on the other, heresy, impurity, and diabolic inspiration."[61] And throughout the ceremony it was made evident that the former had triumphed over the latter. Beyond the basic separation of purity and impurity, the staircases, and those who sat at each level, reflected the hierarchies of power and punishment that were the essence of the Auto. On the bench of honor, the distribution of the seats reflected distinctions among the highest authorities, both civil and religious.[62] At the highest rows sat those who held the positions of greatest political and religious preeminence. Within each row, the central seats were the most important, and the seats to the right of center followed. On the bench of infamy, at the highest rows sat those who were going to receive the harshest punishments.

For each Auto General, there was a unique arrangement of the principals: the monarchy and its representatives, the local authorities, the organizations of civil justice, the Inquisition, and the Church.[63] For the Auto General performed in 1639 in Lima, several benches were needed to accommodate the large number of attendees. The highest bench was for the Viceroy Conde de Chinchón and the inquisitors, hosts of the ceremony. At lower levels were seats assigned to the viceroy's wife, the couple's ten-year-old son, and the wives of audiencia members. Other benches were for bureaucrats of a lesser rank and their spouses, and the additional plain seats were available to members of the religious orders and Lima residents. Twenty-two trees planted for the occasion protected the gathered officials and the public from the sun of the Peruvian summer.[64]

The viceroy Conde de Chinchón sat at the top center, escorted by an inquisitor at each side: Juan de Mañozca y Zamora at his right, Andrés Juan Gaitán at his left. The other two inquisitors, Antonio de Castro y del Castillo and León de Alcayaga Lartaun, sat next to Mañozca and Gaitán. Members of the civil court, the ecclesiastic and secular cabildos, and other organizations, including institutions of higher education, sat toward the bench's edges.[65] Within the most powerful men, those sitting highest, minor variations in the ornamentation of their seats differentiated the most powerful among them. In anticipation of a long ceremony, the viceroy's seat had three yellow pillows, two of them for his feet. His wife's seat was covered in yellow fabric and had a pillow of the same color. The black velvet cushion on Mañozca y Zamora's seat signaled that he was a member of the Supreme Council of the Inquisition. In addition to providing comfort for the authorities attending a long spectacle, the visual combination of elevation and chromatic differentiation signaled to onlookers which authorities were present, and where they were seated. The remaining seats were adorned with silk but had no padded support, according to Montesinos, although the chronicler indicates that the seats for cabildo members had eye-catching rugs, something unseen at Autos before.[66] Of course, the physical arrangements also conveyed relative positions of authority; for example, a bishop's status was lower than that of a viceroy, but higher than that of a governor. But the hierarchical elements, distinctive as they might have been, also embodied the interactions between the state and the Church and the collaboration of the regular clergy, secular orders, and the Inquisition in bringing the Auto General to pass. Occasionally, an Auto General triggered discussions, tensions, and negotiations as to the physical arrangements. If someone disagreed with the arrangement, that person would probably avoid attending it.[67] The allocation of seats on the bench of honor was a striking instance of the unity in the struggle against heresy; however, this unity coalition was not a homogeneous one and was far from perfect harmony, but the Auto General did demand that sometimes conflicting institutions and personalities achieve some degree of equilibrium and consensus in moving forward with the celebration.

Like the bench of honor, the seats at the bench of infamy also displayed a hierarchy, in this case related to the severity of the offenses, the outcomes of the trials, and the tabulation of the punishments. The Inquisition applied scaled punishments according to the characteristics of the offence. In general, the spectrum of punishments included public repentance, reprimands, formal abjurations, derogatory hats and garments to be worn in public after the reconciliation and hung at the church upon the death of the offender, lashes, exile, submission to the galleys, confiscation of property, and death at the stake. At the Auto General, those who were sentenced to die sat in the higher rows, exposed to the public eye throughout the entire ceremony, and those who had committed minor offenses and been received for reconciliation sat in the lower rows.

A Journey of Collective Devotion

The celebration of the Auto General held on Sunday, January 23, 1639, was fairly long, but considerably shorter than some of the annual celebrations that might last for eight or nine days. The Auto officially began on the afternoon of Saturday, January 22, with the procession of the Green Cross, and it ended on the morning of Monday, January 24, when the last prisoners received their punishments.[68] An Auto General of this length was not unusual.[69] The Green Cross, symbol of the tribunal of Holy Office of the Inquisition, was kept at the main house of the tribunal and taken out at 4:00 p.m. on Saturday to begin its journey at the head of the procession to the altar of the tablado on the central plaza. Ironically, the altar faced the Street of Merchants, where the Portuguese New Christians had had their stores prior to the trials of faith.[70] In this procession were the members of the tribunal (familiares, commissaries) together with other members of the Church, the religious orders, the local nobility, the governor of the Chile Captaincy, and other secular authorities. As they walked, the people sang a hymn, accompanied by musicians. It was a long procession. The members of the religious orders alone covered three blocks with their column. The procession was another visual display of how the secular and religious authorities marched together in the struggle against heresy.[71] As at any festival, social hierarchy was expressed in the relative position of the various participants in the procession; those opening the caravan were of a rank lower than the people closing it. The processional order, like the assignment of seats on the steps of the benches on the tablado, sometimes provoked arguments that exposed rivalries and disputes among participants.[72]

That Saturday night, in the prisons of the Lima tribunal, thirteen men learned that they would be burned at the stake. Two of them, Enrique de Paz and Manuel de Espinosa, asked for one more hearing and begged to be admitted for reconciliation; the inquisitors who heard them agreed to spare their lives.[73] Another man, Rodrigo Váez Pereira, also tried to offer a last confession and asked for reconciliation; but the tribunal was not satisfied with it, and Váez Pereira's sentence remained as issued.[74] The eleven men who would die the next day had their last meal.[75] The other sentences, as usual, would be announced later. After the meal, preparation of the rest of the prisoners for the ceremony, those with minor offenses and lesser sentences, began. In the meantime, upstanding leaders of the civil society arrived at the tribunal house and volunteered to escort the eleven prisoners and the single effigy, which on this occasion was carried by two *indios principales*, and to publicly express in this way their support for the task of the Inquisition.[76]

Early Sunday morning, the procession of the prisoners, also known as the procession of infamy, began. Its itinerary covered the central streets of the city, where Lima residents eagerly observed the spectacle. Although he does not provide a count of how many attended, Montesinos explains that five days in advance benches and platforms indicating the route of the penitents' procession were placed at the side of these streets, and he later adds that the audience also occupied adjacent balconies and terraces. Some sense of the size of the watching public can be appreciated in the following fragment: "On the streets where the procession passed, the number of people gathered to see the penitents was so great that it is not possible to determine a total. Suffice it to say that five days in advance benches with a backrest were put in place . . . and behind them platforms on one side [of the street], and [also] on another street where the people were, aside from those who were on the balconies, and windows, and terraces. . . . In many parts there were two sets of platforms and in the plaza three."[77]

As the prisoners left their cells, they received *insignias* (badges) to be worn during the ceremony. An atmosphere of grief and bereavement, enhanced with bells ringing from the cathedral and the other churches, marked the exit of the penitents and the initiation of the journey. Crosses and members of the clergy opened the caravan, and infantry squadrons provided escort.[78] The prisoners followed next, with their distinctive garments, badges, and candles, all under the custody of soldiers and accompanied by friars. Finally, members of the tribunal closed the procession of infamy. In this act everyone participated, from the tribunal secretary to its constable and janitor. One official carried a silver coffer containing the sentences.

The penitents were walked in a processional order that reflected the seriousness of their offenses and the severity of their assigned punishments. Those condemned for sorcery and bigamy walked first, and those accused of heresy followed, wearing sambenitos and corozas and holding Green Crosses. Following the prisoners who had committed minor offenses were the crypto-Jews, the most heinous of heretics. Those whose efforts to abjure and receive reconciliation to the Catholic faith had been successful preceded those to be released to the secular arm. In Montesinos's words: "[Here came] the Judaizers with their sambenitos, and those who would be beaten with thick ropes [tied to] their throats. The last were those to be released in person [to the state], with corozas and sambenitos [decorated with] flames and demons in varied forms, of snakes and dragons, and green Crosses in their hands."[79]

The varied colors and patterns imprinted on the derogatory garments represented different types of sentences. For example, the corozas and sambenitos of those to be executed were decorated with flames, and even the effigies were dressed with sambenitos painted with flames on one side and with the name, offense, and residence of the evoked person on the other.[80] Those who would receive lashes had ropes tied around their necks, with knots symbolizing the number (each knot equivalent to one hundred) of lashes they would receive at the Auto. As they anticipated the ceremony, those who saw the procession could recognize these varied colors and patterns as markers and thus infer the outcome of the ceremony for the passing prisoners.

Let us consider what a spectator might have perceived while watching the procession of infamy pass by. Again, there was a great contrast between the visual codes and display passing before him and the secrecy attached to the Inquisition trials themselves. By deciphering the codes, the local population could not only anticipate the outcome of individual trials but also see into the secret proceedings of the trials that had led to the Auto General. Given the long trajectory of the Inquisition trial from imprisonment to sentencing, we have to remember that the prisoners would have spent months, even years, in dungeons. Many spectators would see people they knew for the first time in months or years and of necessity witness the effects of their imprisonment. It may have been for many years that a prisoner's contact with the outer world, and very likely with the other prisoners in the procession, had been forbidden, or at least reduced to clandestine communications. So narrow was the opportunity for such contact that it was a punishable offense; if such communications were found out, both the prisoner and anyone who might have assisted in accomplishing them were punished.[81]

Many prisoners had endured physical and psychological torment and had probably overheard other inmates' ordeals or agonies. Some inmates, like father and son Juan de Valencia and Juan de Acosta, were members of the same family and received sentences at the same ceremony. Others might have lost relatives who had died during earlier trials, or recognize relatives scheduled to die in the same trial. Some had committed suicide, like Manuel de Paz Estravagante, who was imprisoned in August 1636 and killed himself in November of the same year. Others had lost consciousness during sessions at the torture chambers and died soon after, like Antonio Morón, who was imprisoned in November 1635 and died in March 1638, and his sister-in-law Mencía de Luna, imprisoned in November 1635, who died captive in September 1638.[82] Their respective spouses, Mayor de Luna (Morón's wife and Mencía's sister) and Enrique

Núñez de Espinosa (Mencía's husband), had remained in the Lima prisons until they were reconciled at the 1639 Auto General, as was Isabel Antonia, daughter of Antonio Morón and Mayor de Luna. Montesinos says that Mayor de Luna was a woman "seemingly older than 60 years, although she denied being 40."[83] Now, her husband and sister dead, she was going to be reconciled at the same time as her daughter. At the same ceremony, Mayor de Luna's son-in-law, Rodrigo Váez Pereira, was to be released to the secular arm.

In general, the members of the Complicidad Grande punished in the 1639 Auto General had spent three or four years in the dungeons of the Inquisition. Traces of their suffering and lack of human contact, along with their distinctive garments, dramatically transformed their physical appearance. They looked eerily the same *and* different. They were perfect targets for the disgusted gaze and morbid curiosity created by such a human spectacle. Although Montesinos says nothing about the physical appearance of Jorge de Silva, a man from Estremoz in Portugal who walked with a sambenito and a rope around his neck, we can assume that his years in prison had taken their effect. In Silva's case, the sambenito was for a lifetime, like sentence to exile or the galleys, and he would also face property confiscation and physical punishment. Also in the procession was Juan Rodríguez de Silva, the brother of Jorge de Silva. When Jorge de Silva was first imprisoned in Lima, he wrote to his brother Juan, then in Panama, exhorting him to appear in front of the Lima tribunal at his own initiative and offer a self-denunciation and a spontaneous confession. Juan had followed his brother's advice, but later in the trial revoked his confession; his responses to the tribunal were viewed as negative, and as a result he was to be released to the secular arm.[84]

The prisoners' physical appearance likely would have been unappealing to the crowd that attended the Auto General. As the procession passed by, it would have left an image that fit very well with the representations of Jews, heretics, and other deviants as contaminating agents in the Christian community, a widespread representation in the Spanish and the Spanish American worlds.[85] According to the historian Rosa M. Acosta, each year on Thursday of Holy Week there departed a procession from the church of San Agustín that featured life-size wooden figures representing the role of Jews in Jesus's death. These figures were usually insulted by people attending the festival.[86] On Saturday night, the burning of Judas was a highlight of the annual celebration.[87]

The structure and content of the Auto General de Fe, rare as the event was in colonial Lima, did share some elements with the annual cycle of religious celebrations. The authorities were the same, the members of the Church were the same, the local population was the same. While the tablado was exclusive to the Auto de Fe ceremony, and the stage was adjusted to its specific purposes and the unfolding of its script, the Auto was still celebrated in the same plaza where people attended many other festivals. But its unique elements were far removed from those others. Most rare and distinctive was the presence of "real Jews," people in their flesh and bones who had been members of regular society and had probably participated in festivals as regular residents of the city, prior to their incarcerations. During the Auto General, they walked in the procession of infamy, sat on the benches wearing derogatory garments, read aloud their statements of abjuration, or underwent public physical punishment (burning at the stake took place in a separate ceremony conducted by civil officers).

From this point of view, the Auto General, in addition to providing closure to individual trials of faith, made real the rites of scorn and destruction that were wrought on the wooden figures that moved in procession during Holy Week. This literal execution, then, was conceptually entrenched in colonial society's religiosity through its expression and repetition each year during the Holy Week festival. Furthermore, masks and effigies representing human beings from present and past times, along with those representing mythological and fantastic characters, were commonly present in parades conducted at religious and civic festivals. The effigies had thus a symbolic and religious power that made the application of punishment to an effigy during the Auto General far from a fiction in the eyes of participants.[88]

Visually, the prisoners' appearance during the Auto General probably confirmed that deviants and heretics were in some way subhuman and did not and could not belong to the society of good Christians. They were ugly, old, sick, and weak. They were appalling and sinful. In the case of repeaters, the Inquisition had offered them mercy, forgiveness, and a second opportunity, but look, the ingrates had wasted it and returned to heresy. What the public saw was a group of disgusting people, accused of deviant behaviors that horrified them— the despicable other, the dehumanized heretic, the horrible deviant. The bitter paradox is that what the audience saw was not what these people had looked like as they had lived in society, regardless of their religious beliefs, but what the tribunal and the trial of faith had made out of them.

Finally, at five in the morning, the last group set out in procession. Here walked the living image of the king (in this case, the viceroy), his court, and people from the local elites.[89] In 1639, a herald and a captain leading a company of harquebusiers opened the procession (Montesinos comments that the captain was sick but did not want to excuse himself). This type of armed company usually had fifty men and would be put in charge of protecting the city during Holy Week, Autos Generales, and other festivities.[90] City knights, members of the consulate, and high-ranking doctors and administrators of the royal colleges and the university, all wearing their special robes, followed the harquebusiers.

Walking also were members of the secular and ecclesiastical cabildos, notaries and secretaries of these governing bodies, judges, and distinguished elements of the Lima aristocracy. In representation of the monarchy, the viceroy Chinchón and his personal guard closed the procession, along with the captain and the company of lancers, usually numbering one hundred men. Finally, the Old Christians who had been falsely denounced in the course of the trials of the Complicidad Grande and were to recover their honor during the Auto marched with the royal delegation. As Montesinos puts it: "And to honor those who emerged free from the testimonies of the Jews, the tribunal agreed that they could be accompanied by their godparents, and His Excellency [the viceroy] assigned for them a place with the City: it was a spectacle of admiration, to see at the same time the truth winning and the punishment of the lie, effects of the Holy Office's rectitude."[91]

This last contingent marched from the viceregal palace to the Holy Office facilities, where the tribunal members were waiting. Moving along with the viceroy and the inquisitors, they took one more walk to the plaza, where the penitents had been already seated. Once everyone was accommodated, the ceremony started. As with other aspects of the Auto General, it is likely that the sequence varied slightly from one tribunal to another, and between the Spanish and Portuguese Inquisitions as well. But we can still describe a basic structure that was usually enacted with only minor alterations or local adjustments.[92] The Auto de Fe began with a Mass, followed by an oath, for which everybody (those at the central stage and those at the plaza and on the balconies as well) uncovered their heads and bent down on their knees. In taking this oath, everybody made a shared pledge in the battle against heresy and committed themselves to support the tribunal of the Inquisition and to exclude heretics from public offices. The oath also legitimized the task of the tribunal, an act that was seconded by the reading of a papal decree from Pio V favoring the institution.

A sermon followed the Mass and the collective oath. Usually, someone associated with the Church but not necessarily involved with the tribunal delivered it. For example, it might be a secular priest or a religious friar. In the 1639 Auto, Joseph de Cisneros, a calificador, gave a sermon dedicated to the viceroy, the ultimate head of the tribunal. The sermon addressed four points in its fifteen folios; it was approved for publication in February, and published during the year of the Auto.[93] In the first chapter, Cisneros discussed the imperial scope of the Church. In the second, he exalted the task and glory of the Holy Office of the Inquisition. He described the role and responsibility of the Church and emphasized the relationship between the biblical patriarchs and the Inquisition: "Moses was the world's first Inquisitor . . . and his authority was so vast, that the princes of the people of God surrendered life to his sentence." This point was intended to bestow both biblical antiquity and divine legitimacy on the tribunal.[94] A third chapter provides a list of inquisitors from the Franciscan and Dominican orders, beginning with Pope Gregory IX and the officers who had jurisdiction over France, Italy, Spain, Germany, and Hungary, including San Pedro Mártir de Verona, the patron saint of the tribunal, and Fray Nicolau Eimeric, who authored the core Inquisition procedure manual.

In the fourth chapter of his sermon, Cisneros changed direction to specifically attack Judaism and Jewish perfidy. Supporting his words with biblical references, he discussed Jews' recalcitrance in their refusal to accept Christ; the fact that destiny had left them with no governor, priest, or place of worship; and their deserved sentence: to be embraced by flames.[95] Historical evidence external to the tribunal presents a similarity with Cisneros's choice of words: "Twenty-three Jews, all Portuguese" wrote Fray Diego de Ocaña, referring to those who had received sentences at the 1605 Lima Auto;[96] "Eleven Jews were taken to be burned, and one in a statue," wrote the Lima chronicler about the 1639 ceremony.[97] It is interesting to note, as Bethencourt has, that in the sermons given at the Autos de Fe there are plenty of references to "Jews" rather than "New Christians."[98] Let us remember that after 1492 in Spain and after 1497 in Portugal there were no Jews, at least officially. Those of Jewish descent who had, either by will or by force, converted to Christianity were labeled conversos or New Christians.

Following Bethencourt, the recurrent references to Jews in sermons given at Autos de Fe invite us to question if there is any incongruence between the spoken rhetoric at the ceremony and the written word in the printed sermon. This author also mentions that sermons from different ceremonies are similar and have roots in "medieval anti-Jewish polemic."[99] In my view, these references provide evidence of another important disparity: the gap between the everyday perception of the world in elite and popular culture after the conversions and the formal act of religious conversion. It is probable that, in the view of those who spoke at the Auto de Fe and those who wrote about the ceremony (like Ocaña), the sincerity of the conversions of the New Christians was not even a probability. Indeed, the formal conversions were overlooked in the construction of the sermons—instead of questioning the sincerity of the conversions, the sermons given at Autos simply ignored them. The tribunal had located and uncovered the "real" Jews and offered them opportunities to confess, repent, and reintegrate themselves into the Christian community. The viceregal authority, together with the Holy Office, created a colossal theatrical display in order to punish a few stubborn, untrustworthy, and ever-resistant Jews who were living in colonial Lima.

The Heart of the Auto de Fe: Sentences and Punishment

When all who had marched in the procession were seated, and the Mass and the sermon completed, the core of the ceremony began. This was the proclamation of the cases in summary form and the assignment of sentences. In the 1639 Auto General in Lima, seventy-two prisoners received punishment and one prisoner was punished in effigy. The sentence for two men and a woman who had broken the secrecy of the prisons of the Inquisition was exile from the city.[100] A bigamist received one hundred lashes and was sent to the galleys. Six women accused of sorcery received assorted punishments that included temporary exile from their hometowns, whippings, and abjuration of their practices.[101] Seven men also abjured, under suspicion of believing in the Law of Moses. Each received lashes and suffered either exile or conviction to the galleys, and some also had to pay the Holy Office for their trial expenses. Two women and forty-two men, including the two men who had been reconciled only the night before the Auto, were made to put on the sambenito.

Each penitent had to walk to the altar in the middle of the tablado, escorted by the steward (alcaide) of the secret prisons. The penitent had to make a reverence to the cross and salute the inquisitors. With the penitent exposed to everyone's eyes, a priest read a summary of his or her case that included a synopsis of the offenses and the concluding remarks of the tribunal's discussions of the case. Each of those who were to be reconciled held a candle and was made to read aloud the statement of abjuration. This was a speech that expressed the rejection of any heresy against the Catholic faith, the promise never to return to such practices, and the promise not to join other heretics. Further, the abjuration included the commitment to reveal information about heresies and heretics to the tribunal. Those who were reconciled also received some combination of other penalties that included whippings, assignment to the galleys, exile, perpetual imprisonment in the facilities of the Seville Inquisition, and confiscation of their properties.[102] The worth of the sequestered properties ranged from as little as 136 pesos and 7 reales to as much as 381,342 pesos 7 reales.[103] After a lunch break, the celebration continued, and the people who were reconciled or who had minor punishments now received them.

About 3:00 in the afternoon the reading of the sentences ended, and those about to die at the stake were released to the authorities of the city. The secular officers proceeded with a quick trial and a sentence of death at the stake. This final procession moved from the central plaza to the Plaza de Acho, almost eight blocks away across the Rimac River.[104] The prisoners had two rows of soldiers alongside them "to guard them from the tumultuous crowd that went to see them, which was uncountable"; friars making a last attempt to preach to the prisoners also followed this last caravan.[105] The authorities, including the notary, waited until the prisoners turned into ashes, and wrote a testimony recording the event.[106]

In his manual for inquisitors, written in the fourteenth century, Nicolau Eimeric said: "Burning a heretic is not only for [his/her] own good, but also in particular for the benefit and spiritual edification of the Catholic peoples."[107] As he witnessed the final punishment of those executed in Lima in 1639, Fernando de Montesinos set down a few words about how these men faced their own deaths. The deaths did not represent the idea of good death upheld by honorable members of society, as has been studied by many scholars.[108] Rather, those who perished after the Auto General went through a "bad death," the one suffered by heretics and criminals.[109]

In the resolution of the Complicidad Grande trials, eleven men and one effigy were released to the secular arm for burning at the stake. They were Antonio de Vega, Antonio de Espinosa, Diego López de Fonseca, Francisco Maldonado de Silva, Juan Rodríguez de Silva, Juan de Azevedo, Luis de Lima, Manuel Bautista Pérez, Rodrigo Váez Pereira, Sebastián Duarte, and Tomé Quaresma. Manuel de Paz Estravagante, who had hanged himself in the Lima secret prisons, was released in effigy.[110] Some of these men had relatives who were reconciled on the same day, for example, two siblings of Luis de Lima, Juan and Tomás. Others had siblings, cousins, or in-laws who reconciled, perhaps even wives.

Obviously, each individual reacted differently. In his Relación del Auto de la Fe, our narrator says that Antonio de Espinosa expressed signs of remorse, but that they were not believable.[111] According to Montesinos, Diego López de Fonseca was so stricken that he seemed almost unconscious throughout the entire ceremony and needed to be carried forward to listen to his own sentence, unable even to hold up his head.[112] Francisco Maldonado de Silva openly acknowledged he was dying as a Jew, and as such embraced his punishment.[113] Another man, Luis de Lima, cried and regretted having committed perjury against three men out of personal animosity and publicly asked for forgiveness.[114]

Fernando de Montesinos also took note of how those about to die related to each other. Manuel Bautista Pérez projected an image of majesty, severity, and self-confidence; and he even assessed what other prisoners had done during their trials of faith.[115] According to Montesinos, Pérez looked approvingly at his brother-in-law Sebastián Duarte, who was also about to die, and expressed disapproval with his eyes at those relatives who had confessed and accepted the reconciliation. Sebastián Duarte seemed deeply loyal and in tune with his brother-in-law Pérez when they greeted one another and seemed repentant when he saw the latter dead.[116] Montesinos wrote that the physician Tomé Quaresma also wanted to ask for forgiveness from God and the Church, but changed his mind when he caught the look in Manuel Bautista Pérez's eyes.[117]

In Montesinos's remarks about these seven men together, an interesting point emerges.[118] Even though some of them regretted the perjuries they had committed against others as they approached the end of their lives, these men neither claimed innocence of the heresies of which they were accused nor expressed a change in their religious beliefs. Hence, it is very likely that all these men died in their own minds as Jews, whether they verbally expressed it or not. At least that is the assumption Fernando de Montesinos conveys to the reader: that each died impenitent (*murió impenitente*). The Lima chronicler, on the other hand, mentions that only one man was burned alive because he would not accept conversion (implying that the other ones had done so) and that this caused everyone great sadness. He did not provide penitents' names when describing the Auto General, but presumably he was referring to Francisco Maldonado de Silva, the man who according to Montesinos was burned alive.[119]

From Montesinos as well as other sources, we see a completely different reaction in Rodrigo Váez Pereira, the man mentioned in the introduction to this book, when he faced the stake (his wife Isabel Antonia was reconciled at the ceremony). According to the friar who stood by his side, these were Rodrigo Váez Pereira's words: "'Up to now I have been a Jew and from now on I am a Christian.' . . . Rodrigo Váez Pereira turned toward Señor Tomás Quaresma who was at his side . . . 'for what we have been it is not so much to pay, and we trust in Jesus who is the one who is going to save us.'"[120] Unlike the men just discussed, Rodrigo Váez Pereira acknowledged that he had been a crypto-Jew, and stated that from the present moment on he would be a Christian. With this statement, he made it known that he had finally admitted all his faults, repented, and sincerely accepted Christianity. His soul was now saved from the eternal suffering of the afterlife, unlike the souls of the others who did not die as true Christians. Following the suggestion of the friars who were escorting him, Váez Pereira talked to the other penitents and encouraged them to follow his example of repentance and (now) sincere conversion. Unfortunately, none of the testimonies that address Váez Pereira's conversion report how the others responded. Rodrigo Váez Pereira did what the Inquisition wanted him to do, but the others did not follow his path. The last to be burned was the effigy of Manuel de Paz Estravagante, who had killed himself in his cell. But the event was not complete. There remained an epilogue.

The last sacred act was the rehabilitation of those Old Christians who had been falsely accused by prisoners of the Complicidad Grande. Among the falsely accused were Santiago del Castillo, Alonso Sánchez Chaparro, Antonio de los Santos, Ambrosio de Morales, Francisco Sotelo, Pedro de Soria Arcilla, and Andrés Muñiz.[121] When the ceremony ended and the crowd that attended had left, the reconciled prisoners were taken to the facilities of the Holy Office. On the following day, Monday, January 24, there were more abjurations, explanations of the dangers of being a relapse, and descriptions of the trials that would result should an abjuration be violated. According to Montesinos, the streets were as crowded at eight that morning as they usually were about eleven: the crowd had come to see the penitents. Physical punishments were applied later on Monday afternoon, once again preceded by a procession that departed from the tribunal facilities and walked through the central streets of Lima. The tribunal prohibited the circulation of horses and carts on these paths during the procession so that crowds on foot could follow the prisoners to be scourged one more time.[122]

Despite the dedication of the Lima tribunal in bringing cases related to the Complicidad Grande to the 1639 Auto General, not all cases ended there. The tribunal set free three more men in February.[123] Enrique Jorge Tavares's trial was suspended in 1639 because the tribunal believed that the prisoner was insane. He was relocated to the San Andrés hospital in 1648, an institution that also received mental health patients.[124] Other cases dragged on for years because the tribunal could not agree on a proper sentence or had tabled the cases while officials waited for specific instructions from the Suprema. But the 1639 Auto General had made space in the crowded prisons. In the years just after the ceremony, the tribunal was able to take in and try fourteen prisoners from Cusco, most of whom confessed quickly and were reconciled. The office of the Lima Inquisition, which had reported overcrowded cells during the Complicidad Grande trials, let the Suprema in Madrid know in 1648 that Manuel Henríquez was then the only prisoner. There had been additional cases and new prisoners after the 1639 Auto, but those cases had been resolved by the time of the 1648 report.[125] To the best of our knowledge, the last two people to be sentenced of those imprisoned between 1635 and 1639 were Manuel Henríquez and Mencía de Luna. Henríquez had an extremely long process that lasted for an additional twenty-five years.

In 1664, again on January 23, which this time fell in midweek, Lima celebrated another Auto General. In the opening procession don Manuel de Benavídes (son of the viceroy Conde de Santisteban) carried the banner, followed by knights of Santiago and members of the other religious orders. Twenty-one penitents received sentences in the 1664 ceremony: one was released to the secular arm, another two were released as effigies, three with sambenitos, and two were punished for bigamy, along with other renegade friars and sorcerers. The man burned was the same Manuel Henríquez, the petty peddler born in

Lamego, who had had a trial in Coimbra in the 1620s and was imprisoned in Lima in 1635. According to the declaration he had made at the beginning of his Lima trial, he was then thirty-four years old; when he died at the stake in 1664, he was sixty-three—twenty-nine years had passed. Although he had persisted in revocations and claims of his own insanity for decades; historical evidence indicates that Manuel Henríquez died accepting his punishment as fair.[126] An effigy representing Mencía de Luna, the woman who had traveled from Seville and arrived in Peru in 1629 in the same fleet that carried the viceroy Chinchón, was also burned at the 1664 Auto in Lima; she had died twenty-six years earlier (in 1638) soon after her first session at the torture chambers.[127] Her husband Enrique Núñez de Espinosa had received a sentence of reconciliation at the 1639 Auto General (his second trial in Lima; the first one had been suspended).[128]

Catholic indoctrination included description of the dangers of heresies and the ultimate fate that awaited persistent heretics. But the Auto General de Fe was unique in that it provided the most visual and tangible confirmation of the message. Heretics were a disease that had to be purged and expunged from the social body. As a permanently alert guardian, the Inquisition was always in the shadows, collecting and processing information, aiming to uncover hidden heretics. When the members of the tribunal considered it right to do so, they imprisoned those suspected of deviations and initiated trials against them. Through those trials, the Inquisition attempted to rehabilitate the heretics by placing them in an isolated space so they could examine their consciences and by offering them the remedies of confession, the relief of repentance, and the hope of a second chance. But on occasion, such treatment did not render the expected outcome. Stubborn heretics refused to confess, and deviants previously pardoned relapsed; these heretics were beyond cure. Therefore, on extraordinary occasions, the Inquisition publicly displayed its full strength and power and exercised violence upon irrecoverable heretics. Ecclesiastical and civil authorities participated, and members of the broader society witnessed.

The frequency of Autos Generales in Lima was, by all means, low, as vast scholarship has demonstrated. But as John Lewis Gaddis has noted, "the frequency of events is inversely proportional to their intensity."[129] The actual number of people released to the secular arm was small, but the intensity of the event was amplified to the extreme through theatrical performance and broad participation. The interpretation of the historical meaning of an infrequent but highly dramatic ceremony, therefore, must combine quantitative information and contextual analysis.

This brings us to the reasons for studying the Auto General of 1639 as a singular event. It was exceptional, yes, but at the same time it provides a great number of lenses for looking into the practices of the Lima tribunal. The questions crucial to understanding the history of the tribunal are not the frequency of trials and the number of executions but their historical context, cultural purpose, and indirect impact on the society in which it was an actor. In this chapter, I have focused on the plight of the condemned during the Lima 1639 Auto General to demonstrate this point. The impact of inquisitorial activities was not related to numbers but to the way in which the Inquisition, as an institution, articulated its repressive goals and punitive practices.

Autos Generales de Fe allowed inquisitors to showcase their successes in front of the public whose interests they served. Since in the past the Lima tribunal had had financial difficulties that prevented the organization of larger celebrations, the Lima inquisitors, newly funded by confiscated property, organized a colossal event in 1639 with more than seventy prisoners receiving an array of sentences, including the eleven men burned at the stake. Even though most of their work was conducted in secrecy, inquisitors were part of Lima's social and intellectual life, recognized members of a royal tribunal. They also participated in ceremonies other than the Autos, such as the regular annual celebrations of the Christian calendar, the festival of the patron saint, and other secular public festivities. The Auto General, rare as it was in the seventeenth century, was most assuredly part of the broader context of religious and civic celebrations that were frequent in colonial cities. It did not function in isolation from its broader symbolic and social context. As an event, the 1639 Auto General de Fe in Lima was meant to be an exemplary punishment, a display of the Inquisition's reach and power, and a deterrent to anyone who might deviate from Christian doctrine or practice.

Through its secret procedures the tribunal had removed the false dress to expose crypto-Jews for public punishment. At the Auto General, the appearance of "real Jews" in the city streets, participating in every step of the ceremony, was unusual. Even the effigies that were punished represented concrete individuals who had lived in Lima at some point in their lives. Although the Auto General heightened the focus on Jews to the extreme, the presence of Jews as symbols was already part of society. They had been included, though figuratively, in the regular cycle of the religious fiestas and in the discourse of the sermons given at Autos de Fe.

The display of power and its deterrent effect worked precisely because the authorities applied death at the stake to a low number of heinous offenders in front of large crowds. The elaborate preparation and anticipation of the ceremony created the necessary excitement and a climate for the celebration of bad death. The religious and civil ornamentation, the derogatory garments, and the punitive symbols on display in the processions enhanced the visual power of the ceremony, and thereby its intensity. Finally, the climactic phases of the event and the dire words spoken by the various authorities charged with conducting the ceremony—even the last words of the victims—resounded to the drama and magnitude of the sacred ceremony.

Conclusion

As I stated in the introduction, I have situated my work on the Peruvian Inquisition in the analytical tension between a quantitative and a qualitative approach, and to do so I have focused deliberately on a few cases—not a full representation perhaps, but only in the statistical sense—taken on by the Lima Tribunal of the Inquisition in the seventeenth century. I chose this focus, off-center by definition, because I believe that the activities and events surrounding these cases are so singular and so dramatic that they merit in their own right an empirical basis for analysis, which is the study I have presented here. I have set these stories within the larger rationale of the institution, with the intent to achieve both tension and balance: between the study of institutional practices (highly standardized) and the study of individual lives (clearly unrepeatable). In this way, I tried to retrieve the experiences, inhuman and human as I found them, as they are reflected in these unusual trials.

The Inquisition was established to keep watch on the entire Christian population, first in the Peninsula and later in the colonies, but from its inception it operated under important constraints. First, its aim was not to imprison or eliminate large numbers of people but rather to eradicate certain practices considered heretical or unacceptable according to Christian religion and morality, and its hallmark was a clearly defined protocol. Second, there were significant external constraints in Lima, among them a chronic shortage of personnel and an inadequate number of cells for housing prisoners. These factors, along with the many regulations under which it operated, support the notion that the Inquisition, in spite of its potential reach, did not anticipate large numbers of detainees. The Lima tribunal operated between 1570 and 1820, and following modern scholarship, only forty-eight people died as a result of a trial of faith.

Offenses were precisely outlined and scaled as to severity, and there were published procedures for bringing offenders and suspects to trial and punishment. The latter also instructed officials to offer the accused opportunities for introspection, confession of offenses, and reinsertion into the Christian community. Since the tribunal had at its disposal many lesser levels of punishment, it is reasonable to expect that only a few of the accused would ever come to stand before the tribunal at formal trial, and that even fewer would receive severe and irreversible punishment—execution. Indeed, following the protocols under which it operated, execution was reserved for only the most heinous offenses (heresy) and was assigned in a most specific context. The intent to proceed with a trial of faith, assignment of punishment, and the associated ritual was anchored not in the number of similar cases (quantity) but on the specific characteristics of each offense and the actions and defense of each offender, as played out against the conduct of trial procedures (quality). Again, these are the reasons behind the low number of trials and executions.

Underlying the protocol and procedures for conducting tribunal activities was the fact that it operated under the presumption of guilt and accepted accusation as evidence justifying an investigation. But here again protocol provided both means and constraint: the tribunal could apply physical torment only in selected cases and then only under much-regulated circumstances. Only in extreme cases could the tribunal issue death sentences to be executed by the state (the secular arm), and this it did. It could also confiscate offenders' properties and merge them into the funds it used to finance its own activities. The formality of this system did not, however, preclude failures: even the regulations governing the trial, care, and sentencing of prisoners could not prevent the deaths of some individuals in the Inquisition's own chambers (Mencía de Luna, Antonio Morón).

To carry out its responsibilities, the tribunal counted on educated officials to sit at the top of the hierarchy and lower-rank personnel to run day-to-day operations. Officials were to provide moral guidance and control for the Christian population, suspect or not, and exercise censorship over books, establish criteria and clear boundaries for potential religious offenses, and carry out trials of faith. Outside the tribunal, its officials participated in civic and religious events and hosted the spectacular rituals after which the state administered capital punishment in irredeemable cases. The articulation between secular and religious authorities was not seamless, but the division was strong enough to enable the relatively independent functioning of the institution.

The Lima tribunal also had the authority to communicate with tribunals in Spain, Portugal, and the other Spanish colonies, and this authority allowed it to expand its reach and the reach of the Holy Office beyond its own jurisdiction and beyond the colonies. Thus, as it grew to become a stable institution, the tribunal was transformed into a space for the development of transatlantic careers, whether within the Inquisition itself or in other Church posts, or even in the royal bureaucracy (Juan de Mañozca y Zamora). In step with the process of colonial expansion, the institution adapted its norms to emerging colonial realities, identifying its targets narrowly or broadly as necessary. The establishment of separate jurisdictions for Europeans and Africans (under the eyes of the Inquisition) and for Native Americans (outside the reach of Inquisition, but under tribunals of Extirpation of Idolatries) meant that colonial Inquisition tribunals did not have to spread themselves across entire viceroyalties but instead were able to locate in areas where the populations they were assigned to control tended to enter the country and to reside, that is, in capital and port cities. The presence of European foreigners (non-Spaniards) in the colonies was a matter for concern among civil and religious authorities, and it was the arrival of Portuguese traders of New Christian descent in key colonial centers such as Lima and Potosí that provided a justification for the establishment of the tribunal. These migrants circulated throughout Portugal, Spain, Africa, Brazil, and the Spanish colonies, in itineraries connected to and at times directly reflecting the Atlantic trade.

The New Christians of Portuguese descent who sailed across the Atlantic lived in two worlds. As Iberians, they belonged to the upper layers of colonial society, and some of them (Garci Méndez de Dueñas, Manuel Bautista Pérez) occupied the higher niches of the Atlantic trade. Others, like Joan Vicente or Manuel Henríquez, were artisans or petty merchants, dispersed in the countryside. Whatever their professional dedication or trade, New Christians could become at any time the objects of suspicion—of heresy—and it was this suspicion that marked the limit of their inclusion in colonial society. Once a person came into the sights of the Lima Inquisition and its repressive policies, the case against him or her would very likely advance, albeit slowly. There might be attempts to retrieve information from tribunals in another colony, in Spain, or in Portugal. Even if the trial was built on local evidence, additional information obtained from a distant place could modify a single offense into a relapse if it were later found that the accused had had a previous encounter with the Inquisition. The two worlds in which the Lima Portuguese New Christians lived held them swinging like a pendulum, between the upper layer of colonial society and the dungeons of the Inquisition. For those forced to leave completely the first of those worlds, there could be nothing between them and the *quemadero* at the Plaza de Acho.

While it is certain that the implementation of requests for information among different tribunals across the Atlantic allowed for an expansion of inquisitorial reach and for drawing together a body of evidence to be used in trials, these exchanges had an important secondary effect, redounding to the benefit of the accused. The considerable time necessary for the exchanges resulted in delayed trials, which contributed over time to the general view that the tribunal was slow moving, even semidormant. And even though the purpose of the delays was ostensibly to accumulate and verify evidence, the time was occupied to other purposes: prisoners took the opportunity to build defense strategies and to exercise agency to confound or slow the trial proceedings.

During the 1630s the Lima tribunal showed unusual vitality in its implementation of the Great Complicity detentions: seventeen incarcerations in a single afternoon, some prisoners brought from the countryside, with a total of close to one hundred prisoners. The Portuguese New Christians who resided in the Peruvian viceroyalty endured long trials of faith between 1635 and 1639. Although the religiosity of alleged crypto-Jews might be seen as monolithic resistance to conversion, the Portuguese New Christians who lived in colonial Peru were quite diverse and inconsistent in their religious adherences and exhibited different degrees of knowledge about Jewish practices. Even though the tribunal's interrogations were highly scripted, and confessions extracted under torment are of limited value, I have paid special attention to those elements in the confessions that were *not* standardized by the tribunal, moving beyond the avoidance of pork or the weekly changing of bed linen to distinguish the religiosity of selected individuals. Some prisoners participated in communities of crypto-Jews in Spain, Portugal, and even France. Some could recite full prayers and some could tell biblical stories, but some were not sure about the teachings of one religion or the other or both. Some expressed pragmatism rather than religious conviction as motivation for their participation in crypto-Jewish communities. Some invoked the protection of Christ and the Virgin Mary while in the torture chambers, and some never confessed to crypto-Jewish practices and beliefs, no matter how hard the tribunal tried to expose their alleged activities.

During the trials of the Great Complicity, prisoners could take advantage of the interplay of several factors. The shortage of prison cells and their often inadequate internal security, the corruption of the Inquisition, and the preexisting commercial and familial ties among the members of the Complicity (including their previous participation in the slave trade) offered to these prisoners interstices for deploying limited but important levels of agency, as expressed in strategies for exchanging messages, the revocation of confessions, and the bribing of both lower-ranking members of the tribunal and slaves. Beyond shared religious practices, the Portuguese New Christians held in Inquisition cells were able to activate long-standing community ties and broader networks. These strategies and the prisoners' keen awareness of the interstices in the practices and procedures under which they were held allowed them to confuse and mislead the tribunal and stall tribunal procedures. They could not, however, alter the outcomes of their trials, as we have seen in the cases of Rodrigo Váez Pereira and Manuel Henríquez.

The trials also had a very different and practical outcome: the revenues from the confiscations of the goods of those accused dramatically altered the finances of the Lima office. This outcome was not directly related to religious righteousness, nor to the number of people put on trial: its central effect was to enable the Lima Inquisition to achieve economic independence from the royal treasury. In looking at the cultural theater of the 1639 Auto General, we have shown that the actual number of people formally sentenced and executed has limited significance for understanding the history of the Inquisition and real or suspected Jews. The 1639 Auto General de Fe in Lima was a rare event that provided public closure to secret trials, but financially it represented a great gain for the tribunal. The amount seized during the Complicity trials was about one million pesos, although only about 31 percent of that amount went to the tribunal coffers.

By focusing on the plight of the condemned, I have retrieved a ceremony in which perfidious "Jews" who had endured long confinements and sometimes physical torments were exposed and disgraced in front of the assembled Christian community. Some few were also put to death, and it was those few who embodied the representation of the heinous heretic—the hidden Jew—the enemy within who had to be expunged. It was not necessary to hold frequent autos or to release large numbers of people to the secular arm for burning. The dramatic effect of the procession and pageantry that led to the tablado, and the events that took place there, captivated the attention of all even though the number of people condemned was quite small. And this too, I think, had a practical effect: who among the onlookers would want to be among the accused thus led to an excruciating and shameful death?

The relevance of alleged crypto-Jews as historical subjects stems from neither the frequency of their interactions with the tribunal nor the number of prisoners accused. It does stem from the dramatic intensity and the fearsome connotations of the tribunal's singular and sporadic interactions. The playing out of this drama seems more important for Jewish history than whether the Lima Portuguese of New Christian descent did or did not preserve a hidden faith. It is the overriding image and the story to be told, whether or not the faith of the accused as portrayed in tribunal documents was consistent with canonical Judaism or fragmented and unarticulated because of remote geographic location and a generational gap with formal Jewish practice.

I have portrayed, both directly and indirectly, the colonial elite as a diverse group with varied national and religious affiliations and not as a Spanish Roman Catholic enclave. Rivalries related to the various divisions had different and sometimes unexpected outcomes. For example, tribunal sources tell that the 1635 indictments began when some Old Christians denounced a Portuguese

New Christian and triggered the imprisonments of the Great Complicity. Then, some imprisoned New Christians retaliated by falsely accusing Old Christians of heresy: this payback brought Old Christians into the dungeons of the Inquisition. In the end, the New Christians received exemplary punishment in front of the entire Christian community. Those who had been falsely accused received broad applause and the restitution of their honor. In other words, even across the Atlantic, where all parties concerned were deeply involved in the colonial endeavor, the division between Old and New Christians was not erased. The effects on colonial society and its elites were very clear in the events of the mid-seventeenth century. For understanding the impact of the trials beyond the end of the ceremony over the prisoners and their families, there remain further questions for research: What happened to those who were reconciled? What happened to the spouses and children of those who suffered death at the stake?

It is true that royal restrictions prohibited Jews and New Christians from participating in a public way in the early conquest of the New World, and also true that their participation in the process of colonization was restricted to specific areas and occupations. Nonetheless, their social and economic importance in colonial society is clear. However, in the colonial context, it was "the perfidious Jew," both social and religious construct and powerful symbol, who played a central role in the assertion of colonial religious unity and national identity. Spanish colonizers wanted no challenges to their social cohesion as a Christian community, and they saw defects in purity and in adherence to Christian doctrine and practice as dangerous to their mission. They knew they had to keep an eye on matters of *limpieza de sangre* and potential heresy; thus they supported and respected the Inquisition and participated in its administrative tasks or the collective performance of its main rituals.

Exceptional cases like those of the Great Complicity trials illustrate that this colonial society, with its attention to purity and religious adherence, was constructed not only as a bulwark against the Indian "other" but also to confine and exclude a different "other"—one whose otherness was rooted not in visible racial traits but in hidden blood stains and secret religious practices, all imperceptible to the lay eye. Only the eyes of the Inquisition could locate, expose, and keep under control these secretive practitioners, considered all the more dangerous because their commercial and trade skills and social position put them in contact with all parts of colonial Christian society and beyond the boundaries of the Spanish world.

Notes

Introduction

1. "Hasta aqui he sido judio y desde ahora soy xptiano." Testimonios sobre la conversión y confesión de Rodrigo Váez Pereira antes que le den garrote, Archivo Histórico Nacional (hereafter AHN)–Inquisición, Libro 1031, f. 276r. All translations are mine unless otherwise indicated. I have not modernized the spellings in any original text, including accents. On occasion I have spelled out abbreviations to ensure readability.

2. "El establecimiento del Santo Oficio en el Perú no obedeció únicamente al interés por parte del Estado por perseguir la heterodoxia y controlar la moral sino que dicha medida forma parte de un ambicioso proyecto político colonial puesto en ejecución por Felipe II a fines de la década de 1560, cuyo principal objetivo era el robustecimiento del poder del Estado en el virreinato peruano." Pedro Guibovich Pérez, "Proyecto colonial y control ideológico: El establecimiento de la Inquisición en el Perú," *Apuntes* 35 (1994): 109–116, 110.

3. Bartolomé Escandell Bonet, "Estructura geográfica del dispositivo inquisitorial americano," in *Historia de la Inquisición en España y América*, vol. 2, ed. Joaquín Pérez Villanueva and Bartolomé Escandell Bonet (Madrid: Biblioteca de Autores Cristianos, Centro de Estudios Inquisitoriales, 1993), 48–60.

4. Richard Kagan, *Urban Images of the Hispanic World, 1493–1793* (New Haven, Conn.: Yale University Press, 2000), 169.

5. Fernando Montesinos, *Anales del Perú*, vol. 2, ed. Víctor M. Maúrtua (Madrid: Imprenta de Gabriel L. y del Horno, 1906), 197; Fray Buenaventura de Salinas y Córdova, *Memorial de las historias del nuevo mundo Pirú*, Colección Clásicos Peruanos 1 (Lima: Universidad Mayor Nacional de San Marcos, 1957 [1630]), 245; Fred Bronner, "The Population of Lima, 1593–1637: In Quest of a Statistical Bench Mark," *Ibero-Amerikanisches Archiv* 5, New Series, no. 2 (1979): 107–119; Noble David Cook, *Demographic Collapse: Indian Peru, 1520–1620* (Cambridge: Cambridge University Press, 1981), 151–156.

6. Alejandra B. Osorio, *Inventing Lima: Baroque Modernity in Peru's South Sea Metropolis* (New York: Palgrave Macmillan, 2008), 24.

7. Margarita Suárez, *Desafíos transatlánticos: Mercaderes, banqueros y el estado en el Perú virreinal, 1600–1700* (Lima: Pontificia Universidad Católica del Perú, Instituto

Riva Agüero; Fondo de Cultura Económica; Instituto Francés de Estudios Andinos, 2001).

8. Suárez, *Desafíos transatlánticos*; Osorio, *Inventing Lima*.

9. Suárez, *Desafíos transatlánticos*, 196-197; Daviken Studnicki-Gizbert, *A Nation upon the Ocean Sea: Portugal's Atlantic Diaspora and the Crisis of the Spanish Empire, 1492-1640* (Oxford: Oxford University Press, 2007), 144-145.

10. Studnicki-Gizbert, *A Nation upon the Ocean Sea*, 5. See also Miriam Bodian, "'Men of the Nation': The Shaping of *Converso* Identity in Early Modern Europe," *Past and Present* 143 (1994): 48-76; and Richard L. Kagan and Philip D. Morgan, *Atlantic Diasporas: Jews, Conversos, and Crypto-Jews in the Age of Mercantilism, 1500-1800* (Baltimore: Johns Hopkins University Press, 2009).

11. Miriam Bodian, "Hebrews of the Portuguese Nation: The Ambiguous Boundaries of Self-Definition," *Jewish Social Studies* 15, New Series, no. 1, Sephardi Identities (2008): 66-80; David Graizbord, "Religion and Ethnicity among the 'Men of the Nation': Toward a Realistic Interpretation," *Jewish Social Studies* 15, New Series, no. 1, Sephardi Identities (2008): 32-65.

12. Osorio, *Inventing Lima*, 107.

13. Juan Antonio Llorente, *Historia crítica de la Inquisición en España*, 4 vols., 2nd ed. (Madrid: Hiperión, 1981).

14. According to Bethencourt, Llorente overestimated the number of victims. Therefore, I did not take into account Llorente's work in that regard. Francisco Bethencourt, *The Inquisition: A Global History, 1478-1834*, trans. Jean Birrell, Past and Present Publications (Cambridge: Cambridge University Press, 2009), 10-12.

15. See Henry Charles Lea, *A History of the Inquisition of Spain*, 4 vols. (London: Macmillan, 1906); Henry Charles Lea, *The Inquisition in the Spanish Dependencies* (New York: Macmillan, 1908).

16. Ricardo Palma, *Anales de la Inquisición de Lima* (Lima: Ediciones del Congreso de la República del Perú, 1997 [facsimile edition expanded from the third edition of 1897]), 5-6.

17. On Palma, see Manuel Ballesteros Gaibrois, "La historiografía de la Inquisición en Indias," in *Historia de la Inquisición en España y América*, vol. 1, ed. Joaquín Pérez Villanueva and Bartolomé Escandell Bonet (Madrid: Biblioteca de Autores Cristianos, Centro de Estudios Inquisitoriales, 1984), 40-57; Palma, *Anales*, "Prólogo" by Luis Millones; Teodoro Hampe Martínez, "Ricardo Palma, cronista de la Inquisición," *Quaderni ibero-americani* 95 (2004): 15-30.

18. José Toribio Medina, *Historia del Tribunal del Santo Oficio de la Inquisición de Lima (1569-1820)*, vol. 1 (Santiago: Imprenta Gutenberg, 1887); José Toribio Medina, *La primitiva Inquisición americana: Estudio histórico* (Santiago: Imprenta Elzeviriana, 1914); José Toribio Medina, *La Inquisición en el Río de La Plata* (Buenos Aires: Huarpes, 1945); José Toribio Medina, *Historia del Tribunal del Santo Oficio de la Inquisición en Chile* (Santiago: Fondo Histórico y Bibliográfico, 1952); José Toribio Medina, *Historia del Tribunal de la Inquisición de Lima, 1569-1820*, 2nd ed., vol. 2 (Santiago: Fondo Histórico y Bibliográfico J. T. Medina, 1956); José Toribio Medina, *La Inquisición en Cartagena de Indias*, 2nd ed.

(Bogotá: C. Valencia, 1978); José Toribio Medina, *Historia del Tribunal del Santo Oficio de la Inquisición en México*, 2nd ed. (Mexico City: Dirección de Publicaciones del Consejo Nacional para la Cultura y las Artes, 2010 [1905]).

19. Paulino Castañeda Delgado and Pilar Hernández Aparicio, *La Inquisición de Lima*, vol. 1, *1570–1635* (Madrid: Deimos, 1989), xxi.

20. Henry Charles Lea, *The Inquisition in the Spanish Dependencies*; Boleslao Lewin, *El Santo Oficio en América y el más grande proceso inquisitorial en el Perú* (Buenos Aires: Sociedad Hebraica Argentina, 1950).

21. Throughout the twentieth century, historians of the Spanish colonial period have assessed the Black Legend in different ways. For a revision of American historiography that considers the Black Legend within a broader analytical frame (and not only in connection with the Spanish Inquisition), see Benjamin Keen, "Main Currents in United States Writings on Colonial Spanish America, 1884–1984," *Hispanic American Historical Review* 65, no. 4 (1985): 657–682. For an approach to the Black Legend that does not confirm or deny the level of Spanish colonial exploitation but challenges its unanimity by emphasizing the voices of Indian advocates on the Spanish camp, see Lewis Hanke, *All Mankind Is One: A Study of the Disputation between Bartolomé de Las Casas and Juan Ginés de Sepúlveda in 1550 on the Intellectual and Religious Capacity of the American Indians* (DeKalb: Northern Illinois University Press, 1974). For a critique of the Black Legend that does not question the level of Spanish exploitation or the existence of alternative voices but insists on the need for exploring Indigenous agency, see Steve Stern, "Prologue," in *Peru's Indian Peoples and the Challenge of the Spanish Conquest: Huamanga to 1640* (Madison: University of Wisconsin Press, 1993), xxi–liii. For a new conceptualization that addresses Spain's uniqueness in a comparative analysis, see Margaret Greer, Walter Mignolo, and Maureen Quilligan, eds., *Rereading the Black Legend: The Discourses of Religious and Racial Difference in the Renaissance Empires* (Chicago: University of Chicago Press, 2007).

22. Kimberly Lynn, "Unraveling the Spanish Inquisition: Inquisitorial Studies in the Twenty-First Century," *History Compass* 5, no. 4 (2007): 1280–1293, 1282.

23. Henry A. Kamen, *The Spanish Inquisition: A Historical Revision* (London: Weidenfeld & Nicolson, 1997).

24. Benzion Netanyahu, *The Origins of the Inquisition in Fifteenth Century Spain* (New York: Random House, 1995).

25. David Niremberg, "Race and the Middle Ages," in *Rereading the Black Legend: The Discourses of Religious and Racial Difference in the Renaissance Empires*, ed. Margaret Greer, Walter Mignolo, and Maureen Quilligan (Chicago: University of Chicago Press, 2007), 71–87, 86.

26. Julio Caro Baroja, *El señor inquisidor, y otras vidas por oficio* (Madrid: Alianza Editorial, 1968); Antonio Domínguez Ortiz, *Los judeoconversos en España y en América* (Madrid: Istmo, 1971); Francisco Tomás y Valiente, "Relaciones de la Inquisición con el aparato institucional del Estado," in *Gobierno e instituciones de la España del Antiguo Régimen* (Madrid: Alianza 1982), 13–35; Bartolomé Bennassar, "El poder inquisitorial," in *Inquisición española: Poder político y control social*, ed. Bartolomé Bennassar (Barcelona: Grijalbo, 1984),

68-93; Antonio Domínguez Ortiz, *Los judeoconversos en la España Moderna* (Madrid: Mapfre, 1992).

27. Bartolomé Bennassar, "La Inquisición o la pedagogía del miedo," in *Inquisición española: Poder político y control social*, ed. Bartolomé Bennassar (Barcelona: Grijalbo, 1984), 95-125; Bartolomé Bennassar, "Patterns of the Inquisitorial Mind as the Basis for a Pedagogy of Fear," in *The Spanish Inquisition and the Inquisitorial Mind*, ed. Angel Alcalá (Highland Lakes, N.J.: Atlantic Research and Publications, 1987), 177-184.

28. Jaime Contreras, *El Santo Oficio de la Inquisición de Galicia: Poder, sociedad y cultura* (Madrid: Akal, 1982), 110-115; Jaime Contreras, "Los cambios en la Península," in *Historia de la Inquisición en España y América*, vol. 1, ed. Joaquín Pérez Villanueva and Bartolomé Escandell Bonet (Madrid: Biblioteca de Autores Cristianos, Centro de Estudios Inquisitoriales, 1984), 1156-1176; Stephen Haliczer, *Inquisition and Society in the Kingdom of Valencia, 1478-1834* (Berkeley: University of California Press, 1990), 174; Kamen, *The Spanish Inquisition*, 147-148 and 178-179.

29. Joaquín Pérez Villanueva, ed., *La Inquisición española: Nueva visión, nuevos horizontes* (Madrid: Siglo XXI, 1980); Joaquín Pérez Villanueva and Bartolomé Escandell Bonet, *Historia de la Inquisición en España y América*, 3 vols. (Madrid: Biblioteca de Autores Cristianos, Centro de Estudios Inquisitoriales, 1984, 1993, 2000); Ángel Alcalá, *The Spanish Inquisition and the Inquisitorial Mind* (Highland Lakes, N.J.: Atlantic Research and Publications, 1987). Individual contributions from these collective volumes are also discussed in the core chapters.

30. See among others Contreras, *Inquisición de Galicia*; Solange Alberro, *Inquisición y sociedad en México, 1571-1700* (Mexico City: Fondo de Cultura Económica, 1988); Castañeda Delgado and Hernández Aparicio, *Inquisición de Lima*, vol. 1; Haliczer, *Inquisition and Society*; William Monter, *Frontiers of Heresy: The Spanish Inquisition from the Basque Lands to Sicily* (New York: Cambridge University Press, 1990); Paulino Castañeda Delgado and Pilar Hernández Aparicio, *La Inquisición de Lima*, vol. 2, *1635-1696* (Madrid: Deimos, 1995); René Millar Carvacho, *La Inquisición de Lima*, vol. 3, *1697-1820* (Madrid: Deimos, 1998); Fermina Álvarez Alonso, *La Inquisición en Cartagena de Indias durante el siglo XVII* (Madrid: Fundación Universitaria Española, 1999); Fernando Ayllón Dulanto, *El Tribunal de la Inquisición: De la leyenda a la historia*, 2nd ed. (Lima: Ediciones del Congreso del Perú, 2011).

31. Bethencourt, *The Inquisition*, 29.

32. See also I. S. Revah, "Les Marranes," *Revue des Etudes Juives* 3e série (1959-1960): 29-77; Yosef Hayim Yerushalmi, *From Spanish Court to Italian Ghetto: Isaac Cardoso, a Study in Seventeenth-Century Marranism and Jewish Apologetics* (New York: Columbia University Press, 1971); António José Saraiva, *Inquisição e Cristãos-Novos*, 6th ed. (Lisbon: Editora Estampa, 1994); Benzion Netanyahu, *The Marranos of Spain: From the Late 14th to the Early 16th Century, According to Contemporary Hebrew Sources*, 3rd ed. (Ithaca, N.Y.: Cornell University Press, 1999).

33. Jaime Contreras and Gustav Henningsen, "Forty-four Thousand Cases of the Spanish Inquisition (1540-1570): Analysis of a Historical Data Bank," in *The Inquisition in*

Early Modern Europe, ed. Gustav Henningsen and John Tedeschi (DeKalb: Northern Illinois University Press, 1986), 100–129.

34. Jean Pierre Dedieu, "Los cuatro tiempos de la Inquisición," in *Inquisición Española: Poder político y control social*, ed. Bartolomé Bennassar (Barcelona: Grijalbo, 1984), 15–39.

35. For instance, between 1570 and 1598, of 902 people sentenced in Mexico, 13 (1.44 percent) were "*relajados al brazo secular*" (released to the secular arm), or turned over to the secular authorities, which usually implied being burned at the stake. Bartolomé Escandell Bonet, "La peculiar estructura administrativa y funcional de la Inquisición Española en Indias," in *Historia de la Inquisición en España y América*, vol. 2, ed. Bartolomé Escandell Bonet and Joaquín Pérez Villanueva (Madrid: Biblioteca de Autores Cristianos, Centro de Estudios Inquisitoriales, 1993), 661.

36. Another 1.1 percent (291 people) were released to the secular arm.

37. Another 16 people were released to the secular arm. The numbers are also available in Jaime Contreras, "Estructura de la actividad procesal del Santo Oficio," in *Historia de la Inquisición en España y América*, vol. 2, ed. Joaquín Pérez Villanueva and Bartolomé Escandell Bonet (Madrid: Biblioteca de Autores Cristianos, Centro de Estudios Inquisitoriales, 1993), 588–632.

38. Teodoro Hampe Martínez, "Recent Works on the Inquisition and Peruvian Colonial Society, 1570–1820," *Latin American Research Review* 31, no. 2 (1996): 43–65, 43–44; Teodoro Hampe Martínez, "Estudios recientes sobre Inquisición y sociedad en el Perú colonial," in *Santo Oficio e historia colonial* (Lima: Congreso del Perú, 1998), 103–133.

39. René Millar Carvacho, *Inquisición y sociedad en el virreinato peruano: Estudios sobre el tribunal de la Inquisición de Lima* (Santiago, Chile: Ediciones Universidad Católica de Chile, 1998), 31, 62.

40. Between 1600 and 1700, from a total of 374 cases sentenced by the Lima tribunal, some 13 (3.74 percent) were released to the secular arm for burning at the stake *en persona*, and three others (0.86 percent) were burned *en efigie* (in effigy). For these and other numbers, see Escandell Bonet, "La peculiar estructura." See also Ayllón Dulanto, *El Tribunal de la Inquisición*. Although it focuses on the sixteenth century, a similar perspective based on the impact of low numbers in the relevance of the Inquisition can be found in Juan Carlos Carcelén Reluz, "La persecución a los judíos conversos en el Perú colonial, siglos XVI y XVII," in *Incas e indios cristianos: Elites indígenas e identidades cristianas en los Andes coloniales*, ed. Jean Jacques Decoster (Cusco: CBC/IFEA/Asociación KURAKA, 2002), 373–393. The same idea is implied to some extent in the analysis of Autos de Fe in Lima as presented in Osorio, *Inventing Lima*, 107.

41. See the following fragment: "El conocimiento objetivo de la Inquisición americana se obtiene mediante una sencilla aplicación del método cuantitativo: clasificación de los procesos inquisitoriales por la naturaleza de sus contenidos, cuantificación de cada grupo resultante que muestre su respectivo índice de frecuencia y establecimiento porcentual de sus relaciones de proporcionalidad dentro del conjunto global que constituyen." Bartolomé Escandell Bonet, "Una lectura psico-social de los papeles del Santo Oficio: Inquisición y sociedad peruanas en el siglo XVI," in *La Inquisición española: Nueva*

visión, nuevos horizontes, ed. Joaquín Pérez Villanueva (Madrid: Siglo XXI, 1980), 437–467, 451. See also Pilar Pérez Cantó, "Tribunal del Santo Oficio de Lima: Relación de Causas vistas en la primera mitad del siglo XVIII," in *La Inquisición española: Nueva visión, nuevos horizontes,* ed. Joaquín Pérez Villanueva (Madrid: Siglo XXI, 1980), 469–477; Pilar Pérez Cantó, "El Tribunal de Lima en tiempos de Felipe III," in *Historia de la Inquisición en España y América,* vol. 1, ed. Joaquín Pérez Villanueva and Bartolomé Escandell Bonet (Madrid: Biblioteca de Autores Cristianos, Centro de Estudios Inquisitoriales, 1984), 979–983; Pérez Cantó, "El Tribunal de Lima"; Pilar Pérez Cantó, "La dinámica de las estructuras en el Tribunal de Lima," in *Historia de la Inquisición en España y América,* vol. 1, ed. Joaquín Pérez Villanueva and Bartolomé Escandell Bonet (Madrid: Biblioteca de Autores Cristianos, Centro de Estudios Inquisitoriales, 1984), 1180–1189.

42. See Dedieu, "Los cuatro tiempos"; "Una 'Inquisición' muy dinámica, la de Felipe II, y una 'Inquisición' más reposada, la de sus sucesores," in Contreras, "Estructura de la actividad procesal," 595.

43. See, for example, Manuel Ballesteros Gaibrois, "La historiografía de la Inquisición en Indias"; Alfonso Quiroz Norris, "La expropiación inquisitorial de cristianos nuevos portugueses en Los Reyes, Cartagena y México, 1635–1649," *Histórica* 10, no. 2 (1986): 237–303; Millar Carvacho, *Inquisición y sociedad,* chap. 4.

44. Marcel Bataillon, "La herejía de Fray Francisco de la Cruz y la reacción antilascasiana," in *Estudios sobre Bartolomé de Las Casas* (Barcelona: Península, 1976); Álvaro Huerga, *Historia de los alumbrados,* vol. 3, *Los alumbrados de Hispanoamérica (1570–1605)* (Madrid: Fundación Universitaria Española, Seminario Cisneros, 1986); Vidal Abril Castelló, *Francisco de la Cruz, Inquisición, Actas I* (Madrid: Consejo Superior de Investigaciones Científicas, 1992).

45. Millar Carvacho, *Inquisición y sociedad,* chap. 6.

46. Hampe Martínez, "Recent Works on the Inquisition," 43. For a version in Spanish, see Hampe Martínez, "Estudios recientes." See also Jean Pierre Dedieu, "The Archives of the Holy Office of Toledo as Source for Historical Anthropology," in *The Inquisition in Early Modern Europe,* ed. Gustav Henningsen and John Tedeschi (DeKalb: Northern Illinois University Press, 1986), 158–189; Gustav Henningsen and John Tedeschi, eds., *The Inquisition in Early Modern Europe: Studies on Sources and Methods* (DeKalb: Northern Illinois University Press, 1986).

47. Gabriela Ramos, "El Tribunal de la Inquisición en el Perú, 1605–1666: Un estudio social," *Cuadernos para la Historia de la Evangelización en América Latina* 3 (1988): 93–125; Millar Carvacho, *Inquisición y sociedad,* chap. 7.

48. Maurice Birckel, "Recherches sur la Trésorerie Inquisitoriale de Lima, I, 1569–1610," *Mélanges de la Casa de Velázquez* 5, no. 1 (1969): 223–307; Maurice Birckel, "Recherches sur la Trésorerie Inquisitoriale de Lima, II, 1611–1642," *Mélanges de la Casa de Velázquez* 6, no. 1 (1970): 309–357; Quiroz Norris, "La expropiación inquisitorial"; Gabriela Ramos, "La fortuna del inquisidor: Inquisición y poder en el Perú (1594–1611)," *Cuadernos para la Historia de la Evangelización en América Latina* 4 (1989): 89–122; Millar Carvacho, *Inquisición y sociedad,* chap. 4.

49. See Pedro Guibovich Pérez, *Censura, libros e Inquisición en el Perú colonial, 1570–1754* (Seville: Consejo Superior de Investigaciones Científicas, Escuela de Estudios Hispano-Americanos, Universidad de Sevilla, Diputación de Sevilla, 2003), 19, 223. See also Pedro Guibovich Pérez, "Los libros del inquisidor," *Cuadernos para la Historia de la Evangelización en América Latina* 4 (1989): 47–64; Pedro Guibovich Pérez, "Fray Juan de Almaraz, calificador de la Inquisición de Lima (s. XVI)," *Cuadernos para la Historia de la Evangelización en América Latina* 4 (1989): 31–45; Pedro Guibovich Pérez, "La cultura libresca de un converso procesado por la Inquisición de Lima," *Historia y Cultura*, no. 20 (1990): 133–160.

50. Millar Carvacho, *Inquisición y sociedad*, chap. 9.

51. Ana Sánchez, "Mentalidad popular frente a ideología oficial: El Santo Oficio en Lima y los casos de hechicería (siglo XVII)," in *Poder y violencia en los Andes*, ed. Henrique Urbano (Cusco: Centro de Estudios Rurales Andinos Bartolomé de Las Casas, 1991), 33–51; María Emma Mannarelli, *Hechiceras, beatas y expósitas: Mujeres y poder inquisitorial en Lima* (Lima: Ediciones del Congreso del Perú, 1999).

52. Hampe Martínez, "Recent Works on the Inquisition," 43. The Spanish version reads: "Entre las nuevas aportaciones más sugerentes se halla la imagen de un tribunal del Santo Oficio relativamente inactivo e ineficiente, desconectado de la vigilancia en materias de fe y orientado más bien a promover los intereses comerciales y financieros de sus miembros." Hampe Martínez, "Estudios recientes," 103–104.

53. Bethencourt, *The Inquisition*, 444.

54. In previous pages I have discussed chapters from this book that are reprints of prior publications. Millar Carvacho, *Inquisición y sociedad*, 97; René Millar Carvacho, *La Inquisición de Lima: Signos de su decadencia, 1726–1750* (Santiago: Dirección de Bibliotecas, Archivos y Museos, LOM Ediciones, Centro de Investigaciones Barros Arana, 2004).

55. Irene Silverblatt, *Moon, Sun, and Witches: Gender Ideologies and Class in Inca and Colonial Peru* (Princeton, N.J.: Princeton University Press, 1987); Irene Silverblatt, *Modern Inquisitions: Peru and the Colonial Origins of the Civilized World* (Durham, N.C.: Duke University Press, 2004), 3–53.

56. François Soyer, "An Example of Collaboration between the Spanish and Portuguese Inquisitions: The Trials of the *Converso* Diogo Ramos and his Family (1680–1683)," *Cadernos de Estudos Sefarditas* 6 (2006): 317–340, 317.

57. Silverblatt, *Modern Inquisitions*, 232.

58. Osorio, *Inventing Lima*, 32.

59. Pierre Duviols, *La destrucción de las religiones andinas: Conquista y colonia* (Mexico: Universidad Nacional Autónoma de México, 1977); Silverblatt, *Moon, Sun, and Witches*; Nicholas Griffiths, *The Cross and the Serpent: Religious Repression and Resurgence in Colonial Peru* (Norman: University of Oklahoma Press, 1996); Kenneth Mills, *Idolatry and Its Enemies: Colonial Andean Religion and Extirpation, 1640–1750* (Princeton, N.J.: Princeton University Press, 1997); Iris Gareis, "Repression and Cultural Change: The 'Extirpation of Idolatry' in Colonial Peru," in *Spiritual Encounters*, ed. Nicholas Griffiths and Fernando Cervantes (Lincoln: University of Nebraska Press, 1999), 230–254.

60. Bennassar, "La Inquisición o la pedagogía del miedo."

61. "Se trata de algo profundamente vivo, dramático, sobrecogedor." Consuelo Maqueda Abreu, *El auto de Fe* (Madrid: Istmo, 1992), 11.

62. See, for example, the work of Boleslao Lewin previously quoted; Revah, "Les Marranes"; Yerushalmi, *From Spanish Court*; Cecil Roth, *Los judíos secretos: Historia de los marranos* (Madrid: Altalena, 1979); Haim Beinart, *Conversos on Trial: The Inquisition in Ciudad Real*, trans. Yael Guiladi (Jerusalem: Magnes Press, Hebrew University, 1981).

63. Saraiva, *Inquisição*; Norman Roth, *Conversos, Inquisition, and the Expulsion of the Jews from Spain* (Madison: University of Wisconsin Press, 1995); Netanyahu, *The Marranos of Spain*.

64. Yirmiahu Yovel, *The New Otherness: Marrano Dualities in the First Generation*, 1999 Swig Lecture, September 13 (San Francisco: Swig Judaic Studies Program at the University of San Francisco, 1999).

65. David Gitlitz, *Secrecy and Deceit: The Religion of the Crypto-Jews* (Philadelphia: Jewish Publications Society, 1996), 84. The paragraph continues: "For that matter, a single individual might vary his or her practice over time, might begin believing one thing and end up believing quite another, or might even hold contradictory beliefs simultaneously. It is therefore not useful to try to devise a single descriptor for the wide range of *converso* beliefs and customs. Yet neither is it profitable to talk only about individuals or about small communities at one particular point of time." Also, Nathan Wachtel speaks about a "Marrano religiosity." According to this author, this religiosity was not a clearly defined doctrine, but an assembly of inquiries, practices, and contradictory beliefs. See Nathan Wachtel, "Marrano Religiosity in Hispanic America in the Seventeenth Century," in *The Jews and the Expansion of Europe to the West, 1450–1800*, ed. Paolo Bernardini and Norman Fiering (New York: Berghahn Books, 2001), 149–171.

66. For a recent study of martyrs see Miriam Bodian, *Dying in the Law of Moses: Crypto-Jewish Martyrdom in the Iberian World* (Bloomington: Indiana University Press, 2007).

67. See Gitlitz, *Secrecy and Deceit*, chap. 4.

68. The law of Moses is considered by Christians to have been superseded by the arrival of Jesus and the establishment of the Christian Church and its law.

69. Gretchen Starr-Lebeau, *In the Shadow of the Virgin: Inquisitors, Friars, and Conversos in Guadalupe, Spain* (Princeton, N.J.: Princeton University Press, 2003); Bodian, "Hebrews of the Portuguese Nation," 71; Graizbord, "Religion and Ethnicity among the 'Men of the Nation'"; Juan Ignacio Pulido Serrano, "Plural Identities: The Portuguese New Christians," *Jewish History* 24 (2011): 129–151.

70. Jonathan Schorsch, *Swimming the Christian Atlantic: Judeoconversos, Afroiberians and Amerindians in the Seventeenth Century* (Leiden: Brill, 2009), 62.

71. Starr-Lebeau, *In the Shadow of the Virgin*, 6.

72. Lewin, *El Santo Oficio en América*; Günter Böhm, *Historia de los judíos en Chile*, vol. 1, *Período colonial: El Bachiller Francisco Maldonado de Silva, 1592–1639* (Santiago: Andrés Bello, 1984); Bodian, *Dying in the Law of Moses*, chap. 5; Nathan Wachtel, *La fe del recuerdo: Laberintos marranos*, trans. Sandra Garzonio (Buenos Aires: Fondo de Cultura Económica,

2007), chap. 2; Nathan Wachtel, *The Faith of Remembrance: Marrano Labyrinths*, trans. Nikki Halpern (Philadelphia: University of Pennsylvania Press, 2013), chap. 2.

73. Lucía García de Proodian, *Los judíos en América: Sus actividades en los virreinatos de Nueva Castilla y Nueva Granada, S. XVII*, ed. Instituto Arias Montano (Madrid: Consejo Superior de Investigaciones Científicas, 1966). Böhm also studies the presence of New Christians in different cities: see Günter Böhm, "Crypto-Jews and New Christians in Colonial Peru and Chile," in *The Jews and the Expansion of Europe to the West, 1450–1800*, ed. Paolo Bernardini and Norman Fiering (New York: Berghahn Books, 2001), 203–212.

74. "Complicidad: Compañía en el delito," in Real Academia Española, *Diccionario de Autoridades*, vol. 1, A–C (Madrid: Gredos, S.A., 1990), 453.

75. According to Minchin, "Sería importante señalar que el término 'complicidad,' tal como fue utilizado en la España durante la época Moderna Temprana, no debe ser interpretado como sinónimo de 'conspiración.'" Susie Minchin, "Vuestras Mercedes son capitanes bizarros y peruleros: El Perú visto por la comunidad conversa portuguesa hacia principios del siglo XVII," in *Sobre el Perú: Homenaje a José Agustín de la Puente Candamo*, ed. Margarita Guerra and Oswaldo Olguín (Lima: PUCP, 2002), 863–878, 873 n. 26. For a discussion of the conspiracy in 1630 Lima, see Irene Silverblatt, "The Black Legend and Global Conspiracies: Spain, the Inquisition, and the Emerging Modern World," in *Rereading the Black Legend: The Discourses of Religious and Racial Difference in the Renaissance Empires*, ed. Margaret Greer, Walter Mignolo, and Maureen Quilligan (Chicago: University of Chicago Press, 2007), 99–116.

76. Castañeda Delgado and Hernández Aparicio, *Inquisición de Lima*, 2:427–431.

77. Harry Cross, "Commerce and Orthodoxy: A Spanish Response to Portuguese Commercial Penetration in the Viceroyalty of Peru, 1580–1640," *The Americas* 35, no. 2 (1978): 151–167; Quiroz Norris, "La expropiación inquisitorial"; Castañeda Delgado and Hernández Aparicio, *Inquisición de Lima*, vol. 2, chap. 16; Millar Carvacho, *Inquisición y sociedad*, chap. 4; Linda A. Newson and Susie Minchin, *From Capture to Sale: The Portuguese Slave Trade to Spanish South America in the Early Seventeenth Century*, The Atlantic World 12 (Leiden: Brill, 2007); Silverblatt, "The Black Legend and Global Conspiracies"; Studnicki-Gizbert, *A Nation upon the Ocean Sea*; Seymour B. Liebman, "The Great Conspiracy in Peru," *The Americas* 28, no. 2 (October 1971): 176–190.

78. Yerushalmi, *From Spanish Court*.

79. Wachtel, *The Faith of Remembrance*, 3. See also Wachtel, "Marrano Religiosity." In the following fragment from the introduction to the Spanish translation of his book, Wachtel writes: "Por este último vocablo [marrano] entiendo, no una religión claramente definida por una doctrina teológica, sino un conjunto de inquietudes, prácticas y creencias que se inscriben en una configuración compuesta de elementos variables, incluso contradictorios, cuya diversidad no excluye una manera de unidad, un estilo genérico que permite identificarlo con un término propio, en este caso el de 'marrano.'" Later in the same introduction the French scholar says: "Los miembros de la 'Nación' comparten, más allá de su diversidad, una fe común: la fe del recuerdo." Wachtel, *La fe del recuerdo*, 29. For a comparable approach that combines historical, anthropological, and sociological analysis to discuss the roots of crypto-Judaism in New Mexico and

explores historical continuity up to the beginning of the twenty-first century, see Stanley Hordes, *To the End of the Earth: A History of the Crypto-Jews of New Mexico* (New York: Columbia University Press, 2005).

80. Graizbord, "Religion and Ethnicity among the 'Men of the Nation,'" 39.

81. Josephe de Mugaburu and Francisco de Mugaburu, *Diario de Lima (1640–1694): Crónica de la época colonial*, repr. and with prologue and notes by Don Carlos A. Romero (Lima: Imp. C. Vásquez L., 1935); Juan Antonio Suardo, *Diario de Lima (1629–1639)*, vol. 1, introduction and notes by Rubén Vargas Ugarte, S.J. (Lima: Universidad Católica del Perú, Instituto de Investigaciones Históricas, 1936); Juan Antonio Suardo, *Diario de Lima (1629–1639)*, vol. 2, introduction and notes by Rubén Vargas Ugarte, S.J. (Lima: Universidad Católica del Perú, Instituto de Investigaciones Históricas, 1936); Salinas y Córdova, *Memorial*; Pedro León de Portocarrero, "Descrição geral do reino do Peru, em particular de Lima," in *Descripción del Virreinato del Perú*, ed. and with prologue by Eduardo Huarag Álvarez (Lima: Universidad Ricardo Palma, Editorial Universitaria, 2009).

82. Kamen says that the authorship was shared by two Protestant exiles, Casiodoro de Reina and Antonio del Corro. García Cárcel and Moreno Martínez have determined that the writer of the *Artes* was probably Casiodoro de Reina, while Bethencourt sustains that Montes's real name was Antonio del Corro. Although he provides a third name, in his list of people condemned in the 1559 Auto in Seville, Juan Gil includes Casiodoro de Reina and Antonio del Corro, both friars of the San Isidoro monastery in Seville, both subsequently burned in effigy. Francisco Ruiz de Pablos, who in 2008 published the edition of the *Artes* that I have consulted (a translation to Spanish from the Latin original), recognizes that the real name of González Montes is still unknown but agrees with those scholars already named in situating him in Seville, most likely among the clerics that supported Erasmus. This association would place the writer of the *Artes* very close to the repression of the Seville Protestants during the 1550s. See Ricardo García Cárcel, *Orígenes de la Inquisición española: El Tribunal de Valencia, 1478–1530* (Barcelona: Península, 1976), 18; Kamen, *The Spanish Inquisition*, 307; Ricardo García Cárcel and Doris Moreno Martínez, *Inquisición: Historia crítica, colección Historia* (Madrid: Temas de Hoy SA, 2000), 271; Juan Gil, *Los conversos y la Inquisición sevillana*, vol. 1 (Seville: Universidad de Sevilla, Fundación El Monte, 2000), 344–345; Francisco Ruiz de Pablos, "Errores antiguos y actuales sobre González Montes, debelador de la Inquisición Española," *Hispania Sacra* 55 (2003): 237–251; Reinaldo González Montes, *Artes de la Santa Inquisición Española*, trans. Francisco Ruiz de Pablos (Seville: Editorial MAD S.L., 2008 [1567?]); Bethencourt, *The Inquisition*, 378.

83. Michel Foucault, *Discipline and Punish: The Birth of the Prison* (New York: Pantheon Books, 1977).

84. Castañeda Delgado and Hernández Aparicio, *Inquisición de Lima*, vol. 1; Castañeda Delgado and Hernández Aparicio, *Inquisición de Lima*, vol. 2; Millar Carvacho, *Inquisición de Lima*.

85. Carlo Ginzburg, "Preface to the English Edition," in *The Cheese and the Worms: The Cosmos of a Sixteenth-Century Miller*, trans. John Tedeschi and Anne Tedeschi (Baltimore: Johns Hopkins University Press, 1992).

86. On embracing the debate, see Stern, "Prologue."

87. "This is a problem both of methods and of ethics: can we retain a cold, clinical gaze when reading, for example, dozens of pages in which the court clerk has scrupulously recorded not only the confessions of a prisoner under torture but also his moaning, his groaning, his supplications, even his cries of pain?" Wachtel, *The Faith of Remembrance*, 17. "El problema es de método y de ética a la vez: ¿es posible mantener la frialdad de la mirada clínica después de la lectura—entre muchas otras—de decenas de páginas a lo largo de las cuales un secretario ha anotado escrupulosamente no sólo las confesiones de un prisionero sometido a tortura, sino también todos sus lamentos, sus gemidos, sus súplicas y hasta sus gritos de dolor?" Wachtel, *La fe del recuerdo*, 32–33.

88. Mills, *Idolatry and Its Enemies*, 6.

89. Eric Van Young, *The Other Rebellion: Popular Violence, Ideology, and the Mexican Struggle for Independence, 1810–1821* (Stanford, Calif.: Stanford University Press, 2001), 28.

90. Tomás y Valiente, "Relaciones de la Inquisición," 34–35.

Chapter 1
Heresy and Inquisition in the Iberian World

1. Juan Antonio Suardo, May 1631: "A 12, amanecieron en las calles del barrio de la perrochia de San Sebastian algunos papeles escritos de mano, llenos de mil herejías y blasfemias, los quales se llevaron luego a la Santa Inquisición. A 13, en el barrio de San Lázaro, amanecieron quitadas todas las cruces que estavan puestas en el cimenterio de la yglessia y otras partes públicas que caussó muy grande escandalo y sobre el casso dizen que van haciendo pesquissa los señores inquisidores." Suardo, *Diario*, 1:161. The diary continues until 1639, but in the introduction to the published edition, Rubén Vargas Ugarte clarifies that after 1637 the writer was Diego de Medrano. Ibid., vii.

2. In Llorente's words, "La sustancia estaba en considerar a la herejía como crimen contra las leyes civiles, y punible por el soberano con penas exteriores." Llorente, *Historia crítica*, 1:37. See also Edward Peters, *Inquisition* (New York: Free Press, 1988), 29.

3. The sambenito was a kind of tunic, sewn of rough cloth and usually yellow, that convicted or suspected heretics were ordered to wear for periods ranging from a year to a lifetime. When the period designated was over, the garment was hung at the church in public view as a lesson to others who might consider similar transgressions. See Llorente, *Historia crítica*, 1:28.

4. Bethencourt, *The Inquisition*, 67.

5. Ibid., 68.

6. For an example of a fourteenth-century instruction manual for inquisitors, see Yosef Hayim Yerushalmi, "The Inquisition and the Jews of France in the Time of Bernard Gui," *Harvard Theological Review* 63, no. 3 (1970): 317–376. For a discussion of writers of Inquisition manuals in sixteenth-century Spain, see Kimberly Lynn, "Was Adam the First Heretic? Diego de Simancas, Luis de Páramo, and the Origins of Inquisitorial Practice," *Archiv für Reformationsgeschichte/Archive for Reformation History* 97 (2006): 184–210. For the comments on the systematization provided by Eimeric's manual,

see the "Introducción" written by Luis Sala-Molins to Nicolau Eimeric and Francisco Peña, *El manual de los inquisidores* (Barcelona: Muchnik, 1983 [1376, 1578]), 15–17.

7. See Emilio Grahit y Papell, *El Inquisidor Fray Nicolás Eymerich* (Gerona: Imprenta de Manuel Llach, 1878); Karen Sullivan, *The Inner Lives of Medieval Inquisitors* (Chicago: University of Chicago Press, 2011), chap. 7.

8. Nicolau Eymeric, *Manual de inquisidores* (Bogotá: Planeta, 1999 [1376]). The introduction to this edition states that Eimeric finished the *Manual* in 1356, but Grahit y Papell says it was in 1376, and Sala-Molins gives the same date in his "Introducción" to Eimeric and Peña, *El manual*, 15. I consulted two different editions in Spanish and cited fragments from both of them.

9. "En punto á heregía se ha de proceder llanamente, sin sutilezas de abogado, ni solemnidades en el proceso. . . . Quiero decir que los tramites del proceso han de ser lo más corto que posible fuere, dexandose de dilaciones superfluas, no parandose su sustanciacion ni en los días que huelgan los demás tribunales." Eymeric, *Manual*, 31. In the edition that includes Peña's comments, the text reads: "En los asuntos de fe, el procedimiento debe ser sumario, sencillo, sin complicaciones ni algaradas, ni ostentación de abogados y jueces. No hay obligación de enseñar acta de acusación al acusado ni consentir debate. No se admite recurso dilatorio ni cosas por el estilo." Eimeric and Peña, *El manual*, 139. For the application of these concepts to book censorship, see Martin A. Nesvig, *Ideology and Inquisition: The World of the Censors in Early Mexico* (New Haven, Conn.: Yale University Press, 2009), chap. 2.

10. Eymeric, *Manual*, 111.

11. "¿Que el judío rejudaizante había recibido el bautismo bajo amenaza de muerte, o siendo niño? El delito de rejudaización permanece intacto. Sin embargo, se tratará con menos rigor al niño rejudaizante." Eimeric and Peña, *El manual*, 87.

12. "Nunca estará de sobra la prudencia, la circunspeccion y la entereza del inquisidor en el interrogatorio del reo. Los hereges son muy astutos para disimular sus errores, afectan santidad, y vierten fingidas lagrimas que pudieran ablandar á los jueces mas rigorosos. Un inquisidor se debe armar contra todas estas mañas, suponiendo siempre que le quieren engañar." Eymeric, *Manual*, 43.

13. "La Segunda treta de que se valen es la adicion de una condicion implicita, la *restriccion mental*. Cuando les preguntan *¿si creen en la resurreccion de la carne?* Responde *sí; si Dios quiere*, y suponen que no quiere Dios que crean en este misterio." Ibid., 44. In the edition with Peña's comments, the text reads: "Si le preguntáis: '¿Crees en la resurrección de la carne?' Le oiréis contestar: 'Claro, si a Dios le place' (sobreentendiéndose que Dios no quiere que lo crea)." Eimeric and Peña, *El manual*, 148. For all the strategies, see Eimeric and Peña, *El manual*, 148–151.

14. "Son relajados al brazo seglar 1° los relapsos arrepentidos; 2° los no relapsos pertinaces; 3° los hereges pertinaces y relapsos; 4° los hereges negativos, esto es los que se empeñan en negar, habiendo plena probanza de su delito; 5° los hereges rebeldes, cuando pueden ser aprehendidos en persona, y cuando no, son quemados en estatua." Eymeric, *Manual*, 97.

15. See the prologue written in 1821 by José Marchena Ruíz de Cueto to ibid. See also Lynn, "Was Adam the First Heretic?" Later on the Spanish tribunals also followed the manual written by Francisco Peña in 1578, which was an update of Eimeric's.

16. There is a vast literature covering this period of Spanish history. See, for example, Américo Castro, *España en su historia: Cristianos, moros y judíos* (Buenos Aires: Editorial Losada, 1948); Angus MacKay, "Popular Movements and Pogroms in Fifteenth-Century Castille," *Past and Present* 55, no. 1 (1972); Thomas Glick, *Islamic and Christian Spain in the Early Middle Ages* (Princeton, N.J.: Princeton University Press, 1979); Stanley Payne, *Spanish Catholicism: An Historical Overview* (Madison: University of Wisconsin Press, 1984); Bat Ye'or, *The Dhimmi: Jews and Christians under Islam* (London: Associated University Presses, 1985); John Elliott, "A Europe of Composite Monarchies," *Past and Present*, no. 137 (1992): 48–71; Vivian B. Mann et al., *Convivencia: Jews, Muslims, and Christians in Medieval Spain* (New York: G. Braziller in association with the Jewish Museum, 1992); M. J. Rodríguez Salgado, "Christians, Civilised and Spanish: Multiple Identities in Sixteenth-Century Spain," *Transactions of the Royal Historical Society* 8 (1998): 233–251; María Rosa Menocal, *The Ornament of the World: How Muslims, Jews, and Christians Created a Culture of Tolerance in Medieval Spain* (Boston: Little, Brown, 2002).

17. On the life of Jews in Spain and the 1492 expulsion, see Yitzhak Baer, *A History of the Jews in Christian Spain*, vol. 2 (Philadelphia: Jewish Publication Society of America, 1961). See also Jane Gerber, *The Jews of Spain: A History of the Sephardic Experience* (New York: Free Press, 1992); Esther Benbassa and Aron Rodrigue, *Sephardi Jewry: A History of the Judeo-Spanish Community, 14th–20th Centuries* (Berkeley: University of California Press, 2000).

18. Benbassa and Rodrigue, *Sephardi Jewry*, xxvi.

19. The 1391 conversions in Spain marked a turning point: previous forced conversions in other places of Europe were individual rather than massive. On this matter, see Yerushalmi, "The Inquisition and the Jews of France"; MacKay, "Popular Movements and Pogroms." The forced conversions in 1497 Portugal also involved a cohesive community and fostered new identities, as has been analyzed by Yerushalmi, *From Spanish Court*.

20. The Muslim population of Spain underwent a similar process, but this discussion is outside the limits of this book.

21. Stuart B. Schwartz, *All Can Be Saved: Religious Tolerance and Salvation in the Iberian Atlantic World* (New Haven, Conn.: Yale University Press, 2008), 98.

22. "Limpio se dize comunmente el hombre Christiano viejo sin raza de Moro, ni Iudio." Sebastián de Covarrubias Orozco, *Tesoro de la lengua castellana o española*, 2 pts. in 1 vol. (Madrid: Melchor Sanchez, 1673), pt. 2, 92.

23. For a detailed analysis of the statutes of blood purity, see Albert A. Sicroff, *Los estatutos de limpieza de sangre: Controversias entre los siglos XV y XVII*, trans. Mauro Armiño (Madrid: Taurus Ediciones, 1985). Martínez clarifies many details related to these statutes in both the Old and New Worlds. María Elena Martínez, *Genealogical Fictions: Limpieza de Sangre, Religion, and Gender in Colonial Mexico* (Stanford, Calif.: Stanford University Press, 2008).

24. In Martinez's words: "Early Modern Spanish society came to accept as normal that a candidate for a religious order would present the hierarchy with genealogical information about his Old Christian antecedents, that a Holy Office commissioner would inspect local archives and conduct interrogations about a certain lineage, and that a nobleman or wealthy commoner would pay a genealogist to invent him a pure pedigree." Martínez, *Genealogical Fictions*, 87.

25. Joaquín Pérez Villanueva, "Felipe IV y su política," in *Historia de la Inquisición en España y América*, vol. 1, ed. Joaquín Pérez Villanueva and Bartolomé Escandell Bonet (Madrid: Biblioteca de Autores Cristianos, Centro de Estudios Inquisitoriales, 1984), 1006–1079, 1037–1041; Sicroff, *Los estatutos de limpieza de sangre*, 253–257; Studnicki-Gizbert, *A Nation upon the Ocean Sea*, chap. 5.

26. Silverblatt, *Modern Inquisitions*, 128–139.

27. "Puede esta Vniuersidad enriquezer a toda Europa de sujetos Ilustres en virtudes, Claros en sangre, Insignes en gouierno, y Celebrados en letras." Salinas y Córdova, *Memorial*, 172. For a short biography of Salinas y Córdova, see also Manuel de Mendiburu, *Diccionario histórico-biográfico del Perú*, 8 vols. (Lima: Imprenta de J. Francisco Solís, 1874–1890), 7:174–175. Castañeda Delgado and Hernández Aparicio, on the other hand, say that Fray Buenaventura de Salinas y Córdova's father, Don Lope de Salinas, was a man from Lima who was suspected of having converso lineage like his wife. According to these authors Lope de Salinas was a lawyer at the Lima audiencia, an opponent of the inquisitor Don Antonio Gutiérrez de Ulloa, and a friend of Don Juan Ruiz de Prado during the conflicts associated with the inspection of the tribunal conducted by the latter (1587–1591). As a result of these conflicts, Lope de Salinas was excommunicated and authorized to leave Peru. Paulino Castañeda Delgado and Pilar Hernández Aparicio, "La visita de Ruiz de Prado al Tribunal del Santo Oficio de Lima," *Anuario de Estudios Americanos* 41 (1984): 1–53, 47–49, and n. 130.

28. "Martes 5 de Septiembre de 1673 años, los señores inquisidores mandaron prender a don Sebastián de Aguilar, racionero entero, desta Iglesia de Lima, sobre la información que prestó en el dicho Tribunal que le enviaron de España acerca de la familiatura, que pareció ser falsa." Mugaburu and Mugaburu, *Diario de Lima*, 160.

29. The document in which the request appears is from 1813, but the Inquisition was not fully abolished in the colonies until the end of the Wars of Independence and not until 1834 in Spain. "1813—El Cabildo de Lima felicita a las Cortes españolas reunidas en Cádiz por el decreto de supresión de la Inquisición y pide que se extraiga de los Archivos de la Inquisición todos los libros y papeles infamantes para la buena fama de los ciudadanos perseguidos por ésta y se quemen públicamente." Reproduced in Medina, *Historia del Tribunal de la Inquisición de Lima*, 2:492–494. The Lima population entered the tribunal facilities once the abolishment was decreed. See Palma, *Anales*, 192–195.

30. Various regulations that aimed for the separation between Jews and conversos had been issued since 1393. See Baer, *A History of the Jews*, 2:125. On rites of rejudaization among Spanish conversos, see, for example, Renee Levine Melammed, *Heretics or Daughters of Israel: The Crypto-Jewish Women of Castile* (New York: Oxford University Press, 1999).

31. See Teresa Sánchez Rivilla, "Inquisidores Generales y Consejeros de la Suprema: Documentación biográfica," in *Historia de la Inquisición en España y América*, vol. 3, ed. Joaquín Pérez Villanueva and Bartolomé Escandell Bonet (Madrid: Biblioteca de Autores Cristianos, Centro de Estudios Inquisitoriales, 2000), 228–435, 276; John Edwards, *Torquemada & the Inquisitors* (Stroud, U.K.: Tempus, 2005), 11–33.

32. See Jaime Contreras and Jean Pierre Dedieu, "Estructuras geográficas del Santo Oficio en España," in *Historia de la Inquisición en España y América*, vol. 2, ed. Joaquín Pérez Villanueva and Bartolomé Escandell Bonet (Madrid: Biblioteca de Autores Cristianos, Centro de Estudios Inquisitoriales, 1993), 3–47.

33. See Joseph Pérez, *Crónica de la Inquisición en España* (Barcelona: Ediciones Martínez Roca, 2002), 93–99. Indeed, the initial opposition of Aragon persisted as lack of support, a disapproval of the methods of the Inquisition, and even more extreme actions: In the 1480s, two inquisitors were murdered in Zaragoza. And in Barcelona, in the middle of the sixteenth century, the inquisitors complained that the city authorities did not attend to the celebrations of the Autos de Fe. On this point, see Kamen, *The Spanish Inquisition*, 178. González Montes also refers to the Aragonese opposition in González Montes, *Artes de la Santa Inquisición Española*, 134. For the last named author, see also Ruiz de Pablos, "Errores antiguos y actuales sobre González Montes."

34. "El espíritu de los pueblos castellanos era tan contrario al nuevo establecimiento [of the Inquisition] que aunque los inquisidores llegaron a Sevilla y presentaron sus títulos y cédulas reales, no pudieron ejercer su oficio por falta de auxilio." Llorente, *Historia crítica*, 1:128–129.

35. At this time, the kingdoms of Galicia and Navarre were still independent, and their tribunals were established later.

36. Pérez, *Crónica*, 92.

37. For comprehensive approaches see, among others, Pérez Villanueva and Escandell Bonet, *Historia de la Inquisición*; Kamen, *The Spanish Inquisition*; Pérez, *Crónica*; Bethencourt, *The Inquisition*.

38. Peters, *Inquisition*, 17.

39. "En el proceso inquisitivo el juez tiene por lo menos tanto de policía como de oficial administrador de justicia." Francisco Tomás y Valiente, *El derecho penal de la monarquía absoluta (siglos XVI–XVII–XVIII)* (Madrid: Tecnos, 1969), 168.

40. Tomás y Valiente, "Relaciones de la Inquisición," 13–35, 15.

41. Lea, *A History*, 2:4. For a detailed discussion of the concept of heresy see book 3, chap. 1, of the same volume.

42. Ibid., 2:20.

43. Ibid., 2:26. "El significado de la noción de error es más amplio que el de la noción de herejía, pues si toda herejía es un error, todo error no es una herejía. Y si todo hereje se equivoca, todos los que se equivocan no son necesariamente herejes. Pero en el ámbito de la fe, herejía y error son perfectamente sinónimos." Eimeric and Peña, *El manual*, 61.

44. Eimeric and Peña, *El manual*, 161.

45. On this matter, see Julio Caro Baroja, *El señor inquisidor*; Lynn, "Was Adam the

First Heretic?"; Kimberly Lynn, *Between Court and Confessional: The Politics of Spanish Inquisitors* (Cambridge: Cambridge University Press, 2013).

46. Lea also mentions that laymen were sometimes hired as inquisitors, but only if they were single. Once married, they had to resign the position, probably because the secrecy demands of the Inquisition were incompatible with the idea of marriage. Lea, *A History*, vol. 2, book 4, 234–235; Castañeda Delgado and Hernández Aparicio, *Inquisición de Lima*, 2:8–9.

47. Lynn, *Between Court and Confessional*, 295–296.

48. Lea, *A History*, vol. 2, book 4, 234; Eimeric and Peña, *El manual*, 221–222.

49. For general information, see Mendiburu, *Diccionario histórico-biográfico*, 7:221–222; Rafael Sánchez-Concha Barrios, *Santos y Santidad en el Perú Virreinal* (Lima: Vida y Espiritualidad, 2003), chap. 5. For conflicts between Mogrovejo and the Lima tribunal, see Medina, *Inquisición de Lima*, vol. 1, chap. 12. For the academic training of Lima inquisitors, see Castañeda Delgado and Hernández Aparicio, *Inquisición de Lima*, 2:6–7. The Lic. Pedro de la Gasca was also a member of the Suprema, sent to Peru to preside over the audiencia (royal court) in Lima in 1546. See Sánchez Rivilla, "Inquisidores Generales y Consejeros de la Suprema," 358–359; Lynn, *Between Court and Confessional*, 303.

50. Castañeda Delgado and Hernández Aparicio, *Inquisición de Lima*, 2:222; Millar Carvacho, *Inquisición y sociedad*, 124; Ayllón Dulanto, *El Tribunal de la Inquisición*, 315.

51. For salaries in the Lima tribunal, see Medina, *Inquisición de Lima*, 1:202; Bernabé Cobo, *Historia del Nuevo Mundo*, ed. P. Francisco Mateos, Obras del P. Bernabé Cobo de la Compañía de Jesús, Biblioteca de Autores Españoles (Madrid: Atlas, 1956), 400–401; Salinas y Córdova, *Memorial*, 147–148; Palma, *Anales*, 178–180. To compare finances in Spain, Lima, and Mexico as expressed in *maravedíes*, see Ayllón Dulanto, *El Tribunal de la Inquisición*, 315. For the reference about the income of archbishoprics and bishoprics in the Peruvian viceroyalty, see Salinas y Córdova, *Memorial*, 192. I am thankful to Renzo Honores for helping me to elucidate this information.

52. Pérez Villanueva, "Felipe IV," 1016, 1033.

53. Here is a full transcription of Fonseca's statements on this occasion: "1) que Jesucristo Nuestro Señor siendo Dios ubiese padecido muerte y pasión; 2) que haya nacido de mujer; 3) que cómo nuestra Señora fue Virgen siendo casada; 4) cómo fue Dios el Mesías; 5) como aviendo un Dios son tres personas si son tres no son uno; 6) como el Mesías podia ser Dios si comia bebia y cagaba; 7) si guardamos los fieles la escriptura como eran los judios en guardarla y damos por muerta la ley de Moysen; 8) como es reprobada la circuncision si el mismo Mesías fue circuncidado." AHN-Inquisición, Libro 1030, "Causas despachadas en el auto de fe celebrado el 21 de diciembre de 1625 en Lima," f. 432r. For a summary, see Castañeda Delgado and Hernández Aparicio, *Inquisición de Lima*, 1:436.

54. Schwartz, *All Can Be Saved*, 205.

55. Caro Baroja also points out that, in Spain, the annual salary of the inquisitor was the same of that of a judge of the high court (*audiencia*): 100,000 *maravedís*. See Caro Baroja, *El señor inquisidor*, 25.

56. For synoptic biographies of Juan de Mañozca y Zamora, see Mendiburu, *Diccionario histórico-biográfico*, 5:195–196; Sánchez Rivilla, "Inquisidores Generales y Consejeros de la Suprema," 367–368. For his activities in Quito, see John Leddy Phelan, *The Kingdom of Quito in the Seventeenth Century: Bureaucratic Politics in the Spanish Empire* (Madison: University of Wisconsin Press, 1967). For Mañozca's performance in Lima and in Mexico, see Medina, *Inquisición de Lima*, vol. 2; Jonathan Israel, *Race, Class, and Politics in Colonial Mexico, 1610–1670* (Oxford: Oxford University Press, 1975). For a recent study of his life and career, see Lynn, *Between Court and Confessional*, chap. 5.

57. In January 1631 the Lima viceroy gave to a man named Pedro Sáenz de Mañozca the grant of León de Huánuco. Suardo, *Diario*, 1:132. On the Carvajal family, see Seymour B. Liebman, *The Enlightened: The Writings of Luis de Carvajal, el Mozo* (Coral Gables, Fla.: University of Miami Press, 1967); Martin Cohen, *The Martyr Luis de Carvajal: A Secret Jew in Sixteenth-Century Mexico* (Albuquerque: University of New Mexico Press, 2001).

58. Lynn, *Between Court and Confessional*, 245.

59. Phelan, *Kingdom of Quito*, chaps. 11–13.

60. Suardo wrote in August 1630: "También se supo como Su Magestad avia escrito que le avian informado siniestramente acerca del proceder del señor Licenciado Juan de Mañozca en la Vissita de la Real Audiencia de Quito y mandava que en su lugar fuesse a acavarla el Señor doctor Juan de la Celda, Oydor desta Real Audiencia." Suardo, *Diario*, 1:93.

61. Licenciado Don Fernando de Montesinos, *Auto de la Fe celebrado en Lima a 23 de enero de 1639* (Madrid: Imprenta del Reino, 1640), Biblioteca Nacional del Perú (BNP-Lima), f. 8v, XCS—2896.

62. Mendiburu, *Diccionario histórico-biográfico*, 4:217; Suardo, *Diario*, 1:4.

63. Contreras, *Inquisición de Galicia*, 208–211; Contreras, "Los cambios en la Península," 1156–1176, 1164–1167; Gabriela Ramos, "La privatización del poder: Inquisición y sociedad en el Perú," in *Poder y violencia en los Andes*, ed. Henrique Urbano and Mirko Lauer (Cusco: Centro de Estudios Regionales Andinos Bartolomé de Las Casas, 1991), 75–92; Sánchez Rivilla, "Inquisidores Generales y Consejeros de la Suprema," 272–273.

64. Medina, *Inquisición de Lima*, 2:71; Salinas y Córdova, *Memorial*, 147. For the itinerary of Peruvian viceroys up to 1630, see Salinas y Córdova, *Memorial*, 124–127.

65. Pérez Cantó, "La dinámica de las estructuras en el Tribunal de Lima," 1180–1189, 1180. "El tiempo medio de permanencia en la Inquisición limeña fue de 15 años; si bien alguno superó con creces esta cifra: por ejemplo Gaitán, el más veterano, que sirvió 40 años." Castañeda Delgado and Hernández Aparicio, *Inquisición de Lima*, 2:11.

66. See Salinas y Córdova, *Memorial*, 147. See also Medina, *Inquisición de Lima*, 2:71.

67. See also Mendiburu, *Diccionario histórico-biográfico*, 2:330; Medina, *Inquisición de Lima*, 2:7; Antonio de la Calancha, *Crónica moralizada del Orden de San Agustín en el Perú*, ed. Ignacio Prado Pastor (Lima: Imprenta de la Universidad Mayor de San Marcos, 1974 [1638]), vol. 4, chap. 16; Castañeda Delgado and Hernández Aparicio, *Inquisición de Lima*, 2:10–11, 19.

68. Suardo, *Diario*, 2:169; Medina, *Inquisición de Lima*, 1:286–287; Lea, *The Inquisition in the Spanish Dependencies*, 357–358, 376–380. See also Castañeda Delgado and Hernández

Aparicio, "La visita de Ruiz de Prado"; Pérez Cantó, "El Tribunal de Lima"; Ramos, "La fortuna del Inquisidor"; Ramos, "La privatización del poder"; Millar Carvacho, *Inquisición y sociedad*.

69. Alejandro Cañeque, *The King's Living Image: The Culture and Politics of Viceregal Power in Colonial Mexico* (New York: Routledge, 2004), 117.

70. For the description of the prosecutor's office, see Lea, *A History*, 2:241. For social profiles of inquisitors and prosecutors in Lima during the seventeenth century, see Castañeda Delgado and Hernández Aparicio, *Inquisición de Lima*, vol. 2, chap. 1.

71. Salinas y Córdova, *Memorial*, 148. For all other paid employees, this author mentions sheer amounts of pesos. Palma says that the secretaries also received their salaries from confiscated properties. Palma, *Anales*, 179. For names and brief biographies, see Castañeda Delgado and Hernández Aparicio, *Inquisición de Lima*, vol. 2, chap. 2.

72. Proceso contra Bartolomé de Pradeda, AHN–Inquisición, Leg. 1643, Exp. 15, f. 78r. Pradeda was born in Galicia. See Castañeda Delgado and Hernández Aparicio, *Inquisición de Lima*, 2:89. For names and brief biographies of these lower-level officials, see ibid., 2:89 (table).

73. Millar Carvacho, *Inquisición y sociedad*, 50 n. (c).

74. See Proceso de Antonio Morón, AHN–Inquisición, Leg. 1647, Exp. 18, fs. 141–146.

75. See the testimony of Manuel de Fonseca, relación (he changed this declaration afterward and said he had been baptized); and the procesos of Enrique Jorge Tavares and Manuel Henríquez. Manuel de Fonseca, Relación de Causa, AHN–Inquisición, Libro 1030; Proceso de Enrique Jorge Tavares, AHN–Inquisición, Leg. 1648, Exp. 15; and Proceso de Manuel Henríquez, AHN–Inquisición, Leg. 1647, Exp. 11. Reaching beyond Peru to capture information from the Mexican tribunal, Nathan Wachtel examines the fact that 1650s physicians there checked female prisoners for evidence of a socioreligious practice, allegedly applied to crypto-Jewish women, in which a small piece of flesh from a woman's shoulder was removed, symbolizing a parallel to the male circumcision. Clearly, the Mexican tribunal and its physicians considered such evidence useful, as they recorded their verifications in trial records, but Wachtel's analysis of the primary sources questions its veracity, credibility, and frequency. The French scholar concludes that in a given case, inquisitors may have found a scar and on that basis have come to believe that the removal of a woman's flesh was a common practice, and may have even incorporated the probe into routine examinations. But there is not enough evidence to sustain that it was an extended habit among Mexican crypto-Jews. Here is the quotation: "Se trata, en efecto, de hacer revisar a la acusada por médicos, para que éstos verifiquen si lleva la marca de una 'circuncisión.' Por sorprendente que parezca, los inquisidores se refieren a la 'experiencia' de los procesos instruidos durante la década de 1640, que habrían registrado esta práctica en ciertos judaizantes." Wachtel, *La fe del recuerdo*, 188. In the English version: "They had doctors examining the defendant to verify whether she bore the mark of 'circumcision.' As astonishing as this might seem, the Inquisitors based their action on the 'experience' of trials held in the 1640s, said to attest to such a practice among Judaizers." Wachtel, *The Faith of Remembrance*, 154.

76. Suardo, *Diario*, 1:96; Salinas y Córdova, *Memorial*, 148.

77. Montesinos, *Auto de la Fe*, BNP-Lima. See also Pedro Guibovich Pérez, "The Printing Press in Colonial Peru: Production Process and Literary Categories in Lima, 1584–1699," *Colonial Latin American Review* 10, no. 2 (2001): 168–188.

78. See Salinas y Córdova, *Memorial*, 174; Castañeda Delgado and Hernández Aparicio, *Inquisición de Lima*, 1:67; Guibovich Pérez, "Fray Juan de Almaraz"; Pedro Guibovich Pérez, *La Inquisición y la censura de libros en el Perú virreinal (1570–1813) / The Inquisition and Book Censorship in the Peruvian Viceroyalty (1570–1813)* (Lima: Ediciones del Congreso del Perú, 2000), 26–27; Pedro Guibovich Pérez, *Censura, libros e Inquisición en el Perú colonial, 1570–1754* (Seville: Consejo Superior de Investigaciones Científicas, Escuela de Estudios Hispano-Americanos, Universidad de Sevilla, Diputación de Sevilla, 2003), 63–80.

79. Lea, *The Inquisition in the Spanish Dependencies*, 334–336. For comisarios in Lima during the seventeenth century, see Ramos, "La privatización del poder," 84; Castañeda Delgado and Hernández Aparicio, *Inquisición de Lima*, vol. 2, chap. 4.

80. According to Henry Charles Lea, the Suprema was "on the side of mercy rather than of rigor." Lea, *A History*, vol. 2, book 4, chap. 1, 186. For the construction of inquisitorial power, see also Tomás y Valiente, "Relaciones de la Inquisición"; Bennassar, "El poder inquisitorial."

81. "In the medieval Inquisition the inquisitor had the right to surround himself with armed guards, whether to protect his person or to execute his orders. They were reckoned as members of his family, thence obtaining the name of familiars, entitling them to immunity from justice." Lea, *A History*, 2:273.

82. Ibid., vol. 2, book 4, chap. 3. See also Contreras, *Inquisición de Galicia*, 67; Haliczer, *Inquisition and Society*, chap. 4. For familiares serving as notarios in Lima, see Castañeda Delgado and Hernández Aparicio, *Inquisición de Lima*, 2:110.

83. Suardo, *Diario*, 1:57–58; Suárez, *Desafíos transatlánticos*, 190; Osorio, *Inventing Lima*, 27.

84. Contreras, "Los cambios." For the numbers of familiares in Lima and in Spanish cities, see Castañeda Delgado and Hernández Aparicio, *Inquisición de Lima*, 1:58–61. For a list of merchants who were also familiars in Lima during the seventeenth century, see Cross, "Commerce and Orthodoxy." See also Suárez, *Desafíos transatlánticos*, 192; Osorio, *Inventing Lima*, 31.

85. Eimeric and Peña, *El manual*, 266–268.

86. Birckel, "Recherches sur la Trésorerie Inquisitoriale de Lima, I"; Tomás y Valiente, *El derecho penal*, chap. 3; Birckel, "Recherches sur la Trésorerie Inquisitoriale de Lima, II"; Castañeda Delgado and Hernández Aparicio, *Inquisición de Lima*, vol. 1, chap. 4; Castañeda Delgado and Hernández Aparicio, *Inquisición de Lima*, vol. 2, chap. 8; Millar Carvacho, *Inquisición y sociedad*, chaps. 3–4; Ayllón Dulanto, *El Tribunal de la Inquisición*, chap. 3.

87. Birckel, "Recherches sur la Trésorerie Inquisitoriale de Lima, I," 229; Castañeda Delgado and Hernández Aparicio, "La visita de Ruiz de Prado."

88. The information discussed in this paragraph and in the following one can be found in these sources: Carta del inquisidor Ordóñez y Flórez, Lima, December 30, 1594, reproduced in Birckel, "Recherches sur la Trésorerie Inquisitoriale de Lima, I,"

295–296. See also Medina, *Inquisición de Lima*, 1:342; Lea, *The Inquisition in the Spanish Dependencies*, 342–347; Birckel, "Recherches sur la Trésorerie Inquisitoriale de Lima, II," 329; Castañeda Delgado and Hernández Aparicio, *Inquisición de Lima*, 1:225, 234–238; Millar Carvacho, *Inquisición y sociedad*, 108, 111–120.

89. Suardo, *Diario*, 1:50, 151–152; Pérez Cantó, "El Tribunal de Lima," 1139–1141; Castañeda Delgado and Hernández Aparicio, *Inquisición de Lima*, 2:62; Millar Carvacho, *Inquisición y sociedad*, 112–113. On inquisitorial canonries, see also José Martínez Millán, "Structures of Inquisitorial Finance," in *The Spanish Inquisition and the Inquisitorial Mind*, ed. Ángel Alcalá (Highland Lakes, N.J.: Atlantic Research and Publications, 1987), 159–176.

90. Lea, *The Inquisition in the Spanish Dependencies*, 347; Castañeda Delgado and Hernández Aparicio, *Inquisición de Lima*, 2:226–228, 230–232; Millar Carvacho, *Inquisición y sociedad*, 113–114, 153–154. According to Matthew Warshawsky, at the time of the confiscations, Manuel Bautista Pérez and his brother-in-law Sebastián Duarte owned between them an equivalent of $33 million. Matthew Warshawsky, "Manuel Bautista Pérez and the *Complicidad Grande* in Colonial Peru: Inquisitorial Hysteria or Crypto-Jewish Heresy?," *Journal of Spanish, Portuguese, and Italian Crypto-Jews* 2 (2010): 132–150.

91. "Fui llebado a una carcel debaxo de la tierra a donde no çe ve claridade del cielo sino con luces de noche e de dia." Proceso de Manuel Henríquez, AHN–Inquisición, Leg. 1647, Exp. 11, f. 172v. For a summary of his trial in Lima, see Castañeda Delgado and Hernández Aparicio, *Inquisición de Lima*, 2:449–453.

92. "El lugar que tiene cada uno como cárcel privada, por su estrechez, hedor y, si es subterráneo, humedad, se diría más correctamente que es un sepulcro y no una cárcel de vivos." González Montes, *Artes de la Santa Inquisición Española*, 199.

93. Medina, *Inquisición de Lima*, 1:44.

94. Miguel de la Pinta Llorente, *Las cárceles inquisitoriales españolas* (Madrid: Librería Clío, 1949), 42–43; González Montes, *Artes de la Santa Inquisición Española*, 201.

95. González Montes, *Artes de la Santa Inquisición Española*, 210–211; Eimeric and Peña, *El manual*, 239. For information about the visits to the Lima tribunal prisons toward the end of the sixteenth century, see Medina, *Inquisición de Lima*, vol. 1, chaps. 10–11. There are also many references to viceregal visits to the secular prisons in Lima, for example Mugaburu and Mugaburu, *Diario (1640–1694)*, 97; Suardo, *Diario*, 2:20–21, 25, 128, and 155.

96. See, for example, González Montes, *Artes de la Santa Inquisición Española*, 204–205.

97. See Proceso de Manuel Bautista Pérez, AHN–Inquisición, Leg. 1647, Exp. 13, fs. 344v–345v; see also Wachtel, *La fe del recuerdo*, chap. 3; Wachtel, *The Faith of Remembrance*, chap. 3. For suicide attempts inside the Lima prisons at the end of the sixteenth century, see Medina, *Inquisición de Lima*, 1:309, 322, and Medina, *Inquisición de Lima*, 2:30.

98. See Proceso de Enrique Jorge Tavares, AHN–Inquisición, Leg. 1648, Exp. 15.

99. See Kamen, *The Spanish Inquisition*.

100. For the Lima tribunal and book censorship, see Guibovich Pérez, *La Inquisición y la censura de libros en el Perú virreinal*; Guibovich Pérez, *Censura, libros e Inquisición*. Another

aspect of Inquisition studies (just one of many that lies outside the scope of this book) is the way in which the monarchy manipulated the tribunal for political purposes. On this matter see, for example, Richard Kagan, *Lucrecia's Dreams: Politics and Prophecy in Sixteenth-Century Spain* (Berkeley: University of California Press, 1990); Richard Kagan, "Politics, Prophecy, and the Inquisition in Late-Sixteenth-Century Spain," in *Cultural Encounters: The Impact of the Inquisition in Spain and the New World*, ed. Mary Elizabeth Perry and Anne Cruz (Berkeley: University of California Press, 1991), 105–124.

Chapter 2
The Trial as a Setting for Confession and Repentance

1. In other words, "there was no formal trial, in the sense of a single act carried out in a single room within a set period of time." Kamen, *The Spanish Inquisition*, 196.

2. I consulted two different editions in Spanish of this manual: Eymeric, *Manual*, and Eimeric and Peña, *El manual*.

3. Tomás y Valiente, *El derecho penal*; Peters, *Inquisition*.

4. Eimeric and Peña, *El manual*, 166–168.

5. Guibovich Pérez, *Censura, libros e Inquisición*, 172.

6. Bethencourt, *The Inquisition*, 179–180.

7. Guibovich Pérez, *Censura, libros e Inquisición*, 167–184.

8. Ibid., 180; Bethencourt, *The Inquisition*, chap. 5.

9. See chap. 1.

10. De la Pinta Llorente, *La Inquisición Española*, 92–100; Bethencourt, *The Inquisition*, chap. 5; Eimeric and Peña, *El manual*, 85–86, 132–134. Ricardo Palma provides a full transcription of an edict from the Lima tribunal. Palma, *Anales*, 153–162. See also Gitlitz, *Secrecy and Deceit*, chap. 11.

11. Suardo, *Diario*, 1:63; Castañeda Delgado and Hernández Aparicio, *Inquisición de Lima*, 1:369–371; Millar Carvacho, *Inquisición y sociedad*, chap. 6; Guibovich Pérez, *Censura, libros e Inquisición*, 169–170.

12. Torquemada's instructions had twenty-eight articles that covered the following aspects: (1) establishment of tribunals, (2) the Edict of Faith, (3) grace period, (4) spontaneous confessions, (5) private absolutions, (6) deprivation of penitents from public and honorable positions, (7) monetary penalties to spontaneous confessors, (8) property confiscation for spontaneous confessors who missed the grace period, (9) softer penalties for underaged spontaneous confessors, (10) monetary penalties and duration of offenses, (11) life imprisonment for heretics who sincerely asked for reconciliation while in prison, (12) denial of reconciliation and release to the secular arm if the confession seemed fake, (13) second trial for spontaneous confessors in light of incomplete confessions, (14) consideration as impenitent those who remained without confession (negative), (15) application of torment to those who did not confess, (16) partial release of witnesses' testimonies, (17) requirement that inquisitors conduct hearings, (18) requirement that two inquisitors assist in hearings at the torture chambers, (19) convictions *in absentia*, (20) convictions *post mortem*, (21) mandatory support of the local lords, (22) partial reimbursement for

underaged children of people condemned to death at the stake, (23) procedures when the property of a person condemned was in other hands, (24) liberation of the Christian slaves of people reconciled without confiscation, (25) prohibition for members of the Holy Office on receiving gifts, (26) relationships between inquisitors, (27) supervision of lower rank employees, (28) other issues. See Llorente, *Historia crítica*, 1:145–152. On the assessment of Torquemada's instructions, see also José Luis González Novalín, "Las instrucciones de la Inquisición española: De Torquemada a Valdés (1484–1561)," in *Perfiles jurídicos de la Inquisición Española*, ed. José Antonio Escudero (Madrid: Instituto de Historia de la Inquisición, Universidad Complutense de Madrid, 1989), 91–109.

13. "En adelante el inquisidor no será el intérprete de la Ley, sino un agente que la aplica." Contreras, *Inquisición de Galicia*, 15. See also González Novalín, "Las instrucciones de la Inquisición española"; Bethencourt, *The Inquisition*, 60–62.

14. Gustav Henningsen, "La legislación secreta del Santo Oficio," in *Perfiles jurídicos de la Inquisición Española*, ed. José Antonio Escudero (Madrid: Instituto de Historia de la Inquisición, Universidad Complutense de Madrid, 1989), 163–172.

15. Lea, *A History*, vol. 3, book 6, 36. For the detailed description of the Inquisition trial, see book 6, chap. 8, of the same volume.

16. Enrique Gacto, "Aproximación al Derecho penal de la Inquisición," in *Perfiles jurídicos de la Inquisición Española*, ed. José Antonio Escudero (Madrid: Instituto de Historia de la Inquisición, Universidad Complutense de Madrid, 1989), 175–193.

17. Besides Lea, many other authors described the Inquisition trial, for example: Dedieu, "The Archives of the Holy Office of Toledo," 177–180; Millar Carvacho, *Inquisición y sociedad*, chap. 1; Kamen, *The Spanish Inquisition*, chap. 9; Pérez, *Crónica*, chap. 10. Most primary sources that describe the trial are internal to the tribunal. For a different point of view, see González Montes, *Artes de la Santa Inquisición Española*, 143–236.

18. Montesinos, *Auto de la Fe*, BNP–Lima, f. iv.

19. For descriptions of Argus, also known as Argus Panoptes, see Robert E. Bell, *Dictionary of Classical Mythology: Symbols, Attributes, & Associations* (Oxford: ABC-Clio, 1982); Adrian Room, *NTC's Classical Dictionary: The Origins of the Names of Characters in Classical Mythology* (Lincolnwood, Ill.: National Textbook Company, 1990); Charles Russell Coulter and Patricia Turner, *Encyclopedia of Ancient Deities* (Jefferson, N.C.: McFarland, 2000).

20. Millar Carvacho, *Inquisición y sociedad*, 48.

21. "Durante el interrogatorio conviene que el acusado se siente en una silla más baja, más sencilla que el sillón del inquisidor." Eimeric and Peña, *El manual*, 144.

22. On this matter, see Infieles Judíos o Moros no Baptizados, AHN–Inquisición, Libro 1260, Consejo de la Inquisición, Secretaría de Aragón, Libro de Varios tocantes al Santo Oficio por Don Miguel Lopez de Vitoria y Equinoa Fiscal del Santo Oficio año de 1642, fs. 75r–76r. See also Eva Uchmany, *La vida entre el judaísmo y el cristianismo en la Nueva España, 1580–1606* (Mexico City: Fondo de Cultura Económica, 1992).

23. Lea, *A History*, 3:70; Eimeric and Peña, *El manual*, 155–157.

24. Compare Natalie Zemon Davis, *Fiction in the Archives: Pardon Tales and Their Tellers in Sixteenth-Century France* (Stanford, Calif.: Stanford University Press, 1987); Kathryn

Burns, *Into the Archive: Writing and Power in Colonial Peru* (Durham, N.C.: Duke University Press, 2010), chap. 1.

25. See Proceso de Manuel Henríquez, AHN–Inquisición, Leg. 1647, Exp. 11, fs. 58r–58v.

26. See Proceso de Antonio Morón, AHN–Inquisición, Leg. 1647, Exp. 18, fs. 72v–73r.

27. Millar Carvacho, *Inquisición y sociedad*, 44; Eimeric and Peña, *El manual*, 165, 253–254.

28. Millar Carvacho, *Inquisición y sociedad*, 76.

29. See Proceso de Joan Vicente, AHN–Inquisición, Leg. 1647, Exp. 3. See also Wachtel, *La fe del recuerdo*, chap. 1; Wachtel, *The Faith of Remembrance*, chap. 1.

30. See Proceso de Francisco Vázquez, AHN–Inquisición, Leg. 1647, Exp. 16, doc. 1, f. 86v.

31. "Porque ussan mucho de la hypocresia: jeneralmente, ninguno se prende que no ande cargado de rosarios, reliquias, ymagenes, cinta de San Agustin, cordon de San Francisco, y otras devociones y mucho cilicio y disciplina; saben todo el catecismo y reçan el rosario, y preguntados cuando ya confiesan su delito, que por qué le reçan responden que por que no se les olviden las oraçiones para el tiempo de la necesidad, que es este de la prision, y se muestran devotos para engañar y que los tengan por buenos christianos." See Carta de los Inquisidores Juan de Mañozca, Andrés Juan Gaytán y Antonio de Castro y del Castillo, Lima, May 18, 1636, reproduced in Böhm, *Historia de los judíos en Chile*, 345–367, 362.

32. See introduction.

33. "Habia visto y oido que el reo Franco. Vasquez paseandose con cierta persona q nombro en la plaça de esta ciudad le habia dicho endos o tres ocaciones que para asegurarse que la Inqon no le prendiese abia de embiar la armada de seicientos y treinta y seis dos mil p a españa para q le negociasen una familiatura." Proceso de Francisco Vázquez, AHN–Inquisición, Leg. 1647, Exp. 16, doc. 1, f. 104r.

34. Pedro Guibovich Pérez, "La cultura libresca"; Suárez, *Desafíos transatlánticos*, 80; Studnicki-Gizbert, *A Nation upon the Ocean Sea*, 62–65.

35. Pérez was not the only one who noted differences between tribunals: complaints about the harshness of the Portuguese tribunal compared with the Castilian one, had been expressed by other Portuguese New Christians in Madrid close to the time of Pérez's incarceration. Juan Ignacio Pulido Serrano, *Injurias a Cristo: Religión, política y antijudaísmo en el siglo XVII (análisis de las corrientes antijudías durante la Edad Moderna)* (Alcalá de Henares: Instituto Internacional de Estudios Sefardíes y Andalusíes, Universidad de Alcalá, Servicio de Publicaciones, 2002); Studnicki-Gizbert, *A Nation upon the Ocean Sea*.

36. Suardo, *Diario*, 2:91. See Proceso de Manuel Bautista Pérez, AHN–Inquisición, Leg. 1647, Exp. 13, fs. 263r–269r. In the trial it reads that Pérez spoke in *esdrújulos*. According to Covarrubias, "Esdrúxulo. Es un género de verso italiano que se compone de doce sílabas, cuyo final tiene el acento en la décima o antepenúltima, y las dos últimas parece que se van derrocando abajo y deslizando." Covarrubias Orozco, *Tesoro de la lengua castellana o española*, pt. 1, 260v. On the complaints of Portuguese New Christians

about the harshness of the Portuguese tribunal during the first half of the seventeenth century, see, for example, Pulido Serrano, *Injurias a Cristo*, 60–61.

37. Here is the complete sentence: "El inquisidor no debe mostrarse muy apresurado en aplicar la tortura, pues sólo se recurre a ella a falta de otras pruebas, y corresponde al inquisidor establecerlas." Eimeric and Peña, *El manual*, 184. Peña wrote a similar comment: "Si puede establecerse el hecho de otro modo distinto de la tortura, no se torturará, ya que la tortura únicamente sirve para remediar la falta de pruebas." Ibid., 243.

38. Foucault, *Discipline and Punish*. Also, while focusing on torture within the frame of the Inquisition, we see the differences from our contemporary perception. In the words of Karen Sullivan: "They [Eimeric and Peña] have inherited a penitential tradition which regards the sensation of pain, not as a necessarily negative, world-shattering ordeal, but as a possibly positive, redemptive experience." Sullivan, *Inner Lives*, 181. For our contemporary perception, see the following: "In its basic outlines, torture is the inversion of the trial, a reversal of cause and effect. While the one studies evidence that may lead to a punishment, the other uses punishment to generate the evidence." Elaine Scarry, *The Body in Pain: The Making and Unmaking of the World* (New York: Oxford University Press, 1985), 41.

39. Tomás y Valiente, *El derecho penal*; Kamen, *The Spanish Inquisition*; Burns, *Into the Archive*, chap. 1.

40. Eimeric and Peña, *El manual*, 245–246.

41. The use of specific rooms for torture is also common in our era, like the "guest rooms" in Greece and the "safe houses" in the Philippines mentioned on page 40 of Scarry, *The Body in Pain*. See also Edward Peters, *Torture* (Philadelphia: University of Pennsylvania Press, 1999).

42. "Durante la preparación del suplicio, el obispo y el inquisidor, por sí mismos o por boca de un creyente ferviente, presionan al acusado a que confiese espontáneamente." Eimeric and Peña, *El manual*, 185.

43. Kamen, *The Spanish Inquisition*, 186–192; Millar Carvacho, *Inquisición y sociedad*, 56; Silverblatt, *Modern Inquisitions*, 71.

44. Medina, *Inquisición de Lima*, 1:120; de la Pinta Llorente, *Las cárceles*, chap. 4; Ayllón Dulanto, *El Tribunal de la Inquisición*, chap. 3; Sullivan, *Inner Lives*, 180–190. Palma confuses the different techniques. Palma, *Anales*, 60–61. I am thankful to Fernando Ayllón Dulanto, who kindly responded to my questions about torture.

45. Sullivan, *Inner Lives*, 180. On the following page this author mentions that on some occasions weights were attached to the prisoner's feet. Ibid., 181.

46. Latin: literally, in his/her own head.

47. Latin: literally, in the head of the other.

48. "Le exhortarán a que confiese mientras los verdugos le desnudan. Si aún se resiste, le conducirán aparte, totalmente desnudo, y los buenos creyentes le exhortarán repetidas veces. Mientras le exhortan le dirán que si confiesa no le matarán con tal de que prometa no cometer más delitos. . . . Por lo tanto el inquisidor y el obispo se lo prometan, pues podrán mantener su palabra (salvo si se trata de un relapso en cuyo caso no se prometerá nada)." Eimeric and Peña, *El manual*, 185.

49. Martínez, *Genealogical Fictions*.

50. Carta escrita por el Señor Don Gonzalo Bravo a la Inquisición de Galicia sobre la forma que se tiene en executar los tormentos en Castilla, AHN–Inquisición, Libro 1226, fs. 605r–606v, 1662.

51. Forma de escribir los tormentos según los da regularmente Alonso de Alcalá Ministro executor de Justicia de Madrid, AHN–Inquisición, Libro 1226, fs. 606v–609v, 1690. For a similar document, see "Instructions for Administering Questioning under Torture using the Rack," in *The Inquisition in New Spain, 1536–1820: A Documentary History*, ed. and trans. John F. Chuchiak IV (Baltimore: Johns Hopkins University Press, 2012), 135–138.

52. Sobre cambios en la aplicación de la tortura, AHN–Inquisición, Tribunal de Toledo, Leg. 3123, 1654.

53. Found in Forma de escribir los tormentos según los da regularmente Alonso de Alcalá Ministro executor de Justicia de Madrid, AHN–Inquisición, Libro 1226, f. 606v:

    Empezose esta diligencia a las tantas de la mañana

    Notificase la sentencia de tormento y si apela se manda executar sin embargo y luego se dice

    Fuele dicho diga la Verdad por amor de Dios no se quiera ver en tanto trabajo

    Dixo

    Fuele dicho diga la verdad o se le mandara bajar a la camara del tormento

    Dixo

    Y con tanto fue llevado a la camara del tormento donde fueron los dhos Sres Inquisidores y ordinario y estando en ella

    Fue amonestado el dicho F [Fulano] que por amor de Dios diga la verdad no se querra ver en tanto trabajo

    Dixo

    Fuele dicho diga la verdad o se mandara entrar el Ministro

    Dixo

    Y luego fue mandado entrar y entro el Ministro

    Dixo . . .

    Fuele dicho diga la verdad o se mandara desnudar

    Dixo

    Fue mandado desnudar y se desnudo y estando desnudo fuele dicho diga la verdad no se querra ver en tanto trabajo.

54. We see this procedure described somewhat more precisely in the Carta escrita por el Señor Don Gonzalo Bravo, AHN–Inquisición, Libro 1226, f. 605r: "y antes de mandar desnudar al Reo se le hace la monicion ordinaria que diga la Verdad o se mandara desnudar y desnudo que diga la verdad y puesto en el potro que diga la Verdad o se mandara ligar y pie ligado por el cuerpo: molledos, pie derecho, izquierdo y brazos haciendole cada amonestacion antes de executar cada cosa y se Va escribiendo."

55. Here we can see the following lines of the dialogue found in Forma de escribir los tormentos según los da regularmente Alonso de Alcalá Ministro executor de Justicia de Madrid, AHN–Inquisición, Libro 1226, f. 607v:

> Fuele dicho diga la verdad o se mandara poner en el potro =
> Dixo
> Mandose poner y fue puesto y estando en el
> Fuele dicho diga la verdad no se querra ver en tanto trabajo =
> Dixo
> Fueron mandados entrar F [Fulano] medico y F [Fulano] cirujano para que le reconozcan y habiendo entrado y reconocidole se volvieron a salir o dijeron Estando desnudo suelen entrar para reconocerle mejor o ya ligado como parece pero si el Ministro es diestro el reconoce si hay algun impedimento =
> Fuele dicho diga la verdad o se mandara ligar el cuerpo
> Dixo
> Mandose ligar... y estandose ligando
> Le fue dicho diga la verdad no se querra ver en tanto trabajo
> Dixo
> Fuele dicho diga la verdad o se mandaran ligar los pies para el trampazo
> Dixo
> Mandose ligar y se ligo el pie derecho y
> Dixo
> Fuele dicho diga la verdad o se mandara ligar el pie Izquierdo
> Dixo
> Mandose ligar y se ligo el pie izquierdo
> Dixo
> Fuele dicho diga la verdad o se mandaran ligar los molledos de los brazos
> Dixo

56. This exchange is applicable for torture in general. See Scarry, *The Body in Pain*, 28.

57. "Se le interroga sobre los artículos menos graves al principio, luego sobre los más graves, pues confiesan más fácilmente las faltas más leves que las más graves." Eimeric and Peña, *El manual*, 185.

58. "En el ajustamiento de los tormentos consiste el acierto de las causas y la aberiguazión de la verdad regulado el arbitrio y la prudencia con la piedad que acostumbra el Santo Oficio de manera que no se falte ni se exceda." Carta escrita por el Señor Don Gonzalo Bravo, AHN–Inquisición, Libro 1226, f. 606r.

59. "By Church law, ecclesiastical tribunals could not kill nor could they shed blood." Kamen, *The Spanish Inquisition*, 190.

60. "Algunos Inquisidores suelen escusar condenar al tormento a un Reo por su debilidad flaqueza o tener roto algun brazo y no combiene porque la tortura tiene partes como son la monicion, sentencia, bajarle a la camara, desnudarse, ponerle en el potro, ligarle, darle las bueltas, y siempre combiene llegar hasta donde se puede porque pueden confesar en lo permitido y se pierde esta esperanza por decir no se pueden dar las bueltas, luego escusese todo el medio; y yo he visto confesar a algunos solo con la monicion o pronunciación de la sentencia o desnudarse o ponerlos en el potro que se puede hacer sin riesgo y al fin se ha de parar donde el Medico y cirujano dijeren que no se puede pasar y si el Reo es quebrado no importa como se le ponga un buen braguero

fuerte que se ha de tener siempre prevenido para este efecto y en estos se suele // escusar el trampazo riguroso." Carta escrita por el Señor Don Gonzalo Bravo, AHN–Inquisición, Libro 1226, fs. 606r–606v.

61. The concern with detail went even further, since the guidelines included specific comments about how to regulate the ropes and pressure according to gender variation, and even contemplated the possibility of torturing pregnant women, although Peña wrote that pregnant women should not be scared or tortured until after they had given birth. See, for example: "Se tiran los cordeles de los pies igualmente de manera que hubieren los escalones del potro en los muslos y espinillas de modo que quede lugar para poderle dar Segunda vuelta de trampazo; en las mugeres se ha de hacer esto con mas tiento por la flaqueza de sus huesos." Carta escrita por el Señor Don Gonzalo Bravo, AHN–Inquisición, Libro 1226, f. 605v. "El tormento de la silla que es para quebrados o preñadas o sujetos debiles se executa mandando sentar en la silla y se le faxa y se afianzan los dos garrotes." Forma de escribir los tormentos según los da regularmente Alonso de Alcalá Ministro executor de Justicia de Madrid, AHN–Inquisición, Libro 1226, f. 609v. "¿Qué hay que hacer si el acusado al que hay que interrogar es una mujer encinta? No se la torturará ni aterrorizará, no vaya a ser que dé a luz o aborte. Se intentará arrancarle la confesión por otros medios antes del parto. Después del parto ya no hay obstáculo para la tortura." Eimeric and Peña, *El manual*, 187–188.

62. "Si después de haber sido convenientemente torturado no confiesa, se le enseñará los instrumentos de otro tipo de tormento diciéndole que tendrá que sufrirlos si no confiesa." Eimeric and Peña, *El manual*, 185.

63. See Proceso de Manuel Bautista Pérez, AHN–Inquisición, Leg. 1647, Exp. 13, fs. 386r–390r.

64. For instance, regarding the revocations there is a document that says: "Cuando la confesión se hiço en el tormento o cerca de él como es habiendosele ya notificado la sentencia y // pasadas las veinte y cuatro horas cuando se ha de ratificar la revoca se le repite el tormento una y aún dos veces si no fue suficientemente atormentado conforme fuere la testificación fuerças y edad del reo y otras circunstancias. . . . Hácese la ratificación. Pasadas las 24 horas después de la confesión así hecha en el tormento porque de otra suerte es inválida. . . . Y si dado el tormento suficientemente se ratifica pasadas las 24 horas diciendo que lo que declaró fue por miedo del tormento y no por ser verdad no se repite más el tormento porque sería proceder infinitum si siempre que revocase de usar el tormento." Revocantes de sus Confesiones, AHN–Inquisición, Libro 1260, Consejo de la Inquisición, Secretaría de Aragón, Libro de Varios tocantes al Santo Oficio por Don Miguel López de Vitoria y Equinoa Fiscal del Santo Oficio año de 1642, fs. 23v–24r. On the effects of the repetition of torment, Eimeric says: "Los que ya han sido torturados, éstos aguantan mejor que nadie el tormento pues enseguida tensan los miembros y los endurecen; pero otros salen muy debilitados de las primeras torturas y son incapaces de // aguantar otras. Están los embrujados, que por efecto de sortilegios que utilizan bajo la tortura, se hacen casi insensibles: éstos morirán antes que confesar." Eimeric and Peña, *El manual*, 184–185. For the use of torture in secular trials, see Tomás y Valiente, *El derecho penal*, chap. 3.

65. "Para sus sortilegios, estos embrujados suelen utilizar palabras y oraciones de los salmos de David u otras partes de la Sagrada Escritura que escribían en sus procedimientos supersticiosos en trozos de pergamino crudo que ellos llaman 'papel virgen,' mezclando a veces nombres de ángeles desconocidos. . . . Ocultan esto en un lugar secreto de su cuerpo para hacerse insensibles a la tortura." Eimeric and Peña, *El manual*, 187. See also Sullivan, *Inner Lives*, 182.

66. "Finalmente, ¿Cuándo puede decirse que un acusado ha sido 'torturado suficientemente'? Se dirá cuando sea evidente para los jueces y los expertos que ha sufrido, sin confesar, tormentos de una gravedad comparable a la gravedad de los indicios." Eimeric and Peña, *El manual*, 189.

67. "Yten dixo que despues de algunos dias supo esta declarante que se habia dado tormento a Antonio de Acuña porque asi lo dixo el dicho alcayde en la cocina a esta declarante diciendo Jesus que gran tormento le han dado y le han tenido tres horas y tiene los brazos hechos pedaços y le nombro por su nombre diciendo que era el dicho Antonio de Acuña." Proceso contra Bartolomé de Pradeda, AHN–Inquisición, Leg. 1643, Exp. 15, f. 4r.

68. Scarry, *The Body in Pain*, 29.

69. "Preguntada como son judias su m[adr]e y su hermana Dijo que lo que quissieren Poner ay [ahí] Pongan y decia Jesús que me muero, miren que me sale mucha sangre." Proceso de Mencía de Luna, AHN–Inquisición, Leg. 1647, Exp. 10, f. 59v. See also Lewin, *El Santo Oficio en América*, 122–123.

70. For similar statements in cases of the Spanish tribunal, see Kamen, *The Spanish Inquisition*, 191. For the Portuguese Inquisition, see Graizbord, "Religion and Ethnicity among the 'Men of the Nation.'"

71. "Y en particular un dia estando dando de comer a los presos se le escapa [a] un negro que no reparo qual de ellos era esta declarante un trapito sucio atado y redondo y esta lo alço entendiendo que era algun patacon y se lo metio en la faltriquera sin que nadie la viese y acabado de dar de comer esta declarante se fue a su aposento y desato el dicho trapito y vio que dentro del estaba un papel escrito y dentro del papel estaban quatro pelotillas redondas mas gruesas // algo que granos de maiz las quales le olieron a esta declarante a inciensio y sospecho y tuvo por cierto esta declarante que al negro a quien se le habian caydo las dichas pelotillas las tenia para metellas algun preso de las carceles secretas y esta declarante por no saber leer aunque la letra le parecio de muger llevo el dicho papel a un religioso de San Francisco que no le sabe el nombre y le dixo en confesion lo que le habia pasado y que le leyese el dicho papel el qual decia que tomase la noche antes que le hubiesen de dar tormento una pelotilla de aquellas y otra o todas que no esta bien [claro] en ello quando se lo hubiesen de dar." Proceso contra Bartolomé de Pradeda, AHN–Inquisicion, Leg. 1643, Exp. 15, fs. 6r–6v.

72. See Lea, *A History*, 3:42–50.

73. In the Papal Inquisition, the presence of a defense advocate was exceptional rather than usual. Regarding this point, Eimeric says: "Empero cuando la defensa del acusado parece de derecho natural, todavía se le dejará al reo facultad para usar las que fueren legítimas y conformes á derecho. Las principales son la intervención de un

abogado á quien pueda consultar el reo." Eymeric, *Manual*, 53. According to Peña, "Aunque Eimeric tenga razón respecto al fondo y al desenlace del proceso por sospecha grave, se admitirá, para la forma, la presencia de un defensor." Eimeric and Peña, *El manual*, 106.

74. Medina, *Inquisición de Lima*, 1:43. For the presence of lawyers in colonial Peru, see Renzo Honores, "*Pleytos*, letrados y cultura legal en Lima y en Potosí, 1540–1640," paper presented at the Latin American Studies Association XXVI International Congress (San Juan, Puerto Rico, 2006).

75. On this matter, see Lyman L. Johnson and Sonya Lipsett-Rivera, *The Faces of Honor: Sex, Shame, and Violence in Colonial Latin America* (Albuquerque: University of New Mexico Press, 1998); Ann Twinam, *Public Lives, Private Secrets: Gender, Honor, Sexuality, and Illegitimacy in Colonial Spanish America* (Stanford, Calif.: Stanford University Press, 1999).

76. "*Tacha*: es alegación de uno o más hechos por los cuales el derecho disminuye la fe y crédito que sin esa circunstancia merecería el testigo." Llorente, *Historia crítica*, 1:28.

77. Eimeric and Peña, *El manual*, 166–167.

78. Procesos of Manuel Henríquez, Antonio Morón, Manuel Bautista Pérez, and Francisco Vázquez; see also Proceso de Mencía de Luna, AHN–Inquisición, Leg. 1647, Exp. 10. For Enrique Núñez de Espinosa's, see Montesinos, *Auto de la Fe*, BNP–Lima, f. 14v.

79. Procesos of Joan Vicente (AHN–Inquisición, Leg. 1647, Exp. 3) and Enrique Jorge Tavares (AHN–Inquisición, Leg. 1648, Exp. 15). For Joan Vicente, see also Wachtel, *La fe del recuerdo*, chap. 1; Wachtel, *The Faith of Remembrance*, chap. 1.

80. Eimeric and Peña, *El manual*, 171–177.

81. An interesting case in New Spain illustrates this plea. See Uchmany, *La vida entre el judaísmo y el cristianismo*.

82. Procesos of Enrique Tavares and Manuel Henríquez.

83. Kamen, *The Spanish Inquisition*, 196–197.

84. See, for example, the following quote: "Yten dixo que sabe esta declarante que todas las consultas que en este santo oficio se hacian las oia el dicho alcayde Bartolome de Pradeda porque en habiendo consulta se metia en las carceles y se ponia a escuchar junto a la ventana que cae a la sala de tubos y alli encima de un bufete se ponia a escuchar." Proceso contra Bartolomé de Pradeda, AHN–Inquisición, Leg. 1643, Exp. 15, f. 2v. I will return to the gap between theory and reality inside the world of the Lima Inquisition and the circulation of secret information in later chapters.

85. Bennassar, "La Inquisición o la pedagogía del miedo."

86. See Medina, *Inquisición de Lima*, 1:125 n. 12.

87. "Mandamos a las dichas personas que así hanse ido o fueren condenadas por los dichos Inquisidores y a cada una de ellas que no vuelvan ni tornen a los dichos nuestros Reynos e señorío por alguna via manera causa o razón so pena de muerte e de perdimiento de bienes. La cual pena queremos y mandamos que por esto mismo fecho incurran: e queremos que la tercia parte de los dichos bienes sea para la persona que lo acusare e la tercia para la justicia e la otra tercia parte para nuestra Cámara." Decreto de los Reyes Católicos Don Fernando y Doña Isabel para que se castiguen y se secuestren

la tercera parte de los bienes de los penitenciados por el Santo Oficio aún trayendo habilitación de otros tribunales de Inquisición para arbitrar en estos reynos, BN–Madrid, MSS 718, f. IV.

88. Here I transcribe a fragment from the form of the abjuration: "Yo Fulano . . . abjuro y detesto y anatematizo toda especia de herejia y apostasia que se levante contra la santa fee catolica y ley evangelica de nuestro Redemptor y Salvador Jesuchristo y contra la Santa Sede Appostolica iglesia Romana especialmente aquella de que yo en vuestro juizio he sido acussado y estoy gravemente sospechosso y juro y prometo de tener y guardar siempre aquella santa fee que tiene y guarda la sancta madre yglessia y que ser siempre obediente a nuestro señor el Papa y a su sucessor que canonicamente sucedieren en la santa silla appostolica y a sus determinaciones y confiesso que todos aquellos que contra esta sancta fee catholica vinieren sean dignos de condenacion y prometo que nunca me juntar con ellos y que en cuanto en mi fuere los perseguire y las heregias que de ellos supiere las rebelare y notifficare a qualquier inquisidor de la heretica pravedad y prelado de la santa madre Yglesia donde quier que me hallare y juro y prometo que recibire humildemente y con paciencia la penitencia que me ha sido o fuere impuesta con todas mis fuerças y poder y la cunmplire en todo y por todo sin ir ni venir contra ello ni contra cossa alguna ni parte dello y quiero y consiento y me plaze // que si yo en algun tiempo lo que Dios no quiere y fuere o viniere contra las cossas suso dichas o contra qualquier cossa o parte dellas que en tal casso sea habido y tenido por relapso y me someto a la correccion y severidad de los sacros canones para que en mi como en perssona que abjura de Vehementi sean executadas las cien juras y penas en ellos contenidas y consiento que aquellas me sean dadas y las haya de sufrir quando quier que algo se me provare haber quebrantado de lo suso dicho por mi abjurado y ruego al presente notario que me lo de por testimonio y a los presentes que dello sean testigos." Reproduced in "La forma de la abjuracion de Vehemente," BN–Madrid, MS 2987, fs. 171v–172v.

89. González Montes, *Artes*, 235.

90. During the sixteenth century Juan Ginés de Sepúlveda used this rationale to argue in favor of wars against the Indigenous population. Juan Ginés de Sepúlveda, *Demócrates Segundo o De las justas causas de las guerras contra los indios*, critical bilingual edition with Spanish translation, introduction, notes, and indexes by Ángel Losada, 2nd ed. (Madrid: Consejo Superior de Investigaciones Científicas, Instituto Francisco de Vitoria, 1984), 88–91. For how these penalties influenced secular verdicts in Spain, see Tomás y Valiente, *El derecho penal*, chap. 3.

91. Castañeda Delgado and Hernández Aparicio, *Inquisición de Lima*, 2:218.

92. For examples of research based on sources related to property confiscations, see René Millar Carvacho, "Las confiscaciones de la Inquisición de Lima a los comerciantes de origen judeo-portugués de la 'Grand Complicidad' de 1635," *Revista de Historia de Indias* 42, no. 171 (1983): 27–58; Quiroz Norris, "La expropiación inquisitorial"; Guibovich Pérez, "La cultura libresca"; Pilar Huerga Criado, *En la raya de Portugal: Solidaridad y tensiones en la comunidad judeoconversa* (Salamanca: Universidad de Salamanca, 1993).

93. Eimeric and Peña, *El manual*, 125–126; see also Millar Carvacho, *Inquisición y sociedad*, 73–74.
94. Eimeric and Peña, *El manual*, 233–234.
95. Millar Carvacho, *Inquisición y sociedad*, 62–63; Eimeric and Peña, *El manual*, 231–233.
96. When the trial continued after her death, she was also accused of impenitence. See Proceso de Mencía de Luna, fs. 67r–67v. For more on people who died in the prisons of the Inquisition, see Difuntos, AHN–Inquisición, Libro 1260, Consejo de la Inquisición, Secretaría de Aragón, Libro de Varios tocantes al Santo Oficio por Don Miguel López de Vitoria y Equinoa Fiscal del Santo Oficio año de 1642, fs. 37r–39v.
97. The quote is from Lea, *A History*, 3:85. For the example, see Proceso de Garci Méndez de Dueñas, AHN–Inquisición, Leg. 1648, Exp. 16.
98. Bartolomé Escandell Bonet, "Las adecuaciones estructurales: Establecimiento de la Inquisición en Indias," in *Historia de la Inquisición en España y América*, vol. 1, ed. Joaquín Pérez Villanueva and Bartolomé Escandell Bonet (Madrid: Biblioteca de Autores Cristianos, Centro de Estudios Inquisitoriales, 1984), 713–730, 717.

Chapter 3
A Cobbler and a Merchant

1. "Todos los portugueses que andan por el mundo que son bulliciosos como no sean labradores o Marineros Son Judios." Testimonio de Álvaro Cardoso de Silba, in Proceso de Garci Méndez de Dueñas, AHN–Inquisición, Leg. 1648, Exp. 16, f. 55v.
2. For the reaction of the Lima bishops, see Castañeda Delgado and Hernández Aparicio, *La Inquisición de Lima*, 1:176–182.
3. "Por provisión de el Señor rey Don Phelipe 2º de 7 de febrero de 1569 se mandó erigir el tribunal de la Ynquisición en la ciudad de Lima de los reynos del Perú," *Origen y fundación de las Inquisiciones de España*, Biblioteca Nacional (hereafter BN—Madrid), MS 6591, f. 18v; and "Por provisión del Señor Rey Don Phelipe Segundo de 16 de Agosto de 1570 [ref] se mandó erigir Tribunal de la Ynquisición en la Ciudad de Mexico de los reynos de Nueva España," ibid., f. 19v. On the Junta Magna, see Demetrio Ramos Pérez, "La crisis indiana y la Junta Magna de 1568," *Jahrbuch für Geschichte von Staat, Wirtschaft und Gesselschaft Lateinamerikas* 23 (1986): 1–61. The bibliography about the Lima tribunal is vast and will be discussed in depth later in this chapter. See Medina, *Inquisición de Lima*, vol. 2; Bataillon, "La herejía de Fray Francisco de la Cruz"; Ramos, "El Tribunal de la Inquisición en el Perú"; Lee Penyak, "Más que sólo la destrucción de la Leyenda Negra: Un vistazo a los estudios actuales sobre la Inquisición española," *Cuadernos para la Historia de la Evangelización en América Latina* 4 (1989): 77–88; Teodoro Hampe Martínez, "Inquisición y sociedad en el Perú colonial (1570–1820): Una lectura crítica de la bibliografía reciente," *Histórica* 19 (1995): 1–28; Fernando Iwasaki Cauti, *Inqvisiciones Pervanas* (Lima: Promoción Editorial El Inca S.A., 1996); Palma, *Anales*; Pedro Guibovich Pérez, *En defensa de Dios: Estudios y documentos sobre la Inquisición en el Perú* (Lima: Congreso de la República del Perú, 1998); Hampe Martínez, *Santo Oficio e historia colonial*; Millar Carvacho,

Inquisición y sociedad; Guibovich Pérez, *Censura*; Silverblatt, *Modern Inquisitions*; Ayllón Dulanto, *El Tribunal de la Inquisición*.

4. See Reginaldo de Lizárraga, *Descripción breve de toda la tierra del Perú, Tucumán, Rio de la Plata y Chile*, preliminary study by Don Mario Hernández Sánchez-Barba, Biblioteca de Autores Españoles (Madrid: Atlas, 1968), 160–161. See also the preliminary study in this work by Don Mario Hernández Sánchez-Barba. For the establishment of the Inquisition in Lima, see Salinas y Córdova, *Memorial*, 146; Calancha, *Crónica*, vol. 4, chap. 16. See also Medina, *Inquisición de Lima*, vol. 1, chaps. 1–4, 7, and 10.

5. John F. Schwaller, *The History of the Catholic Church in Latin America: From Conquest to Revolution and Beyond* (New York: New York University Press, 2011), 51.

6. Martínez, *Genealogical Fictions*, chap. 7.

7. See, for example, Griffiths, *The Cross and the Serpent*; Gareis, "Repression and Cultural Change," 230–254.

8. Escandell Bonet, "Estructura geográfica del dispositivo inquisitorial americano," 48–60.

9. See chap. 2.

10. For the definition of these roles in Inquisition tribunals, see chap. 1.

11. Medina, *Inquisición de Lima*, 1:199–200; Castañeda Delgado and Hernández Aparicio, *Inquisición de Lima*, 1:209.

12. Following Salinas y Córdova: "Á tres de Octubre, de 1576, el Virrey del Pirú don Francisco de Toledo, hizo merced a la dicha Vniuersidad, del sitio, y casas que tiene oy en la plaçuela de la santa Inquisicion quatro cuadras de la plaza principal desta ciudad." Salinas y Córdova, *Memorial*, 163. According to the historian Durán Montero, "Una de las zonas más cotizadas fue la plazuela de la Inquisición y sus inmediaciones." María Antonia Durán Montero, *Lima en el siglo XVII: Arquitectura, urbanismo y vida cotidiana*, Sección Historia, "Nuestra América," no. 1 (Seville: Diputación Provincial de Sevilla, 1994), 21. The buildings were destroyed and rebuilt after the 1746 earthquake, and toward the end of the nineteenth century the former building of the Lima Inquisition served as a penitentiary facility for people detained for all kinds of crimes. Manuel Atanasio Fuentes, *Lima: Apuntes históricos, descriptivos, estadísticos y de costumbres* (Lima: Librería Escolar e Imprenta E. Moreno, 1925 [1867]), 35; Palma, *Anales*, 199.

13. Mendiburu, *Diccionario histórico-biográfico*, 5:37; Medina, *La primitiva Inquisición americana*, 370. Francisco de Aguirre, former governor of the Province of Tucumán, faced inquisitorial trial twice. Medina, *La primitiva Inquisición Americana*, chap. 19.

14. Relación verdadera de un auto de Inquisición que se hiço en la ciudad de los Reyes a 13 de Abril año de 1578, BN–Madrid, MS 721, fs. 121r–122v. For references to María Pizarro and Mateo Salcedo, see also Silverblatt, *Modern Inquisitions*, 65–69; Andrew Redden, *Diabolism in Colonial Peru* (London: Pickering & Chatto, 2008), chap. 2; Schwartz, *All Can Be Saved*, 156–157, 167–168.

15. José Toribio Medina, *La Inquisición en Cartagena de Indias*, 2nd ed. (Bogotá: C. Valencia, 1978).

16. Escandell Bonet, "Las adecuaciones estructurales," 713–730, 719.

17. Que se embie Relacion al q° de los estrangeros que hay en Potosí y en esta

provincia y de los ynconvenientes que resultan de su estado en estas partes, 1581, BN-Madrid, MS 2927, f. 48r.

18. "In Cartagena and in Mexico City they [Portuguese settlers] accounted for an estimated 5 to 6 percent of the urban European settler population, a percentage that, if extrapolated across the cities and towns of Spanish America, would render an estimated five thousand to seven thousand individuals." Studnicki-Gizbert, *A Nation upon the Ocean Sea*, 44. According to Nathan Wachtel, the Portuguese represented probably more than 15 percent of the resident population in the early seventeenth century, mainly in urban settlements such as Buenos Aires, Potosí, Veracruz, Zacatecas, and Mexico City. Wachtel, *La fe del recuerdo*, 21–22; Wachtel, *The Faith of Remembrance*, 8–9.

19. Castañeda Delgado and Hernández Aparicio, "La visita de Ruiz de Prado."

20. Medina, *Inquisición de Lima*, 2:65. For the lack of *calificadores* (clerics who evaluated if a given statement was heretical) in Lima during the sixteenth century, see also Guibovich Pérez, *La Inquisición y la censura de libros en el Perú*, 27. For changes in Lima's population over the sixteenth and seventeenth centuries, see the introduction.

21. Fray Diego de Ocaña, *Un viaje fascinante por la América hispana del siglo XVI* (Madrid: Stvdivm Ediciones, 1969 [1608]), 83–84, and 89.

22. The sentence reads: "Extranjeros inficionados de los errores que hay en sus tierras [Protestants], y los portugueses, que son todos judíos." Letter from Ordoñez y Florez, Los Reyes, April 28, 1600, quoted in Medina, *Inquisición en Cartagena*. See also Tomás Escribano Vidal, "Recesión, estancamiento administrativo, infiltración judía y extranjera," in *Historia de la Inquisición en España y en América*, vol. 1, ed. Joaquín Pérez Villanueva and Bartolomé Escandell Bonet (Madrid: Biblioteca de Autores Cristianos, Centro de Estudios Inquisitoriales, 1984), 1002–1005. For general biographical information on the inquisitor, see Mendiburu, *Diccionario histórico-biográfico*, 6:161.

23. Wachtel, *La fe del recuerdo*, 21–22; Wachtel, *The Faith of Remembrance*, 8–9.

24. "Que de cien Portugueses q ay en Potosi los noventa y cinco son hijos de Judios." Declaración de Gregorio Díaz Tavares, in Proceso de Joan Vicente, doc 1, f. 19r.

25. "Pero no se entienda, que aqueste es el mayor vltraje deste Reyno, verse solo, y cercado de enemigos de la Fé, que lo inquietan, y amenazan por la mar. Mayor peligro tiene en tierra, mayor daño daño [*sic*] recibe esta Ciudad de Lima, Guancauelica, Potosi, con los forasteros, que passan todos los años al comercio, y viuen con nosotros chupando la tierra como esponjas." Salinas y Córdova, *Memorial*, 275. See also Jonathan Israel, *Diasporas within a Diaspora: Jews, Crypto-Jews and the World Maritime Empire (1540–1740)* (Leiden: Brill, 2002), chap. 4.

26. "Y ansí nos ha parecido advertir a V. S. que esta Inquisición [de Lima] sola no puede acudir al gobierno de tantos reinos y que es necesario en esta Inquisición haya tres inquisidores y a lo menos tres secretarios." Quoted in Medina, *Inquisición en Cartagena*, 18.

27. For example, Kimberly Lynn traces down different members of a family of inquisitors who across generations participated in trials for crypto-Judaism in Mexico (1590s), Lima (1630s), and Mexico (1640s). See Lynn, *Between Court and Confessional*, chap. 5.

28. See Lea, *The Inquisition in the Spanish Dependencies*, 337–342; Studnicki-Gizbert, *A Nation upon the Ocean Sea*, 159–160.

29. It is interesting to note that although the Spanish American colonies belonged to the Crown of Castile, the Tribunals of the Inquisition of the Spanish American colonies responded to the Secretaría of Aragon. I was unable to find an explanation for this, nor any bibliography addressing this question.

30. Escandell Bonet, "Las adecuaciones estructurales," 717–718.

31. See Relaçion de el processo de Duarte nuñez de cea Portugues q' esta presso en la inqon de los Reyes en los Reynos de el Piru por judio remettida al 9 de abril de 1596, AHN–Inquisición, Leg. 1648, Exp. 7. For Duarte Méndez, see also Silverblatt, *Modern Inquisitions*, 93.

32. See Proceso de Joan Vicente, AHN–Inquisición, Leg. 1647, Exp. 3. For a portrait of this case, see also Wachtel, *La fe del recuerdo*, chap. 1; Wachtel, *The Faith of Remembrance*, chap. 1.

33. "Bento Adonay nosso Deus Rey de Sempre que nos sanctificou suas encomendanças." In the proceso of Joan Vicente (AHN–Inquisición, Leg. 1647, Exp. 3) these materials are at the end of the folder titled in Portuguese "Treslado das confissões de Joao Vicente meo xpao novo çapateiro de campo maior," f. 2r.

34. "Potosí dá barras para enriquezer a España." Salinas y Córdova, *Memorial*, 172.

35. Enrique Tandeter, *Coacción y mercado: La minería de la plata en el Potosí colonial, 1692–1826* (Buenos Aires: Editorial Sudamericana, 1992); Kendall Brown, *A History of Mining in Latin America: From the Colonial Era to the Present* (Albuquerque: University of New Mexico Press, 2012).

36. See also Lewis Hanke, "The Portuguese in Spanish America, with Special Reference to the Vila Imperial of Potosí," *Revista de Historia de América* 51 (1961): 1–48.

37. "De las naciones extranjeras hay muchos hombres, que si no los hubiera no perdiera nada el reino." Lizárraga, *Descripción breve*, 91.

38. Ibid. See also Portocarrero, "Descrição geral do reino do Peru." Guillermo Lohmann Villena says that Pedro de León Portocarrero was a New Christian born in Portugal in 1576, whose father had been released to the secular arm by the Coimbra tribunal while his mother died in the prisons of the Inquisition. Portocarrero had also been reconciled by the Toledo tribunal in 1600, prior to his migration to the New World. He lived and got married in Lima, and as a merchant participated in the same networks in which Garci Méndez de Dueñas operated. Portocarrero appears in testimonies given to the Lima tribunal in Méndez de Dueñas's trial and had another encounter with the institution upon his return to Spain. See Proceso de Garci Méndez de Dueñas, AHN–Inquisición, Leg. 1648, Exp. 16; and Guillermo Lohman Villena, "Una incógnita despejada: La identidad del judío portugués autor de la 'Discriçion General del Piru,'" *Revista de Indias* 30, nos. 119–122 (1970): 315–387.

39. Carlos Sempat Assadourian, "Chile y El Tucumán en el siglo XVI: Una correspondencia de mercaderes," *Historia* 9 (1970): 65–109; Zacarías Moutoukias, *Contrabando y control colonial en el siglo XVII: Buenos Aires, el Atlántico y el espacio peruano* (Buenos Aires: Centro Editor de América Latina, 1988); Israel, *Diasporas within a Diaspora*, chap. 4.

40. For biographical information on inquisitor Francisco Verdugo, see Mendiburu, *Diccionario histórico-biográfico*, 8:307; Medina, *Inquisición de Lima*, 1:329.

41. Nathan Wachtel dates Vicente's first use of this argument of his defense in 1609, by which time Lima had received the Évora materials. In my reading of the primary source, the first meeting of Vicente with his attorney Lic. Pardo del Castillo took place years earlier, and it was very shortly thereafter that this defense was first made. The first meeting was on Friday, September 19, 1603; the argument made in the hearing on Monday, September 22, 1603, starts with "*Joan Vicente presso en las carceles secretas.*" Lima did not question whether or not the Évora procedure had taken place; what it set out to verify was Vicente's spontaneous confession as a trigger to the Évora reconciliation. Once the Évora evidence was received in Lima, prisoner and lawyer reintroduced the defense in 1609, following a meeting between Vicente and Pardo del Castillo on September 4, 1609. There had also been interrogations of Vicente regarding discrepancies between his declarations of 1601 and 1609. A hearing took place on Friday, September 11, 1609, in which Pardo del Castillo and Vicente reintroduced the spontaneous-confession defense, adding to it the issue of Vicente's age and the lack of proper assistance at the time the Évora events took place and referring to "*Joan Vicente presso cerca de diez años ha.*" See Proceso de Joan Vicente, AHN–Inquisición, Leg. 1647, Exp. 3, doc. 2, fs. 59v–63v and 67v–69v; Wachtel, *La fe del recuerdo*, chap. 1; Wachtel, *The Faith of Remembrance*, chap. 1.

42. Eimeric and Peña, *El manual*, 171–173.

43. For the difference between the roles of *letrados* and *curadores*, see Honores, "*Pleytos*, letrados y cultura legal en Lima y en Potosí.*"

44. Relación de las causas despachadas en el Auto que la Inquisición del Perú hizo en la capilla de la dicha Inquisición domingo de la Santísima Trinidad 17 de junio de 1612, AHN–Inquisición, Libro 1029, fs 485r–585r. For the celebration at the chapel, see Medina, *Inquisición de Lima*, vol. 2, chap. 16.

45. For a portrait of Vicente in his last days, see Wachtel, *La fe del recuerdo*, chap. 1; Wachtel, *The Faith of Remembrance*, chap. 1.

46. Writing in the seventeenth century but referring to the creation of the Inquisition tribunals, jurist Juan de Solórzano Pereira summarized the control of the Inquisition in the Indies: "Si algún herege o judaizante, que ha cometido estos delitos en España, se pasa a las Indias, podrá en ellas ser preso y juzgado y castigado por los Inquisidores que allí residen, sin necesidad de remitirle al lugar de su origen o domicilio, o adonde cometió el delito." Juan de Solórzano Pereira, *Política indiana*, 2 vols., ed. Luis García Arias, Breviarios del Pensamiento Español (Madrid: Editorial Nacional, 1947 [1647]), 2:68. See also, Medina, *Inquisición de Lima*, 1:9.

47. Medina, *Inquisición de Lima*, 1:173. For trials *in absentia*, see chap. 2.

48. Relación de las causas pendientes en el Santo Oficio de la Inquisición de la ciudad de Los Reyes por el mes de marzo de 1597, AHN–Inquisición, Libro 1028, fs. 476r–477v.

49. See the testimony of Manuel de Fonseca, in Proceso de Garci Méndez de Dueñas, AHN–Inquisición, Leg. 1648, Exp. 16, fs. 38v–39r. See also Medina, *Inquisición de Lima*, 2:31; Castañeda Delgado and Hernández Aparicio, *Inquisición de Lima*, 1:436.

50. Proceso de Manuel Henríquez, AHN–Inquisición, Leg. 1647, Exp. 11.

51. Proceso de Garci Méndez de Dueñas, AHN–Inquisición, Leg. 1648, Exp. 16; Castañeda Delgado and Hernández Aparicio, *Inquisición de Lima*, 1:438–440. Andrés Juan Gaitán arrived in Lima to serve on the tribunal in 1611.

52. Proceso de Garci Méndez de Dueñas, AHN–Inquisición, Leg. 1648, Exp. 16, f. 69v.

53. Murdo MacLeod, *Spanish Central America: A Socioeconomic History, 1520–1720* (Berkeley: University of California Press, 1973), chap. 14. See also Portocarrero, "Descrição geral do reino do Peru," 223.

54. Causas despachadas en el auto de fe celebrado el 21 de diciembre de 1625 en Lima, AHN–Inquisición, Libro 1030, fs. 402r–406v; Medina, *Inquisición de Lima*, 2:28.

55. Castañeda Delgado and Hernández Aparicio, *Inquisición de Lima*, vol. 1, chap. 12; Silverblatt, *Modern Inquisitions*; Wachtel, *La fe del recuerdo*, chap. 1; Wachtel, *The Faith of Remembrance*, chap. 1.

56. Wachtel, *La fe del recuerdo*, 35; Wachtel, *The Faith of Remembrance*, 19.

57. For people from colonial Brazil whose trials of faith were processed under the Lisbon tribunal, see Rachel Mizrahi Bromberg, *A Inquisição no Brasil: Um capitão-mor judaizante* (São Paulo: FFLH/USP Centro de Estudos Judaicos, 1984); Anita Novinsky and Maria Luiza Tucci Carneiro, *Inquisição: Ensaios sobre mentalidade, heresias e arte; Trabalhos apresentados no I Congresso Internacional—Inquisição, Universidade de São Paulo, maio 1987* (Rio de Janeiro; São Paulo: Expressão e Cultura; EDUSP, 1992); Lina Gorenstein Ferreira da Silva, *Heréticos e impuros: A inquisição e os cristãos-novos no Rio de Janeiro, século XVIII* (Rio de Janeiro: Prefeitura da Cidade do Rio de Janeiro, Secretaria Municipal de Cultura, Departamento Geral de Documentação e Informação Cultural, Divisão de Editoração, 1995); Ronaldo Vainfas, *Santo Oficio da Inquisição de Lisboa: Confissões da Bahia* (Sao Paulo, 1997); James Sweet, *Domingos Alvares, African Healing, and the Intellectual History of the Atlantic World* (Chapel Hill: University of North Carolina Press, 2011). For the Goa tribunal, created in 1560, see Ana Cannas da Cunha, *A Inquisição no Estado da India: Origens (1539–1560)* (Lisbon: Arquivos Nacionais/Torre do Tombo, 1995). For a Portuguese inquisitor's suggestion that a tribunal be established in Brazil, see Schwartz, *All Can Be Saved*, 180.

58. Fernanda Olival, "Los virreyes y gobernadores de Lisboa (1583–1640): Características generales," in *El mundo de los virreyes en las monarquías de España y Portugal*, ed. Pedro Cardim and Joan-Lluís Palos (Madrid: Iberoamericana–Vervuert, 2012), 287–316; Joan-Lluís Palos and Joana Fraga, "Tres capitales virreinales: Nápoles, Lisboa y Barcelona," in *El mundo de los virreyes en las monarquías de España y Portugal*, ed. Pedro Cardim and Joan-Lluís Palos (Madrid: Iberoamericana–Vervuert, 2012), 345–390.

59. "Su propio nombre es Manuel de Fonseca y que para no quitar de todo punto el nombre de su apellido se llamaua Diego de Andrada Fonseca y que tambien se ha llamado Diego de Guzman a los principios que passo a este Reyno porque compro una Lic[encia] en Sevilla para enbarcarse de este nombre y apellido." Testimony of Manuel de Fonseca, in Proceso de Garci Méndez de Dueñas, AHN–Inquisición, Leg. 1648, Exp. 16, f. 38v. And from another witness in Méndez de Dueñas's trial: "Esteban Cardoso que es su nombre de Baptismo y que para pasar a este Reyno en Sevilla entro por criado

de un Antonio Gomez y porque traia lic[encia] para Vn criado que se llamaua Alv°[aro] de Silba este tomo este nombre y con el passo a las Yndias." Testimony of Álvaro Cardoso de Silva, in Proceso de Garci Méndez de Dueñas, AHN–Inquisición, Leg. 1648, Exp. 16, f. 51v.

60. Antonio Domínguez Ortiz, "Los extranjeros en la vida española durante el siglo XVII," in *Los extranjeros en la vida española durante el siglo XVII y otros artículos*, ed. León Carlos Álvarez Santaló (Seville: Diputación de Sevilla, Área de Cultura y Ecología, 1996); Solange Alberro, "Crypto-Jews and the Mexican Holy Office in the Seventeenth Century," in *The Jews and the Expansion of Europe to the West, 1450–1800*, ed. Paolo Bernardini and Norman Fiering (New York: Berghahn Books, 2001), 172–185; Eva Uchmany, "The Participation of New Christians and Crypto-Jews in the Conquest, Colonization, and Trade in Spanish America, 1521–1660," in *The Jews and the Expansion of Europe to the West, 1450–1800*, ed. Paolo Bernardini and Norman Fiering (New York: Berghahn Books, 2001), 186–202. For the Portuguese presence in Seville and the process of naturalization, see Santiago de Luxán Melendez, "A colónia portuguesa de Sevilha: Uma ameaça entre a Restauração portuguesa e a conjura de Medina Sidónia?," *Penélope: Fazer e Desfazer a História* 9/10 (1993): 127–134; Herzog, "'A Stranger in a Strange Land'"; Jesús Aguado de los Reyes, "El apogeo de los judíos portugueses en la Sevilla americanista," *Cadernos de Estudos Sefarditas* 5 (2005): 135–157; Studnicki-Gizbert, *A Nation upon the Ocean Sea*, 27–28, 44. Herzog also explains that the process in peninsular Spain was "easier" than in the Spanish colonies.

61. Yosef Hayim Yerushalmi, *The Lisbon Massacre of 1506 and the Royal Image in the Shebet Yehudah* (Cincinnati: Hebrew Union College, Jewish Institute of Religion, 1976).

62. Claude Stuczynski, "New Christian Political Leadership in Times of Crisis: The Pardon Negotiations of 1605," in *Leadership in Times of Crisis*, ed. Moises Orfali (Ramat Gan, Israel: Bar-Ilan University Press, 2007), 45–70, 56.

63. For a definition of "men of the Portuguese nation," see the introduction of this book.

64. Bernardo López Belinchón, "Olivares contra los portugueses. Inquisición, conversos y guerra económica," in *Historia de la Inquisición en España y América*, vol. 3, ed. Joaquín Pérez Villanueva and Bartolomé Escandell Bonet (Madrid: Biblioteca de Autores Cristianos, Centro de Estudios Inquisitoriales, 2000), 499–530; Pulido Serrano, *Injurias a Cristo*, 52–56; Stuczynski, "New Christian Political Leadership."

65. Castañeda Delgado and Hernández Aparicio, *Inquisición de Lima*, 1:425; Wachtel, *La fe del recuerdo*, 42–43; Wachtel, *The Faith of Remembrance*, 24–25.

66. Decreto de SM remitido a su Consejo de la Santa y General Inquisición año de 1619—Acerca de los portugueses que se pasan a Francia con sus familias y haciendas, BN–Madrid, MS 718, fs. 255r–256r.

67. López Belinchón, "Olivares contra los portugueses," 520–523; Israel, *Diasporas within a Diaspora*, chap. 7; Wachtel, *La fe del recuerdo*, chaps. 4 and 6; Juan Ignacio Pulido Serrano, "Jesuitas y cristianos nuevos portugueses en el siglo XVII: El Padre Hernando de Salazar y sus proyectos de repatriación," *Cadernos de Estudos Sefarditas* 9 (2009): 35–74; Wachtel, *The Faith of Remembrance*, chaps. 4 and 6.

68. Papel sobre si la Inquisicion de Castilla y Portugal reciprocamente deben remitir los reos que se hallan delatados en cada Reyno y que cometieron el delito en el y después se ausentaron, BN–Madrid, MS 10994. For exchanges of information between tribunals of Lima and Portugal (Évora and Coimbra), see Proceso de Joan Vicente, AHN–Inquisición, Leg. 1647, Exp. 3; and Proceso de Manuel Henríquez, AHN–Inquisición, Leg. 1647, Exp. 11.

69. Treaty for the Extradition of Prisoners (1570), Arquivo Nacional da Torre do Tombo (hereafter ANTT)–Lisbon, Inquisição, Conselho Geral, Livro 481, f. 114r, reproduced in François Soyer, "The Extradition Treaties of the Spanish and Portuguese Inquisitions (1500–1700)," in *Estudios de Historia de España* (Buenos Aires: Universidad Católica Argentina, Facultad de Filosofía y Letras, Instituto de Historia de España, 2008), 201–238, 237–238.

70. Culpas do judaismo: culpas vindas das inquisições espanholas contra judaizantes de Portugal, ANTT–Lisbon, Inquisição de Coimbra, Livro 70; Papel sobre si la Inquisicion de Castilla y Portugal reciprocamente deben remitir los reos que se hallan delatados en cada Reyno y que cometieron el delito en el y después se ausentaron, BN–Madrid, MSS 10994, fs. 161r–164r. See also Borrador del Voto de mano de D Pedro de Neyla en lo de las Inquisiciones de Portugal y Castilla, BN–Madrid, MSS 10994, fs. 169r–172v; and Soyer, "The Extradition Treaties." For the information about Goa, see James C. Boyajian, *Portuguese Trade in Asia under the Habsburgs, 1580–1640* (Baltimore: Johns Hopkins University Press, 1993), 180.

71. Wachtel also mentions that Vicente's wife had an affair with a more prominent Portuguese New Christian. See Wachtel, *La fe del recuerdo*, chap. 1; Wachtel, *The Faith of Remembrance*, chap. 1. For the Lima tribunal sending information to its Mexican counterpart in a different case, see Wachtel, *La fe del recuerdo*, chap. 4; Wachtel, *The Faith of Remembrance*, chap. 4.

72. Eymeric, *Manual*; Eimeric and Peña, *El manual*.

73. Osorio, *Inventing Lima*, 3.

74. The list of institutions is based on Antonio Vázquez de Espinosa, *Compendio y descripción de las Indias Occidentales*, ed. Balbino Velasco Bayón (Madrid: Historia 16, 1992). Salinas y Córdova, writing in 1630, gives the number of churches and chapels. Salinas y Córdova, *Memorial*, 195. He also notes that there were twenty-eight public schools in the city. Salinas y Córdova, *Memorial*, 257.

75. Gonçalo de Reparaz, *Os portugueses no Vice-Reinado do Peru (séculos XVI e XVII)* (Lisbon: Instituto de Alta Cultura, 1976), 90.

76. See, for example, Rafael Ramos Sosa, *Arte festivo en Lima Virreinal (siglos XVI–XVII)* (Andalusia: Junta de Andalucía, Consejería de Cultura y Medio Ambiente, Asesoría Quinto Centenario, 1992); Rosa María Acosta de Arias Schreiber, *Fiestas coloniales urbanas (Lima–Cuzco–Potosí)* (Lima: Otorongo Producciones, 1997); José R. Jouve Martín, "Public Ceremonies and Mulatto Identity in Viceregal Lima: A Colonial Reenactment of the Fall of Troy (1631)," *Colonial Latin American Review* 16, no. 2 (2007): 170–201; Osorio, *Inventing Lima*; Ana Schaposchnik, "Exemplary Punishment in Colonial Lima: The 1639 *Auto de Fe*," in *Death and Dying in Colonial Spanish America*, ed. Martina Will de Chaparro and Miruna Achim (Tucson: University of Arizona Press, 2011), 121–141.

77. See also Cobo, *Historia del Nuevo Mundo*, 320.

78. "Todos tratam e são mercadores, ainda que por mão alheia e dissimuladamente." Portocarrero, "Descrição geral do reino do Peru," 176. See also "Y por una vía y por otra, todos emplean y todos son mercaderes," in Ocaña, *Un viaje fascinante*, 96.

79. For Portocarrero's biography, see Lohman Villena, "Una incógnita despejada."

80. Fernando Montesinos, *Anales del Perú*, vol. 2, ed. Víctor M. Maúrtua (Madrid: Imprenta de Gabriel L. y del Horno, 1906), 197; Cobo, *Historia*, 306; Salinas y Córdova, *Memorial*, 245. For an analysis of these numbers, see Bronner, "The Population of Lima." See also Honores, "*Pleytos*, letrados y cultura legal en Lima y en Potosí."

81. Suárez, *Desafíos transatlánticos*, 24–39.

82. Medina, *Inquisición de Lima*, vol. 1, chap. 11.

83. Assadourian, "Chile y El Tucumán en el siglo XVI."

84. See Portocarrero, "Descrição geral do reino do Peru"; see also Salinas y Córdova, *Memorial*.

85. Suárez says that de la Cueva also had a warehouse next to the bank, but that the commodities stored there did not belong to him. Suárez, *Desafíos transatlánticos*, 75, 79–94, 99, and 432.

86. Salinas y Córdova, *Memorial*; Reparaz, *Os portugueses*, 89–91, and 109. For salaries and finances of the Lima tribunal, see also chap. 1.

87. Reparaz, *Os portugueses*, 109; Castañeda Delgado and Hernández Aparicio, *Inquisición de Lima*, 1:237–238.

88. Suárez, *Desafíos transatlánticos*, 82.

89. Suardo, *Diario*, 1:20–21, 26–27, 98–99, and 129–130; Medina, *Inquisición de Lima*, 2:18.

90. Portocarrero, "Descrição geral do reino do Peru," 168.

91. Lea, *A History*, vol. 2, book 3, chaps. 2–3.

92. On the creation of institutions to govern the colonies, see José María Ots y Capdequí, *El Estado Español en las Indias*, 3rd ed. (Mexico: Fondo de Cultura Económica, 1957).

93. Attempts to introduce it in Naples and Milan encountered local resistance. See Lea, *The Inquisition in the Spanish Dependencies*.

Chapter 4
A Community under Trial in Colonial Peru

1. See, for example, Quaderno de la Complicidad del Judaísmo que se empeçó en esta Ynquisiçion De la ciudad de Los Reyes del rreyno del Pirú desde principio de Abril del año De 1635, AHN–Inquisición, Libro 1030, fs. 426–495; and Auto que se celebro a los 23 de Hen° de seys° y treinta y nueve y execucion de las sentencias (hereafter Auto que se celebro . . .), AHN–Inquisición, Libro 1031, fs. 10r–30v. The following description excludes material related to people punished in the 1639 Auto de Fe who did not live in Lima prior to their arrest, such as Francisco Maldonado de Silva, who before his trial had lived in Concepción (Chile).

2. For this and the following paragraphs, see Relación de la causa de Antonio Cordero portugués que fue preso por judaizante, AHN–Inquisición, Libro 1031,

fs. 153r–168r. See also Castañeda Delgado and Hernández Aparicio, *Inquisición de Lima*, vol. 2, chap. 14. In several instances the documentation shows that the customers wanted to buy *rengos* (or *rencos*), the Portuguese term for a type of fabric. In a dictionary of Portuguese words present among the population of the Canary Islands, we find: "*rengo*. Tela de mala calidad. Port. *Rengo* 'tecido liso e transparente em que se fazem bordados.'" Marcial Morera, *Diccionario etimológico de los portuguesismos canarios* (Puerto del Rosario, Las Palmas: Excmo. Cabildo Insular de Fuerteventura, Servicio de Publicaciones, 1996), 318. From a Portuguese-English dictionary: "*rengo, rengue*: gauze, transparent cotton muslin used for lacework." H. Michaelis and Fritz Pietzschke, *Nôvo Michaelis, dicionário ilustrado* (São Paulo: Edições Melhoramentos, 1958), 1084. In the documents, all these conversations appear in Spanish, not only the dialogues with the tribunal but also the conversations among Lima residents, whether they were Old or New Christian, born in Spain or in Portugal. However, all parties used this Portuguese term when telling of this event.

3. "El viernes siguiente entró en el dicho almacén el testigo [Joan de Salazar Negrete] como a las ocho de la mañana y vio que el dicho Cordero estaba comiendo pan y manzana y le dijo el testigo sin reparar que era viernes pues ahora de mañana come pan y manzana no pudiera comer un pedazo de tocino a lo cual había dicho el dicho reo [Antonio Cordero] pues como he de comer yo lo que no comio mi padre." Relación de la causa de Antonio Cordero, AHN–Inquisición, Libro 1031, f. 153v. These two encounters between Antonio Cordero and Joan de Salazar Negrete are confirmed in the accounts of Joan Agustin and Pedro de Mendoza, who were also at the store and testified in Cordero's Inquisition trial as well. Joan Agustin said that he himself did not hear Cordero's answer, but saw Pedro de Mendoza and Joan de Salazar making the sign of the cross and praying. When Joan Agustin asked his companions why were they doing that, they explained that Cordero would not sell on a Saturday. Relación de la causa de Antonio Cordero, AHN–Inquisición, Libro 1031, fs. 154r–155r.

4. "Y que [Joan de Salazar Negrete] se acuerda que cuando pasó lo del sábado dio por disculpa el reo despues de haber dicho que en sábado no podía vender que también había de ir a cobrar por las tiendas y que le pareció al testigo flaca escusa y que antes le había causado sospecha y que habiendo comunicado lo suso dicho con un hombre docto y preguntadole si era acaso que debía denunciar dél le dijo que sí y que así lo había fecho." Relación de la causa de Antonio Cordero, AHN–Inquisición, Libro 1031, f. 154r.

5. "Fue este [Cordero] presso sin secresto de bienes, y con grandifsimo secreto, y en mucho tiempo no se supo del, por lo cual no se podia persuadir los demas se huviesse hecho tal prision por la Inquisicion." Montesinos, *Auto de la Fe*, BNP–Lima, f. 1v.

6. See for instance the following excerpt: "En 14 de mayo de 1620 = Fue testificado el reo Manuel Baptista por testigos mayores de toda excepción de que se había puesto un libelo en la esquina de la plaza pública desta ciudad que decía = Quien quisiese observar la ley de Moisés acuda a los señores Diego de Ovalle, fulano de Avila, y Manuel Baptista Perez que ellos se la enseñaran." Relación para el Consejo supremo de la causa de Manuel Baptista Pérez, relajado por este Santo Oficio en el auto de 23 de enero de

1639 años, AHN–Inquisición, Libro 1031, fs. 169r–185v. See also the following fragment: "Habia ocho o nueve años que Manuel Bautista Perez tenia culpas en esta inquisición y que su señoria no habia querido prenderle por guardarle para mejor ocasion." Proceso contra Bartolomé de Pradeda, AHN–Inquisición, Leg. 1643, Exp. 15, f. 26r. For other approaches to his case, see Silverblatt, *Modern Inquisitions*, 29–53; Wachtel, *La fe del recuerdo*, chap. 3; Wachtel, *The Faith of Remembrance*, chap. 3.

7. Alberro, "Crypto-Jews and the Mexican Holy Office," 172–185, 180.

8. Ramos, "El Tribunal de la Inquisición en el Perú"; Hampe Martínez, "Inquisición y sociedad en el Perú colonial"; Hampe Martínez, "Recent Works on the Inquisition"; Millar Carvacho, *Inquisición y sociedad*; Guibovich Pérez, *Censura*; Ayllón Dulanto, *El Tribunal de la Inquisición*. For an extended discussion of the bibliography, see introduction.

9. Contreras, "Estructura de la actividad procesal," 588–632, 627. I thank Kimberly Lynn for sharing with me her transcription of Mañozca's letter, and here I reproduce a selection of fragments: "Estos años alo que parece, se ha desembarazado Portugal de infinita cantidad de Judios, que se han passado a Castilla y auecindandose en Seuilla, y de ocho años aesta parte han venido flotas enteras dellos a estos Reynos . . . escriuimos con el secreto acostumbrado alos comissarios del distrito (que es inmenso) nos enbiasen con todo recato el numero cierto, delos que cada uno tenia en su partido." Cartas del inquisidor Juan de Mañozca, solicitando dinero de las Cajas Reales al ser insuficientes las rentas de sus canonjías; Y cuentas de rentas dela Canonjía del Cuzco, AHN–Inquisición, Leg. 4797, Exp. 1, f. 2v.

10. "Estando las cossas en este estado se siruio Dios de dar principio por un cossa bien ligera al parecer, alamayor complicidad que hamas se vio." Cartas del inquisidor Juan de Mañozca.

11. See for illustration the title of this document: Relacion de las causas determinadas y pendientes en esta Inquisicion de los reinos del Piru desde veynte y seys de mayo de mill y seiscientos y treinta y cinco años y auto que se celebro a los diez y siete de agosto del mismo año en la capilla por *desembaraçar las cárceles habiendo sobrevenido la grande complicidad de los años pasados*, AHN–Inquisición, Libro 1031, fs. 4–30 (emphasis mine).

12. In a letter the Lima inquisitors wrote: "En carta de 10 de diciembre del año pasado de 636 recibida en esta Inquisicion a 31 de agosto de 637 se sirve V Alteza aprobar la relacion que se ymbio al Consejo del principio que tuvo la complicidad en que se esta entendiendo desde dos de abril de 635 y nos manda V Alteza que para mayor acierto no se de paso sin grande fundamento." Carta de los Inquisidores de Lima, AHN–Inquisición, Libro 1031, f. 31r.

13. Castañeda Delgado and Hernández Aparicio, *Inquisición de Lima*, 2:413. For a brief social profile of crypto-Jews put under trial in Lima between 1621 and 1700, see also Pérez Cantó, "La dinámica de las estructuras en el Tribunal de Lima."

14. See Proceso de Enrique Tavares, AHN–Inquisición, Leg. 1648, Exp. 15. Castelo Branco is a Portuguese city located close to the Spanish region of Extremadura, and Fundão is a town close to Castelo Branco. For the presence of New Christians and crypto-Jews in this area, see Huerga Criado, *En la raya de Portugal*.

15. Studnicki-Gizbert, *A Nation upon the Ocean Sea*, 73.
16. Isabel Antonia was sixteen years old. See also Castañeda Delgado and Hernández Aparicio, *Inquisición de Lima*, 2:420.
17. Ibid., 419.
18. See Ida Altman, *Emigrants and Society: Extremadura and America in the Sixteenth Century* (Berkeley: University of California Press, 1989); Alexandra Cook and Noble David Cook, *Good Faith and Truthful Ignorance: A Case of Transatlantic Bigamy* (Durham, N.C.: Duke University Press, 1991); Susan Migden Socolow, *The Women of Colonial Latin America* (Cambridge: Cambridge University Press, 2000).
19. For the relevance of women in crypto-Judaism and the treatment of women under the Inquisition, see Mary Giles, ed., *Women in the Inquisition: Spain and the New World* (Baltimore: Johns Hopkins University Press, 1998); Melammed, *Heretics or Daughters of Israel*; Wachtel, *La fe del recuerdo*, chap. 4; Wachtel, *The Faith of Remembrance*, chap. 4.
20. García de Proodian, *Los judíos en América*, chap. 8; Castañeda Delgado and Hernández Aparicio, "La visita de Ruiz de Prado," 13.
21. Proceso de Manuel Henríquez, AHN–Inquisición, Leg. 1647, Exp. 11.
22. Proceso de Luis de Valencia, AHN–Inquisición, Leg. 1647, Exp. 12.
23. Proceso de Mencía de Luna, AHN–Inquisición, Leg. 1647, Exp. 10, f. 39r. Coincidentally, the name of the viceroy's younger sister was also doña Mencía. See Fred Bronner, "Advertencia privada de un virrey peruano del siglo XVII a su presunto sucesor," *Revista de Indias* 41, nos. 163–164 (1981): 55–77.
24. Domínguez Ortiz, "Los extranjeros en la vida española." See also Portocarrero, "Descrição geral do reino do Peru," 186.
25. "Entro en el patio Francisco Basques corredor que es un hombre alto de cuerpo algo descolorido de cara y en su abla parece portugues o gallego." Declaración de Juan de Acevedo, in Proceso de Francisco Vázquez, AHN–Inquisición, Leg. 1647, Exp. 16, f. 29v. Another mention is found in the declaración of Bartolomé de León, also in Proceso de Francisco Vázquez, f. 50r: "[Francisco Vázquez] corredor y portugues aunque el ha dho a este confesante que es portugues con los portugueses gallego con los gallegos con los extremeños se hace extremeño."
26. There is a vast literature on the Sephardic diaspora and its commercial activities. Regarding the Spanish and Portuguese colonies in the New World, see, for example, Hanke, "The Portuguese in Spanish America," 1–48; Anita Novinsky, *Cristãos Novos na Bahia* (Sao Paulo: Perspectiva, 1972); Enriqueta Vila Vilar, "Los asientos portugueses y el contrabando de negros," *Anuario de Estudios Americanos* 30 (1973): 557–609; Silva, *Heréticos e impuros*; Hordes, *To the End of the Earth*; Studnicki-Gizbert, *A Nation upon the Ocean Sea*; Kagan and Morgan, *Atlantic Diasporas*.
27. See Proceso de Manuel Bautista Pérez, AHN–Inquisición, Leg. 1647, Exp. 13.
28. Yosef Hayim Yerushalmi, "Between Amsterdam and New Amsterdam: The Place of Curaçao and the Caribbean in Early Modern Jewish History," *American Jewish History* 72, no. 2 (1982): 172–192, 177.
29. Guibovich Pérez, "La cultura libresca"; Newson and Minchin, *From Capture to Sale*, introduction and chaps. 1 and 2; Studnicki-Gizbert, *A Nation upon the Ocean Sea*,

chaps. 3 and 4; Wachtel, *La fe del recuerdo*, chap. 3; Wachtel, *The Faith of Remembrance*, chap. 3.

30. Luis de Valencia, Proceso de Fe, AHN–Inquisición, Leg. 1647, Exp. 12, f. 113v; Carta de los Inquisidores Juan de Mañozca, Andrés Juan Gaytan y Antonio de Castro y del Castillo, Lima, May 18, 1636, in Böhm, *Historia de los judíos en Chile*, 345–367.

31. Carta de los Inquisidores Juan de Mañozca et al., Lima, May 18, 1636, in Böhm, *Historia de los judíos en Chile*, 349.

32. Frederick P. Bowser, *The African Slave in Colonial Peru, 1524–1650* (Stanford, Calif.: Stanford University Press, 1974), chap. 2; Boyajian, *Portuguese Trade in Asia*, chap. 6; Newson and Minchin, *From Capture to Sale*, chap. 1; Wachtel, *La fe del recuerdo*, chap. 3; Wachtel, *The Faith of Remembrance*, chap. 3. For a map illustrating Pérez's itinerary, see Newson and Minchin, *From Capture to Sale*, 103.

33. According to James Boyajian there was a decline in cloth shipments from India to Lisbon after 1610, but 1618 was probably the best year during that decade. Boyajian, *Portuguese Trade in Asia*, 130.

34. Studnicki-Gizbert, *A Nation upon the Ocean Sea*, 98.

35. Ibid., 109.

36. Castañeda Delgado and Hernández Aparicio, *Inquisición de Lima*, 1:133.

37. Cross, "Commerce and Orthodoxy"; Newson and Minchin, *From Capture to Sale*, 9, 70–71, 145–146.

38. Cross, "Commerce and Orthodoxy," 162–164. Since the appointment as a familiar required proof of blood purity, hence the possibility that merchants acting as familiares (Spanish Old Christians) could have used the tribunal to eliminate the Portuguese New Christian trading networks.

39. López Belinchón, "Olivares contra los portugueses"; Pulido Serrano, *Injurias a Cristo*, chap. 1; Studnicki-Gizbert, *A Nation upon the Ocean Sea*, chap. 5.

40. Sicroff, *Los estatutos de limpieza de sangre*, 253–257. In using the concept of "legal inequality" I follow the work of Claude Stuczynski, "New Christian Political Leadership."

41. John Elliott, *The Count-Duke of Olivares: The Statesman in an Age of Decline* (New Haven, Conn.: Yale University Press, 1986), 295–308; Boyajian, *Portuguese Trade in Asia*, chap. 8; Pulido Serrano, *Injurias a Cristo*, 86–105.

42. Elliott, *The Count-Duke of Olivares*, 303; Pulido Serrano, *Injurias a Cristo*, 90–92.

43. Quoted from Pulido Serrano: "Los discursos antijudíos que se levantaron entonces equipararon al cristiano nuevo, al converso, con el judío. Algo, que como se sabe, fue sólo producto de la animadversión y de la estereotipación descalificadora." Pulido Serrano, *Injurias a Cristo*, 107. See also Studnicki-Gizbert, *A Nation upon the Ocean Sea*, 162. And see the following sentence: "El punto central de la nueva corriente anti-conversa era la firme creencia de que los portugueses se dedicaban a *sacar la sustancia al reino*." López Belinchón, "Olivares contra los portugueses," 511.

44. "No parece dudoso que estos portugueses contaron con el apoyo del Conde Duque [de Olivares] que veía en ellos un apoyo importante para salir de la crisis." Pérez Villanueva, "Felipe IV," 1006–1079, 1044; Elliott, *The Count-Duke of Olivares*, 324–325. For an example of a Jew from Amsterdam who joined Olivares's entourage, see

Jonathan Israel, *Empires and Entrepots: The Dutch, the Spanish Monarchy and the Jews, 1585–1713* (London: Hambledon Press, 1990), chaps. 9 and 10. Israel also points out connections between Olivares and the prosperity of the Portuguese New Christians in the colonies.

45. The full quotation from Pulido Serrano: "Creemos que estos aspectos mencionados son muy vagos como para afirmar una actitud favorable a los judíos y al judaísmo por parte de Olivares. Elementos muy vagos para dotarle de la virtud de la tolerancia." Pulido Serrano, *Injurias a Cristo*, 50–51.

46. Bernardo López Belinchón, *Honra, libertad y hacienda (Hombres de negocios y judíos sefardíes)* (Alcalá de Henares: Instituto Internacional de Estudios Sefardíes y Andalusíes, Universidad de Alcalá Servicio de Publicaciones, 2001), 311–335.

47. Stephen Fortune, *Merchants and Jews: The Struggle for British West Indian Commerce, 1650–1750* (Gainesville: University Presses of Florida, 1984). For the concept of the "royal alliance," see chap. 1.

48. Stuart Schwartz, "Panic in the Indies: The Portuguese Threat to the Spanish Empire, 1640–1650," *Colonial Latin American Review* 2, nos. 1–2 (1993): 165–187.

49. On the economic motivations of the Lima tribunal and the monetary outcome of the Complicidad Grande, see Quiroz Norris, "La expropiación inquisitorial"; Millar Carvacho, "Las confiscaciones de la Inquisición de Lima"; Millar Carvacho, *Inquisición y sociedad*.

50. "Habia ocho o nueve años que Manuel Bautista Perez tenia culpas en esta Ynquisicion y que su señoria no habia querido prenderle por guardarle para mejor ocasión." Proceso contra Bartolomé de Pradeda, AHN-Inquisición, Leg. 1643, Exp. 15, f. 26r. Kimberly Lynn mentions that in 1618 in Cartagena, when Mañozca was inquisitor of that tribunal, there also were charges against Manuel Bautista Pérez for bribes related to the slave trade. Lynn, *Between Court and Confessional*, 252.

51. Quiroz Norris, "La expropiación inquisitorial"; Lynn, *Between Court and Confessional*.

52. For the Inquisitions's use of "complicity," see Susie Minchin, "Vuestras Mercedes son capitanes bizarros y peruleros," 863–878, 873, and n. 826. For discussion of the conspiracy, see Silverblatt, "The Black Legend and Global Conspiracies."

53. Castañeda Delgado and Hernández Aparicio, *Inquisición de Lima*, 2:420–425; Millar Carvacho, *Inquisición y sociedad*, chap. 4; López Belinchón, "Olivares contra los portugueses," 527–530; Studnicki-Gizbert, *A Nation upon the Ocean Sea*, chap. 6; Osorio, *Inventing Lima*, chap. 4; Lynn, *Between Court and Confessional*, 262–270.

54. On this matter, see also Antonio Domínguez Ortiz, *Los judeoconversos en España y en América* (Madrid: Istmo, 1971); Silverblatt, "The Black Legend and Global Conspiracies"; Studnicki-Gizbert, *A Nation upon the Ocean Sea*, chap. 6; Lynn, *Between Court and Confessional*.

55. "Lo primero para que por el consejo de Estado y el de Portugal se advierta al Santo Oficio de aquel Reyno la atención y desvelo con que es bien que esté porque sin duda en la gente común y en particular la que trata de la mercancía debe ser generalísimo el estrago de sus graves culpas." Carta de los Inquisidores de Lima (sin firma), Lima, May 13, 1636, in Böhm, *Historia de los judíos en Chile*, 333–334.

56. Jonathan Israel, *The Dutch Republic and the Hispanic World, 1606–1661* (Oxford: Clarendon Press, 1982), 281.

57. Israel, *Diasporas within a Diaspora*, chap. 4.

58. See Salinas y Córdova, *Memorial*, 204. See also Pedro Rodríguez Crespo, "El peligro holandés en las costas peruanas a principios del siglo XVII: La expedición de Spilbergen y la defensa del Virreynato," *Histórica* 26, Supplement (1962): 259–310; Jonathan Israel, *Dutch Primacy in World Trade, 1585–1740* (Oxford: Clarendon Press, 1989); Israel, *Empires and Entrepots*. For the San Cristóbal battle, see Suardo, *Diario*, 1:48. Between 1629 and 1639 Lima received information regarding Dutch ships from Buenos Aires, Quito, and Panama; also relayed were measures taken in anticipation of a Dutch invasion. See Suardo, *Diario*, 1:81, 87, 89, 100, 117, 134, 136, and 140. See also ibid., 2:33, 92–94, 107, 120, and 121.

59. For the inquisitor's account, see Carta de Antonio de Castro y del Castillo, AHN–Inquisición, Libro 1031, f. 264v; and for the inquisitors' report to Madrid, see Mendiburu, *Diccionario histórico-biográfico*, 6:273; López Belinchón, "Olivares contra los portugueses," 516.

60. "Fue mandado llevar el dicho reo a la cámara del tormento y habiéndole desnudado y puesto en la cincha atados los molledos de los brazos para la mancuerda le fue mandado dar y apretar la primera vuelta della y estando el ministro apretándosela dijo no aprietes que confesaré la verdad y de nuevo confesó ser judío observante de la ley de Moisés y haberse comunicado en esta ciudad de los Reyes en la guardia y observancia della y en sus ritos y ceremonias con el dicho su amo Antonio de Acuña y con Diego Lopez de Fonseca, compañero y camarada del dicho Antonio de Acuña y con Manuel de la Rosa." Relación de la causa de Antonio Cordero, AHN–Inquisición, Libro 1031, f. 159r. Manuel de la Rosa was Diego López de Fonseca's servant. In a later hearing, Cordero revealed that his wife was also crypto-Jewish. Ibid., f. 159v.

61. "Y preguntado en qué forma llamaba o se encomendaba a su Dios de Ysrael = dijo que no sabía oración particular por no haber tenido escuela ni quien se la enseñase y que en la forma que llamaba a su Dios de Ysrael era pedille que como había librado a Joseph de las prisiones y del testimonio que le habían levantado y al pueblo de Ysrael del cautiverio de Egipto y poder del Rey faraón y como había librado a aquellos inocentes del horno de babylonia y como había librado al pueblo de Ysrael de la traición que le había armado aquel vasallo del Rey de asuero y como había librado la arca del testamento de poder de sus enemigos así librara al reo de sus trabajos." Relación de la causa de Antonio Cordero, AHN–Inquisición, Libro 1031, f. 159v.

62. Suardo, *Diario*, 2:80.

63. Cross, "Commerce and Orthodoxy," 161; Suárez, *Desafíos transatlánticos*, 79–94. Chinchón wrote: "Con la ocasion de las haciendas que se han embargado ha quedado tan enflaquecido el comercio que apenas pueden llevar las cargas ordinarias" Carta de Conde de Chinchón, Doctor Galdós de Valencia, Licenciado Don Blas de Torres, Doctor Don Gabriel de Sanabria, Licenciado Cristóbal Cacho de Santillana, Licenciado Luis Henríquez, Doctor don Martín de Arriola, Doctor don Andrés de Billela, Lima, May 18, 1636, in Böhm, *Historia de los judíos en Chile*, 341.

64. "Andan las gentes como asombradas, y no se fian unos de otros, porque cuando menos piensan se hallan sin el amigo o compañero." Carta de los Inquisidores Juan de Mañozca, Andrés Juan Gaytan y Antonio de Castro y del Castillo, Lima, May 18, 1636, in Böhm, *Historia de los judíos en Chile*, 361.

65. "Y dixo a este confessante voto a Dios que cada dia ban prendiendo mas gente uno a uno nos an de llevar alla atodos." Declaración de Fernando de Espinosa, in Proceso de Francisco Vázquez, AHN-Inquisición, Leg. 1647, Exp. 16, document 1, f. 62v. For the indictment and first hearing see the following pages of the same document. In the 1640s the Mexican tribunal conducted about three hundred imprisonments. In discussing these cases Wachtel cites the example of a woman who had a first encounter with the tribunal. She was not imprisoned but had ongoing nightmares in which the Inquisition would indict her again. Wachtel, *La fe del recuerdo*, 128; Wachtel, *The Faith of Remembrance*, 98.

66. Suardo, *Diario*, 2:90–92. See also Silverblatt, *Modern Inquisitions*, 61–65.

67. The seven were Enrique de Paz, Diego de Ovalle, the Licenciado Tomé Quaresma, and Antonio Negrón, his wife, daughter, and sister-in-law. Suardo, *Diario*, 2:106.

68. On December 10 the following men were arrested: Francisco Fernández, Francisco Márquez Montesinos, Amaro Dionis Coronel, Luis de Vega, Antonio de Vega, and Pasqual Díaz. Ibid., 109–110. The prisoner Enrique Lorenzo was sent from Panama in January. See the Carta de los Inquisidores Juan de Mañozca, Andrés Juan Gaytan y Antonio de Castro y del Castillo, Lima, May 18, 1636, in Böhm, *Historia de los judíos en Chile*, 345–367. On the gathering of the public to follow the inquisitors, see Carta del Licenciado Don Antonio de Castro y del Castillo, AHN-Inquisición, Libro 1031, fs. 264r–266r; see also Medina, *Inquisición de Lima*, 2:50 n. 3.

69. "Ha caussado grande admiraçion en esta ciudad su prission por aber sido efecto de providençia particular de Dios, que esta açion mostro muy piadosos los ojos con que mira a este Reyno." Carta del inquisidor don León de Alcayaga Lartaun, Lima, May 15, 1636, in Böhm, *Historia de los judíos en Chile*, 337.

70. Lynn, *Between Court and Confessional*, 267–268.

71. Some of the arrests made between February and May: Luis de Lima, Francisco Vázquez, and Juan Rodríguez Duarte in February; Simón Correa, Tomás Rodríguez and Baltasar Gómez de Acosta in March; Pascual Núñez, Fernando de Espinosa, Rodrigo de Ávila el Viejo, Antonio de Santos, Pedro de Farías, a barber's apprentice whose name is not recorded, Sebastián Delgado, and Gerónimo de Acevedo in April; and Joan Ramos, Santiago del Castillo, Alonso Sánchez Chaparro, the captain Martín Morato, Francisco Sotelo, Andrés Muñiz, Ambrosio de Morales, Matías de Paz, Francisco de Vergara, and Fernando de Fonseca (plus the men brought from Huánuco) in May. Suardo, *Diario*, 2:113–136, 160, 176, 179, 183, 195. For honor restitutions in 1639, see Montesinos, *Auto de la Fe*, BNP-Lima, f. 25r; and Osorio, *Inventing Lima*, chap. 4. For details of the detentions, see Medina, *Inquisición de Lima*, 2:51–70.

72. On this matter and on the role of notaries, see also Davis, *Fiction in the Archives*; Burns, *Into the Archive*.

73. See Proceso de Antonio Morón, AHN–Inquisición, Leg. 1674, Exp. 18; and Proceso de Manuel Henríquez, AHN–Inquisición, Leg. 1647, Exp. 11.

74. Here I present a brief summary and list the work of some authors I included in the introduction. They are Gitlitz, *Secrecy and Deceit*; Starr-Lebeau, *In the Shadow of the Virgin*; Bodian, "Hebrews of the Portuguese Nation"; Graizbord, "Religion and Ethnicity among the 'Men of the Nation'"; Pulido Serrano, "Plural Identities."

75. See Wachtel, *La fe del recuerdo*, chaps. 1, 2, and 3; Wachtel, *The Faith of Remembrance*, chaps. 1, 2, and 3.

76. See Castañeda Delgado and Hernández Aparicio, *Inquisición de Lima*, vol. 2, chap. 14.

77. "Quando se habia comunicado con Araujo en Guancavelica le habia preguntado si sabia algunas Palabras en hebreo y deciendole que si y Araujo q las dixese avia dho çama ysrael y que al punto habia dho araujo adonay elueno y que el habia dho adonay exag y que araujo le habia abrazado." Manuel de Fonseca, Relación de su causa, AHN–Inquisición, Libro 1030, f. 431v.

78. "Quieren que sea judio yo no lo soy siempre he sido xpiano y lo he de ser ya no puedo mas que quiere que sea soy judio soy judio soy judio mill vezes soy judio." Luis de Valencia, Proceso de Fe, AHN–Inquisicion, Leg. 1647, Exp. 12, f. 111v. Similar examples showing a desperate attempt to guess what the inquisitors wanted to hear appear in Mencía de Luna's trial, as I have already brought up in chapter 2.

79. Proceso de Luis de Valencia, AHN–Inquisición, Leg. 1647, Exp. 12, f. 112r.

80. Here I transcribe a fragment from a confession: "Dixo que ya ha dicho que lo principal es amar un dios criador de todas las cosas guardar el sabado por fiesta reservarlo que es natural con el proximo hacer ayunos en orden a penitencia de salvarse como son de sol a sol lo principal tener quenta con las estrellas y el cielo que dios crio y con las maravillas que en el se ven de aquel ynmenso dios que todo crio que yo adoro y amo y que eso hace en orden a la ley de Moyses porque esa es la verdad a lo que entiende para salvarse y que el no hace otras cosas porque no lo mando dios y que esta es la verdad." Proceso de Enrique Jorge Tavares, AHN–Inquisición, Leg. 1648, Exp. 15, f. 185r.

81. *Poniendo ropa limpia en persona mesa y cama*, in the jargon of the Inquisition.

82. Drawing on information from the Mexican tribunal, Nathan Wachtel finds a broader meaning for fasting among the crypto-Jews of the early seventeenth century. He establishes differences between a Christian fast, often undertaken for its ascetic value, and a fast mandated by crypto-Jewish society, which encompassed shared secrets and affection among friends or relatives, and perhaps even an erotic component between lovers. Wachtel remarks that this combination between fast and eroticism was uncommon, and that it was probably related to a cabbalistic tradition disseminated in the Old World toward the end of the sixteenth century that believed in inversion of values and transgression. "Según los adeptos más radicales del movimiento, se trataba de transgredir las leyes de la Torá del mundo inferior—el del exilio—con la esperanza de provocar la llegada de la verdadera Torá, la del mundo superior, hasta entonces escondida." Wachtel, *La fe del recuerdo*, 125. From the English version: "According to the most radical believers, the idea was to transgress the laws of the Torah of the lower world, the world of exile, in

the hope of hastening the advent of the true Torah, that of the upper world, which had thus far remained concealed." Wachtel, *The Faith of Remembrance*, 96.

83. The image and inspiration of Queen Esther persisted among Portuguese crypto-Jews until the twentieth century, and it affected the gendered power balance in their communities, for example, in the crypto-Jewish community of Belmonte (Portugal). See Maria Antonieta Garcia, *Judaísmo no feminino: Tradição popular e ortodoxia em Belmonte*, ed. Instituto de Sociologia e Etnologia das Religiões (Lisbon: Universidade Nova de Lisboa, 1999).

84. David Gitlitz maintains that crypto-Jewish rejection of pork was related not only to adherence to Kosher dietary laws but also to immigrants' rejection of their Iberian environment, in which pork is broadly present. See Gitlitz, *Secrecy and Deceit*, chap. 19.

85. "Si miramos al pescado, pocas Ciudades tiene Europa, que gozen todo el año de tanta abundancia como esta de los Reyes." Salinas y Córdova, *Memorial*, 251. For other descriptions of the fish, fruits, and vegetables available in Lima in the early seventeenth century, see Portocarrero, "Descrição geral do reino do Peru," 40, 168; and Ocaña, *Un viaje fascinante*, 104.

86. See, for example, Antonio Cordero's answer transcribed and translated earlier in this chapter.

87. For another example of women from different generations within the same family facing Inquisition trials, see Richard Kagan, "Keeping the Faith: Doña Blanca Méndez de Rivera," in *Inquisitorial Inquiries: Brief Lives of Secret Jews and Other Heretics*, ed. Richard Kagan and Abigail Dyer (Baltimore: Johns Hopkins University Press, 2004), 152–188.

88. Relación de la causa de Tomé Quaresma, AHN–Inquisición, Libro 1031, fs. 206r–212v.

89. Pulido Serrano, "Plural Identities."

90. Reparaz, *Os portugueses*, 125.

91. "Siendo el reo [Rodrigo Váez Pereira] de 13-a 14 años le dijo un primo suyo llamado Duarte Rodriguez que el reo era cristiano nuevo y que si se atreviera a hacer un ayuno en guarda de la ley de Dios del cielo sin comer en todo el dia y que el reo le dijo que si y los dos ayunaron aquel dia sin comer hasta la noche que cenaron huevos, garbanzos, y comidas de viernes; y que otro dia ayuno con el dicho su primo no comiendo en todo el dia hasta la noche que cenaron comidas de viernes y que hizo los dichos ayunos como muchacho a persuasion del dicho su primo." Extracted from Relación de la causa de Rodrigo Váez Pereira, AHN–Inquisición, Libro 1031, fs. 198r–205r, f. 201r. In one of his confessions Manuel Henríquez said that his parents introduced him into crypto-Judaism when he was twelve years old. Enrique Jorge Tavares said his grandmother introduced him to crypto-Jewish practices when he was about eight years old.

92. See Böhm, *Historia de los judíos en Chile*; Bodian, *Dying in the Law of Moses*, chap. 5; Wachtel, *La fe del recuerdo*, chap. 2; Wachtel, *The Faith of Remembrance*, chap. 2.

93. Reparaz, *Os portugueses*, 132.

94. It turned out this man had indeed been reconciled under the Coimbra tribunal, in 1625 as recorded in the Lista das pessoas que sairao no Auto da Fee que se celebrou na Praça desta Cidade de Coimbra a 4 de Maio de 625 asistido nelle o snor Dor Joam Alvrez Brandao do Conselho de Sua Magestade e do Geral da Sta Inquisição Ldo Gaspar Borges Dazevedo o Los Po da Silva o Dtor Lopo Soares de Castro Pregou o Pe Mel Fagundes da Compa de Jesus, ANTT–Lisbon, Inquisição de Coimbra, Livro 4, fs. 249r–255v. This record was sent by the Coimbra tribunal to Lima.

95. Proceso de Manuel Henríquez, AHN–Inquisición, Leg. 1647, Exp. 11, f. 62r. Excerpts of this long trial from the years of 1645–46, 1646–47, 1647–48, 1650–51, 1660–62, 1659–60–64, and 1666 also appear in different summaries of his trial now preserved in Madrid. See AHN–Inquisición, Libro 1031. For Manuel Henríquez's death at the stake in the 1664 Auto de Fe in Lima, see Relaciones de Causas de Fe, Lima, años 1659, 1660 y 1664, AHN–Inquisición, Leg. 5345, Exp. 1, fs. 13r–16r.

96. "Los dichos D Simon Ossorio y P⁰ Lopez Montesinos a la hora del comer volvieron a decir a este confesante [Manuel Henríquez] que lo que le importaba era guardar la ley de Moyses y hazer sus ritos y ceremonias porq asi saldria de necesidad y le daria Dios riquezas y q entendiesse le Aconsejaban y persuadian lo que le estaba bien a la salvacion de su alma y a tener hazienda y estimacion y que guardando la dicha ley ambos le ayudarian y q escusandose este confesante le dixeron que si no seguia la ley de Moses ni le harian bien ni le ayudarian y se quedaria perdido pobre y necesitado como otros muchos que habia en las Yndias que no tenian quien les diesse la mano en que le hizieron mucha fuerça y viendose este pobre miserable y Aflixido y considerando que si le hechaba Don Simon de su casa no tenia que comer ni çapatos que ponerse y q habia dejado mujer y una hija en Madrid con summa pobreza instandole mucho el dicho P⁰ Lopez Montesinos que hiziese lo que decia el dicho D Simon Ossorio que el tambien le ayudaria vencido de su necessidad Dixo q guardaria la Ley de Moyses y que al punto que dixo este confesante la dicha palabra sin comer le llebo el dicho D Simon Ossorio y le Acredito en cassa de Antonio Rodriguez Ferrerin mercader portugues que le dio listones y otras mercadurias para que este buscasse su vida por las calles." Proceso de Manuel Henríquez, AHN–Inquisición, Leg. 1647, Exp. 11, f. 62r.

97. For references to crypto-Jewish fasts performed in Italy, Mexico, and Cartagena, see, for instance, Luis de Valencia, Proceso de Fe, AHN–Inquisición, Leg. 1647, Exp. 12.

98. Proceso de Enrique Jorge Tavares, AHN–Inquisición, Leg. 1648, Exp. 15, f. 123v and 171v–172r.

99. Neither Enrique Jorge Tavares nor Manuel Henríquez were sentenced at the 1639 Auto General de Fe. The similarity in these cases is that the tribunal doubted if these men were mentally sane to face the responsibility of their heretical acts, but they differ in the resolution. Tavares was declared insane and moved to the Hospital de San Andrés in 1648. Henríquez, on the other hand, was declared sane and therefore responsible for relapsing into heresy, and as such burned at the stake in 1664.

100. Here I transcribe what the doctor reported as Tavares's answer: "Respondio [Enrique Jorge Tavares] que en Dios no habia esta diversidad de personas sino que dios

era uno y que no tenia hijo pues no tenia ynstrumentos para poderlos engendrar nombrandolos por sus propios nombres deshonestos y replicandole a este declarante [el doctor Joan de Vega] que en dios para hacer hombres solo basto su voluntad respondio [Tavares] que aquello habia sido creacion y no generacion de lo qual colige este declarante [Vega] y de otras raçones que pasaron que el dicho Henrique Tavares no es loco sino que esta firme y consequente en los errores referidos." Proceso de Enrique Jorge Tavares, AHN–Inquisición, Leg. 1648, Exp. 15, f. 51v–52r. Another doctor named Gerónimo de la Rocha provided a similar testimony and conclusion. Ibid., f. 55r–v. It appears from the trial that there was a disagreement among the examiners (priests and doctors) about whether or not Tavares was sane and whether there was consistency in his heresy.

101. "Adverti en las respuestas de dicho reo muchas proposiciones hereticas contra nra sta fee catholica en articulos expresamente contenidos en el nuevo testamento Como que sin baptismo se puede uno salvar y que de hecho se salvaron sin el los indiecitos que . . . murieron antes que los españoles viniesen a estas partes." Proceso de Enrique Jorge Tavares, AHN–Inquisición, Leg. 1648, Exp. 15, f. 201r.

102. "Y es el caso que viniendo de España embarcado por el año de treinta y uno en la Almiranta de Napoles en compañía de Antonio de Acuña y Manuel de Espinosa que venian por pasajeros en la misma nao queste confesante [Enrique Jorge Tavares] el dicho Antonio de Acuña le tomo amistad particular y ya de antes eran conocidos de Sevilla y le persuadio a este confesante muchas y diferentes veces a solas que siguiese la ley de Moises sus ritos y ceremonias porque era la buena y en ella se habia de salvar y no en otra." Proceso de Enrique Jorge Tavares, AHN–Inquisición, Leg. 1648, Exp. 15, f. 129r.

103. Manuel Henríquez said that "el dho Jacinto Henrriquez Dixo que *habia estado por alla en aquellas partes de Francia y que alla le habian enseñado la ley de Moyses* sin decir en que lugar." Proceso de Manuel Henríquez, AHN–Inquisición, Leg. 1647, Exp. 11, f. 69r (emphasis mine). Another example appears in the trial of Luis de Valencia, who confessed that he turned to crypto-Judaism in Florence, Italy. Proceso de Luis de Valencia, AHN–Inquisición, Leg. 1647, Exp. 12, f. 112r.

104. Relación de la causa de Juan de Ortega, AHN–Inquisición, Libro 1030, f. 376v.

105. Bernardo Serrano said "que despues de avellos desposado y velado un clerigo francess catholico cura de la parroquia . . . según orden de la sta me yglessia catholica aquel mismo dia despues de comer habia ydo a cassa de la dha Bernarda Serrana su muger duarte sanches portugues hombre hijo con el doctor Duarte Henrriques medico y Fernando Morero portugueses y que todos tres juntos habian entrado en la sala donde estaba con la dha su muger y la habian dho ya VM me casso y velo esta mañana esta bien hecho agora es menester hazer otra diligencia a nro modo y que diciendole haga VM lo que ha de hazer q yo no lo se el dho Duarte Sanches en presencia de los susso dhos y de las mujeres de cassa y Antonio Fernandez habia tomado un anillo de oro que llevaba consigo y le habia dho metaselo a su muher en el dedo y habiendosele puesto se habia quedado con el la dha Bernarda Serrano para siempre y que luego habia pedido el dho Duarte un basso de vidrio lleno de bino y habiendole tomado en su mano se le

habia dado para que beviese un poquito y le dijo que diese luego de bever a su muger y que habiendo bevido el y la dha su muher habia vuelto a tomar el vasso y el dho Duarte Sanchez con el vino que habia sobrado y dejandolo caer en el suelo se habia hecho pedaços y que quando le habia dado el anillo y el vasso le habia dho que dizese unas palabras en español de que no se acordaba aunque las entendio y dizo quando se lo mando y que con aquello habia quedado cassado conforme a las ceremonias de la ley de moyses." Relación de la causa de Bernardo López Serrano, AHN–Inquisición, Libro 1030, f. 381r.

106. See, for example, what Nathan Wachtel concludes about Pérez: "El aspecto cristiano de su religiosidad se manifiesta según las modalidades ostentosas de su época, conteniendo al mismo tiempo un trasfondo de duda e incertidumbre, mientras que su fidelidad a la ley de Moisés sería de orden más conmemorativo e histórico que verdaderamente religioso." Wachtel, *La fe del recuerdo*, 94. From the English version of the same book: "The Christian side of his religiosity was expressed through the flamboyant modes of his epoch, albeit with a reserve of doubts and uncertainties; while his faithfulness to the Law of Moses would be more commemorative and historical than truly religious." Wachtel, *The Faith of Remembrance*, 68. See also Warshawsky, "Manuel Bautista Pérez and the *Complicidad Grande* in Colonial Peru."

Chapter 5
The Inner World of the Lima Prisons

1. "Cuentas de gastos, jornales y cartas de pago por las obras de las casas del Tribunal del Santo Oficio de la Inquisición de Lima (1584)," paleographic transcription by Percy Vargas Valencia, Lima, June 1972, available at the website of the Museo del Congreso y de la Inquisición, 2012, http://www4.congreso.gob.pe/museo/inquisicion/cuentas-gastos.html. See also Medina, *Inquisición de Lima*, 1:200–202; Fuentes, *Lima*, 35; José Flores Aráoz, "El local del Tribunal del Santo Oficio de Lima," *Cultura Peruana* (Supplement) (1946); Cobo, *Historia*, 401; Emilio Harth-Terré and Alberto Márquez Abanto, "Las bellas artes en el Virreynato del Perú en el siglo XVI: Las casas del Real Tribunal de la Inquisición," *Revista del Archivo Nacional del Perú* 22 (1958): 194–217; Birckel, "Recherches sur la Trésorerie Inquisitoriale de Lima, 1:277 and 289; Castañeda Delgado and Hernández Aparicio, *Inquisición de Lima*, 1:212, 224, and 239.

2. De la Pinta Llorente, *Las cárceles*; González Montes, *Artes de la Santa Inquisición Española*.

3. Castañeda Delgado and Hernández Aparicio, *Inquisición de Lima*, 2:283–284; Kamen, *The Spanish Inquisition*, 184; Pérez, *Crónica*, 321–322.

4. See Proceso de Antonio Morón, AHN–Inquisición, Leg. 1647, Exp. 18; and Proceso de Manuel Bautista Pérez, AHN–Inquisición, Leg. 1647, Exp. 13.

5. The primary and secondary sources I used to develop my understanding of the trial of faith are discussed in chapter 2.

6. For example, Kathryn Burns shows how nuns interacted with the world beyond the convent walls in colonial Cuzco. See Kathryn Burns, "Nuns, Kurakas, and Credit:

The Spiritual Economy of Seventeenth-Century Cuzco," *Colonial Latin American Review* 6, no. 2 (1997): 185–203.

7. On this matter see, for example, de la Pinta Llorente, *Las cárceles*, 25–26; Millar Carvacho, *Inquisición y sociedad*, 71; Ana Cristina Cuadro García, "Las cárceles inquisitoriales del tribunal de Córdoba," *Hispania* 65/2, no. 220 (2005): 443–464.

8. "En lo que toca al modo que se tuvo en la execucion de las prisiones de los reo lo que tengo que informar a V Alt° es que la primera que se hiço de Antonio Cordero el descubridor de tamaña complicidad fue con tanto secreto que sus mismos amos Antonio de Acuña y Diego Lopez de Fonseca echando varios juicios por muchos dias dieron quenta de su falta a los Alcaldes de Corte para que averiguasen si en alguna casa de esta ciudad le habian muerto." Lic. Don Antonio de Castro y de Castillo to the Suprema, AHN–Inquisición, Libro 1031, f. 265v.

9. Alberro, *Inquisición y sociedad en México*, 227.

10. Monter, *Frontiers of Heresy*; Jaime Contreras, *Sotos contra Riquelmes: Regidores, inquisidores y criptojudíos* (Madrid: Anaya & M. Muchnik, 1992); Starr-Lebeau, *In the Shadow of the Virgin*.

11. See, for example, Stern, *Peru's Indian Peoples*; Inga Clendinnen, *Ambivalent Conquests: Maya and Spaniard in Yucatan, 1517–1570*, 2nd ed. (New York: Cambridge University Press, 2003).

12. See the materials cited in n. 1; and Lea, *A History*, vol. 2, book 6, chap. 4.

13. De la Pinta Llorente, *Las cárceles*, 30–32; Contreras, *Inquisición de Galicia*, 308–313; Lea, *A History*, vol. 2, book 6, chap. 4.

14. De la Pinta Llorente, *Las cárceles*, 30 and 110–111.

15. See Proceso de Antonio Morón, AHN–Inquisición, Leg. 1647, Exp. 18, f. 100.

16. De la Pinta Llorente, *Las cárceles*, 102. For viceregal visits to secular prisons between 1629 and 1634, see Suardo, *Diario*, 1:45, 116, 118, 119, and 128.

17. Castañeda Delgado and Hernández Aparicio, "La visita de Ruiz de Prado." The inspection is also summarized in Medina, *Inquisición de Lima*, vol. 1, chap. 11.

18. González Montes, *Artes de la Santa Inquisición Española*, 201–204.

19. Contreras, *Inquisición de Galicia*, 350–351; Alberro, *Inquisición y Sociedad en México*, 243; Lea, *A History*, vol. 2, book 6, chap. 4. For circulation and exchanges among prisoners of the Mexican tribunal, see Wachtel, *La fe del recuerdo*, chap. 4; Wachtel, *The Faith of Remembrance*, chap. 4.

20. Kagan, *Lucrecia's Dreams*, chap. 6.

21. "Diosele [a Isabel Antonia] por compañera de carcel a una muher llamada doña Beatriz de la Bandera que quando entro en compañía de Doña Isabel era acabada de llegar del Cuzco 150 leguas de aquí sin haber pisado mas calles de Lima que las que la trajeron del camino a esta inquisicion sin hablar con nadie. Con esta pues pasado algun tiempo que les dio a las dos familiar amistad quejandose doña Ysabel de sus trabajos comunico que el agujero que se habia començado a hacer en el almacen de la polvora de Guadalupe habia sido por orden de sus deudos y para volar la ciudad y que se comunicaban con los holandeses y que los aguardaban." Lic. Don Antonio de Castro y del Castillo to the Suprema, AHN–Inquisición, Libro 1031, 264v.

22. Boleslao Lewin, "'Las Confidencias' of Two Crypto-Jews in the Holy Office Prison of Mexico (1654–1655)," *Jewish Social Studies* 30, no. 1 (1968): 3–22; Alberro, *Inquisición y Sociedad en México*, 247; Wachtel, *La fe del recuerdo*, chap. 4; Wachtel, *The Faith of Remembrance*, chap. 4.

23. See, for example, Proceso contra Bartolomé de Pradeda, AHN–Inquisición, Leg. 1643, Exp. 15. For brief summaries of the issues addressed in this trial and punishments applied to Pradeda and others who helped the prisoners, see Pérez Cantó, "El Tribunal de Lima," 1133–1141, 1134–1135; Castañeda Delgado and Hernández Aparicio, *Inquisición de Lima*, 2:544–547.

24. Castañeda Delgado and Hernández Aparicio, *Inquisición de Lima*, vol. 1, chap. 15; Castañeda Delgado and Hernández Aparicio, *Inquisición de Lima*, vol. 2, chap. 18.

25. Medina, *Inquisición de Lima*, 2:50–51.

26. Here I reproduce the heading of the accusation: "Digo que [Bartolomé de Pradeda] siendo Alcayde de las carceles secretas desta ynquisicion y el cargo de los de mayor confianza y secreto y jurado de guardarlo contraviniendo al dicho juramento y a las demas ordenes establecidos por instrucciones cartas acordadas y censuras con poco temor de Dios nuestro Señor y en gran cargo de su conciencia y condenacion de su alma olvidado de sus obligaciones e inviolable secreto lo ha quebrantado muchas y diversas veces siendo infiel en el dicho officio en gran deshonor deste tribunal y sus ministros." Proceso contra Bartolomé de Pradeda, AHN–Inquisición, Leg. 1643, Exp. 15, f. 104r.

27. "Y en especial para que se vea al descuydo y poca atencion con que el dicho alcayde vivia era tan grande que entre las muchas veces que se dejo las puertas de las carceles abiertas un dia por el año de 39 habiendose ido a la plaza estuvo desde las nueve de la mañana hasta las doce del mediodia en el quel tiempo entraron en dichas carceles secretas algunas personas." Proceso contra Bartolomé de Pradeda, AHN–Inquisición, Leg. 1643, Exp. 15, f. 104v.

28. "Y que este mismo criado vio cierta persona que venia de quatro en quatro noches a casa del dicho alcayde y hablaba con el en secreto y algunas noches traya muchos generos de conservas asi cajas como tarros y en una ocasión trajo una frasquera llena de vino y otros muchos regalos y el dicho Alcayde lo recibia y guardaba en su despensilla y de todo ello daba muy poco al dicho presso." Proceso contra Bartolomé de Pradeda, AHN–Inquisición, Leg. 1643, Exp. 15, f. 106r.

29. There is also a document claiming that Bartolomé de Pradeda owed payment for the rent of a house in Lima in 1640, but this is not included in his criminal trial. Archivo Nacional (hereafter AN)–Lima, So–Co, Ca 94, Doc. 647.

30. See, for example, the trials of faith of Enrique Jorge Tavares (AHN–Inquisición, Leg. 1648, Exp. 15) and Manuel Bautista Pérez (AHN–Inquisición, Leg. 1647, Exp. 13). For other members of the tribunal personnel who circulated messages among prisoners, see Medina, *Inquisición de Lima*, 2:59–60.

31. Castañeda Delgado and Hernández Aparicio, *Inquisición de Lima*, vol. 1, chap. 7; Ruth Magalí Rosas Navarro, "El Tribunal de la Santa Inquisición y los negros esclavos en América," *Hispania Sacra* 55 (2003): 535–567; Robert Ferry, "Don't Drink the

Chocolate: Domestic Slavery and the Exigencies of Fasting for Crypto-Jews in Seventeenth-Century Mexico," *Nuevo Mundo, Mundos Nuevos*, no. 5 (2005): 2–16; Schorsch, *Swimming the Christian Atlantic*, chap. 4.

32. Castañeda Delgado and Hernández Aparicio, *Inquisición de Lima*, 1:286–287.

33. "Cuentas de gastos, jornales y cartas." See n. 1.

34. Rosas Navarro, "El Tribunal de la Santa Inquisición y los negros esclavos," 565.

35. See Cannas da Cunha, *A Inquisição no Estado da India*. For an example of testimony provided by black slaves, see Proceso de Antonio Morón, AHN–Inquisición, Leg. 1647, Exp. 18.

36. Wachtel, *La fe del recuerdo*, 96; Wachtel, *The Faith of Remembrance*, 71.

37. "Los sirvientes para tanta gente eran negros boçales que es el servicio de por aca y aunque lo eran los reos como tratantes en esta mercaduria trayendo gruesas partidas de ellos desde Cartagena les hablaban en su lengua y daban recados que llevasen los unos a los otros y muchas veces les daban papeles escritos con çumo de limones que los pedian para achaques que fingian o para sainete de su comida y aunque al parecer iban blancos los papeles puestos al fuego salian las letras." Carta de Antonio de Castro y del Castillo, AHN–Inquisición, Libro 1031, f. 265r; also available in Böhm, *Historia de los judíos en Chile*, 371–374. On Spain, see Kagan, *Lucrecia's Dreams*; Lu Ann Homza, *Religious Authority in the Spanish Renaissance* (Baltimore: Johns Hopkins University Press, 2000); Pulido Serrano, "Jesuitas y cristianos nuevos portugueses." On the reference to messages written on pieces of cloth, see Medina, *Inquisición de Lima*, 2:88. For communication between merchants and slaves, see Silverblatt, *Modern Inquisitions*, 150. On the Mexican prisons, see Alberro, *Inquisición y Sociedad*, 223–279; Wachtel, *La fe del recuerdo*, chap. 4; Schorsch, *Swimming the Christian Atlantic*, chap. 6; Wachtel, *The Faith of Remembrance*, chap. 4.

38. "Y que en una ocasión vio cierta persona que un criado de uno de los presos que estaban dentro de las carceles trajo un papel cerrado y se lo dio al dicho alcayde y luego que le recibio se entro con el en las carceles y de alli a un rato salio sin papel y la persona juzgo que se le debia de haber dado al dicho preso por haberle traydo su criado." Proceso contra Bartolomé de Pradeda, AHN–Inquisición, Leg. 1643, Exp. 15, f. 106r. For transgressions found in Lima at different times during the sixteenth century, such as violation of secrecy, female slaves' assistance in carrying messages outside of the prisons, and communications among prisoners in secret cells, see Medina, *Inquisición de Lima*, 1:52, 144–145, and 262. For information on the Silva brothers, see Montesinos, *Auto de la Fe*, BNP-Lima, fs. 17r and 22r; and Medina, *Inquisición de Lima*, 2:59. On messages sent into and out of Mexican prisons, see Alberro, *Inquisición y Sociedad*, 236–237; Wachtel, *La fe del recuerdo*, chap. 5; Wachtel, *The Faith of Remembrance*, chap. 5. The example from Cartagena is quoted in Schorsch, *Swimming the Christian Atlantic*, 247.

39. Schorsch, *Swimming the Christian Atlantic*.

40. "Yten dixo que sabe esta declarante [María de la Cruz] que el dicho alcayde Bartolome de Pradeda de ordinario dexava los calaboços abiertos sin llave mas que hechado el cerrojo." Proceso contra Bartolomé de Pradeda, AHN–Inquisición, Leg. 1647, Exp. 15, f. 11r.

41. See Medina, *Inquisición de Lima*, 1:200–201; Flores Aráoz, "El local del Tribunal."

42. A couple of years after the 1639 Auto, the inquisitor Antonio de Castro y del Castillo reported his performance in the events related to the Complicidad Grande: "Hallose esta inquisicion en la complicidad referida de tanto numero de presos con diez y seys carceles donde fueron menester mas de ciento tomaronse casas circunvecinas y propias." Lic. Don Antonio de Castro y del Castillo to the Suprema, AHN–Inquisición, Libro 1031, fs. 264v–265r. See also Emilio Harth-Terré and Alberto Márquez Abanto, "Las bellas artes en el Virreynato del Perú en el siglo XVI: Las casas del Real Tribunal de la Inquisición," *Revista del Archivo Nacional del Perú* 22 (1958): 194–217.

43. Medina, *Inquisición de Lima*, 1:149.

44. Contreras, *Inquisición de Galicia*, 329.

45. Lewin, *El Santo Oficio en América*; Böhm, *Historia de los judíos en Chile*; Bodian, *Dying in the Law of Moses*, chap. 5; Wachtel, *La fe del recuerdo*, chap. 2; Wachtel, *The Faith of Remembrance*, chap. 2.

46. See note 42 and the text that follows: "tomaronse casas circunvecinas y propias abrieronse puertas atajaronse aposentos *no con la division que se debia sino con la comodidad que el tiempo y prisas daban lugar*." Lic. Don Antonio de Castro y del Castillo to the Suprema, AHN–Inquisición, Libro 1031, f. 265r (emphasis mine). See also Flores Aráoz, "El Local del Tribunal." The Mexican tribunal faced a similar situation in the following decade, as noted by Alberro, *Inquisición y Sociedad*, 224.

47. He was moved on December 16, 1636. "Dixeron que por quanto se han acabado de hazer las carceles nuevas secretas para los reos deste judaysmo que ha sobrevenido es conveniente mudar a Enrique Jorge Tavares de la carcel numero 2 en que esta a la carcel numero 81 por los inconvenientes que se ha seguido de comunicación." Proceso de Enrique Jorge Tavares, AHN–Inquisición, Leg. 1648, Exp. 15, f. 152r.

48. "Otras [veces, los prisioneros] se valian para las carceles circunvecinas de golpes de piedras señalando un golpe la a dos la B y asi por las demas letras y quando llegaba a la letra de que se habian de valer para la comunicación daban en ella un repiquete y el que estaba escuchando los golpes la escribia en el suelo o en la pared y juntas despues todas las letras sacaban la edicion entera." Lic. Don Antonio de Castro y del Castillo to the Suprema, AHN–Inquisición, Libro 1031, f. 265r.

49. See Proceso de Manuel Henríquez, AHN–Inquisición, Leg. 1647, Exp. 11, f. 166r.

50. Alberro, *Inquisición y Sociedad*, 241; Wachtel, *La fe del recuerdo*, 131–132; Sweet, *Domingos Álvares*; Wachtel, *The Faith of Remembrance*, 101–102.

51. "Nos manda V Alteza que para mayor acierto no se de paso sin grande fundamento particularmente en lo tocante a xpianos viejos testificados por haberse experimentado en ese reino *que los de la nacion hebrea de proposito declaran falsamente contra los catholicos por hacelles daño*" (emphasis mine). The Lima Inquisitors to the Suprema, AHN–Inquisición, Libro 1031, fs. 31r–33r, f. 31r. This motive is confirmed in the declaration of Enrique Jorge Tavares: "Para que se descubriera la verdad que este viene a decir y es la maldad que los portugueses han querido hacer contra los castellanos en levantarle falsos testimonios y traerlos a padecer ynjustamente lo que no deben solo movidos de hacer mal y traer a padecer a los xpianos porque los portugueses que lo han hecho no

estan arrepentidos." Proceso de Enrique Jorge Tavares, AHN–Inquisición, Leg. 1648, Exp. 15, f. 152v.

52. "Y que era tan grande la licencia que tenian los negros de que se servia [Bartolomé de Pradeda] que entraban solos en las carceles y se comunicaban con los presos de donde resulto que a un negro se le cayo un trapo atado y cierta persona cogio y vio si tenia en el un papel escrito y enviaban de fuera para uno de los presos y con el quatro pelotillas al parecer de incienso porque leyendo dicho papel decia en el como se habia de usar de dichas pelotillas el dia que se hubiese de dar tormento." Proceso contra Bartolomé de Pradeda, AHN–Inquisición, Leg. 1643, Exp. 15, f. 106r. In her testimony against Pradeda, María de la Cruz explains how she found out about this: "En particular un dia estando dando de comer a los presos se le escapa [a] un negro que no reparo qual de ellos era esta declarante [María de la Cruz] un trapito sucio atado y redondo y esta lo alço entendiendo que era algun patacon y se lo metio en la faltriquera sin que nadie la viese y acabado de dar de comer esta declarante se fue a su aposento y desato el dicho trapito y vio que dentro del estaba un papel escrito y dentro del papel estaban quatro pelotillas redondas mas gruesas algo que granos de maiz las quales le olieron a esta declarante a incienso y sospecho y tuvo por cierto esta declarante que al negro a quien se le habian caydo las dichas pelotillas las tenia para metellas algun preso de las carceles secretas y esta declarante por no saber leer aunque la letra le parecio de muger llevo el dicho papel a un religioso de San Francisco que no le sabe el nombre y le dixo en confesion lo que le habia pasado y que le leyese el dicho papel el qual decia que tomase la noche antes que le hubiesen de dar tormento una pelotilla de aquellas y otra o todas que no esta bien en ello quando se lo hubiesen de dar." Proceso contra Bartolomé de Pradeda, AHN–Inquisición, Leg. 1643, Exp. 15, fs. 6r–6v.

53. Eimeric and Peña, *El manual*, 187.

54. Proceso de Manuel Bautista Pérez, AHN–Inquisición, Leg. 1647, Exp. 13, fs. 323v–333v; Wachtel, *La fe del recuerdo*, chap. 3; Wachtel, *The Faith of Remembrance*, chap. 3.

55. Starr-Lebeau, *In the Shadow of the Virgin*, chap. 6.

56. See Rodrigo Váez Pereira, Relación de su causa, AHN–Inquisición, Libro 1031, fs. 198r–205r.

57. "[Enrique Núñez de Espinosa] fue el mas perjudicial Iudio que ha auido en este Reyno, por auer dicho a los de su profefsion [*sic*], lo que passaua en el Santo Officio, y el modo de procesar." Montesinos, *Auto de la Fe*, BNP–Lima, f. 14v. For information about Montesinos, see Sabine Hyland, *The Quito Manuscript: An Inca History Preserved by Fernando de Montesinos* (New Haven, Conn.: Yale University Press, 2007), chap. 2.

58. "Las revocaciones tuvieron principio de unos golpes que oyeron los presos se daban en la capilla desta Ynquisicion para asentar en ella unas puertas nuevas con clavaçon de bronce. Entendieron que era hacer tablado para auto de fe y *como esperaban con mucha certidumbre que habia de venilles perdon de V Altº por la muchedumbre a que decian que mas facilmente a que mas facilmente* [*sic*] *se perdonaba* para dilatar el auto trataron por sus señas y golpes corriendo la palabra por las mas de las carceles de revocar y hacer la imposible que esta nombre dieron a esta traça diabolica. Declarando asi algunos de los presos que vinieron a asentar en sus primeras confesiones y es cierto" (emphasis mine). Lic. Don

Antonio de Castro y del Castillo to the Suprema, AHN–Inquisición, Libro 1031, f. 265v. A similar explanation for the motives behind the revocations is offered in this fragment: "Las demas [causas] se van siguiendo y muchas dellas estan sentenciadas y otras conclusas de que se ymbia relacion al consejo con que se dispone la celebridad del auto para antes de Navidad con el favor divino el qual estuviera mucho ha fenecido si las comunicaciones de carceles tan perniciosas al buen progreso no lo hubieran estorbado y dado motivo a las revocaciones que los mas de los presos hicieron pareciendoles que con la dilacion y hacer la cosa imposible mejorarian su causa metiendola a barata y llegaria en tanto perdon general de su santidad y Magd real asi se ha coligido de las declaraciones de muchos reos y que de yntento ponian unos a otros las testificaciones verdaderas muchas falsas para confundir lo que era cierto con lo mentiroso que no dexan traça que no ynteneten ni malicia que no alcancen." The Lima Inquisitors to the Suprema, f. 32r, AHN–Inquisición, Libro 1031, fs. 31r–33r.

59. Schwartz, *All Can Be Saved*, 116–117.

Chapter 6
The Plight of the Condemned

An earlier version of this chapter was published as Ana Schaposchnik, "Exemplary Punishment in Colonial Lima: The 1639 *Auto de Fe*," in *Death and Dying in Colonial Spanish America*, ed. Martina Will de Chaparro and Miruna Achim (Tucson: University of Arizona Press, 2011), © 2011 The Arizona Board of Regents. Reprinted by permission of the University of Arizona Press.

1. "En la ciudad de Lima, reino del Peru, a 23 de enero de 1639, hubo un auto general de fe con setenta y dos reos." Llorente, *Historia crítica*, 4:12. The exact number of sentences issued in this Auto General de Fe was seventy-three. Seventy-two prisoners received punishment at the ceremony. One man committed suicide and received punishment in effigy.

2. "Es la lectura pública y solemne de los sumarios de procesos del Santo Oficio, y de las sentencias que los inquisidores pronuncian estando presentes los reos o efigies que los representen, concurriendo todas las autoridades y corporaciones respetables del pueblo y particularmente el juez real ordinario, a quien se le entregan allí mismo las personas y estatuas condenadas a relajación, para que luego pronuncie sentencias de muerte y fuego conforme a las leyes del reino contra los herejes." Llorente, *Historia crítica*, 1:19–20.

3. Osorio, *Inventing Lima*, chap. 4.

4. "Puestos de rodillas los penitentes ante el juez, éste les presentaba un libro de los Evangelios que ellos tocaban para garantía de su juramento, se entonaba el salmo *Miserere*, y durante su canto eran golpeados, más o menos simbólicamente, por los clérigos presentes con unas varas al efecto dispuestas." Miguel Jiménez Monteserín, "Modalidades y sentido histórico del Auto de Fé," in *Historia de la Inquisición en España y América*, vol. 2, ed. Joaquín Pérez Villanueva and Bartolomé Escandell Bonet (Madrid: Biblioteca de Autores Cristianos, Centro de Estudios Inquisitoriales, 1993), 559–587, 562. The medieval

ceremony was itself based on earlier Christian penitential ceremonies that combined excommunication and reconciliation. On this matter, see Francisco Bethencourt, "The *Auto da Fé*: Ritual and Imagery," *Journal of the Warburg and Courtauld Institutes* 55 (1992): 155–168. Consuelo Maqueda Abreu describes how the Auto de Fe of the Spanish Inquisition changed over time. See Maqueda Abreu, *El auto de Fe*.

5. Bethencourt, "The *Auto da Fé*," 156.
6. García Cárcel and Moreno Martínez, *Inquisición*.
7. See Medina, *Inquisición de Lima*, vol. 1, chap. 4; Llorente, *Historia crítica*, 1:19–20.
8. Osorio, *Inventing Lima*, 104, 119.
9. "Es la ciudad, según yo experimenté en dos años que // estuve en ella, y muy falta de fiestas de plaza, que entristece más a la gente; pues en estos dos años no hubo juegos de cañas ni de toros, ni otras fiestas semejantes, con que la gente se suele alegrar. Pero lo que falta de estas fiestas, sobra de Iglesias; pues no hay domingos ni días de fiesta en que en alguna iglesia no haya fiesta, adonde la gente acude a rezar y con este achaque a pasear." Ocaña, *Un viaje fascinante*, 94–95. "Tiene esta Ciudad mas de quarenta Iglesias, y Capillas." Salinas y Córdova, 195.
10. Ocaña, *Un viaje fascinante*, 100–101. For a discussion of the duration of Fray Diego de Ocaña's visit to Lima and his possible presence at the 1605 Auto de Fe, see the notes of the editor in the same volume. See also Osorio, *Inventing Lima*, 113.
11. "La Magestad con que estos grandes Ministros celebran en esta ciudad los Autos Generales de la Fé, es incomparable: y assi se an admirado, y ayudado mucho los Virreyes en cuyo tiempo se hizieron." Salinas y Córdova, *Memorial*, 149; Fred Bronner, "Acerca de un olvidado manuscrito del 'Memorial' de Fr. Buenaventura Salinas," *Revista de Historia de América* 84 (1977): 235–240.
12. For details of the ceremony of 1625, see Causas despachadas en el auto de fe celebrado el 21 de diciembre de 1625 en Lima, AHN–Inquisición, Libro 1030, fs. 293r–434r; Medina, *Inquisición de Lima*, 2:18–32; Osorio, *Inventing Lima*, 9. On the infrequency of public Autos, see also Pérez Villanueva, "Felipe IV," 1021; Kamen, *The Spanish Inquisition*, 212.
13. For recent scholarship that discusses this ceremony in places other than Lima, see Maqueda Abreu, *El auto de Fe*; Alejandro Cañeque, "Theater of Power: Writing and Representing the Auto de Fe in Colonial Mexico," *The Americas* 52, no. 3 (1996): 321–343; García Cárcel and Moreno Martínez, *Inquisición*, 179–188; Cañeque, *The King's Living Image*, chap. 4.
14. Salinas y Córdova, *Memorial*, 252–254.
15. For bullfights in the plaza, see Suardo, *Diario*, 1:7, 117, 119–120, 125, and 133. Manuel Atanasio Fuentes reported that a ring for that purpose was built at a different plaza in 1768. Fuentes, *Lima*.
16. See José A. Maravall, *La cultura del Barroco* (Barcelona: Ariel, 1975); and Acosta de Arias Schreiber, *Fiestas coloniales urbanas*. See also Ramos Sosa, *Arte festivo*; Linda Ann Curcio-Nagy, "Giants and Gypsies: Corpus Christi in Colonial Mexico City," in *Rituals of Rule, Rituals of Resistance: Public Celebrations and Popular Culture in Mexico*, ed. William H. Beezley, Cheryl E. Martin, and William E. French (Wilmington, Del.: Scholarly

Resources Inc., 1994), 1–26; Clara García Ayluardo, "A World of Images: Cult, Ritual, and Society in Colonial Mexico City," in *Rituals of Rule, Rituals of Resistance: Public Celebrations and Popular Culture in Mexico*, ed. William H. Beezley, Cheryl E. Martin, and William E. French (Wilmington, Del.: Scholarly Resources Inc., 1994), 77–93; Linda Ann Curcio-Nagy, *The Great Festivals of Colonial Mexico City: Performing Power and Identity* (Albuquerque: University of New Mexico Press, 2004); José R. Jouve Martín, "Public Ceremonies and Mulatto Identity"; Osorio, *Inventing Lima*; Solange Alberro, "Los efectos especiales en las fiestas virreinales de Nueva España y Perú," *Historia Mexicana* 59, no. 3 (2010): 837–875.

17. Acosta de Arias Schreiber, *Fiestas coloniales urbanas*; Osorio, *Inventing Lima*; Alberro, "Los efectos especiales." For the financial aspects of the viceroy's arrival in 1628, see also Margarita Suárez, *Desafíos transatlánticos*, 127.

18. "Fue tan grande el fuego, y estallido, que en esta ciudad de los Reyes se pudiera leer vna carta después de auer cerrado la noche, que fue quando se leuantó el incendio." Salinas y Córdova, *Memorial*, 133.

19. See, for example, Suardo, *Diario*, 1:84, 112–113, 116, and 127; Suardo, *Diario*, vol. 2. Suardo also reported that on December 31, 1630, the merchants' guild organized a gala fire festival that included floats the shapes of caimans, unicorns, whales, serpents, and rhinos. Costumed Indians and blacks also participated in the parade. The fireworks that closed the festival lasted for an hour, and many commented that the pyrotechnics were the best the city had ever seen. Suardo, *Diario*, 1:129–130.

20. See Olinda Celestino and Albert Meyers, *Las cofradías en el Perú: Región central* (Frankfurt am Main: Vervuert, 1981), chap. 1; Guillermo Reverter-Pezet, *Las cofradías en el Virreynato del Perú* (Lima, 1985); Acosta de Arias Schreiber, *Fiestas coloniales urbanas*; Paul Charney, "A Sense of Belonging: Colonial Indian Cofradías and Ethnicity in the Valley of Lima, Peru," *The Americas* 54, no. 3 (1998): 379–407.

21. For years in which there were earthquakes in Lima during the sixteenth and seventeenth centuries, see Durán Montero, *Lima en el siglo XVII*, 36–47; Osorio, *Inventing Lima*, appendix 4.

22. See María Águeda Méndez, "La fiesta de San Pedro Mártir: Preparativos y vicisitudes de la Inquisición novohispana," *Caravelle* 73 (1988): 61–70.

23. Medina, *Inquisición de Lima*, 2:21; Méndez, "La fiesta de San Pedro Mártir"; Acosta de Arias Schreiber, *Fiestas coloniales urbanas*, 66. According to Bethencourt: "Its symbolism [of the Green Cross] was fairly transparent: green liturgical colour of Ordinary Time, is associated with the idea of hope. The cross was covered, a common practice in some areas of Europe during part of Lent, and which symbolized the contemplation of the Church in preparation for Christ's resurrection. In this case [the Auto General], it was meant to be a reminder of the offence committed by heresy against Christ's sacrifice and of the wound inflicted by heretics on the Christian community as a whole." Bethencourt, *The Inquisition*, 262.

24. Mendiburu, *Diccionario histórico-biográfico*, 2:356; Suardo, *Diario*, vol. 2. See also chap. 4 of this book.

25. Suardo, *Diario*, 2:126, 168, and 196–197; Medina, *Inquisición de Lima*, vol. 2, chap. 18.

26. Medina, *Inquisición de Lima*, 1:181. For Autos performed in Lima during the sixteenth and seventeenth centuries, see Pérez Cantó, "El Tribunal de Lima," 1136; Osorio, *Inventing Lima*, appendix 3.

27. Relación verdadera de un auto de Inquisición que se hiço en la ciudad de los Reyes a 13 de abril año de 1578, BN–Madrid, MSS 721, fs. 121r–122v.

28. Guibovich Pérez, "The Printing Press in Colonial Peru." The remaining categories are: materials from the civil authority, related to the university and intellectual life, and materials dealing with applied sciences. For accounts of other festivities, see also Osorio, *Inventing Lima*, 98.

29. For biographical information on Fernando de Montesinos, see Sabine Hyland, *The Quito Manuscript*, chap. 2. A brief paragraph can be found in Mendiburu, *Diccionario histórico-biográfico*, 5:341.

30. Montesinos, *Auto de la Fe*, BNP–Lima. The quotation is from Hyland, *The Quito Manuscript*, 28.

31. On Chinchón's life and government, see José Luis Muzquiz de Miguel, *El conde de Chinchón, virrey del Perú* (Madrid: Escuela de Estudios Hispano-Americanos de la Universidad de Sevilla, 1945).

32. Lima celebrated a public Auto in 1608. Gaitán arrived in 1611 and left in 1651. The other public ceremony was in 1664.

33. Lynn, *Between Court and Confessional*, chap. 5.

34. Suardo, *Diario*, 1:4, 16, 108, 129, and 161–162; Bethencourt, *The Inquisition*, 126. Suardo clarifies that Mañozca did not attend the debate because he felt indisposed.

35. On August 6, 1629, the inquisitors attended a celebration at the Santa Clara convent. Suardo, *Diario*, 1:19.

36. Ibid., 2:44.

37. See Mugaburu and Mugaburu, *Diario de Lima (1640–1694)*, 79–80.

38. Suardo, *Diario*, 1:147, editor's footnote. The historian José Luis Muzquiz de Miguel says that Chinchón and his wife attended the 1631 Auto (performed at the Inquisition chapel) *de incógnito*. Muzquiz de Miguel, *El conde de Chinchón*, 68. See also Castañeda Delgado and Hernández Aparicio, *Inquisición de Lima*, 1:159.

39. Maqueda Abreu, *El auto de Fe*.

40. This is probably valid for continental Europe. According to Michel Foucault: "In France, as in most European countries, with the notable exception of England, the entire criminal procedure, right up to the sentence, remained secret: that is to say, opaque, not only to the public but also to the accused himself." Foucault, *Discipline and Punish*, 35.

41. "Public torture and execution was by no means the most frequent form of punishment." Ibid., 32.

42. See Suardo, *Diario*, 1:19, 60, 82, 90–91, and 105; and Suardo, *Diario*, 2:17–18, 40, 89, 95, 98–101, 102, 109, 114, 143, 152, 154, and 178. See also Mugaburu and Mugaburu, *Diario de Lima (1640–1694)*, 84, 98, 101, 105, 167, 184, and 194; and Osorio, *Inventing Lima*, 107–109.

43. For punishments for homosexuality, including scourging and sentencing to the galleys, see Suardo, *Diario*, 1:10–11, 113, and 115. For the crime of monetary forgery, see

"Quemaron al monedero falso," in Mugaburu and Mugaburu, *Diario de Lima (1640-1694)*, 167.

44. For a semiotic analysis of the Auto de Fe as a representation of the Last Judgment, see Maureen Flynn, "Mimesis of the Last Judgment: The Spanish *Auto de Fe*," *Sixteenth Century Journal* 22, no. 2 (1991): 281–297.

45. Maqueda Abreu, *El auto de Fe*, 10.

46. "Retardose este Auto, aunque la diligencia de la Inquisicion fue con todo cuydado, por culpa, y pretension, de los mismos reos. Fue el caso que aviendose puesto vnas puertas nueuas en la Capilla de la Inquisicion, que cae a la plaça della. . . . Para adorno pues de las puertas, se guarnecieron con clavaçon de bronce, y el ruido que se hizo al clauarlas, les dio tanto que entender a los Iudios, que con notables estratajemas se trataron de comunicar, como lo hizieron, diziendo: ya se llega la ora en que se nos ha de seguir algun gran daño que nos esta aparejado, no ay sino reuoquemos nuestras confefsiones, y con ello retardaremos el Auto, y para mejor traigamos muchos Christianos viejos a estas prisiones, y aura [habrá] perdon general y podra ser nos escapemos. Afsi lo hicieron, que fue la causa de que durasse tanto tiempo la liquidacion de la verdad." Montesinos, *Auto de la Fe*, BNP–Lima, f. 2r–2v.

47. Ibid., f. 2r; Suardo, *Diario*, 2:194–195.

48. "Antes de publicarse el Auto, se encerraron todos los negros que seruian en las carceles, en parte donde no pudieron oir, saber, ni entender de la publicacion, porque no diessen noticia a los reos, pues aunque la Inquisicion vsaua para esto de negros boçales, acabados de traer de partida . . . eran ladinos para los Portugueses, que como los traen de Guinea sabian sus lenguas, y afsi esto les ayudo mucho." Montesinos, *Auto de la Fe*, BNP–Lima, f. 3r. The term *bozal* refers to a black who only knows his or her own language. "Bozal: el negro que no sabe otra lengua que la suya." Covarrubias Orozco, *Tesoro de la lengua castellana o española*, pt. 1, 99. In general, the term *ladino* refers to an Indian who speaks Spanish. In this particular context, it refers to the fact that the Portuguese spoke African languages as a result of their participation in the slave trade.

49. See *Libros de Cabildos de Lima*, ed. Juan Bromley, IV Centenario de la Fundación de la Ciudad (Lima: Torres Aguirre S.A., 1961), 217. See also Medina, *Inquisición de Lima*, vol. 1, chap. 15; Medina, *Inquisición de Lima*, vol. 2, chaps. 16 and 17. For the cost of elaborated Autos, see Kamen, *The Spanish Inquisition*, 212.

50. *Libros de Cabildos de Lima*, 238, 243.

51. Millar Carvacho, *Inquisición y sociedad*, 145–169. Millar Carvacho also explains that the information about the use of the money is complex because the tribunal recorded together moneys from confiscations of 1639 and 1641. See also Quiroz Norris, "La expropiación inquisitorial." According to Suárez, the bankruptcy of Juan de la Cueva was evaluated at 1,068,284 pesos; as she explains, this bankruptcy together with the confiscations related to the Great Complicity affected the credit system of the entire viceroyalty. The tribunal itself became a creditor of de la Cueva. See Suárez, *Desafíos transatlánticos*, 85, 93–94, 98–99.

52. Suardo, *Diario*, 1:50, 151 and 152. For salaries of tribunal members, see Salinas y Córdova, *Memorial*, 147–148. For tribunal finances in the second half of the seventeenth century, see Millar Carvacho, *Inquisición y sociedad*.

53. See Bethencourt, "The *Auto da Fé*," 157. See also Bethencourt, *The Inquisition*, for figures and illustrations of stages for other Autos.

54. See Bethencourt, "The *Auto da Fé*," 161.

55. See Montesinos, *Auto de la Fe*, BNP-Lima, f. 4r; Portocarrero, "Descrição geral do reino do Peru," 150–151; Medina, *Inquisición de Lima*, vol. 2, chap. 17; Lohman Villena, "Una incógnita despejada."

56. Montesinos, *Auto de la Fe*, BNP-Lima, f. 3v. The coroza was an elongated paper cone, marked with a symbol that alluded to the crime committed by its wearer. Real Academia Española, *Diccionario de la lengua española*, 22nd ed., 2 vols. (Madrid: Editorial Espasa Calpe, 2001), http://lema.rae.es/drae/.

57. Montesinos, *Auto de la Fe*, BNP-Lima, f. 4v; Ramos Sosa, *Arte Festivo*, 240, 242. For the number of carpenters in Lima, see Salinas y Córdova, *Memorial*, 256.

58. Bethencourt, *The Inquisition*, 258.

59. Bethencourt, "The *Auto da Fé*," 157.

60. "Encima de la grada [de los penitenciados] estaua la media naranja, que formauan tres figuras de horrendos demonios." Montesinos, *Auto de la Fe*, BNP-Lima, f. 4v.

61. Bethencourt, *The Inquisition*, 259. See also Bethencourt, "The *Auto da Fé*."

62. Bethencourt, *The Inquisition*, 260–261.

63. For example, in seventeenth-century Madrid, the monarchy occupied a podium at the center, with the inquisitors at a podium to the right. This particular distribution had a meaning related to both: the centrality of the Spanish monarchy and the preeminent role the monarchy gave to the Inquisition throughout that century. But this arrangement was not necessarily adopted by other tribunals. Apparently, the inquisitors occupied the central seat of the highest row in the Tribunal of Cartagena de Indias, the bishop sat at the right of the inquisitors, and the governor at the left. As Bethencourt has noted, the distribution of the seats in the staircases among the authorities varied between the Spanish and the Portuguese Inquisitions, and even among the different tribunals of the same monarchy. Ibid., chap. 7.

64. In *Auto de la Fe*, f. 9v (BNP-Lima), Montesinos reports that the Viceroy Chinchón's child was present, seated next to his wife Francisca Enríquez de Rivera. The boy, Francisco Fausto Antonio Melchor, was born in Lambayeque, Peru, on the couple's journey to Lima, where Chinchón assumeed his office at the viceroyalty (January 1629). See Muzquiz de Miguel, *El conde de Chinchón*; Salinas y Córdova, *Memorial*; Montesinos, *Auto de la Fe*, BNP-Lima, fs. 3v–4v. José Toribio Medina mentions the presence of the viceroy's daughters at the 1625 Auto but does not mention Chinchón's son at the 1639 ceremony. Medina, *Inquisición de Lima*, 2:21. For the description of the Lima tablado in this ceremony, see also Medina, *Inquisición de Lima*, 2:99–101; Osorio, *Inventing Lima*, 114.

65. "Su Excelencia [el Virrey], y los señores Inquisidores se pusiero en sus lugares, estuvo en medio del señor Licenciado don Iuan de Mañozca, que estuuo a la mano derecha, y del señor Licenciado Andres Iuan Gaytan, que estuuo a la siniestra. A la mano derecha del señor Mañozca, estuuo el señor Licenciado don Antonio de Castro, y

a la siniestra del señor Gaytan, el señor Licenciado D. Leon de Arcayaga Lartau. Y luego por vn lado y otro se seguian los señores de la Real Audiecia, y los del Tribunal mayor de Cuentas, los Cabildos Eclesiastico, y secular, Vniversidad, Colegios, y Comunidades, en sus lugares." Montesinos, *Auto de la Fe*, BNP Lima, f. 9r. For disagreements between the leaders of the armed forces about the seats at the 1664 Lima Auto de Fe, see Mugaburu and Mugaburu, *Diario de Lima (1640–1694)*, 63.

66. "Tuuo su Excelencia [el Virrey] tres almohadas de estrado (que en este Reyno vulgarmente se llaman coxines) vna para asiento, y dos a los pies, de rica tela amarilla. Y el señor don Iuan de Mañozca tuuo su almohada negra de terciopelo, por Consejero de su Magestad, en el de la General, y santa Inquisicion. Lo restante donde estuuieron los señores de la Real Audiencia estuuo curiosamente adornado con ricos brocateles." Montesinos, *Auto de la Fe*, BNP Lima, f. 9v; Osorio, *Inventing Lima*, 114. According to Medina's account of the 1625 ceremony, the viceroy was the only authority who had a pillow for his feet, again in a yellow fabric. Medina, *Inquisición de Lima*, 2:25. For a discussion of the meaning of these elements, see also Cañeque, *The King's Living Image*, chap. 4.

67. See also Osorio, *Inventing Lima*, 111; Bethencourt, *The Inquisition*, 260–261. For the way in which politics influenced royal processions, see James Flaks, "The Death of the Monarch as a Colonial Sacrament," in *Death and Dying in Colonial Spanish America*, ed. Martina Will de Chaparro and Miruna Achim (Tucson: University of Arizona Press, 2011), 100–120.

68. Montesinos, *Auto de la Fe*, BNP Lima, fs. 27r–28r.

69. For descriptions of Autos de Fe in places other than Lima, see, for example, Lea, *A History*; Flynn, "Mimesis of the Last Judgment"; Bethencourt, "The *Auto da Fé*"; Maqueda Abreu, *El auto de Fe*; Kamen, *The Spanish Inquisition*; García Cárcel and Moreno Martínez, *Inquisición*; Pérez, *Crónica*; Bethencourt, *The Inquisition*.

70. "Afsi camino la procefsion co toda magestad hasta la plaça de la ciudad, y sin torcer llegó a las puertas principales de Palacio, y desde alli tomo la buelta a coxer las del tablado, que mirauan a la calle de los Mercaderes." Montesinos, *Auto de la Fe*, BNP Lima, f. 6r.

71. "Seguiãse los Religiosos de todas ordenes que en tanto numero, y concierto, que cogían tres calles en largo." Montesinos, *Auto de la Fe*, BNP Lima, fs. 5v–6r.

72. In general, in a regular festivity of the annual cycle, Native groups usually opened a procession, followed by leaders and representatives of the Inca nobility, followed by Spanish soldiers, guild associates, nobles, and members of the religious orders. Closing the procession were civil and religious authorities. See Acosta de Arias Schreiber, *Fiestas coloniales urbanas*; Osorio, *Inventing Lima*; Bethencourt, *The Inquisition*, 262–265.

73. "Poco despues de notificadas las sentencias a los relaxados, boluiero en si Enrique de Paz, y Manuel de Espinosa, y co el vno hizo Audiecia el señor Inquisidor Andres Iua Gayta y co el otro el señor Inquisidor D. Antonio de Castro, hasta las tres de la mañana, y a aquella hora se llamo a cosulta en q se hallaron co los señores Inquisidores, el señor Licéciado D. Iua de Cabrera, Tesorero de la santa Iglesia, Prouisor

en Sedeuacate [Sede vacante], y ordinario del Santo Oficio y los señores. . . . En esta Consulta se admitieron a reconciliacion a los dichos." Montesinos, *Auto de la Fe*, BNP–Lima, f. 6v.

74. "La noche antes del auto de 22 de enero del dicho año habiéndosele notificado que estaba condenado a relajar y habiéndosele puesto las insignias de relajado [Rodrigo Váez Pereira] pidió misericordia y dijo que quería declarar los cómplices con quienes se había comunicado en la ley de Moisés y declaró contra algunos y no pareció satisfacer bastantemente demás de tener contra sí los muchos testimonios que levantó a inocentes." Relación de la causa de Rodrigo Váez Pereira para el consejo supremo de la Santa y General Ynquisición el cual fue relajado en persona en el auto de 23 de enero de 1639 años, fol. 204v, AHN–Inquisición, Libro 1031, fs. 198r–205r.

75. "Dioseles de almorçar a los penitenciados este dia a las tres, para cuyo efeto se mando llamar vn pastelero tres dias antes, y debaxo de juramento de secreto, se le mando cuydasse desto, de modo que antes de la hora dicha, estuuiesse el almuerço en casa del Alcayde, que se hizo con toda puntualidad." Montesinos, *Auto de la Fe*, BNP–Lima, f. 6v.

76. "A la hora señalada acudieron muchos Republicanos honrados, con deseo, que se les cupiesse algun penitenciado, q acompañar, para mostrar en lo q podian el afecto con que deseavan seruir a tan santo Oficio. Pero para que se entienda ser esto mocio[n] de Dios, y para exemplar de todos los fieles: sucedio que don Saluador Velazquez Indio principal, Sargento mayor de la milicia de los naturales, entro en el santo Oficio, a la misma hora que los Republicanos, de gala, con espada, y daga plateada, y pidio, que le honrassen a el, dandole vna estatua de las que auian para salir en el Auto, que a esso solo iva, y visto su afecto se le concedio lo que pedia y a otro compañero suyo." Montesinos, *Auto de la Fe*, BNP–Lima, f. 6v.

77. For the procession of the penitents in general, see ibid., fs. 7r–7v. For the description of the audience: "Por las calles por donde pafso la procefsion el numero de gente que ocurriô a ver los penitenciados, que no es pofsible sumarla, baste decir que cinco dias antes se pusieron escaños para este efeto, y detras dellos, tablados por vna vanda, y por otra de las calles, donde estaua la gente dicha, fuera de la que auia en los balcones, y ventanas, y techos, y en muchas partes auia dos ordenes de tablados, y en la plaça tres." Montesinos, *Auto de la Fe*, BNP–Lima, f. 7v.

78. The sequence of the processions varied in different settings. For another sequence, see Bethencourt, "The *Auto da Fé*," 158.

79. "Los Iudayzantes con sus sambenitos, y los que auían de ser açotados con sogas gruessas a las gargantas, los vltimos ivan los relaxados en persona, con coroças, y sambenitos de llamas, y demonios en diuersas formas, de sierpes, y dragones, y en las manos Cruzes verdes." Montesinos, *Auto de la Fe*, BNP–Lima, f. 7r. See also Bodian, *Dying in the Law of Moses*, 144.

80. See Lea, *A History*, vol. 3.

81. For this case and context, there is evidence showing that prisoners could circumvent such restrictions and communicate with one another. They received letters from family members and other close associates and were probably allowed to take

walks around the Inquisition patio. See, for example, Proceso contra Bartolomé de Pradeda, AHN–Inquisición, Leg. 1643, Exp. 15, already discussed in this book. But this was a fragmented interaction limited to a narrow social circle. It could not reverse the negative effects of years of reclusion and confinement.

82. See Relación de la causa de Manuel de Paz Estravagante relajado en estatua en el auto de veinte y tres de enero de mil y seiscientos y treinta y nueve años, AHN–Inquisición, Libro 1031, fs. 226r–228r; Proceso de Mencía de Luna, AHN–Inquisición, Leg. 1647, Exp. 10; and Proceso de Antonio Morón, AHN–Inquisición, Leg. 1647, Exp. 18. Manuel Bautista Pérez hurt himself with a knife as reported by Montesinos, *Auto de la Fe*, BNP–Lima, f. 23r. Considering the irregularities of the prisons and the leaks of information I analyzed, it is very likely that other prisoners had learned about these events.

83. "[Doña Mayor de Luna] de edad al parecer, de mas de 60 años, aunque ella nego ser de 40." Montesinos, *Auto de la Fe*, BNP–Lima, f. 14v.

84. Ibid., fs. 17r, 22r.

85. For the intellectual discussion about the humanity and special physical traits of Jews in seventeenth-century Spain, see Yerushalmi, *From Spanish Court*. For an extension of this debate to colonial Peru, see Irene Silverblatt, "New Christians and New World Fears in Seventeenth-Century Peru," *Comparative Studies in Society and History* 42, no. 3 (2000): 524–546.

86. "El Jueves Santo salía del templo de San Agustín de Lima una gran procesión que contaba con el mayor número de andas en la ciudad. De igual modo, sacaban unos figurones de madera de aspecto horrible que tenían el tamaño de un hombre y representaban a los judíos. El pueblo, movido por el celo religioso del momento, insultaba a los muñecos como si fueran verdaderos verdugos de carne y hueso." Acosta de Arias Schreiber, *Fiestas coloniales urbanas*, 64. This author bases her description on Fuentes, *Lima*. The edition is from 1925, but Fuentes's work was initially published in 1867. Suardo mentions the solemnity and the attendance at the procession of the San Agustín *cofradía* on Holy Thursday of 1630 and 1634; however, he does not provide information about who walked in the procession. Suardo, *Diario*, 1:66–67, 2:21. See also Reverter-Pezet, *Las cofradías en el Virreynato*. In a book written to promote tourism in Lima, Guillermo Lohman Villena describes processions that took place during the Holy Week in the seventeenth century but does not provide specific information related to effigies representing Jews; he does mention them, following Atanasio Fuentes also, but for the 1800s. Guillermo Lohman Villena, *La Semana Santa de Lima* (Lima: Fondo de Promoción Turística del Perú, Banco Crédito del Perú, 1996), 40–41. On rituals during the Holy Week in the Iberian Peninsula, see David Niremberg, *Communities of Violence: Persecution of Minorities in the Middle Ages* (Princeton N.J.: Princeton University Press, 1996), chap. 7.

87. Fuentes, *Lima*, 77–79.

88. Suardo, *Diario*, 1:142–144.

89. On the representation of the king, see also Cañeque, *The King's Living Image*, chap. 4; Osorio, *Inventing Lima*, chap. 3.

90. At the beginning of the seventeenth century Fray Diego de Ocaña wrote: "Hay en esta ciudad en particular, dos compañías de gentileshombres muy honrados, la una es de arcabuces y la otra es de lanzas. La compañía de arcabuces tiene cincuenta hombres . . . la compañía de las lanzas tiene cien hombres." Describing their duties Ocaña continues: "y los Jueves Santos y cuando hay Auto de Inquisición, guardan la ciudad y las bocas de las calles de la plaza para más seguridad de la ciudad." Ocaña, *Un viaje fascinante*, 99–100. See also Salinas y Córdova, *Memorial*, 141. For the viceroy's convoy, see Suardo, *Diario*, 2:196–197.

91. "Y para dar toda honra a los que salieron libres de los testimonios de los Iudios, acordó el Tribunal, que fuessen en este acompañamiento con sus padrinos, y su Excelencia [el Virrey] les mandó señalar lugar con la Ciudad: fue espectáculo de admiración, ver a vn mismo tiempo, triunfar la verdad, y castigarse la mentira, efectos de la rectitud del S. Oficio." Montesinos, *Auto de la Fe*, BNP–Lima, f. 8v; Osorio, *Inventing Lima*, 116–117.

92. The following description is based on Bethencourt, *The Inquisition*, 273–277.

93. Fr. José de Cisneros ó Zisneros, *Discurso qve en el insigne Auto de la Fe, celebrado en esta Real ciudad de Lima, aueinte y tres de Enero de 1639 años, predicó el M. R. P. Fray Joseph de Cisneros* (printed in Lima by Gerónymo de Contreras, 1639), BNP–Lima, X 282 56.

94. "El primer Inquisidor del mundo, fue Moyses . . . que fue tanta su autoridad, que los Príncipes del pueblo de Dios, rindiero la vida a su sentencia." Ibid., f. 7r. For a similar and contemporary reference, see also Calancha, *Crónica*, vol. 4, chap. 16. For Inquisition writings in sixteenth-century Spain that also referred to Moses as the first inquisitor, see Lynn, "Was Adam the First Heretic?" For references to King Solomon, see Flaks, "The Death of the Monarch."

95. "Y si proteruos, y duros perseverais en vuestra perfidia judaica, méritamente soys condenados por este santo Tribunal, a muerte de fuego, que el pérfido, q otra muerte merece, sino abrasadoras llamas." Cisneros, *Discurso*, f. 15r.

96. "Salieron en este último auto [de 1605] veintitrés judíos, todos portugueses." Ocaña, *Un viaje fascinante*, 100.

97. "Fueron llevados a quemar onze judíos y a uno en estatua," Suardo, *Diario*, 2:197.

98. Bethencourt, *The Inquisition*, 273–277.

99. Ibid., 274.

100. Montesinos, *Auto de la Fe*, BNP–Lima, fs. 10v–11r.

101. Ibid., fs. 11r–11v. To abjure meant to admit guilt and reject the offense, to ask for forgiveness under the promise of not relapsing, and to offer further cooperation in denouncing those who offended Christian dogma to the Inquisition.

102. Mugaburu and Mugaburu record that in December 1667 people condemned to the El Callao galley arrived at the city prisons and were then sent to the mercury mines of Huancavelica. Mugaburu, *Diario de Lima (1640–1694)*, 97.

103. Millar Carvacho, *Inquisición y sociedad*, 162. According to Matthew Warshawsky, the wealth accumulated by Pérez and Duarte was probably equivalent to $33 million. Warshawsky, "Manuel Bautista Pérez and the *Complicidad Grande* in Colonial Peru."

104. According to Fuentes, the Plaza de Acho had had a ring for bullfights since 1768. Fuentes, *Lima*, 53–54.

105. "Ivan los justiciados entre dos hileras de soldados, para guardarlos del tropel de la gente, que fue sin numero la que ocurrio a verlos, y muchos religiosos de todas ordenes para predicarles." Montesinos, *Auto de la Fe*, BNP–Lima, f. 26v. In an earlier version of this chapter, published in 2011, I wrote that two guardians escorted each prisoner, and here I have corrected that to two lines of guards. The copy of Montesinos's document available to me at the first writing did not allow me to read the word *hileras*.

106. "Asistio el Alguacil Mayor a la justicia, y Diego Xaramillo, de Andrade, Escrivano Publico, y los ministros, y no se aparto hasta que el Secretario dio fee [fe] como todos quedauan convertidos en ceniça." Montesinos, *Auto de la Fe*, BNP–Lima, f. 26v.

107. "El quemar á un herege no solo es por su bien, sino mas particularmente para el provecho y edificacion espiritual del pueblo católico." Eymeric, *Manual*, 105. See also Kamen, *The Spanish Inquisition*, 174; Sullivan, *Inner Lives*, 190–196.

108. See, for example, Claudia Silva Cogollos Amaya and Martín Eduardo Poo, "Sociedad, muerte y prácticas de enterramiento en el Santa Fé colonial," *Universitas Humanística* 22, no. 37 (1993): 35–42; Irma Barriga Calle, "Sobre el discurso Jesuita en torno a la muerte presente en la Lima del siglo XVII," *Histórica* 19, no. 2 (1995): 165–195; Martín Eduardo Poo and Claudia Silvia Cogollos Amaya, "La teología de la muerte: Una visión española del fenómeno durante los siglos XVI al XVII," in *Inquisición, muerte y sexualidad en la Nueva Granada*, ed. Jaime Borja Gómez (Bogotá: Ariel, 1996), 117–142. See also Martina Will de Chaparro and Miruna Achim, *Death and Dying in Colonial Spanish America* (Tucson: University of Arizona Press, 2011).

109. See Carlos N. M. Eire, *From Madrid to Purgatory: The Art and Craft of Dying in Sixteenth-Century Spain* (Cambridge: Cambridge University Press, 1995).

110. Montesinos, *Auto de la Fe*, BNP–Lima, fs. 20v–24v. Francisco Maldonado de Silva was a surgeon who had been imprisoned in Lima for thirteen years. He was not part of the Complicidad Grande and did not live in Lima before his imprisonment, but his trial of faith was contemporary to those of the Complicidad and ended at the same Auto General. See, among others, Lewin, *El Santo Oficio en América*; Böhm, *Historia de los judíos en Chile*; Bodian, *Dying in the Law of Moses*; Wachtel, *La fe del recuerdo*; Wachtel, *The Faith of Remembrance*.

111. "[Antonio de Espinosa] Dio muestras de arrepentimiento en el tablado, mas no fueron verdaderas." Montesinos, *Auto de la Fe*, BNP–Lima, f. 21r.

112. "[Diego López de Fonseca] iva tan desmayado al Auto que fue necessario lleuarlo en braços, y al ponello en la grada a oir sentencia, le huuieron de tener hasta la cabeça." Ibid., f. 21r.

113. "Se levantó vn viento tan recio que afirman vezinos antiguos desta ciudad, no auer visto otro tan fuerte en muchos años. Rompió con toda violencia la vela que hazia sombra al tablado, por la misma parte, y lugar donde estaua este condenado [Francisco Maldonado de Silva], el qual mirando al cielo, dixo: *esto lo ha dispuesto assi el Dios de Israel, para verme cara a cara desde el cielo*." Ibid., f. 22r (emphasis mine). As has been noted earlier, Maldonado de Silva was not a Lima merchant.

114. "[Luis de Lima] en el tablado, auiendosele acabado de leer su sentencia, estando en la grada, con muchas lagrimas pidio perdon a Santiago del Castillo, Pedro de Soria Arçila, y a Francisco Sotelo, delante de todo el pueblo, dixiendoles les auia levantado falso testimonio, por la enemistad que les tuuo, y en general pidio perdon a los demas que auia leuantado testimonios, y que rogasen a Dios le perdonasse." Ibid., f. 22v.

115. "[Manuel Bautista Pérez] dio muestras de su deprauado animo, y de dissimulado Iudio en el osculo de Paz que dio a su cuñado Sebastian Duarte, relaxado, en el cadahalso, y de las demostraciones de ira que con los ojos hazia contra aquellos que de su casa y familia auian confessado y estauan alli con sambenito, oyó su sentencia con mucha seberidad y magestad, murio impenitente, pidie[n]do al verdugo hiziesse su oficio." Ibid., f. 23v. Pérez's attitude probably interested Montesinos more than what others said before dying, because he wrote about it twice. He introduced it with more detail at the beginning of his text, even before he introduced the preparation of the ceremony, and later repeated the exchange: "Salieron al cadahalso el dia del Auto tres cuñados, Manuel Bautista Perez, a quien todos llamauan el Capitan grande (era Vicario de Moysen) y Sebastian Duarte, y Garcia Vaez, este con insignias de reconciliado, los otros de quemados, por negatiuos, Ofreciose a ir el Duarte a la gradilla a oir sentencia, passar por muy cerca del Manuel Bautista, con notable afecto, se dieron el vno al otro y el otro al otro, el osculum pacis Iudayco, sin q se pudiesse estoruar, y se enternecieron como sectaricos [sectarios] de vna ley, e igualmente sentenciados, dandose el parabien de su firmeza con claras demostraciones. Passado esto, fue necessario ir por el mismo paraje el otro cuñado Garcia Vaez, y el negativo Manuel Bautista, no solo no hizo con él las demostraciones de amistad que con el otro, pero lo miro con ojos tan sesgos, y estudiadas acciones de desestima, y menosprecio, que leyeron los circunstantes en el rostro le dezia: mal Iudiguelo, y algunos han afirmado lo dixo. Lo cierto es que lo desestimo, y no hizo caso del, por parecerle auia confessado la verdad." Ibid., f. 2r.

116. "En el tablado se dieron el [Sebastián Duarte] y su cuñado Manuel Bautista Perez osculo de Paz al modo Iudaico, sin poderlos apartar los padrinos. En el quemadero viendo ya muerto a su cuñado Manuel Bautista Perez, dio señales de arrepentimiento." Ibid., f. 24r–24v.

117. "[Tomé Quaresma] en el tablado pidio a vozes misericordia: auiendo baxado el señor Inquisidor don Antonio de Castro y del Castillo, de debaxo del dosel a ver lo que quería, se arrepintio de auer dado muestras de pedirla: dize que porque al baxar le miro Manuel Bautista Perez, como afeadole semejante accion, y assi murio impenitente." Ibid., f. 24v.

118. Montesinos did not write with the same detail about each of the eleven men who died at the stake in the ceremony. Of Antonio de Vega and Juan Rodríguez de Silva he wrote only that they died impenitent. For Juan de Azevedo there is only the summary of his trial. Rodrigo Váez Pereira's death is discussed in the following paragraphs.

119. "Entre los onze fue quemado uno de ellos bibo [vivo], que causó mucha lástima a todos, que no quiso jamás convertirse a nuestra santa fee católica," Suardo, *Diario*, 2:197.

120. "Hasta aquí he sido judío y desde ahora soy xptiano ... y dijo el dicho Rodrigo Vaez Pereira volviéndose al señor Tomás Quaresma que estaba a su lado compañeros pues que lo hemos sido no es mucho que lo paguemos y confiemos en Jesucristo que es el que nos ha de salvar." Testimonios sobre la conversión y confesión de Rodrigo Váez Pereira antes que le den garrote, AHN–Inquisición, Libro 1031, f. 267r. Montesinos wrote a similar description of this particular event. For another example, see Kamen, *The Spanish Inquisition*, 211–212.

121. "Tiene el escudo de armas de la Inquisicion a vn lado de la Cruz, vna espada, y vn ramo de Oliua, y al otro vna Palma. La espada significa el rigor de la justicia. La Oliua, la suauidad de la misericordia. Estos atributos ya los hemos visto en lo referido, en los relaxados, que no quisieron valerse de la piedad, lo riguroso de la ley en los reconciliados, q reconocieron lo tierno, y suaue de la misericordia. La Palma significa el honor que se da al que por testimonios falsos ha padecido. La inoce[n]cia de su alma y el triunfo de sus trabajos. Porque si bien regularmente habla[n]do en las causas de Fe nadie es declarado por inocente por sentencia definitiva; sino tan solamente absuelto dela instancia, co todo esso, si por testigos falsos fue vno acusado, y consta de su inoce[n]cia por reuocacion de los mismos, ha de ser por sentencia, declarado por inocente, y libre de tal crimen, y el Iuez que otra cosa hiziere, peca mortalmente. Esta es opinion de grandes Autores." Montesinos, *Auto de la Fe*, BNP–Lima, f. 25r; Osorio, *Inventing Lima*, 108.

122. Montesinos, *Auto de la Fe*, BNP–Lima, f. 27v; Suardo, *Diario*, 2:197.

123. Suardo, *Diario*, 2:198.

124. Medina, *Inquisición de Lima*, 2:157; Salinas y Córdova, *Memorial*, 196.

125. See Medina, *Inquisición de Lima*, vol. 2, chap. 19; Palma, *Anales*, 38. On the cases from Cusco, see Castañeda Delgado and Hernández Aparicio, *Inquisición de Lima*, vol. 2, chap. 15. For delayed trials, see Kamen, *The Spanish Inquisition*, 197. For information related to some of the people reconciled in Lima in 1639 who were living in Seville afterward, see García de Proodian, *Los judíos en América*.

126. "Al pie del madero [Manuel Henríquez] dixo que moria justamente." Relaciones de Causas de Fe, Lima, años 1659, 1660 y 1664, AHN–Inquisición, Leg. 5345, Exp. 1, fs. 15v–16r.

127. The other effigy represented a man named Luis Ribero. See ibid., fs. 1r–6r. Mugaburu and Mugaburu describe the 1664 Auto but do not include the names of those punished at the ceremony. See Mugaburu and Mugaburu, *Diario*, 62–63.

128. Montesinos, *Auto de la Fe*, BNP–Lima, f. 14v.

129. John Lewis Gaddis, *The Landscape of History: How Historians Map the Past* (Oxford: Oxford University Press, 2002), 85. See also the following quote: "The famous and elaborate autos of the seventeenth century were few and far between." Kamen, *The Spanish Inquisition*, 206.

Bibliography

Archival Documents

Archivo Histórico Nacional (AHN)–Madrid, Sección Inquisición

Legajo 1643

Expediente 15: Bartolomé de Pradeda, Proceso Criminal

Legajo 1647

Expediente 3: Proceso de Joan Vicente
Expediente 10: Proceso de Mencía de Luna
Expediente 11: Proceso de Manuel Henríquez
Expediente 12: Proceso de Luis de Valencia
Expediente 13: Proceso de Manuel Bautista Pérez
Expediente 16: Proceso de Francisco Vázquez
Expediente 18: Proceso de Antonio Morón

Legajo 1648

Expediente 7: Duarte Núñez de Cea, Relación de Causa
Expediente 15: Proceso de Enrique Jorge Tavares
Expediente 16: Proceso de Garci Méndez de Dueñas

Legajo 3123

Sobre cambios en la aplicación de la tortura

Legajo 4797

Expediente 1: Cartas del inquisidor Juan de Mañozca, solicitando dinero de las Cajas Reales al ser insuficientes las rentas de sus canonjías. Y cuentas de rentas dela Canonjía del Cuzco.

Note: The nonnumeric entries in the archival documents are alphabetized for ease of reference.

Legajo 5345

Expediente 1: Relaciones de Causas de Fe, Lima, años 1659, 1660, y 1664

Libro 1028

Relación de las causas pendientes en el Santo Oficio de la Inquisición de la ciudad de Los Reyes por el mes de marzo de 1597

Libro 1029

Relación de las causas despachadas en el Auto que la Inquisición del Perú hizo en la capilla de la dicha Inquisición domingo de la Santísima Trinidad 17 de junio de 1612

Libro 1030

Antonio de la Oliva, Relación de Causa
Bernardo López Serrano, Relación de Causa
Causas despachadas en el auto de fe celebrado el 21 de diciembre de 1625 en Lima
Juan de Ortega, Relación de Causa
Manuel de Fonseca, Relación de Causa
Quaderno de la Complicidad del Judaísmo que se empeçó en esta Ynquisiçión De la ciudad de Los Reyes del rreyno del Pirú desde principio de Abril del año De 1635

Libro 1031

Antonio Cordero, Relación de Causa
Auto que se celebro a los 23 de hen° de seys° y treinta y nueve y execucion de las sentencias
Carta de los Inquisidores de Lima to the Suprema
Carta del Licenciado Don Antonio de Castro y del Castillo to the Suprema
Manuel Bautista Pérez, Relación de Causa
Manuel de Paz Estravagante, Relación de Causa
Relación de las causas determinadas y pendientes en esta Inquisicion de los reinos del Piru desde veynte y seys de mayo de mill y seiscientos y treinta y cinco años y auto que se celebro a los diez y siete de agosto del mismo año en la capilla por desembaraçar las cárceles habiendo sobrevenido la grande complicidad de los años pasados
Relaciones de Causas de los años 1645–46, 1646–47, 1647–48, 1650–51, 1660–62, 1659–60–64, y 1666
Rodrigo Váez Pereira, Relación de Causa
Testimonios sobre la conversión y confesión de Rodrigo Váez Pereira antes que le den garrote
Tomé Quaresma, Relación de Causa

Libro 1226

Carta escrita por el Señor Don Gonzalo Bravo a la Inquisición de Galicia sobre la forma que se tiene en ejecutar los tormentos en Castilla
Forma de escribir los tormentos según los da regularmente Alonso de Alcalá Ministro executor de Justicia de Madrid

Libro 1260

Difuntos
Infieles Judíos o Moros no Baptizados
Revocantes de Ssus Confesiones

Archivo Nacional (AN)-Lima

Juan de Herrera Padilla contra Bartolomé de Pradeda, por cantidad de pesos de arrendamiento

*Arquivo Nacional da Torre do Tombo (ANTT)-Lisbon,
Inquisição de Coimbra*

Livro 4

Lista das pessoas que sairao no Auto da Fee que se celebrou na Praça desta Cidade de Coimbra a 4 de Maio de 1625 asistido nelle o snor Dor Joam Alvrez Brandao do Conselho de Sua Magestade e do Geral da Sta Inquisição Ldo Gaspar Borges Dazevedo o Los Po da Silva o Dtor Lopo Soares de Castro Pregou o Pe Mel Fagundes da Compa de Jesus

Livro 70

Culpas do judaismo—Culpas vindas das inquisições espanholas contra judaizantes de Portugal

Biblioteca Nacional (BN)-Madrid

MS 718

Decreto de los Reyes Católicos Don Fernando y Doña Isabel para que se castiguen y se secuestren la tercera parte de los bienes de los penitenciados por el Santo Oficio aún trayendo habilitación de otros tribunales de Inquisición para arbitrar en estos reynos

Decreto de SM remitido a su Consejo de la Santa y General Inquisición año de 1619—Acerca de los portugueses que se pasan a Francia con sus familias y haciendas

MS 721

Relación verdadera de un auto de Inquisición que se hiço en la ciudad de los Reyes a 13 de Abril año de 1578

MS 2927

Copia del carta que El Rey nuestro Señor mando escribir al presidente y oydores [de la ciudad de Los Reyes] sobre lo tocante a el asiento y acompañamiento del virrey del dia del auto, 1589

Que se embie Relacion al q° de los estrangeros que hay en Potosí y en esta provincia y de los ynconvenientes que resultan de su estado en estas partes, 1581

MS 2987

La forma de la abjuracion de Vehemente

MS 6591

Origen y fundación de las Inquisiciones de España

MS 10994

Borrador del Voto de mano de D Pedro de Neyla en lo de las Inquisiciones de Portugal y Castilla

Papel sobre si la Inquisicion de Castilla y Portugal reciprocamente deben remitir los reos que se hallan delatados en cada Reyno y que cometieron el delito en el y después se ausentaron

Biblioteca Nacional del Perú (BNP)–Lima

Cisneros ó Zisneros, Fr. José de. *Discurso qve en el insigne Avto de la Fe, celebrado en esta Real ciudad de Lima, aueinte y tres de Enero de 1639 años, predicó el M. R. P. Fray Joseph de Cisneros.* Printed in Lima by Gerónymo de Contreras, 1639.

Montesinos, Don Fernando de, Licenciado. *Auto de la Fe Celebrado en Lima a 23 de enero de 1639.* Madrid: Imprenta del Reino, 1640.

Museo del Congreso y de la Inquisición—Lima

Cuentas de gastos, jornales y cartas de pago por las obras de las casas del Tribunal del Santo Oficio de la Inquisición de Lima (1584). Paleographic transcription by Percy Vargas Valencia, Lima, June 1972. http://www4.congreso.gob.pe/museo/inquisicion/cuentas-gastos.html.

Published Documents

1813—El Cabildo de Lima felicita a las Cortes españolas reunidas en Cádiz por el decreto de supresión de la Inquisición y pide que se extraiga de los Archivos de la Inquisición todos los libros y papeles infamantes para la buena fama de los ciudadanos perseguidos por ésta y se quemen públicamente. Reproduced in José Toribio Medina, *Historia del Tribunal de la Inquisición de Lima, 1569-1820*, vol. 2, 2nd ed., 492-494. Santiago de Chile: Fondo Histórico y Bibliográfico J. T. Medina, 1956.

Calancha, Antonio de la. *Crónica moralizada del Orden de San Agustín en el Perú.* Edited by Ignacio Prado Pastor. Lima: Imprenta de la Universidad Mayor de San Marcos, 1974 [1638].

Carta de Conde de Chinchón, Doctor Galdós de Valencia, Licenciado Don Blas de Torres, Doctor Don Gabriel de Sanabria, Licenciado Cristóbal Cacho de Santillana, Licenciado Luis Henríquez, Doctor don Martín de Arriola, Doctor don Andrés de Billela, Lima, May 18, 1636. Reproduced in Günter Böhm, *Historia de los judíos en Chile*, vol. 1, *Período Colonial: El Bachiller Francisco Maldonado de Silva, 1592–1639*, 341. Santiago: Andrés Bello, 1984.

Carta del Inquisidor Ordóñez y Flórez, Lima, December 1594. Reproduced in Maurice Birckel, "Recherches sur la Trésorerie Inquisitoriale de Lima, I, 1569–1610," *Mélanges de la casa de Vélasquez* 5, no. 1 (1969): 223–307.
Carta del Licenciado Ordóñez y Flores, Los Reyes, April 28, 1600. Reproduced in José Toribio Medina, *La inquisición en Cartagena de Indias*, 2nd ed., 19. Bogotá: C. Valencia, 1978.
Carta de los Inquisidores de Lima (sin firma), Lima, May 13, 1636. Reproduced in Günter Böhm, *Historia de los judíos en Chile*, vol. 1, *Período Colonial: El Bachiller Francisco Maldonado de Silva, 1592–1639*, 333–334. Santiago: Andrés Bello, 1984.
Carta de los Inquisidores Juan de Mañozca, Andrés Juan Gaytan y Antonio de Castro y del Castillo, Lima, May 18, 1636. Reproduced in Günter Böhm, *Historia de los judíos en Chile*, vol. 1, *Período Colonial: El Bachiller Francisco Maldonado de Silva, 1592–1639*, 345–367. Santiago: Andrés Bello, 1984.
Cobo, Bernabé. *Historia del Nuevo Mundo*. Edited by P. Francisco Mateos. Obras del P. Bernabé Cobo de la Compañía de Jesús. Biblioteca de Autores Españoles. Madrid: Atlas, 1956.
Eimeric, Nicolau, and Francisco Peña. *El manual de los inquisidores*. Barcelona: Muchnik, 1983 [1376, 1578].
Eymeric, Nicolau. *Manual de Inquisidores*. Bogotá: Planeta, 1999 [1376].
Fuentes, Manuel Atanasio. *Lima: Apuntes históricos, descriptivos, estadísticos y de costumbres*. Lima: Librería Escolar e Imprenta E. Moreno, 1925 [1867].
González Montes, Reinaldo. *Artes de la Santa Inquisición Española*. Translated by Francisco Ruiz de Pablos. Seville: Ed. MAD S.L., 2008 [1567?].
"Instructions for Administering Questioning under Torture using the Rack." In *The Inquisition in New Spain, 1536–1820: A Documentary History*, edited and translated by John F. Chuchiak IV, 135–138. Baltimore: Johns Hopkins University Press, 2012.
Libros de Cabildos de Lima. Edited by Juan Bromley. IV Centenario de la Fundación de la Ciudad. Lima: Torres Aguirre S.A., 1961.
Lizárraga, Reginaldo de. *Descripción breve de toda la tierra del Perú, Tucumán, Rio de la Plata y Chile*. Preliminary study by Don Mario Hernández Sánchez-Barba. Biblioteca de Autores Españoles. Madrid: Atlas, 1968.
Montesinos, Fernando de. *Anales del Perú*. Vol. 2. Edited by Víctor M. Maúrtua. Madrid: Imprenta de Gabriel L. y del Horno, 1906.
Mugaburu, Josephe de, and Francisco de Mugaburu. *Diario de Lima (1640–1694): Crónica de la época colonial*. Reprinted and with prologue and notes by Don Carlos A. Romero. Lima: Imp. C. Vásquez L., 1935.
Ocaña, Fray Diego de. *Un viaje fascinante por la América hispana del siglo XVI*. Madrid: Stvdivm Ediciones, 1969 [1608].
"Poder de inquisidores á los obispos de las Indias é á sus oficiales é á cada uno en sus districtos." Madrid, July 22, 1517. Reproduced in José Toribio Medina, *La primitiva Inquisición Americana: Estudio Histórico*, 69–70. Santiago: Imprenta Elzeviriana, 1914.
Portocarrero, Pedro León de. "Descrição geral do reino do Peru, em particular de Lima." In *Descripción del Virreinato del Perú*, edited and with prologue by Eduardo

Huarag Álvarez, 137–232. Lima: Universidad Ricardo Palma, Editorial Universitaria, 2009.
Salinas y Córdova, Fray Buenaventura de. *Memorial de las historias del nuevo mundo Pirú*. Colección Clásicos Peruanos 1. Lima: Universidad Mayor Nacional de San Marcos, 1957 [1630].
Sepúlveda, Juan Ginés de. *Demócrates Segundo o De las justas causas de las guerras contra los indios*. Critical bilingual edition with Spanish translation, introduction, notes, and indexes by Ángel Losada. 2nd ed. Madrid: Consejo Superior de Investigaciones Científicas, Instituto Francisco de Vitoria, 1984.
Solórzano Pereira, Juan de. *Política indiana*. 2 vols. Edited by Luis García Arias. Breviarios del Pensamiento Español. Madrid: Editorial Nacional, 1947 [1647].
Suardo, Juan Antonio. *Diario de Lima (1629–1639)*. 2 vols. Published with introduction and notes by Rubén Vargas Ugarte, S.J. Lima: Universidad Católica del Perú, Instituto de Investigaciones Históricas, 1936.
Treaty for the Extradition of Prisoners (1570). Reproduced in François Soyer, "The Extradition Treaties of the Spanish and Portuguese Inquisitons (1500–1700)," in *Estudios de Historia de España*, 201–238. Buenos Aires: Universidad Católica Argentina, Facultad de Filosofía y Letras, Instituto de Historia de España, 2008.
Vázquez de Espinosa, Antonio. *Compendio y descripción de las Indias Occidentales*. Edited by Balbino Velasco Bayón. Madrid: Historia 16, 1992.

Secondary Sources

Abril Castelló, Vidal. *Francisco de la Cruz, Inquisición, Actas I*. Madrid: Consejo Superior de Investigaciones Científicas, 1992.
Acosta, Antonio. "La extirpación de las idolatrías en el Perú: Origen y desarrollo de las campañas; A propósito de cultura andina y represión, de Pierre Duviols." *Revista Andina* 5, no. 1 (1987): 171–195.
Acosta de Arias Schreiber, Rosa María. *Fiestas coloniales urbanas (Lima–Cuzco–Potosí)*. Lima: Otorongo Producciones, 1997.
Aguado de los Reyes, Jesús. "El apogeo de los judíos portugueses en la Sevilla americanista." *Cadernos de Estudos Sefarditas* 5 (2005): 135–157.
Alberro, Solange. "Crypto-Jews and the Mexican Holy Office in the Seventeenth Century." In *The Jews and the Expansion of Europe to the West, 1450–1800*, edited by Paolo Bernardini and Norman Fiering, 172–185. New York: Berghahn Books, 2001.
———. "El Tribunal del Santo Oficio de la Inquisición en Nueva España: Algunas modalidades de su actividad." *Cuadernos para la Historia de la Evangelización en América Latina* 4 (1989): 9–29.
———. *Inquisición y sociedad en México, 1571–1700*. Mexico City: Fondo de Cultura Económica, 1988.
———. "Los efectos especiales en las fiestas virreinales de Nueva España y Perú." *Historia Mexicana* 59, no. 3 (2010): 837–875.

Alcalá, Ángel. *The Spanish Inquisition and the Inquisitorial Mind*. Highland Lakes, N.J.: Atlantic Research and Publications, 1987.

Altman, Ida. *Emigrants and Society: Extremadura and America in the Sixteenth Century*. Berkeley: University of California Press, 1989.

Álvarez Alonso, Fermina. *La Inquisición en Cartagena de Indias durante el siglo XVII*. Madrid: Fundación Universitaria Española, 1999.

Assadourian, Carlos Sempat. "Chile y El Tucumán en el siglo XVI: Una correspondencia de mercaderes." *Historia* 9 (1970): 65–109.

Ayllón Dulanto, Fernando. *El Tribunal de la Inquisición: De la leyenda a la historia*. 2nd ed. Lima: Ediciones del Congreso del Perú, 2011.

Baer, Yitzhak. *A History of the Jews in Christian Spain*. Vol. 2. Philadelphia: Jewish Publication Society of America, 1961.

Ballesteros Gaibrois, Manuel. "La historiografía de la Inquisición en Indias." In *Historia de la Inquisición en España y América*, vol. 1, edited by Joaquín Pérez Villanueva and Bartolomé Escandell Bonet, 40–57. Madrid: Biblioteca de Autores Cristianos, Centro de Estudios Inquisitoriales, 1984.

Barriga Calle, Irma. "Sobre el discurso Jesuita en torno a la muerte presente en la Lima del siglo XVII." *Histórica* 19, no. 2 (1995): 165–195.

Bat Ye'or [pseud.]. *The Dhimmi: Jews and Christians under Islam*. London: Associated University Presses, 1985.

Bataillon, Marcel. "La herejía de Fray Francisco de la Cruz y la reacción antilascasiana." In *Estudios sobre Bartolomé de Las Casas*, 353–367. Barcelona: Península, 1976.

———. "Santo Domingo Era Portugal." In *Historia y Sociedad en el mundo de habla española: Homenaje a José Miranda*, edited by García Martínez et al., 113–120. Mexico City: El Colegio de México, 1970.

Beinart, Haim. *Conversos on Trial: The Inquisition in Ciudad Real*. Translated by Yael Guiladi. Jerusalem: Magnes Press, Hebrew University, 1981.

Benbassa, Esther, and Aron Rodrigue. *Sephardi Jewry: A History of the Judeo-Spanish Community, 14th–20th Centuries*. Berkeley: University of California Press, 2000.

Bennassar, Bartolomé. "El poder inquisitorial." In *Inquisición Española: Poder político y control social*, edited by Bartolomé Bennassar, 68–93. Barcelona: Grijalbo, 1984.

———. "La Inquisición o la pedagogía del miedo." In *Inquisición Española: Poder político y control social*, edited by Bartolomé Bennassar, 95–125. Barcelona: Grijalbo, 1984.

———. "Patterns of the Inquisitorial Mind as the Basis for a Pedagogy of Fear." In *The Spanish Inquisition and the Inquisitorial Mind*, edited by Ángel Alcalá, 177–184. Highland Lakes, N.J.: Atlantic Research and Publications, 1987.

Bernardini, Paolo, and Norman Fiering. *The Jews and the Expansion of Europe to the West, 1450 to 1800*. New York: Berghahn Books, 2001.

Bethencourt, Francisco. "The *Auto da Fé*: Ritual and Imagery." *Journal of the Warburg and Courtauld Institutes* 55 (1992): 155–168.

———. *The Inquisition: A Global History, 1478–1834*. Translated by Jean Birrel. Past and Present Publications. Cambridge: Cambridge University Press, 2009.

Birckel, Maurice. "Recherches sur la Trésorerie Inquisitoriale de Lima, I, 1569–1610." *Mélanges de la Casa de Velázquez* 5, no. 1 (1969): 223–307.

———. "Recherches sur la Trésorerie Inquisitoriale de Lima, II, 1611–1642." *Mélanges de la Casa de Velázquez* 6, no. 1 (1970): 309–357.

Bodian, Miriam. *Dying in the Law of Moses: Crypto-Jewish Martyrdom in the Iberian World.* Bloomington: Indiana University Press, 2007.

———. *Hebrews of the Portuguese Nation: Conversos and Community in Early Modern Amsterdam.* Bloomington: Indiana University Press, 1997.

———. "Hebrews of the Portuguese Nation: The Ambiguous Boundaries of Self-Definition." *Jewish Social Studies* 15, New Series, no. 1, Sephardi Identities (2008): 66–80.

———. "'Men of the Nation': The Shaping of *Converso* Identity in Early Modern Europe." *Past and Present* 143 (1994): 48–76.

Böhm, Günter. "Crypto-Jews and New Christians in Colonial Peru and Chile." In *The Jews and the Expansion of Europe to the West, 1450–1800*, edited by Paolo Bernardini and Norman Fiering, 203–212. New York: Berghahn Books, 2001.

———. *Historia de los judíos en Chile.* Vol. 1, *Período Colonial: El Bachiller Francisco Maldonado de Silva, 1592–1639.* Santiago: Andrés Bello, 1984.

Bowser, Frederick P. *The African Slave in Colonial Peru, 1524–1650.* Stanford, Calif.: Stanford University Press, 1974.

Boyajian, James C. *Portuguese Bankers at the Court of Spain, 1626–1650.* New Brunswick, N.J.: Rutgers University Press, 1983.

———. *Portuguese Trade in Asia under the Habsburgs, 1580–1640.* Baltimore: Johns Hopkins University Press, 1993.

Brackman, Harold. *Farrakhan's Reign of Historical Error: The Truth Behind the Secret Relationship Between Blacks and Jews.* Los Angeles: Simon Wiesenthal Center, 1992.

Bromberg, Rachel Mizrahi. *A Inquisição no Brasil: Um capitão-mor judaizante.* São Paulo: FFLH/USP Centro de Estudos Judaicos, 1984.

Bromley, Juan, and José Barbagelata. *Evolución urbana de la ciudad de Lima.* Lima: Consejo Provincial de Lima, 1945.

Bronner, Fred. "Acerca de un olvidado manuscrito del 'Memorial' de Fr. Buenaventura Salinas." *Revista de Historia de América* 84 (1977): 235–240.

———. "Advertencia privada de un virrey peruano del siglo XVII a su presunto sucesor." *Revista de Indias* 41, nos. 163–164 (1981): 55–77.

———. "The Population of Lima, 1593–1637: In Quest of a Statistical Bench Mark." *Ibero-Amerikanisches Archiv* 5, New Series, no. 2 (1979): 107–119.

Brown, Kendall. *A History of Mining in Latin America: From the Colonial Era to the Present.* Albuquerque: University of New Mexico Press, 2012.

Burns, Kathryn. *Into the Archive: Writing and Power in Colonial Peru.* Durham, N.C.: Duke University Press, 2010.

———. "Nuns, Kurakas, and Credit: The Spiritual Economy of Seventeenth-Century Cuzco." *Colonial Latin American Review* 6, no. 2 (1997): 185–203.

Cañeque, Alejandro. *The King's Living Image: The Culture and Politics of Viceregal Power in Colonial Mexico.* New York: Routledge, 2004.

———. "Theater of Power: Writing and Representing the Auto de Fe in Colonial Mexico." *The Americas* 52, no. 3 (1996): 321–343.
Cannas da Cunha, Ana. *A Inquisição no estado da Índia: Origens (1539–1560)*. Lisbon: Arquivos Nacionais/Torre do Tombo, 1995.
Carcelén Reluz, Juan Carlos. "La persecución a los judíos conversos en el Perú colonial, siglos XVI y XVII." In *Incas e indios cristianos: Elites indígenas e identidades cristianas en los Andes coloniales*, edited by Jean Jacques Decoster, 373–393. Cusco: CBC–IFEA–Asociación KURAKA, 2002.
Caro Baroja, Julio. *El Señor Inquisidor, y otras vidas por oficio*. Madrid: Alianza Editorial, 1968.
Carvalho, António. *Os judeus do desterro de Portugal*. Lisbon: Quetzal, 1999.
Castañeda Delgado, Paulino, and Pilar Hernández Aparicio. *La Inquisición de Lima*. Vol. 1, *1570–1635*. Madrid: Deimos, 1989.
———. *La Inquisición de Lima*. Vol. 2, *1635–1696*. Madrid: Deimos, 1995.
———. "La visita de Ruiz de Prado al Tribunal del Santo Oficio de Lima." *Anuario de Estudios Americanos* 41 (1984): 1–53.
Castro, Américo. *España en su historia: Cristianos, moros y judíos*. Buenos Aires: Editorial Losada, 1948.
Celestino, Olinda, and Albert Meyers. *Las cofradías en el Perú: Región central*. Frankfurt am Main: Vervuert, 1981.
Cesarani, David. *Port Jews: Jewish Communities in Cosmopolitan Maritime Trading Centres, 1550–1950*. London: Frank Cass, 2002.
Charney, Paul. "A Sense of Belonging: Colonial Indian Cofradías and Ethnicity in the Valley of Lima, Peru." *The Americas* 54, no. 3 (1998): 379–407.
Clendinnen, Inga. *Ambivalent Conquests: Maya and Spaniard in Yucatan, 1517–1570*. 2nd ed. New York: Cambridge University Press, 2003.
———. "Disciplining the Indians: Franciscan Ideology and Missionary Violence in Sixteenth-Century Yucatan." *Past and Present* 94 (1982): 27–48.
Cogollos Amaya, Silvia Claudia, and Martín Eduardo Poo. "Sociedad, muerte y prácticas de enterramiento en el Santa Fé colonial." *Universitas Humanistica* 22, no. 37 (1993): 35–42.
Cohen, Martin. *The Martyr Luis de Carvajal: A Secret Jew in Sixteenth-Century Mexico*. Albuquerque: University of New Mexico Press, 2001.
———, and Abraham J. Peck. *Sephardim in the Americas*. Judaic Studies Series. Tuscaloosa: University of Alabama Press, 1993.
Contreras, Jaime. *El Santo Oficio de la Inquisición de Galicia: Poder, sociedad y cultura*. Madrid: Akal, 1982.
———. "Estructura de la actividad procesal del Santo Oficio." In *Historia de la Inquisición en España y América*, vol. 2, edited by Joaquín Pérez Villanueva and Bartolomé Escandell Bonet, 588–632. Madrid: Biblioteca de Autores Cristianos, Centro de Estudios Inquisitoriales, 1993.
———. "Los cambios en la Península." In *Historia de la Inquisición en España y América*, vol. 1, edited by Joaquín Pérez Villanueva and Bartolomé Escandell Bonet, 1156–1176. Madrid: Biblioteca de Autores Cristianos, Centro de Estudios Inquisitoriales, 1984.

———. *Sotos contra Riquelmes: Regidores, inquisidores y criptojudíos.* Madrid: Anaya & M. Muchnik, 1992.

Contreras, Jaime, and Jean Pierre Dedieu. "Estructuras geográficas del Santo Oficio en España." In *Historia de la Inquisición en España y América,* vol. 2, edited by Joaquín Pérez Villanueva and Bartolomé Escandell Bonet, 3–47. Madrid: Biblioteca de Autores Cristianos, Centro de Estudios Inquisitoriales, 1993.

Contreras, Jaime, and Gustav Henningsen. "Forty-four Thousand Cases of the Spanish Inquisition (1540–1570): Analysis of a Historical Data Bank." In *The Inquisition in Early Modern Europe,* edited by Gustav Henningsen and John Tedeschi, 100–129. Dekalb: Northern Illinois University Press, 1986.

Cook, Alexandra, and Noble David Cook. *Good Faith and Truthful Ignorance: A Case of Transatlantic Bigamy.* Durham, N.C.: Duke University Press, 1991.

Cook, Noble David. *Demographic Collapse: Indian Peru, 1520–1620.* Cambridge: Cambridge University Press, 1981.

Cross, Harry. "Commerce and Orthodoxy: A Spanish Response to Portuguese Commercial Penetration in the Viceroyalty of Peru, 1580–1640." *The Americas* 35, no. 2 (1978): 151–167.

Cuadro García, Ana Cristina. "Las cárceles inquisitoriales del tribunal de Córdoba." *Hispania* 65/2, no. 220 (2005): 443–464.

Curcio-Nagy, Linda Ann. "Giants and Gypsies: Corpus Christi in Colonial Mexico City." In *Rituals of Rule, Rituals of Resistance: Public Celebrations and Popular Culture in Mexico,* edited by William H. Beezley, Cheryl E. Martin, and William E. French, 1–26. Wilmington, Del.: Scholarly Resources, 1994.

———. *The Great Festivals of Colonial Mexico City: Performing Power and Identity.* Albuquerque: University of New Mexico Press, 2004.

Davis, Natalie Zemon. *Fiction in the Archives: Pardon Tales and Their Tellers in Sixteenth-Century France.* Stanford, Calif.: Stanford University Press, 1987.

Dedieu, Jean Pierre. "The Archives of the Holy Office of Toledo as Source for Historical Anthropology." In *The Inquisition in Early Modern Europe,* edited by Gustav Henningsen and John Tedeschi, 158–189. Dekalb: Northern Illinois University Press, 1986.

———. "Los cuatro tiempos de la Inquisición." In *Inquisición Española: Poder político y control social,* edited by Bartolomé Bennassar, 15–39. Barcelona: Grijalbo, 1984.

de la Pinta Llorente, Miguel. *La Inquisición Española.* Madrid: Archivo Agustiniano, 1948.

———. *Las cárceles inquisitoriales españolas.* Madrid: Librería Clío, 1949.

Domínguez Ortiz, Antonio. "Los extranjeros en la vida española durante el siglo XVII." In *Los extranjeros en la vida española durante el siglo XVII y otros artículos,* edited by León Carlos Álvarez Santaló. Seville: Diputación de Sevilla, Área de Cultura y Ecología, 1996.

———. *Los judeoconversos en España y en América.* Madrid: Istmo, 1971.

———. *Los judeoconversos en la España Moderna.* Madrid: Mapfre, 1992.

Drescher, Seymour. "Jews and New Christians in the Atlantic Slave Trade." In *The Jews and the Expansion of Europe to the West, 1450 to 1800,* edited by Paolo Bernardini and Norman Fiering, 439–470. New York: Berghahn Books, 2001.

———. "The Role of Jews in the Transatlantic Slave Trade." *Immigrants and Minorities* 12, no. 2 (1993): 113–125.
Durán Montero, María Antonia. *Lima en el siglo XVII: Arquitectura, urbanismo y vida cotidiana.* Sección Historia, "Nuestra América," no. 1. Seville: Diputación Provincial de Sevilla, 1994.
Duviols, Pierre. *La destrucción de las religiones andinas: Conquista y colonia.* Mexico: Universidad Nacional Autónoma de México, 1977.
Edwards, John. *Torquemada & the Inquisitors.* Stroud, U.K.: Tempus, 2005.
Eire, Carlos N. M. *From Madrid to Purgatory: The Art and Craft of Dying in Sixteenth-Century Spain.* Cambridge: Cambridge University Press, 1995.
Elliott, John. *The Count-Duke of Olivares: The Statesman in an Age of Decline.* New Haven, Conn.: Yale University Press, 1986.
———. "A Europe of Composite Monarchies," *Past and Present*, no. 137 (1992): 48–71.
Escandell Bonet, Bartolomé. "Estructura geográfica del dispositivo inquisitorial americano." In *Historia de la Inquisición en España y América*, vol. 2, edited by Joaquín Pérez Villanueva and Bartolomé Escandell Bonet, 48–60. Madrid: Biblioteca de Autores Cristianos, Centro de Estudios Inquisitoriales, 1993.
———. "La peculiar estructura administrativa y funcional de la Inquisición Española en Indias." In *Historia de la Inquisición en España y América*, vol. 2, edited by Bartolomé Escandell Bonet and Joaquín Pérez Villanueva, 633–665. Madrid: Biblioteca de Autores Cristianos, Centro de Estudios Inquisitoriales, 1993.
———. "Las adecuaciones estructurales: Establecimiento de la Inquisición en Indias." In *Historia de la Inquisición en España y América*, vol. 1, edited by J. Pérez Villanueva and Bartolomé Escandell Bonet, 713–730. Madrid: Biblioteca de Autores Cristianos, Centro de Estudios Inquisitoriales, 1984.
———. "Una lectura psico-social de los papeles del Santo Oficio: Inquisición y sociedad peruanas en el siglo XVI." In *La Inquisición española: Nueva visión, nuevos horizontes*, edited by Joaquín Pérez Villanueva, 437–467. Madrid: Siglo XXI, 1980.
Escribano Vidal, Tomás. "Recesión, estancamiento administrativo, infiltración judía y extranjera." In *Historia de la Inquisición en España y América*, vol. 1, edited by Joaquín Pérez Villanueva and Bartolomé Escandell Bonet, 1002–1005. Madrid: Biblioteca de Autores Cristianos, Centro de Estudios Inquisitoriales, 1984.
Faber, Eli. *Jews, Slaves, and the Slave Trade: Setting the Record Straight.* New York: New York University Press, 1998.
Ferry, Robert. "Don't Drink the Chocolate: Domestic Slavery and the Exigencies of Fasting for Crypto-Jews in Seventeenth-Century Mexico." *Nuevo Mundo, Mundos Nuevos*, no. 5 (2005): 2–16.
Flaks, James, "The Death of the Monarch as a Colonial Sacrament." In *Death and Dying in Colonial Spanish America*, edited by Martina Will de Chaparro and Miruna Achim, 100–120. Tucson: University of Arizona Press, 2011.
Flores Aráoz, José. "El local del Tribunal del Santo Oficio de Lima." *Cultura Peruana* (supplement), 1946.
Flynn, Maureen. "Mimesis of the Last Judgment: The Spanish *Auto de Fe*." *Sixteenth Century Journal* 22, no. 2 (1991): 281–297.

Fortune, Stephen. *Merchants and Jews: The Struggle for British West Indian Commerce, 1650–1750*. Gainsville: University Presses of Florida, 1984.
Foucault, Michel. *Discipline and Punish: The Birth of the Prison*. New York: Pantheon Books, 1977.
Gacto, Enrique. "Aproximación al Derecho penal de la Inquisición." In *Perfiles jurídicos de la Inquisición Española*, edited by José Antonio Escudero, 175–193. Madrid: Instituto de Historia de la Inquisición, Universidad Complutense de Madrid, 1989.
Gaddis, John Lewis. *The Landscape of History: How Historians Map the Past*. Oxford: Oxford University Press, 2002.
Garcia, Maria Antonieta. *Judaísmo no feminino: Tradição popular e ortodoxia em Belmonte*. Edited by Instituto de Sociologia e Etnologia das Religiões. Lisbon: Universidade Nova de Lisboa, 1999.
García Ayluardo, Clara. "A World of Images: Cult, Ritual, and Society in Colonial Mexico City." In *Rituals of Rule, Rituals of Resistance: Public Celebrations and Popular Culture in Mexico*, edited by William H. Beezley, Cheryl E. Martin and William E. French, 77–93. Wilmington, Del.: Scholarly Resources Inc., 1994.
García Cárcel, Ricardo. *Orígenes de la Inquisición española: El Tribunal de Valencia, 1478–1530*. Barcelona: Península, 1976.
García Cárcel, Ricardo, and Doris Moreno Martínez. *Inquisición: Historia crítica, colección Historia*. Madrid: Temas de Hoy SA, 2000.
García de Proodian, Lucía. *Los judíos en América: Sus actividades en los virreinatos de Nueva Castilla y Nueva Granada, S. XVII*. Edited by Instituto Arias Montano. Madrid: Consejo Superior de Investigaciones Científicas, 1966.
Gareis, Iris. "Repression and Cultural Change: The 'Extirpation of Idolatry' in Colonial Peru." In *Spiritual Encounters*, edited by Nicholas Griffiths and Fernando Cervantes, 230–254. Lincoln: University of Nebraska Press, 1999.
Gerber, Jane. *The Jews of Spain: A History of the Sephardic Experience*. New York: Free Press, 1992.
Gil, Juan. *Los conversos y la Inquisición sevillana*. Vol. 1. Seville: Universidad de Sevilla, Fundación El Monte, 2000.
Giles, Mary, ed. *Women in the Inquisition: Spain and the New World*. Baltimore: Johns Hopkins University Press, 1998.
Ginzburg, Carlo, *The Cheese and the Worms: The Cosmos of a Sixteenth-Century Miller*. Translated by John Tedeschi and Anne Tedeschi. Baltimore: Johns Hopkins University Press, 1992.
Gitlitz, David. *Secrecy and Deceit: The Religion of the Crypto-Jews*. Philadelphia: Jewish Publications Society, 1996.
Glick, Thomas. *Islamic and Christian Spain in the Early Middle Ages*. Princeton, N.J.: Princeton University Press, 1979.
Gonçalves de Mello, José Antonio. *Gente da nação*. Edited by FUNDAJ. Recife: Massangana, 1989.
González Novalín, José Luis. "Las instrucciones de la Inquisición española: De Torquemada a Valdés (1484–1561)." In *Perfiles jurídicos de la Inquisición Española*,

edited by José Antonio Escudero, 91–109. Madrid: Instituto de Historia de la Inquisición, Universidad Complutense de Madrid, 1989.

Gose, Peter. *Invaders as Ancestors: On the Cultural Making and Unmaking of Spanish Colonialism in the Andes*. Toronto: University of Toronto Press, 2008.

Grahit y Papell, Emilio. *El Inquisidor Fray Nicolás Eymerich*. Gerona: Imprenta de Manuel Llach, 1878.

Graizbord, David. "Religion and Ethnicity among the 'Men of the Nation': Toward a Realistic Interpretation." *Jewish Social Studies* 15, New Series, no. 1, Sephardi Identities (2008): 32–65.

Greenleaf, Richard. *The Mexican Inquisition in the Sixteenth Century*. Albuquerque: University of New Mexico Press, 1969.

Greer, Margaret, Walter Mignolo, and Maureen Quilligan, eds. *Rereading the Black Legend: The Discourses of Religious and Racial Difference in the Renaissance Empires*. Chicago: University of Chicago Press, 2007.

Griffiths, Nicholas. *The Cross and the Serpent: Religious Repression and Resurgence in Colonial Peru*. Norman: University of Oklahoma Press, 1996.

Guibovich Pérez, Pedro. *Censura, libros e Inquisición en el Perú colonial, 1570–1754*. Seville: Consejo Superior de Investigaciones Científicas; Escuela de Estudios Hispano-Americanos, Universidad de Sevilla, Diputación de Sevilla, 2003.

———. *En defensa de Dios: Estudios y documentos sobre la Inquisición en el Perú*. Lima: Congreso de la República del Perú, 1998.

———. "Fray Juan de Almaraz, calificador de la Inquisición de Lima (s. XVI)." *Cuadernos para la Historia de la Evangelización en América Latina* 4 (1989): 31–45.

———. "La cultura libresca de un converso procesado por la Inquisición de Lima." *Historia y Cultura*, no. 20 (1990): 133–160.

———. *La Inquisición y la censura de libros en el Perú virreinal (1570–1813) / The Inquisition and Book Censorship in the Peruvian Viceroyalty (1570–1813)*. Lima: Ediciones del Congreso del Perú, 2000.

———. "Los libros del inquisidor," *Cuadernos para la Historia de la Evangelización en América Latina* 4 (1989): 47–64.

———. "The Printing Press in Colonial Peru: Production Process and Literary Categories in Lima, 1584–1699." *Colonial Latin American Review* 10, no. 2 (2001): 168–188.

———. "Proyecto colonial y control ideológico: El establecimiento de la Inquisición en el Perú." *Apuntes* 35 (1994): 109–116.

Haliczer, Stephen. *Inquisition and Society in the Kingdom of Valencia, 1478–1834*. Berkeley: University of California Press, 1990.

Hampe Martínez, Teodoro. "Control moral y represión ideológica: La Inquisición en el Perú (1570–1820)." *Boletín del Instituto Riva Agüero*, no. 16 (1989): 225–256.

———. "Estudios recientes sobre Inquisición y sociedad en el Perú colonial." In *Santo Oficio e historia colonial*, 103–133. Lima: Congreso del Perú, 1998.

———. "Inquisición y sociedad en el Perú colonial (1570–1820): Una lectura crítica de la bibliografía reciente." *Histórica* 19 (1995): 1–28.

———. "Recent Works on the Inquisition and Peruvian Colonial Society, 1570–1820," *Latin American Research Review* 31, no. 2 (1996): 43–65.
———. "Ricardo Palma, cronista de la Inquisición." *Quaderni ibero-americani*, no. 95 (2004): 15–30.
———. *Santo Oficio e historia colonial*. Lima: Congreso del Perú, 1998.
Hanke, Lewis. *All Mankind Is One: A Study of the Disputation between Bartolomé de Las Casas and Juan Ginés de Sepúlveda in 1550 on the Intellectual and Religious Capacity of the American Indians*. DeKalb: Northern Illinois University Press, 1974.
———. "The Portuguese in Spanish America, with Special Reference to the Vila Imperial of Potosí." *Revista de Historia de América*, no. 51 (1961): 1–48.
Harth-Terré, Emilio, and Alberto Márquez Abanto. "Las bellas artes en el Virreynato del Perú en el siglo XVI: Las casas del Real Tribunal de la Inquisición." *Revista del Archivo Nacional del Perú* 22 (1958): 194–217.
Henningsen, Gustav. "La legislación secreta del Santo Oficio." In *Perfiles jurídicos de la Inquisición Española*, edited by José Antonio Escudero, 163–172. Madrid: Instituto de Historia de la Inquisición, Universidad Complutense de Madrid, 1989.
Henningsen, Gustav, and John Tedeschi, eds. *The Inquisition in Early Modern Europe: Studies on Sources and Methods*. Dekalb: Northern Illinois University Press, 1986.
Herculano, Alexandre. *História da origem e estabelecimento da Inquisição em Portugal*. Lisbon: Viuva Bertrand & Cia, Sucesores de Carvalho & Cia, 1879.
Herzog, Tamar. "'A Stranger in a Strange Land': The Conversion of Foreigners into Community Members in Colonial Latin America (17th–18th Centuries)." *Social Identities* 3, no. 2 (1997): 247–263.
Homza, Lu Ann. *Religious Authority in the Spanish Renaissance*. Baltimore: Johns Hopkins University Press, 2000.
Honores, Renzo. "*Pleytos*, letrados y cultura legal en Lima y en Potosí, 1540–1640." Paper presented at the Latin American Studies Association, XXVI International Congress, San Juan, Puerto Rico, 2006.
Hordes, Stanley. "The Crypto-Jewish Community of New-Spain, 1620–1649: A Collective Biography." PhD dissertation, Tulane University, 1980.
———. "Historiographical Problems in the Study of the Inquisition and the Mexican Crypto-Jews in the Seventeenth Century." *American Jewish Archives* 34, no. 2 (1982): 138-152.
———. "The Inquisition as Economic and Political Agent: The Campaign of the Mexican Holy Office against the Crypto-Jews in the Mid-Seventeenth Century." *The Americas* 39, no. 1 (1983): 23–38.
———. *To the End of the Earth: A History of the Crypto-Jews of New Mexico*. New York: Columbia University Press, 2005.
Huerga, Álvaro. *Historia de los alumbrados*. Vol. 3, *Los alumbrados de Hispanoamérica (1570–1605)*. Madrid: Fundación Universitaria Española, Seminario Cisneros, 1986.
Huerga Criado, Pilar. *En la raya de Portugal: Solidaridad y tensiones en la comunidad judeoconversa*. Salamanca: Universidad de Salamanca, 1993.

Hyland, Sabine. *The Quito Manuscript: An Inca History Preserved by Fernando de Montesinos.* New Haven, Conn.: Yale University Press, 2007.

Israel, Jonathan. *Diasporas within a Diaspora: Jews, Crypto-Jews and the World Maritime Empire (1540–1740).* Leiden: Brill, 2002.

———. *Dutch Primacy in World Trade, 1585–1740.* Oxford: Clarendon Press, 1989.

———. *The Dutch Republic and the Hispanic World, 1606–1661.* Oxford: Clarendon Press, 1982.

———. *Empires and Entrepots. The Dutch, the Spanish Monarchy and the Jews, 1585–1713.* London: Hambledon Press, 1990.

———. *Race, Class, and Politics in Colonial Mexico, 1610–1670.* Oxford: Oxford University Press, 1975.

Iwasaki Cauti, Fernando. *Inqvisiciones Pervanas.* Lima: Promoción Editorial El Inca S.A., 1996.

Jiménez Monteserín, Miguel. "Modalidades y sentido histórico del Auto de Fé." In *Historia de la Inquisición en España y América*, vol. 2, edited by Joaquín Pérez Villanueva and Bartolomé Escandell Bonet, 559–587. Madrid: Biblioteca de Autores Cristianos, Centro de Estudios Inquisitoriales, 1993.

Johnson, Lyman L., and Sonya Lipsett-Rivera. *The Faces of Honor: Sex, Shame, and Violence in Colonial Latin America.* Albuquerque: University of New Mexico Press, 1998.

Jouve Martín, José R. "Public Ceremonies and Mulatto Identity in Viceregal Lima: A Colonial Reenactment of the Fall of Troy (1631)." *Colonial Latin American Review* 16, no. 2 (2007): 170–201.

Kagan, Richard. "Keeping the Faith: Doña Blanca Méndez de Rivera." In *Inquisitorial Inquiries: Brief Lives of Secret Jews and Other Heretics*, edited by Richard Kagan and Abigail Dyer, 152–188. Baltimore: Johns Hopkins University Press, 2004.

———. *Lucrecia's Dreams: Politics and Prophecy in Sixteenth-Century Spain.* Berkeley: University of California Press, 1990.

———. "Politics, Prophecy, and the Inquisition in Late-Century Spain." In *Cultural Encounters: The Impact of the Inquisition in Spain and the New World*, edited by Mary Elizabeth Perry and Anne Cruz, 105–124. Berkeley: University of California Press, 1991.

———. *Urban Images of the Hispanic World, 1493–1793.* New Haven, Conn.: Yale University Press, 2000.

Kagan, Richard L., and Philip D. Morgan. *Atlantic Diasporas: Jews, Conversos, and Crypto-Jews in the Age of Mercantilism, 1500–1800.* Baltimore: Johns Hopkins University Press, 2009.

Kamen, Henry A. *The Spanish Inquisition: A Historical Revision.* London: Weidenfeld & Nicolson, 1997.

Kaplan, Yosef. *From Christianity to Judaism: The Story of Isaac Orobio de Castro.* Oxford: Published for the Littman Library by Oxford University Press, 1989.

Keen, Benjamin. "Main Currents in United States Writings on Colonial Spanish America, 1884–1984." *Hispanic American Historical Review* 65, no. 4 (1985): 657–682.

La Fuente Macháin, Ricardo de. *Los portugueses en Buenos Aires (siglo XVII)*. Madrid: Tipografía de Archivos, 1931.

Lea, Henry Charles. *A History of the Inquisition of Spain*. 4 vols. London: Macmillan, 1906.

———. *The Inquisition in the Spanish Dependencies*. New York: Macmillan, 1908.

Lewin, Boleslao. *El Santo Oficio en América y el más grande proceso inquisitorial en el Perú*. Buenos Aires: Sociedad Hebraica Argentina, 1950.

———. *La Inquisición en Hispanoamérica (Judíos, Protestantes y Patriotas)*. Buenos Aires: Editorial Proyección, 1962.

———. *La Inquisición en México: Siglo XVI*. Puebla: Editorial Cajica, 1968.

———. "'Las Confidencias' of Two Crypto-Jews in the Holy Office Prison of Mexico (1654–1655)." *Jewish Social Studies* 30, no. 1 (1968): 3–22.

———. *Los judíos bajo la Inquisición en Hispanoamérica*. Buenos Aires: Dédalo, 1960.

———. *Mártires y conquistadores judíos en la América Hispana*. Buenos Aires: Candelabro, 1954.

Liebman, Seymour B. *The Enlightened: The Writings of Luis de Carvajal, el Mozo*. Coral Gables, Fla.: University of Miami Press, 1967.

———. "The Great Conspiracy in Peru." *The Americas* 28, no. 2 (October 1971): 176–190.

———. "Tomás Treviño de Sobremonte: A Jewish Mexican Martyr." *Jewish Social Studies* 42, no. 1 (1980): 63–74.

Llorente, Juan Antonio. *Historia crítica de la Inquisición en España*. 4 vols. 2nd ed. Madrid: Hiperión, 1981.

Lohman Villena, Guillermo. *La Semana Santa de Lima*. Lima: Fondo de Promoción Turística del Perú, Banco Crédito del Perú, 1996.

———. "Una incógnita despejada: La identidad del judío portugués autor de la Discriçion General del Piru." *Revista de Indias* 30, nos. 119–122 (1970): 315–387.

López Belinchón, Bernardo. *Honra, libertad y hacienda (Hombres de negocios y judíos sefardíes)*. Alcalá de Henares: Instituto Internacional de Estudios Sefardíes y Andalusíes, Universidad de Alcalá Servicio de Publicaciones, 2001.

———. "Olivares contra los portugueses: Inquisición, conversos y guerra económica." In *Historia de la Inquisición en España y América*, vol. 3, edited by Joaquín Pérez Villanueva and Bartolomé Escandell Bonet, 499–530. Madrid: Biblioteca de Autores Cristianos, Centro de Estudios Inquisitoriales, 2000.

Luxán, Santiago de. "A Colónia Portuguesa de Sevilha: Uma Ameaça entre a Restauração Portuguesa e a Conjura de Medina Sidónia?" *Penélope: Fazer e Desfazer a História* 9/10 (1993): 127–134.

Lynn, Kimberly. *Between Court and Confessional: The Politics of Spanish Inquisitors*. Cambridge: Cambridge University Press, 2013.

———. "Unraveling the Spanish Inquisition: Inquisitorial Studies in the Twenty-First Century." *History Compass* 5, no. 4 (2007): 1280–1293.

———. "Was Adam the First Heretic? Diego de Simancas, Luis de Páramo, and the Origins of Inquisitorial Practice." *Archiv für Reformationsgeschichte / Archive for Reformation History* 97 (2006): 184–210.

MacCormack, Sabine. *On the Wings of Time: Rome, the Incas, Spain, and Peru*. Princeton, N.J.: Princeton University Press, 2007.

———. *Religion in the Andes: Vision and Imagination in Early Colonial Peru*. Princeton, N.J.: Princeton University Press, 1991.

MacKay, Angus. "Popular Movements and Pogroms in Fifteenth-Century Castile." *Past and Present* 55, no. 1 (1972): 33–67.

MacLeod, Murdo. *Spanish Central America: A Socioeconomic History, 1520–1720*. Berkeley: University of California Press, 1973.

Mann, Vivian B., Jerrilynn Denise Dodds, Thomas F. Glick, and Jewish Museum (New York). *Convivencia: Jews, Muslims, and Christians in Medieval Spain*. New York: G. Braziller, in association with the Jewish Museum, 1992.

Mannarelli, María Emma. *Hechiceras, beatas y expósitas: Mujeres y poder inquisitorial en Lima*. Lima: Ediciones del Congreso del Perú, 1999.

Maqueda Abreu, Consuelo. *El auto de Fe*. Madrid: Istmo, 1992.

Maravall, José A. *La cultura del Barroco*. Barcelona: Ariel, 1975.

Martínez, María Elena. *Genealogical Fictions: Limpieza de Sangre, Religion, and Gender in Colonial Mexico*. Stanford, Calif.: Stanford University Press, 2008.

Martínez Millán, José. "Structures of Inquisitorial Finance." In *The Spanish Inquisition and the Inquisitorial Mind*, edited by Ángel Alcalá, 159–176. Highland Lakes, N.J.: Atlantic Research and Publications, 1987.

Medina, José Toribio. *Historia del Tribunal de la Inquisición de Lima, 1569–1820*. Vol. 2. 2nd ed. Santiago: Fondo Histórico y Bibliográfico J. T. Medina, 1956.

———. *Historia del Tribunal del Santo Oficio de la Inquisición de Lima (1569–1820)*. Vol. 1. Santiago: Imprenta Gutenberg, 1887.

———. *Historia del Tribunal del Santo Oficio de la Inquisición en Chile*. Santiago: Fondo Histórico y Bibliográfico, 1952.

———. *Historia del Tribunal del Santo Oficio de la Inquisición en México*. 2nd ed. Mexico: Dirección de Publicaciones del Consejo Nacional para la Cultura y las Artes, 2010 [1905].

———. *La Inquisición en Cartagena de Indias*. 2nd ed. Bogotá: C. Valencia, 1978.

———. *La Inquisición en el Río de La Plata*. Buenos Aires: Huarpes, 1945.

———. *La primitiva Inquisición Americana: Estudio histórico*. Santiago: Imprenta Elzeviriana, 1914.

Melammed, Renee Levine. *Heretics or Daughters of Israel: The Crypto-Jewish Women of Castile*. New York: Oxford University Press, 1999.

Méndez, María Águeda. "La fiesta de San Pedro Mártir: Preparativos y vicisitudes de la Inquisición novohispana." *Caravelle* 73 (1988): 61–70.

Menocal, María Rosa. *The Ornament of the World: How Muslims, Jews, and Christians Created a Culture of Tolerance in Medieval Spain*. Boston: Little Brown, 2002.

Millar Carvacho, René. *Inquisición y sociedad en el virreinato peruano: Estudios sobre el tribunal de la Inquisición de Lima*. Santiago, Chile: Ediciones Universidad Católica de Chile, 1998.

———. *La Inquisición de Lima*. Vol. 3, *1697–1820*. Madrid: Deimos, 1998.

———. *La Inquisición de Lima: Signos de su decadencia, 1726–1750*. Santiago: Dirección de Bibliotecas, Archivos y Museos, LOM Ediciones, Centro de Investigaciones Barros Arana, 2004.

———. "Las confiscaciones de la Inquisición de Lima a los comerciantes de origen judeo-portugués de la 'Gran Complicidad' de 1635." *Revista de Historia de Indias* 42, no. 171 (1983): 27–58.

Mills, Kenneth. *Idolatry and Its Enemies: Colonial Andean Religion and Extirpation, 1640–1750*. Princeton, N.J.: Princeton University Press, 1997.

Minchin, Susie. "Vuestras Mercedes son capitanes bizarros y peruleros: El Perú visto por la comunidad conversa portuguesa hacia principios del siglo XVII." In *Sobre el Perú: Homenaje a José Agustín de la Puente Candamo*, edited by Margarita Guerra and Oswaldo Holguín, 863–878. Lima: PUCP, 2002.

Monter, William. *Frontiers of Heresy: The Spanish Inquisition from the Basque Lands to Sicily*. New York: Cambridge University Press, 1990.

Moreno, Doris. *La invención de la Inquisición*. Madrid: Fundación Carolina, Centro de Estudios Hispánicos e Iberoamericanos, Marcial Pons Historia, 2004.

Moutoukias, Zacarías. *Contrabando y control colonial en el siglo XVII: Buenos Aires, el Atlántico y el Espacio Peruano*. Buenos Aires: Centro Editor de América Latina, 1988.

Muzquiz de Miguel, José Luis. *El conde de Chinchón, virrey del Perú*. Madrid: Escuela de Estudios Hispano-Americanos de la Universidad de Sevilla, 1945.

Nesvig, Martin A. *Ideology and Inquisition: The World of the Censors in Early Mexico*. New Haven, Conn.: Yale University Press, 2009.

Netanyahu, Benzion. *The Marranos of Spain from the Late 14th to the Early 16th Century, According to Contemporary Hebrew Sources*. 3rd ed. Ithaca, N.Y.: Cornell University Press, 1999.

———. *The Origins of the Inquisition in Fifteenth Century Spain*. New York: Random House, 1995.

Newson, Linda A., and Susie Minchin. *From Capture to Sale: The Portuguese Slave Trade to Spanish South America in the Early Seventeenth Century*. The Atlantic World 12. Leiden: Brill, 2007.

Niremberg, David. *Communities of Violence: Persecution of Minorities in the Middle Ages*. Princeton, N.J.: Princeton University Press, 1996.

———. "Race and the Middle Ages." In *Rereading the Black Legend: The Discourses of Religious and Racial Difference in the Renaissance Empires*, edited by Margaret Greer, Walter Mignolo, and Maureen Quilligan, 71–87. Chicago: University of Chicago Press, 2007.

Novinsky, Anita. *Cristãos Novos na Bahia*. São Paulo: Perspectiva, 1972.

Novinsky, Anita, and Maria Luiza Tucci Carneiro. *Inquisição: Ensaios sobre mentalidade, heresias e arte; Trabalhos apresentados no I Congresso Internacional—Inquisição, Universidade de São Paulo, maio 1987*. Rio de Janeiro: Expressão e Cultura, EDUSP, 1992.

Olival, Fernanda. "Los virreyes y gobernadores de Lisboa (1583–1640): Características generales." In *El mundo de los virreyes en las monarquías de España y Portugal*, edited by Pedro Cardim and Joan-Lluís Palos, 287–316. Madrid: Iberoamericana-Vervuert, 2012.

Osorio, Alejandra B. *Inventing Lima: Baroque Modernity in Peru's South Sea Metropolis*. The Americas in the Early Modern Atlantic World. New York: Palgrave MacMillan, 2008.

Ots y Capdequí, José María. *El Estado Español en las Indias*. 3rd ed. Mexico: Fondo de Cultura Económica, 1957.

Palma, Ricardo. *Anales de la Inquisición de Lima*. Lima: Ediciones del Congreso de la República del Perú, expanded facsimile of the third edition of 1897, 1997.

Palos, Joan-Lluís, and Joana Fraga. "Tres capitales virreinales: Nápoles, Lisboa y Barcelona." In *El mundo de los virreyes en las monarquías de España y Portugal*, edited by Pedro Cardim and Joan-Lluís Palos, 345–390. Madrid: Iberoamericana-Vervuert, 2012.

Payne, Stanley. *Spanish Catholicism: An Historical Overview*. Madison: University of Wisconsin Press, 1984.

Penyak, Lee. "Más que solo la destrucción de la Leyenda Negra: Un vistazo a los estudios actuales sobre la Inquisición española." *Cuadernos para la Historia de la Evangelización en América Latina* 4 (1989): 77–88.

Pérez, Joseph. *Crónica de la Inquisición en España*. Barcelona: Ediciones Martínez Roca, 2002.

Pérez Cantó, Pilar. "El Tribunal de Lima." In *Historia de la Inquisición en España y América*, vol. 1, edited by Joaquín Pérez Villanueva and Bartolomé Escandell Bonet, 1133–1141. Madrid: Biblioteca de Autores Cristianos, Centro de Estudios Inquisitoriales, 1984.

———. "El Tribunal de Lima en tiempos de Felipe III." In *Historia de la Inquisición en España y América*, vol. 1, edited by Joaquín Pérez Villanueva and Bartolomé Escandell Bonet, 979–983. Madrid: Biblioteca de Autores Cristianos, Centro de Estudios Inquisitoriales, 1984.

———. "La dinámica de las estructuras en el Tribunal de Lima." In *Historia de la Inquisición en España y América*, vol. 1, edited by Joaquín Pérez Villanueva and Bartolomé Escandell Bonet, 1180–1189. Madrid: Biblioteca de Autores Cristianos, Centro de Estudios Inquisitoriales, 1984.

———. "Tribunal del Santo Oficio de Lima: Relación de Causas vistas en la primera mitad del siglo XVIII." In *La Inquisición española: Nueva visión, nuevos horizontes*, edited by Joaquín Pérez Villanueva, 469–477. Madrid: Siglo XXI, 1980.

Pérez Villanueva, Joaquín. "Felipe IV y su política." In *Historia de la Inquisición en España y América*, vol. 1, edited by Joaquín Pérez Villanueva and Bartolomé Escandell Bonet, 1006–1079. Madrid: Biblioteca de Autores Cristianos, Centro de Estudios Inquisitoriales, 1984.

———. *La Inquisición española: Nueva visión, nuevos horizontes*. Madrid: Siglo XXI, 1980.

Pérez Villanueva, Joaquín, and Bartolomé Escandell Bonet. *Historia de la Inquisición en España y América*. 3 vols. Madrid: Biblioteca de Autores Cristianos, Centro de Estudios Inquisitoriales, 1984, 1993, and 2000.

Peters, Edward. *Inquisition*. New York: Free Press, 1988.

———. *Torture*. Philadelphia: University of Pennsylvania Press, 1999.

Phelan, John Leddy. *The Kingdom of Quito in the Seventeenth Century: Bureaucratic Politics in the Spanish Empire*. Madison: University of Wisconsin Press, 1967.

Poo, Martín Eduardo, and Claudia Silvia Cogollos Amaya. "La teología de la muerte: Una visión española del fenómeno durante los siglos XVI al XVII." In *Inquisición, muerte y sexualidad en la Nueva Granada*, edited by Jaime Borja Gómez, 117–142. Bogotá: Ariel, 1996.

Pulido Serrano, Juan Ignacio. *Injurias a Cristo: Religión, política y antijudaísmo en el siglo XVII (análisis de las corrientes antijudías durante la Edad Moderna)*. Alcalá de Henares, Madrid: Instituto Internacional de Estudios Sefardíes y Andalusíes, Universidad de Alcalá, Servicio de Publicaciones, 2002.

———. "Jesuitas y cristianos nuevos portugueses en el siglo XVII: El Padre Hernando de Salazar y sus proyectos de repatriación." *Cadernos de Estudos Sefarditas* 9 (2009): 35–74.

———. "Plural Identities: The Portuguese New Christians." *Jewish History* 24 (2011): 129–151.

Quiroz Norris, Alfonso. "La expropiación inquisitorial de cristianos nuevos portugueses en Los Reyes, Cartagena y México, 1635–1649." *Histórica* 10, no. 2 (1986): 237–303.

Ramos, Gabriela. "El Tribunal de la Inquisición en el Perú, 1605–1666: Un estudio social." *Cuadernos para la Historia de la Evangelización en América Latina* 3 (1988): 93–125.

———. "La fortuna del Inquisidor: Inquisición y poder en el Perú (1594–1611)." *Cuadernos para la Historia de la Evangelización en América Latina* 4 (1989): 89–122.

———. "La privatización del poder: Inquisición y sociedad en el Perú." in *Poder y violencia en los Andes*, edited by Henrique Urbano and Mirko Lauer, 75–92. Cusco: Centro de Estudios Regionales Andinos Bartolomé de Las Casas, 1991.

———. "Política eclesiástica y extirpación de la idolatría: Discursos y silencios en torno al Taqui Onqoy." *Revista Andina* 10, no. 1 (1992): 147–167.

Ramos Pérez, Demetrio. "La crisis indiana y la Junta Magna de 1568." *Jahrbuch für Geschichte von Staat, Wirtschaft und Gesselschaft Lateinamerikas* 23 (1986): 1–61.

Ramos Sosa, Rafael. *Arte festivo en Lima virreinal (siglos XVI–XVIII)*. Andalusia: Junta de Andalucía, Consejería de Cultura y Medio Ambiente, Asesoría Quinto Centenario, 1992.

Redden, Andrew. *Diabolism in Colonial Peru*. London: Pickering & Chatto, 2008.

Reparaz, Gonçalo de. *Os portugueses no Vice-Reinado do Peru (séculos XVI e XVII)*. Lisbon: Instituto de Alta Cultura, 1976.

Revah, I. S. "Les Marranes." *Revue des Études Juives* 3e série (1959–1960): 29–77.

Reverter-Pezet, Guillermo. *Las cofradías en el Virreynato del Perú*. Lima: G. Reverter-Pezet, 1985.

Rodríguez Crespo, Pedro. "El peligro holandés en las costas peruanas a principios del siglo XVII: La expedición de Spilbergen y la defensa del Virreynato." *Histórica* 26, supplement (1962): 259–310.

Rodríguez Salgado, M. J. "Christians, Civilised and Spanish: Multiple Identities in Sixteenth-Century Spain." *Transactions of the Royal Historical Society* 8 (1998): 233–251.

Rosas Navarro, Ruth Magalí. "El Tribunal de la Santa Inquisición y los negros esclavos en América." *Hispania Sacra* 55 (2003): 535–567.

Roth, Cecil. *Los judíos secretos: Historia de los marranos*. Madrid: Altalena, 1979.

Roth, Norman. *Conversos, Inquisition, and the Expulsion of the Jews from Spain.* Madison: University of Wisconsin Press, 1995.
Ruiz de Pablos, Francisco. "Errores antiguos y actuales sobre González Montes, debelador de la Inquisición Española." *Hispania Sacra* 55 (2003): 237–251.
Sánchez, Ana. "Mentalidad popular frente a ideología oficial: El Santo Oficio en Lima y los casos de hechichería (siglo XVII)." In *Poder y violencia en los Andes*, edited by Henrique Urbano, 33–51. Cusco: Centro de Estudios Rurales Andinos Bartolomé de Las Casas, 1991.
Sánchez-Concha Barrios, Rafael. *Santos y Santidad en el Perú Virreinal.* Lima: Vida y Espiritualidad, 2003.
Sánchez Rivilla, Teresa. "Inquisidores Generales y Consejeros de la Suprema: Documentación biográfica." In *Historia de la Inquisición en España y América*, vol. 3, edited by Joaquín Pérez Villanueva and Bartolomé Escandell Bonet, 228–435. Madrid: Biblioteca de Autores Cristianos, Centro de Estudios Inquisitoriales, 2000.
Saraiva, António José. *A Inquisição Portuguesa.* Lisboa: Publicações Europa-America, 1956.
———. *Inquisição e Cristãos-Novos.* 6th ed. Lisbon: Editora Estampa, 1994.
Scarry, Elaine. *The Body in Pain: The Making and Unmaking of the World.* New York: Oxford University Press, 1985.
Schaposchnik, Ana. "Exemplary Punishment in Colonial Lima: The 1639 *Auto de Fe*." In *Death and Dying in Colonial Spanish America*, edited by Martina Will de Chaparro and Miruna Achim, 121–141. Tucson: University of Arizona Press, 2011.
———. "Under the Eyes of the Inquisition: Crypto-Jews in the Ibero-American World (Peru, 1600s)." PhD dissertation, University of Wisconsin–Madison, 2007.
Schorsch, Jonathan. *Swimming the Christian Atlantic: Judeoconversos, Afroiberians and Amerindians in the Seventeenth Century.* Leiden: Brill, 2009.
Schwaller, John F. *The History of the Catholic Church in Latin America: From Conquest to Revolution and Beyond.* New York: New York University Press, 2011.
Schwartz, Stuart. *All Can Be Saved: Religious Tolerance and Salvation in the Iberian Atlantic World.* New Haven, Conn.: Yale University Press, 2008.
———. "Panic in the Indies: The Portuguese Threat to the Spanish Empire, 1640–1650." *Colonial Latin American Review* 2, nos. 1–2 (1993): 165–187.
The Secret Relationship between Blacks and Jews. 2nd ed. Chicago: Historical Research Department of the Nation of Islam, 1991.
Sicroff, Albert A. *Los estatutos de limpieza de sangre: Controversias entre los siglos XV y XVII.* Translated by Mauro Armiño. Madrid: Taurus Ediciones, 1985.
Silva, Lina Gorenstein Ferreira da. *Heréticos e impuros: A inquisição e os cristãos-novos no Rio de Janeiro, século XVIII.* Rio de Janeiro: Prefeitura da Cidade do Rio de Janeiro, Secretaria Municipal de Cultura, Departamento Geral de Documentação e Informação Cultural, Divisão de Editoração, 1995.
Silva Cogollos Amaya, Claudia, and Martín Eduardo Poo. "Sociedad, muerte, y prácticas de enterramiento en el Santa Fé colonial." *Universitas Humanistica* 22, no. 37 (1993): 35–42.

Silverblatt, Irene. "The Black Legend and Global Conspiracies: Spain, the Inquisition, and the Emerging Modern World." In *Rereading the Black Legend: The Discourses of Religious and Racial Difference in the Renaissance Empires*, edited by Margaret Greer, Walter Mignolo, and Maureen Quilligan, 99–116. Chicago: University of Chicago Press, 2007.

———. *Modern Inquisitions: Peru and the Colonial Origins of the Civilized World*. Durham, N.C.: Duke University Press, 2004.

———. *Moon, Sun, and Witches: Gender Ideologies and Class in Inca and Colonial Peru*. Princeton, N.J.: Princeton University Press, 1987.

———. "New Christians and New World Fears in Seventeenth-Century Peru." *Comparative Studies in Society and History* 42, no. 3 (2000): 524–546.

Socolow, Susan Migden. *The Women of Colonial Latin America*. Cambridge: Cambridge University Press, 2000.

Sorkin, David. "The Port Jew: Notes Toward a Social Type." *Journal of Jewish Studies* 50, no. 1 (1999): 87–97.

Soyer, François. "An Example of Collaboration between the Spanish and Portuguese Inquisitions: The Trials of the *Converso* Diogo Ramos and his Family (1680–1683)." *Cadernos de Estudos Sefarditas* 6 (2006): 317–340.

Starr-Lebeau, Gretchen. *In the Shadow of the Virgin: Inquisitors, Friars, and Conversos in Guadalupe, Spain*. Princeton, N.J.: Princeton University Press, 2003.

Stern, Steve. *Peru's Indian Peoples and the Challenge of the Spanish Conquest: Huamanga to 1640*. Madison: University of Wisconsin Press, 1993.

Stuczynski, Claude. "New Christian Political Leadership in Times of Crisis: The Pardon Negotiations of 1605." In *Leadership in Times of Crisis*, edited by Moises Orfali, 45–70. Ramat Gan, Israel: Bar-Ilan University Press, 2007.

Studnicki-Gizbert, Daviken. *A Nation upon the Ocean Sea: Portugal's Atlantic Diaspora and the Crisis of the Spanish Empire, 1492–1640*. Oxford: Oxford University Press, 2007.

Suárez, Margarita. *Desafíos transatlánticos: Mercaderes, banqueros y el estado en el Perú virreinal, 1600–1700*. Lima: Pontificia Universidad Católica del Perú, Instituto Riva Agüero, Fondo de Cultura Económica, Instituto Francés de Estudios Andinos, 2001.

Sullivan, Karen. *The Inner Lives of Medieval Inquisitors*. Chicago: University of Chicago Press, 2011.

Sweet, James. *Domingos Álvares, African Healing, and the Intellectual History of the Atlantic World*. Chapel Hill: University of North Carolina Press, 2011.

Tandeter, Enrique. *Coacción y mercado: La minería de la plata en el Potosí colonial, 1692–1826*. Buenos Aires: Editorial Sudamericana, 1992.

Tomás y Valiente, Francisco. *El derecho penal de la monarquía absoluta (siglos XVI–XVII–XVIII)*. Madrid: Tecnos, 1969.

———. "Relaciones de la Inquisición con el aparato institucional del Estado." In *Gobierno e instituciones de la España del Antiguo Régimen*, 13–35. Madrid: Alianza, 1982.

Truhan, Debora, and Jesús Paniagua Pérez. "Los portugueses en América: La ciudad de Cuenca del Perú (1580–1640)." *Revista de Ciencias Históricas* 12 (1997): 201–220.

Twinam, Ann. *Public Lives, Private Secrets: Gender, Honor, Sexuality, and Illegitimacy in Colonial Spanish America*. Stanford, Calif.: Stanford University Press, 1999.

Uchmany, Eva. *La vida entre el judaísmo y el cristianismo en la Nueva España, 1580–1606*. Mexico City: Fondo de Cultura Económica, 1992.

———. "The Participation of New Christians and Crypto-Jews in the Conquest, Colonization, and Trade of Spanish America, 1521–1660." In *The Jews and the Expansion of Europe to the West, 1450–1800*, edited by Paolo Bernardini and Norman Fiering, 186–202. New York: Berghahn Books, 2001.

Vainfas, Ronaldo. *Santo Ofício da Inquisição de Lisboa: Confissões da Bahia*. São Paulo, 1997.

Van Young, Eric. *The Other Rebellion: Popular Violence, Ideology, and the Mexican Struggle for Independence, 1810–1821*. Stanford, Calif.: Stanford University Press, 2001.

Vieira Maia, Angela. *A sombra do medo: Cristãos Velhos e Cristãos Novos nas Capitanias do Açucar*. Rio de Janeiro: OFICINA Cadernos de Poesia, 1995.

Vila Vilar, Enriqueta. "Los asientos portugueses y el contrabando de negros." *Anuario de Estudios Americanos* 30 (1973): 557–599.

Wachtel, Nathan. *The Faith of Remembrance: Marrano Labyrinths*. Translated by Nikki Halpern. Philadelphia: University of Pennsylvania Press, 2013.

———. *La fe del recuerdo: Laberintos Marranos*. Translated by Sandra Garzonio. Buenos Aires: Fondo de Cultura Económica, 2007.

———. "Marrano Religiosity in Hispanic America in the Seventeenth Century." In *The Jews and the Expansion of Europe to the West, 1450 to 1800*, edited by Paolo Bernardini and Norman Fiering, 149–171. New York: Berghahn Books, 2001.

Warshawsky, Matthew. "Manuel Bautista Pérez and the *Complicidad Grande* in Colonial Peru: Inquisitorial Hysteria or Crypto-Jewish Heresy?" *Journal of Spanish, Portuguese, and Italian Crypto-Jews* 2 (2010): 132–150.

Will de Chaparro, Martina, and Miruna Achim. *Death and Dying in Colonial Spanish America*. Tucson: University of Arizona Press, 2011.

Wiznitzer, Arnold. *Jews in Colonial Brazil*. New York: Columbia University Press, 1960.

Yerushalmi, Yosef Hayim. "Between Amsterdam and New Amsterdam: The Place of Curaçao and the Caribbean in Early Modern Jewish History." *American Jewish History* 72, no. 2 (1982): 172–192.

———. *From Spanish Court to Italian Ghetto: Isaac Cardoso, A Study in Seventeenth-Century Marranism and Jewish Apologetics*. New York: Columbia University Press, 1971.

———. "The Inquisition and the Jews of France in the Time of Bernard Gui." *Harvard Theological Review* 63, no. 3 (1970): 317–376.

———. *The Lisbon Massacre of 1506 and the Royal Image in the Shebet Yehudah*. Cincinnati: Hebrew Union College, Jewish Institute of Religion, 1976.

Yovel, Yirmiahu. *The New Otherness: Marrano Dualities in the First Generation*. 1999 Swig Lecture, September 13. San Francisco: Swig Judaic Studies Program at the University of San Francisco, 1999.

Reference Works

Bell, Robert E. *Dictionary of Classical Mythology, Symbols, Attributes, & Associations*. Oxford: ABC-Clio, 1982.

Coulter, Charles Russell, and Patricia Turner. *Encyclopedia of Ancient Deities.* Jefferson, N.C.: McFarland, 2000.

Covarrubias Orozco, Sebastián de. *Tesoro de la lengua castellana o española.* 2 parts in 1 volume. Madrid: Melchor Sanchez, 1673.

Mendiburu, Manuel de. *Diccionario histórico-biográfico del Perú.* 8 vols. Lima: Imprenta de J. Francisco Solís, 1874-1890.

Michaelis, H., and Fritz Pietzschke. *Nôvo Michaelis, dicionário ilustrado.* São Paulo: Edições Melhoramentos, 1958.

Morera, Marcial. *Diccionario etimológico de los portuguesismos canarios.* Puerto del Rosario, Las Palmas: Excmo. Cabildo Insular de Fuerteventura, Servicio de Publicaciones, 1996.

Real Academia Española. *Diccionario de Autoridades.* Vol. 1, *A–C.* Madrid: Gredos, S.A., 1990.

———. *Diccionario de la lengua española.* 22nd ed. 2 vols. Madrid: Editorial Espasa Calpe, 2001. http://lema.rae.es/drae/.

Room, Adrian. *NTC's Classical Dictionary: The Origins of the Names of Characters in Classical Mythology.* Lincolnwood, Ill.: National Textbook Company, 1990.

Index

abjuration, 73–74, 142, 174, 252n101
abonos (asserting prisoner's honor), 69–70, 120
Abril Castelló, Vidal, 13
Acevedo, Gerónimo de, 232n71
Acevedo, Juan de, 107
Acosta, Duarte de, 122
Acosta, Juan de, 169
Acosta, Rosa M., 170
Acuña, Antonio de, 67, 100, 108–109, 116–117
Acuña, Sebastián de, 117
African languages used by prisoners, 142–143
Aguado de los Reyes, Jesús, 90
Aguilar, Sebastián de, 34–35
Alberro, Solange, 101, 134, 139, 142–143
alcaides de las cárceles secretas (stewards of the secret prisons), 44, 136–137, 139. See also Pradeda, Bartolomé de
Alcayaga Lartaun, León de, 166
Alfar, Gaspar de, 139
alguaciles (constables), 38, 44
Amsterdam Sephardim, 114
Anales de la Inquisición de Lima (Palma), 8, 204n71, 210n44
Anríquez, Manuel, 82
anti-Semitism, 9. See also Jews
Antonia, Isabel, 58, 105–106, 115, 123, 139, 170, 176, 228n16
arbitristas, 34
Archivo General de la Nación (AGN; Lima), 24
Archivo Histórico Nacional (AHN; Madrid), 24
Argos divino de la Fe (divine Argus of the Faith), 56
Arquivo Nacional da Torre do Tombo (ANTT; Lisbon), 24
Artes de la Santa Inquisición Española (González Montes), 24–25, 196n82, 201n33

asientos (licenses for trade in African slaves), 109
Assadourian, Carlos Sempat, 95
Auto de la Fe Celebrado (Montesinos), 158, 170, 251n82
Auto General de Fe (Lima, 1573), 79
Auto General de Fe (Lima, 1578), 79, 157
Auto General de Fe (Lima, 1581), 79
Auto General de Fe (Lima, 1605), 153, 173
Auto General de Fe (Lima, 1608), 246n32
Auto General de Fe (Lima, 1625), 152–154, 156, 164–165, 245n23
Auto General de Fe (Lima, 1639), 151–180; audience size, 168; chronicle of, 45; as collective devotion, 167–173; duration of, 167; finances of, 163–164; Great Complicity members in, 170, 175–177; Green Crosses used in, 167–168; number of deaths in, 3, 100, 243n1; number of prisoners in, 151, 243n1; overview of, 7, 17, 28–29, 179–180, 185; Portuguese New Christian community decimated by, 100; preparations for, 161–167, 249n66; prisoners' isolation/mistreatment in the dungeons, 169–170, 250–251n81 (see also torture); procession for (civil/religious officials), 156–157, 167, 171–172; procession of infamy for (prisoners), 168–171; public nature of, 158–161; rehabilitation of falsely accused prisoners, 176–77; scale/drama of punishments in, 114, 151; seating arrangements at, 165–166, 249n66; sentences/punishments of, 166–169, 174–178, 252n101; sermon at, 172–173; terror exerted by, 153; witness/official accounts of, 148–149, 153–158

281

282 Index

Auto General de Fe (Lima, 1664), 157, 177–178, 255n127
Auto Particular de Fe (Lima, 1631), 159–160
Auto Particular de Fe (Lima, 1635), 159
Autos Generales de Fe, generally: accounts of, 157–158, 175; as celebrations hosted by the Inquisition, 151–153, 159–160; vs. civil/religious festivals, 157, 170–171, 179; definition/goals of, 74, 152; early, 35, 79; frequency of, 12, 25, 178, 255n129; Mass and sermon at, 172; number of deaths in, 98–99, 179–180; oath at, 172; Ocaña on, 153; Alejandra Osorio on, 16–18, 152; public nature of, 19, 152, 160–161; scale/drama of, 151–154, 178, 180; scholarship on, 19; vs. single trials, 25; suspensions of, 111; types of, 152; wealthy traders punished in, 96
Ávila, Rodrigo de, 117
Ávila el Viejo, Rodrigo de, 232n71
Azevedo, Juan de, 175

Ballesteros Gaibrois, Manuel, 8
baptism, 31–32, 71
Bar Mitzvah, 124
Bataillon, Marcel, 13
beatifications, 156
Benavídes, Manuel de, 177
Benbassa, Esther, 33
Bennassar, Bartolomé, 10, 19, 72
Bethencourt, Francisco, 188n14, 196n82, 248n63; on the Auto General de Fe, 164–165, 173, 245n23; on executions of minorities, 15–16; on González Montes, 25; on the Inquisition's focus on heresy, 31; on inquisitors in public, 159; on Llorente, 7; on medieval vs. Spanish and Portuguese Inquisitions, 10–11, 151
Biblioteca Nacional (BN; Madrid), 24
Biblioteca Nacional de Perú (BNP; Lima), 24
Birckel, Maurice, 13, 47
Black Legend, 9, 189n21
blasphemy, 15, 31, 52, 54, 76, 78–79, 133
blood purity, 33–35, 69, 200n24
Bodian, Miriam, 21
bolitas verdes (little green pellets), 68. *See also* pelotillas
Bourbon reforms, 97

Boyajian, James, 93, 229n33
Brandon, Beatriz, 115, 231n60
Brazil, Dutch invasion of, 112, 114–115, 231n58
Buenos Aires, 40, 77, 81, 83–84, 115
bullfights, 154, 244n15, 253n104
Bustamante, Andrés de, 76

Calderón, Bartolomé, 164–165
calificadores (assessors), 38–40, 45, 219n20
Calle de las Mantas (Lima), 95–96
Calle de los Mercaderes (Lima), 95–96, 100–101, 249n70
Cañeque, Alejandro, 43
Cannas da Cunha, Ana, 142
canonizations, 156
Capitanía de Chile, 84
cárcel de la penitencia (penitential prison), 133–134
cárceles medias (intermediate cells), 134
cárceles secretas (secret cells), 133, 144
cárcel perpetua/cárcel de la misericordia (perpetual prison/prison of mercy), 133–134
Cardoso, Bento, 83, 85
Cardoso de Silba, Álvaro, 76, 90
Caro Baroja, Julio, 10, 202n55
Cartagena, Portuguese immigrants to, 219n18
Cartagena tribunal (Colombia), 4, 41, 77, 79, 81–82, 143, 220n29
Carvajal family, 41
Casa de Contratación (Seville), 97
Castañeda Delgado, Paulino: on confiscations, 49; on demographics of Great Complicity prisoners, 105–106; on the Great Complicity, 22, 49, 121; on inquisitors as priests, 39; on the Lima tribunal, 25, 47, 103, 105, 113, 121; on Lope de Salinas, 200n27; on Medina, 8; on obstructions by tribunal officials, 139; on prison facilities, 78; on prison inspections, 137; on slaves, 141
Castelo Branco (Portugal), 105, 227n14
Castilla, Cristóbal de, 160
Castillo, Santiago del, 176–177, 232n71
Castro y del Castillo, Antonio de, 42–43, 115, 117, 134, 143–146, 159, 166, 241n42
Cerezuela, Serván de, 76
Charcas *audiencia*, 4, 77, 79–81, 91
Chinchón, Conde de, Viceroy, 42, 107, 116, 158–159, 165–166, 172, 246n38, 248n64, 249n66

Cisneros, Joseph de, 172–173
City of Kings. *See* Lima
Clement VIII, Pope, 91
cofradías (confraternities), 156, 170, 251n86
Coimbra tribunal (Portugal), 49, 89, 125, 178
comisarios (commissioners), 45
Complicidad Grande. *See* Great Complicity
confiscation of property, 73–74; distribution of properties, 73; of the Great Complicity, 49, 163–164, 185, 247n51; Lima tribunal funded by, 47–49, 204n71; for Portuguese travelers without travel permits, 91–92; reversals of, 91
Consejo de Indias (Seville), 97
consultas de Fe (consultations of faith), 45, 71–72
consultores, 45, 71
contadores (accountants), 44
Contreras, Jaime, 10–12, 15, 46, 102, 135, 138–139, 144–145
convents, 133
conversos. *See* New Christians
Cordero, Antonio, 100–102, 108–109, 115–117, 225–226nn2–3, 231n60
corozas, 164, 168–169, 248n56
Correa, Simón, 232n71
Corro, Antonio del, 196n82
Council of Trent, 4
Cross, Harry, 22, 110
crypto-Jews: children introduced to practices of, 123–124, 234n91; circumcision, evidence of, 44, 204n75; in Lima, 120–129 (*see also* Auto General de Fe (Lima, 1639); Great Complicity; Pérez, Manuel Bautista; Vicente, Joan); markers of, 101, 120–123; networking by, 125–127; number of deaths of, 12; number of trials for, 12; relevance as historical subjects, 185; religiosity of, 19–24, 184, 194n65, 194n68; strategies used by, 59; torture of, 62. *See also* New Christians
crypto-Judaism: definition of, 3; elements of, 120–123; female role in, 106; as heresy, 3, 54; practices of, 54

Dedieu, Jean Pierre, 11–12
de la Cruz, Francisco, 13, 79
de la Cruz, Mateo, 118
de la Cueva, Juan, 59, 96–97, 116, 225n85, 247n51

de la Peña, Pedro, 78, 131
de la Pinta Llorente, Miguel, 131, 136
de la Rosa, Manuel, 108–109, 231n60
Delgado, Sebastián, 232n71
de los Reyes, Melchor, 118
de los Santos, Antonio, 118, 176–177
devil, pacts with/worship of, 31, 54, 78–79
Díaz, Felipe, 118
Díaz, Pasqual, 232n68
Díaz Tavares, Gregorio, 80
Dionis Coronel, Amaro, 232n68
dogmatists, 111
Domínguez Ortiz, Antonio, 10
Duarte, Juan Rodríguez, 108
Duarte, Sebastián, 59, 108, 117, 147, 175–176, 206n90, 252n103
Dutch invasion, 112, 114–115, 231n58
Duviols, Pierre, 17

ecclesiastical writing, 157–158
edictos (edicts), 53–55
Eimeric, Nicolau: on financing of tribunals, 46–47; on heresy, 38; as inquisitor, 173; irregularities during trials of faith, 71; life of, 31; *Manual de Inquisidores*, 31–33, 53, 56–58, 85, 93, 147, 175, 198n8; on testimony of a mortal enemy, 70; on torture, 61, 63–66, 147
El Callao (Peru), 4–5, 77, 80, 252n102
Enríquez, Guiomar, 59, 108
Enríquez, Isabel, 59, 108
Escandell Bonet, Bartolomé, 12, 81
Espinosa, Antonio de, 175
Espinosa, Fernando de, 117, 232n71
Espinosa, Manuel de, 117, 167
Esther, Queen (biblical figure), 123, 234n83
Évora tribunal (Portugal), 82–86, 89, 93, 221n41
excommunication, 73
exile, 73
Extirpation of Idolatries, 17, 77, 94, 157, 183

familiares (familiars), 46, 205n81
Farías, Pedro de, 232n71
fasting, 123–124, 233n82
Ferdinand of Aragon, 33, 35–37
Fernández, Francisco, 232n68
Fernández, Gaspar, 118
Fernández, Rodrigo, 118

Fernández, Rui, 88
festivals: vs. Autos Generales de Fe, 157, 170–171, 179; Holy Week, 170–171, 251n86; in Lima, 154–156, 245n19; processional order at, 249n72; religious, mandated, 156–157; San Pedro de Verona, 156, 245n23
fiscales (prosecutors), 38–39, 43, 58
Fonseca, Fernando de, 232n71
Fonseca, Manuel de, 40, 44, 86, 90, 93, 122, 204n75
Foucault, Michel, 25, 61, 246n40
Fraga, Joana, 89–90
France, 92, 246n40
French Inquisition (1209), 30, 151, 243–244n4
Fuentes, Manuel Atanasio, 244n15, 253n104
Fundão (Portugal), 57, 104 (table), 105, 227n14

Gaddis, John Lewis, 178
Gaitán, Andrés Juan, 42–43, 87, 117, 159, 166, 222n51, 246n32
Galicia, 79, 144–145, 201n35
Galician language, 107
García, Manuel, 118
García Cárcel, Ricardo, 10, 196n82
García de Proodian, Lucía, 22, 106
Gareis, Iris, 17
garrucha, 62, 210n45
Gasca, Pedro de la, 202n49
Gil, Juan, 196n82
Ginés de Sepúlveda, Juan, 216n90
Ginzburg, Carlo, 25
Gitlitz, David, 20–21, 23, 54, 59, 120–121, 194n65, 234n84
Goa tribunal (India), 89, 142
Gobernación del Tucumán, 83–84
Gómez de Acosta, Antonio, 57, 107, 117
Gómez de Acosta, Baltasar, 232n71
González Montes, Reinaldo, 49–50, 131, 138; *Artes de la Santa Inquisición Española*, 24–25, 196n82, 201n33
Grahit y Papell, Emilio, 198n8
Graizbord, David, 21, 23
Great Complicity (Complicidad Grande; 1635–1639), 100–130; arrests/trials of, 100, 115–118, 184–186, 225n1, 232nn67–68, 232n71; in the Auto General de Fe (Lima, 1639), 170, 175–77; confiscations during/following, 49, 163–164, 185, 247n51; crypto-Jews affected by, 120–129, 184; documentation of, 119–120; economic impact of, 116; and gender, 106; meaning of name of, 22; migration paths of Portuguese New Christians, 106–107; number/demographics of prisoners, 68, 103–115, 104 (table), 117; overview of, 28, 100–103, 129–130, 186, 225–226nn2–3; Portuguese New Christians affected by, 128–129; and Portuguese secession from Spain, 114; prisoners' strategies during, 148–150; scholarship on, 13, 22; sentencing in, 100, 118 (*see also* Auto General de Fe); severity of, 113; slaves' involvement in carrying messages, 143; uncovering of, 102–103
Green Cross, 160, 167–168, 245n23
Gregory IX, Pope, 173
Griffiths, Nicholas, 17
Guibovich Pérez, Pedro, 4, 14, 53–54, 102, 157–158
Gutiérrez de Quintanilla, Juan, 42
Gutiérrez de Ulloa, Antonio, 43, 76, 95, 138, 200n27
Gutiérrez Flores, Juan, 42, 159

Haliczer, Stephen, 10
Hampe Martínez, Teodoro, 8, 12, 14–15, 102
Hebrew prayers, 122
Henningsen, Gustav, 11–12
Henríquez, Manuel: burned at the stake, 125, 177–178, 235n99; *discurso* of, 57; imprisonment of, 57, 177; insanity plea by, 44, 71, 204n75; introduced to crypto-Judaism, 125, 127, 234n91; on the jails of Coimbra, 49; knocking trick learned by, 146; migration path of, 106–107; trading by, 124–125, 183; trials of, 70, 86, 93, 125, 177–178; wealthy connections of, 93
Henríquez, Mateo, 118
heresy: Catholic indoctrination on dangers of, 178; classification of, 31; confession/pardon for, 37–38; crypto-Judaism as, 3, 54; death penalty for, 55, 175, 182 (*see also* Auto General de Fe (Lima, 1639); Autos Generales de Fe, generally); defenses by heretics, 32; general pardon for heretics (1605), 48,

91, 149; identifying heretics, 31; Millar Carvacho on, 13; New Christians suspected of, 4, 6, 183; religiosity of those accused of, 19–24, 184, 194n65, 194n68; as religious (sin) and secular (crime) matter, 30, 37–38, 55; rhetorical tactics of heretics, 32; seriousness of the offense, 154, 182; and treason, 139; types of, 38, 54. *See also* abjuration; crypto-Judaism; trials of faith

Hernández, Gerónimo, 108–109

Hernández Aparicio, Pilar: on confiscations, 49; on demographics of Great Complicity prisoners, 103, 105–106; on inquisitors as priests, 39; on the Lima tribunal, 47, 113, 121; on Lope de Salinas, 200n27; on Medina, 8; on obstructions by tribunal officials, 139; on prisons, 78, 137; on slaves, 141

Herzog, Tamar, 90, 223n60

Historia crítica (Llorente), 7

Holy Office of the Inquisition: abolition of, 35, 200n29; vs. civil courts, 160, 246n40; constraints on, 181–182; critique of primary sources on, 11; effectiveness of, 10; establishment of, 4, 30; establishment of tribunals in the colonies, 76; evolution of, 15; expanded to Spanish colonies, 4; *familiares*' role in, 10; financing of, 46–49; fragments of records kept by, 21–22; general pardon issued for prisoners of (1605), 48, 91, 149; goals of, 4, 37, 181, 186; heresy/heretics in records of, 20; jurisdiction of, 4, 97–98; and literature, 14; Llorente on, 7, 30, 36–37, 151, 188n14; local community's role in, 10; longevity of, 9, 15, 18, 37; Medina on, 8–10, 164, 248n64, 249n66; and New World expansion, 89–94, 97–98; officials' role, overview of, 182; pedagogy of fear by, 10, 18–19, 72; percentage of deaths following trials, 11–12; records kept by, 6, 11; religiosity of crypto-Jews/*marranos* accused of heresy, 19–24, 184, 194n65, 194n68; scholarship on, 7–19; secrecy of, 134, 139, 161; secular/religious authorities' participation, scope of, 18–19, 161; studies of, generally (*see* Bethencourt); surveillance by, 97. *See also* inquisitors; Lima Inquisition; medieval Inquisition; Mexican Inquisition; Portuguese Inquisition; Spanish Inquisition

Holy Week rituals, 170–171, 251n86

homens da nação (men of the [Portuguese] nation), 5–6

Homza, Lu Ann, 143

honor, 69–70, 120

Huerga, Álvaro, 13

Ibarra, Álvaro de, 160

Iberian Peninsula, history of, 33, 199n19. *See also* Portugal

indigenous societies, campaigns against, 17. *See also* Extirpation of Idolatries

infidels, 31. *See also* Jews; Muslims; New Christians

Inquisition. *See* Holy Office of the Inquisition; Lima Inquisition; medieval Inquisition; Mexican Inquisition; Portuguese Inquisition; Spanish Inquisition

inquisitors: armed guards for, 46, 205n81; complaints against, 137–138; conflict among, 43; duties of, 40; guidelines for, 55 (see also *Manual de Inquisidores*); laymen as, 202n46; in Lima, 42–43; networks of, 42–44; number per tribunal, 38; priests as, 39; in the public eye, 159–160, 246n35; qualifications for, 39; salaries of, 39–40, 48–49, 96, 163, 202n55; stereotypes of, 39; upward mobility of, 41–42; writings of, 39

Isabella of Castile, 33, 35

Islam, conversion from. *See* New Christians

Israel, Jonathan, 114, 230n44

Italian Inquisition (1224), 30

jails. *See* prisons of Lima

Jesus, 21, 170, 194n68

Jews: under British and Dutch domain, 108; dogmatists, 111; expulsion from France, 92; expulsion from Spain, 36, 90, 97; importance in colonial society, 186; massive forced conversion of, 33, 90, 199n19 (*see also* New Christians); New Christians' social connections with, 35, 200n30; in the procession of infamy, 170–171; represented as contaminating agents, 170, 185;

Jews (*continued*)
  role in Jesus's death, 170; royal alliance, 33, 112; Sephardic, 6, 33, 107–108, 114; sermons attacking, 173
Junta Magna, 76

Kagan, Richard, 139, 143
Kamen, Henry, 9–10, 51–52, 62, 196n82, 207n1, 212n59
Kosher dietary laws, 234n84

ladino (Indian who speaks Spanish), 162, 247n48
Law of Moses, 21, 59, 101, 122–123, 174, 194n68
Lea, Henry Charles, 7–10, 37–39, 46, 49, 55, 136–38, 202n46, 205nn80–81
León, Bartolomé de, 107–109, 117
León, Lucrecia de, 139
Lewin, Boleslao, 8–9
Liebman, Seymour B., 22
Lima (City of Kings): carpenters in, 164–165; celebrations in, 95; Chilean occupation of, 8; churches and schools in, 94–95, 224n74; commercial consortia in, 5; crypto-Jews in, 120–129; festivals in, 154–156, 245n19; founding of, 4; influence of, 94–98; meaning of nickname, 94; merchants and banks in, 4–5; plaza events in, 154–156, 244n15; population of, 4, 79–80; printed works in, 157–158, 246n28; as a trade center, 4–5, 77, 95–96
Lima, Luis de, 175, 232n71
Lima Inquisition, 76–99, 220n29; abolition of, 131; blood purity's role in, 34; book censorship by, 14; vs. Castilian tribunal, 60, 209n35; and colonial expansion, 182–183; duties of, 76; early proceedings against crypto-Jews (*see* Vicente, Joan); early trials of, 78–79; establishment of, 76–78; facilities of, 78, 131, 144, 181, 218n12 (*see also* prisons of Lima); *familiares* of, 110, 229n38; finances of, 13–14, 47–49, 78, 163, 185; focus of, 6; goals/motivations of, 25, 102, 113–114, 181; as an immaterial panoptic, 102; inactivity/inefficiency of, relative, 14–15; information gathering by, 102–103; inquisitors of, 42–43; jurisdiction of, 76–77, 79–81, 102, 112–113, 182–183; Lewin on, 8–9; life at tribunal facilities, 49–51 (*see also* prisons of Lima); longevity of, 181; loopholes sought by prisoners, 93–94; moral control/discipline via, 15, 18, 181; number of deaths following trials, 12, 181–182, 191n40; overview of, 28, 76–82; Palma on, 8, 204n71, 210n44; procedures for, 78, 181–182; prominence/prestige of, 80; qualitative vs. quantitative analysis of, 17–18; records of, 26, 103; scholarship on, 7, 12–16, 24–29; severity of prosecutions by, 112–113; slaves condemned by, 141–142; vs. Spanish Inquisition, 27, 81–82; vs. Tribunal Mayor de Cuentas, 43; tribunal members vs. archbishops/bishops, 43. *See also* Great Complicity; Holy Office of the Inquisition
Lisbon tribunal, 89
Lizárraga, Reginaldo de, 76, 84
Llorente, Juan Antonio, 30, 36–37, 151, 188n14; *Historia crítica*, 7
Lohmann Villena, Guillermo, 84, 164, 251n86
López, Joan, 82
López, Manuel, 82
López Belinchón, Bernardo, 112–113
López de Fonseca, Diego, 100, 108–109, 116–117, 175, 231n60
López Montesinos, Pedro, 125
López Serrano, Bernardo, 127
Lorenzo, Enrique, 232n68
Loyola, San Ignacio de, 156
Luna, Mayor de, 105–106, 123, 169–170
Luna, Mencía de, 106, 123, 158, 217n96; burned in effigy, 178; death of, 68, 74, 169, 178; family background of, 105; imprisonment/suffering of, 67–68, 70; sentencing of, 177; travels of, 107
Lynn, Kimberly, 39, 41, 114, 118, 219n27, 230n50

MacLeod, Murdo, 88
Madrid, tribunals networked via, 97–98
Maldonado de Silva, Francisco, 22, 124, 145, 175–176, 225n1, 253n110, 253n113
mancuerda, 62
Mannarelli, María Emma, 14
Mañozca y Zamora, Juan de, 40–43, 65, 102, 112–115, 117–118, 159, 166, 246n34

Manual de Inquisidores (Eimeric), 31–33, 53, 56–58, 85, 93, 147, 175, 198n8
Maqueda Abreu, Consuelo, 19, 160–161
Márquez Montesinos, Francisco, 232n68
Marranism, 23, 194n65. *See also* crypto-Jews; crypto-Judaism
medieval Inquisition: in France, 30, 151, 243–244n4; in Italy, 30; vs. Spanish Inquisition, 10–11, 37, 51, 151
Medina, José Toribio, 8–10, 164, 248n64, 249n66
Medrano, Diego de, 197n1
Melchor, Francisco Fausto Antonio, 248n64
Méndez, Duarte, 82
Méndez de Dueñas, Garci, 74, 87–90, 94, 96–98, 183, 220n38
Merchant's Guild, 110
Mexican Inquisition, 101, 220n29; *alcaides* of, 139; duties of, 76; establishment of, 76; jurisdiction of, 76; number of imprisonments by, 232n65; percentage of deaths following trials, 12; vs. secular authorities, 43; vs. Spanish Inquisition, 81–82; spies used by, 143
Mexico City, 219n18
Milan, 225n93
Millar, Juan, 79
Millar Carvacho, René: on book censorship, 14; on confiscations following Great Complicity trials, 49, 163–164, 247n51; on financial impact of detentions, 22; on heresy trials, 13; on the Lima tribunal, 13, 25, 47, 102, 113–114; on the modernity of the Inquisition, 16; on percentage of deaths following Inquisition trials, 12; on sorcery trials, 13; on torture, 61–62; on trials of faith, 58
Millones, Luis, 8
Mills, Kenneth, 17, 26
Minchin, Susie, 22
minority groups, 15
Mogrovejo, Toribio de, 39
Moncada, Juan de, 164
Monter, William, 135
Montesinos, Fernando de, 164; on the *Argos divino de la Fe*, 56; *Auto de la Fe Celebrado*, 158, 170, 251n82; on the Auto General de Fe (Lima, 1639), 168–169, 172, 175–176, 254n115, 254n118; background of, 158; on blacks serving in the prisons, 162; on Cordero, 101; death of, 158; on Mayor de Luna, 170; on Núñez de Espinosa, 148; on Manuel Bautista Pérez, 175–176; on Prieto, 41–42; travels of, 158
Moors, 33
Morales, Ambrosio de, 176–177, 232n71
Morato, Martín, 232n71
Moreno Martínez, Doris, 10, 196n82
Morón, Antonio, 105, 123, 137; defense strategy of, 70; *discurso* of, 57–58; family of, 105–106; first hearing at his trial of faith, 58; testimonies questioned by, 132; torture/death of, 44, 68, 169
Moses, 172–173. *See also* Law of Moses
Mugaburu, Francisco de, 252n102
Mugaburu, Josephe de, 24, 252n102
Muñiz, Andrés, 118, 176–177, 232n71
Museo del Congreso y de la Inquisición (Lima), 131
Muslims, 33, 97
Muzquiz de Miguel, José Luis, 246n38

Naples, 225n93
Native Americans, 76–77, 183. *See also* Extirpation of Idolatries
naturalization decrees, 90, 223n60
Navarre, 201n35
Negrón, Antonio, 232n67
Netanyahu, Benzion, 9, 11
New Christians (conversos): conspiracy among (*see* Great Complicity); designation of, 3–4, 173 (see also *homens da nação*); Edict of Grace for, 111; frictions among, 132; government policies toward, 107–108; importance in colonial society, 186; imprisonment of, 132–133 (*see also* prisons of Lima); influence on inquisitorial procedures, 90–91; Jews' social connections with, 35, 200n30; Lisbon massacre of (1506), 90; vs. Old Christians, 90, 128, 186; Portuguese, 6, 89–94, 96, 128–129, 223n60 (*see also* Portuguese immigrants; Portuguese merchants); Portuguese, African languages learned by, 142–143, 162, 247n48; Portuguese, loyalties

New Christians (*continued*)
of, 112–113; Portuguese, relationship with Count-Duke of Olivares, 110–112, 230n44; religiosity of, 35–36, 111, 184; Sephardic Jews' descendants, 6; social mobility of, 35, 129; strategies used by, 132, 161–162, 183–184; suspected of heresy/Judaism, 4, 6, 183; types of, 20–21, 194n65. *See also* crypto-Jews

Newson, Linda, 22
Niremberg, David, 9
notarios (notaries), 38, 44
nuncios (messengers), 44
Núñez, Antonio, 82
Núñez, Duarte, 117
Núñez, Enrique, 117
Núñez, Pascual, 232n71
Núñez, Roque, 117
Núñez de Cea, Duarte, 82
Núñez de Espinosa, Enrique, 70, 105–106, 123, 148, 169–170, 178
Núñez de Olivera, Francisco, 82

Ocaña, Diego de, 80, 153, 173
Old Christians: definition of, 34; and evidence of lineage, 34, 200n24; vs. New Christians, 90, 128, 186; plot to denounce, 146; rehabilitation of, 176–177
Olival, Fernanda, 89–90
Olivares, Count-Duke of, 110–112, 230n44
Ordóñez y Florez, Pedro, 43, 48, 80–81, 84
Ortega, Juan de, 127
Osorio, Alejandra, 4–7, 17–18, 94, 114, 151–153, 155; *Inventing Lima*, 16
Osorio, Simón, 125
Ovalle, Diego de, 232n67

Palacio, Gabriel del, 160
Palma, Ricardo: *Anales de la Inquisición de Lima*, 8, 204n71, 210n44
Palos, Joan-Lluís, 89–90
pasadizos (passages), 164
Paz, Enrique de, 167, 232n67
Paz, Matías de, 232n71
Paz Estravagante, Manuel de, 169, 175–176
pelotillas (pellets used to lessen pain of torture), 147. See also *bolitas verdes*

Peña, Francisco: commentary on Eimeric's *Manual*, 31, 56–58, 198n8; on confiscation of property, 74; on destruction of heretics' residences, 74; on financing of tribunals, 46–47; on heresy, 38; on inspections of prisons, 50; irregularities during trials of faith, 71; on torture, 61, 66, 147, 213n61
Pérez, Manuel Bautista: arrest of/accusations against, 59–60, 101, 112, 117, 209n36, 230n50, 251n82; attitude before dying, 175–176, 254n115; burned at the stake, 175; career of, 109, 183; coded messages used by, 147–148; confiscation of his property, 49; defense strategy of, 69–70; and Duarte, 59, 147, 175–176; family home of, 74, 108; family/network of, 59, 108–109, 116; interactions with other prisoners, 51; on the Portuguese Inquisition, 60, 107–108, 209n35; religiosity of, 127, 237n106; slave trips by, 22, 109; testimonies questioned by, 132; torture of, 65–66; travels of, 109; wealth of, 49, 59, 206n90, 252n103
Pérez Cantó, Pilar, 12, 139
Peru, 12, 96. *See also* Lima Inquisition
peruleros (Peruvian merchants), 4–5
Peruvian Inquisition. *See* Great Complicity; Lima Inquisition
Phelan, John Leddy, 41
Philip II, king of Spain (Philip I of Portugal), 12, 76, 79, 86, 155
Philip III, king of Spain (Philip II of Portugal), 41–42, 91
Philip IV, king of Spain, 42, 92, 110–112, 159–60, 163
pine pitch, 88
Pio V, Pope, 172
Pizarro, Francisco, 4
Pizarro, María, 13, 79
Plaza de Acho (Lima), 174, 183, 253n104
Poma de Ayala, Guamán, 34
pork, avoiding, 101, 123, 234n84
porteros (janitors), 44
Portocarrero, Pedro León de, 24, 84, 95–96, 164, 220n38
Portugal: forced conversions in, 90, 199n19; history of, 33, 89–90, 105; secession from Spain, 114

Portuguese immigrants, 77, 79, 90–94, 97, 219n18
Portuguese Inquisition: Bethencourt on, 10–11, 151; collaboration with Spanish Inquisition, 16, 92–93, 96–97, 114; Manuel Bautista Pérez on, 60, 107–108, 209n35; tribunal facilities, 49; tribunals created by, 89. *See also* Coimbra tribunal; Évora tribunal; Lisbon tribunal
Portuguese language, 107
Portuguese merchants: careers/trade activities of, 109–110; houses/networks of, 108–109; imprisonment of, 132–133 (*see also* prisons of Lima); involvement in slave trade, 109–110, 141; Spanish vs. Portuguese trade networks, 110, 229n38. *See also* New Christians
Potosí (Bolivia), 83–84, 155
potro (rack), 62
Pradeda, Bartolomé de, 239n29; as *alcaide*, 44, 67, 87, 89, 112, 140, 159; criminal trial for misconduct, 67–68, 139–141, 143, 147; leniency toward prisoners, 68, 140–141, 146–147
Prieto, Francisco, 41–42
prisons of Lima, 131–150; *alcaides* at, 44, 136–137; defense preparations at, 137; harshness of, 131–132; insanity pleas by prisoners, 44; inspections of/irregularities in, 50, 137–140; institutional alienation by, 133, 141; isolation/mistreatment of prisoners in, 169–170, 250–251n81; isolation of prisoners, 133–134, 141, 145–146; lack of space in, 144–145; layout of, 136; meals at, 137; networking by prisoners in, 132–133; organization/workings of, 136–140; overview of, 28, 131–136, 149–150; physicians for prisoners, 44, 204n75; porosity, corruption, and agency in, 132, 135–137, 140–150, 184; secrecy in, 134; slaves in, 143, 146–147; spies placed in cells, 51, 139; strategies used by prisoners, 148–150, 161–162, 183–184; suicide in, 74; types of cells in, 50, 133–134, 144–145
property confiscation. *See* confiscation of property
Protestants' trials in Seville, 15

publicaciones, 134
Pulido Serrano, Juan Ignacio, 21, 112, 143
Purim, 123

Quaresma, Tomé, 123, 127, 175–176, 232n67
Quiroz Norris, Alfonso, 13, 22

Ramos, Gabriela, 13, 43, 102
Ramos, Joan, 232n71
receptores (receivers), 44
Reconquista, 33
Reina, Casiodoro de, 196n82
relación del auto de fe (chronicle of the Auto General), 157–158, 175
religion and ethnicity, 5–6
Ribero, Luis, 255n127
Rodrigue, Aron, 33
Rodríguez, Domingo, 118
Rodríguez, Duarte, 124
Rodríguez, Tomás, 232n71
Rodríguez de Acosta, Jorge, 117
Rodríguez Duarte, Juan, 232n71
Rosas Navarro, Ruth Magalí, 141
Ruiz de Pablos, Francisco, 196n82
Ruiz de Prado, Juan, 43, 48, 79, 106, 137–138, 200n27

Sáenz de Mañozca, Pedro, 40–41, 203n57
Sáenz de Mañozca y Murillo, Juan, 41
Sala-Molins, Luis, 198n8
Salazar Negrete, Joan de, 100–102, 116–117, 226n3
Salcedo, Mateo, 79
Salinas, Lope de, 200n27
Salinas y Córdova, Buenaventura de, 115; association with Lima tribunal, 24; on Autos Generales, 153–154; on blood purity, 34; on confiscated properties, 44; on functionaries' salaries, 39–40, 44, 204n71; life of, 34; on Lima, 123, 164, 224n74; on Potosí, 83
sambenitos (tunic for heretics), 31, 58, 73, 83, 168–169, 197n3
San Agustín *cofradía*, 170, 251n86
Sánchez, Ana, 14
Sánchez Chaparro, Alonso, 118, 176–177, 232n71
San Pedro, Mártir de Verona, 156, 173

San Pedro de Verona festival, 156, 245n23
Santos, Antonio de, 232n71
Saturday Sabbath observances, 101, 122–123
Scarry, Elaine, 67
Schorsch, Jonathan, 21, 141–144
Schwaller, John, 76
Schwartz, Stuart, 34, 40
secretarios (secretaries), 44, 204n71
secular authorities, death at the stake by, 3, 74, 151, 191nn35–37. *See also* Auto General de Fe (Lima, 1639); Autos Generales de Fe, generally
Sephardim, 6, 33, 107–108, 114
Sermo Publicus (Public Sermon)/Sermo Generalis de Fide (General Sermon of Faith), 151, 243–244n4
Seville, 97
Shema prayer, 122
shrimp, avoiding, 123
Sicily, 98
Silva, Jorge de, 117, 143, 170
Silva, Juan Rodríguez de, 143, 170, 175, 254n118
silver, 5
Silverblatt, Irene, 16–17, 22, 62, 113
Sixtus IV, Pope, 35
slaves, 5, 109–110, 141–144, 146–147
sorcery trials/punishments, 13, 174
Soria Arcilla, Pedro de, 176–177
Sosa, Antonio de, 117
Sotelo, Francisco, 118, 176–177, 232n71
Sotomayor, Antonio de, 42
Soyer, François, 16
Spanish Inquisition, 30–52, 36; blood purity's role in, 33–35, 200n24; collaboration with Portuguese Inquisition, 16, 92–93, 96–97, 114; vs. colonial tribunals, 81–82; colonial tribunals created by, 89; Dominican friars as inquisitors, 36; establishment of, 27, 35; functionaries of, 38–39 (see also *familiares*; inquisitors; *and other specific functionaries*); goals of, 51–52; and Iberian Peninsula history, 33, 51, 199n19; Lea on, 7–10, 37–39, 46, 49, 55, 136–138, 202n46, 205nn80–81; vs. Lima Inquisition, 27; Llorente on, 7; manuals for inquisitors, 31–33 (see also *Manual de Inquisidores*); vs. medieval Inquisition, 10–11, 37, 51, 151; and New World expansion, 97–98; opposition of Aragon and Castile, 36–37, 201n33; overview of, 27, 30–34, 51–52; Portuguese migration managed by, 91–92; rationale for, 27, 35–36; scale/drama of, 151; scholarship on, 7, 11; secular authorities vs. tribunal, 43; torture used by, 62; tribunals, creation of, 36, 201n35; tribunals, organization of, 11–12, 37–46. *See also* Holy Office of the Inquisition; Supreme Council of the Inquisition
Starr-Lebeau, Gretchen, 21, 59, 135, 148
Stuczynski, Claude, 91
Studnicki-Gizbert, Daviken, 5, 22, 105, 113
Suardo, Juan Antonio: arrests recorded by, 116–118; on bullfights, 154; crimes reported by, 96; diary of, 24, 30, 197n1; on festivals, 245n19; on inquisitors' salaries, 48; on Mañozca, 41, 246n34; on privilege of carrying weapons, 46; on the San Agustín cofradía, 251n86
Suárez, Antonio, 115
Suárez, Margarita, 4–5, 95–96, 225n85, 247n51
suicide, 74
Sullivan, Karen, 62, 210n38, 210n45
Supreme Council of the Inquisition (Madrid), 24, 40, 45–46, 48, 78, 97, 205n80

tablados (central stages), 164–65
tachas (questioning testimony based on witness's motives), 69–70, 120, 134
Tavares, Enrique Jorge: defense of, 70; family of, 105; imprisonment of, 145, 241n47; insanity plea by, 44, 51, 71, 126, 177, 204n75, 235–236nn99–100; introduced to crypto-Judaism, 234n91; on the plot to denounce Old Christians, 146
textile trade, 109, 229n33
Toledo, Francisco de, 76, 78–80
Toledo Inquisition, 63, 73, 92, 139, 220n38
Tomás y Valiente, Francisco, 10, 26
Torquemada, Tomás de, 36, 38, 42, 55, 61, 207–208n12
tortura del agua (water torture), 62
torture: for civil trials, 61, 160, 246n41; confession as goal of, 65, 68; confessions under, 66, 184; contemporary perceptions of, 61, 210n38; deaths from, 68, 74; Foucault on, 61; *in capud alienum*, 62; *in capud proprium*, 62; killing/shedding blood during, 65,

212n59; legality of, 62–63; methods of, 62–65, 210n45; pain/threat of pain from, 65; of pregnant women, 213n61; used for trials of faith, 60–68, 210n45
torture chambers: contemporary use of, 210n41; inquisitors and physicians present in, 61; interactions among prisoners/personnel in, 51, 67–68; *pelotillas* used by prisoners in, 147; prisoners' aid to fellow prisoners, 68; records from, 26, 61, 63, 67–68, 197n87; secrecy of, 61–62; uniform procedures in, 63–65, 68
trials of faith, 53–75; abjuration/reconciliation following, 73–74; in absentia, 74; characteristics/outcomes established for, 31, 133; confession/conviction as goals of, 55–56, 61, 75, 133; confession during, 53, 55, 60–61, 72, 148–49 (*see also under* torture); *consultas de Fe* (consultations of faith), 45, 71–72; *edictos* (edicts) for, 53–55; guidelines for, 31–32 (see also *Manual de Inquisidores*); and honor of prisoners/witnesses, 69–70, 120; for insane prisoners, 71; intelligible questions vs. deception during, 57; length of, 50, 72, 148, 184; manipulation of, 148–149; for minors, 70–71; obstruction of, 52; officials/associates participating in, 43–45; overview of, 27–28, 53–55, 75; prisoner defense in, 69–72, 214n73; procedures for, 55–60, 148, 207–208n12; punishment following (*see* Autos Generales de Fe, generally); punishment in effigy, 74; sentences, 71–74 (*see also* Autos Generales de Fe, generally; secular authorities); suspension of, 72–73; theologians' (*patrones teólogos*) assistance to prisoners, 71; torture used for, 60–68, 210n45; witness names unveiled (*publicación de testigos*), 71
trials of faith, stages of, 53, 75, 207n11; accusation (*acusación*), 58; *denuncia* (denunciation), 56; *discurso de vida* (life speech or life story), 57; hearings (*audiencias*), 56–58; imprisonment, 56; *testificación* (deposition), 56
Tribunal Mayor de Cuentas, 43
Tribunal of the Inquisition, 30

University of San Marcos, 78

Váez, Isabel, 82–84, 106, 224n71
Váez Machado, Francisco, 82
Váez Pereira, Rodrigo, 3, 5, 105–106, 117, 123–124, 148, 167, 170, 175–176
Váez Sevilla, Simón, 109, 142
Valencia, Juan de, 169
Valencia, Luis de, 105, 107–108, 122, 236n103
Van Young, Eric, 26
Vargas Ugarte, Rubén, 197n1
Vázquez, Francisco, 59, 65, 70, 107, 117–118, 232n71
Vega, Antonio de, 175, 232n68, 254n118
Vega, Juan de, 108
Vega, Luis de, 232n68
Verdugo, Francisco, 84
verdugos (public executioners), 44
Vergara, Francisco de, 232n71
Vicente, Joan, 183; accusations against, 58, 85–86; arrest of, 84; background/family of, 82; burned at the stake, 93; Cartagena trial of, 85; Évora trial of, 82–86, 93, 221n41; ineligibility for pardon, 91; Lima trial of, 71, 84–85, 89, 93, 221n41; reconciliation of, 85; travels of, 83–84, 89–90, 98; wealthy connections of, 93
Viceroy. *See* Chinchón, Conde de, Viceroy
Visigoths, 33

Wachtel, Nathan: on circumcision, 204n75; on fasting, 233n82; on Marranism, 23–24, 194n65; on Manuel Bautista Pérez, 127, 237n106; on Portuguese immigrants, 219n18; primary sources used to study individuals, 121; on slaves, 142–143; on torture chamber records, 26, 197n87; on transgressing Torah laws, 233–234n82; on Isabel Váez, 224n71; on Vicente, 85, 89, 221n41
Warshawsky, Matthew, 206n90, 252n103
women, 14, 106

Yom Kippur, 123
Yovel, Yirmiahu, 20–21

www.ingramcontent.com/pod-product-compliance
Lightning Source LLC
Chambersburg PA
CBHW070724160426
43192CB00009B/1301